Handbook of Tobacco Taxation: Theory and Practice

by Arthur B. Laffer, Ph.D.

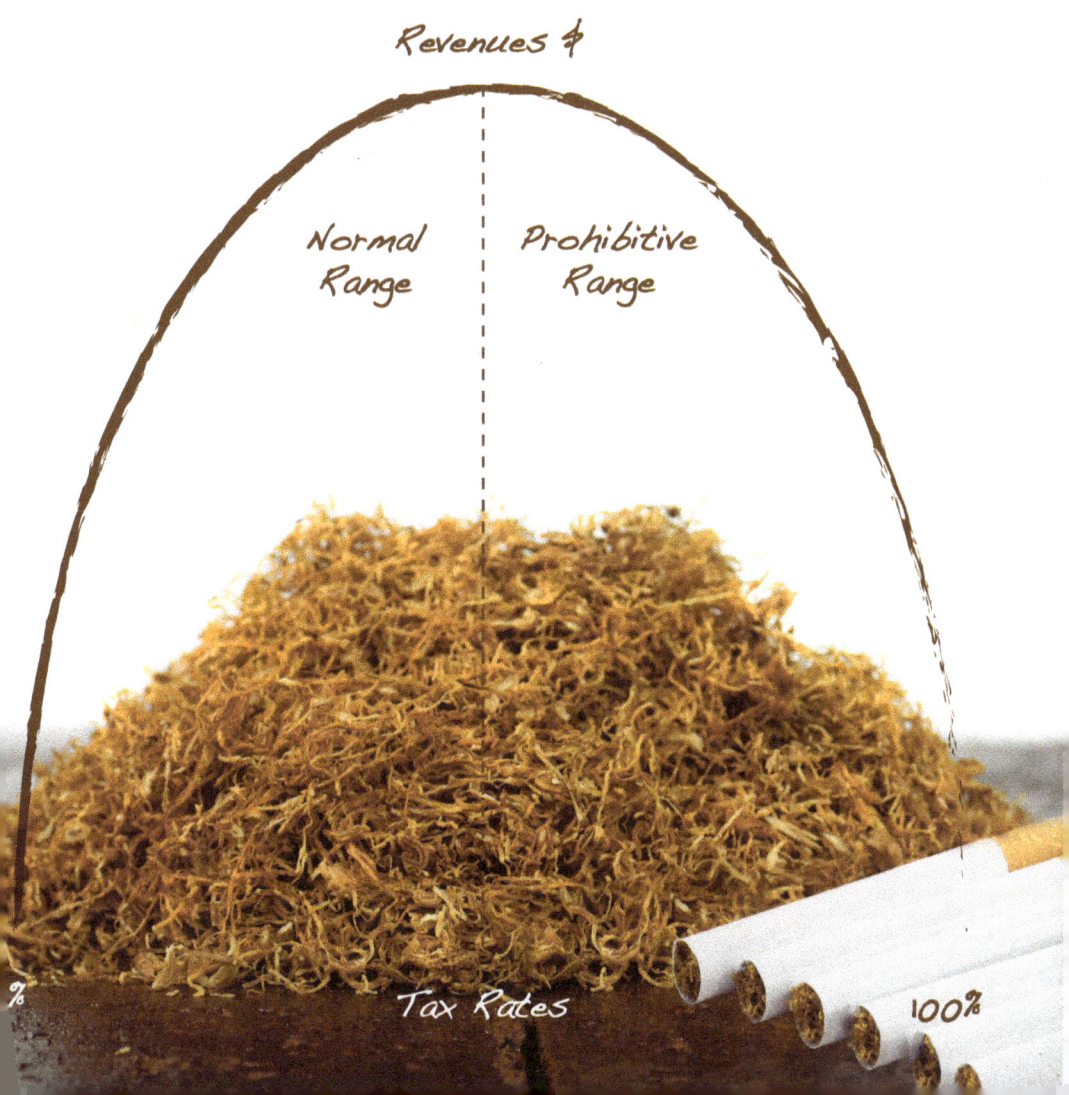

Revenues $

Normal Range

Prohibitive Range

%

Tax Rates

100%

Handbook of Tobacco Taxation:
Theory and Practice

Tobacco Taxation: Theory and Practice
by Arthur B. Laffer, Ph.D.

ISBN-13: 978-1-934276-15-0

The Laffer Center at the Pacific Research Institute
One Embarcadero Center, Suite 350
San Francisco, CA 94111
Tel: 415-989-0833
Fax: 415-989-2411
www.pacificresearch.org

Handbook of Tobacco Taxation: Theory and Practice

by
Arthur B. Laffer, Ph.D.

THE
LAFFER
CENTER
at the Pacific Research Institute

Contents

Acknowledgments

I had loads of help in bringing this book to fruition. And for this help I am truly grateful, for the project would neither have been undertaken nor completed on my own.

First and foremost, Philip Morris International (PMI) deserves credit for their efforts globally to ensure that tobacco taxation is applied responsibly in reaching the public health and public finance goals of each country. I personally am no longer a smoker and actually am now quite hostile toward cigarettes, but I am also a realist and acknowledge that people are going to continue to smoke. Accordingly, the industry should be taxed and regulated based upon sound economic theory.

How to achieve public policy goals via taxation is what this book is all about, and that desire on the part of PMI to work with governments toward reaching these goals is admirable and should not go unnoticed. They sponsored this effort and for that I am grateful. In particular, I would like to thank Huub Savelkouls and Declan Coyne for the countless hours they spent with us providing ample practical examples of the theoretical points made.

Additionally, Collette Wheeler has to be singled out as the *primum primorum* of those to whom Huub, Declan and I owe so much. In every aspect of the research, organization and writing, this book simply would not have been possible without her tireless efforts.

We would also like to say thank you to our friends, colleagues and family members for all they have done to edit, comment, support and critique the themes and ideas presented in this book. We would especially like to thank Paul Abelkop, Ali Ansari, John Burke, Nicholas Drinkwater, Rachael Hamilton, Chase Harriman, Thomas Jepsen, Evangelos Kolovos, Allison Laffer, Kenneth Petersen, Roberto Picchizzolu, Zach Saei, Ford Scudder, Emily Williams, and Drew Zinder.

Finally, we would like to thank the entire team at the Laffer Center at the Pacific Research Institute for all of their hard work in publishing this book, especially on such a short timeframe.

Foreword

As a non-smoker whose mother died of cancer after smoking her whole life, I might not seem to be a natural supporter of smokers. Indeed, I am actually hostile towards cigarettes and the act of smoking. But my personal feelings do not suspend the laws of economics.

Many people believe that policy toward objectionable products like guns, alcohol and tobacco should be made on purely moral grounds, without consideration of economics. On the contrary, however, there is a rich history in economics of how to address non-economic objectives in the most efficient way possible. It is from the latter vantage that any policymaker should approach the tax and regulatory process surrounding tobacco, and that is precisely the approach taken in this book.

The aim of this book is to serve as a handbook or reference guide for everyone interested in or involved in setting tobacco taxation policy. The topic is very relevant and timely from a domestic standpoint and international standpoint. Tobacco taxes represent an essential source of tax revenue for most countries across the globe, and the public health goals of reducing smoking incidence cannot be understated. However, certain actors are seeking to curtail the policy process at the national level and instead create an overarching tobacco tax structure and level for every country across the globe. Such an effort is detrimental to the goals of tobacco taxation.

Tobacco regulation and taxation are complex matters that require consideration of a number of political, economic, and demographic factors prior to deciding on a tobacco tax structure and level. Amongst these factors are: elasticity of demand, affordability, regressivity of the tax, the tax multiplier of *ad valorem* taxes, unintended consequences such as illegal trade, smuggling, and decreased revenues.

Before even beginning to delve into these considerations, however, the first and foremost task in order to enact any agenda vis-à-vis tobacco is to have politicians across the globe understand that tobacco companies are not their enemy. If anything, tobacco companies should be partners and instruments of public policy. As much as possible, tobacco sales should go through legitimate tobacco companies and government should have constructive relations with tobacco companies. In other words, you don't want to tax cigarettes to the point that consumers are no longer purchasing cigarettes from tobacco companies and instead are smuggling, dealing in illicit trade, etc. Instead, you want to work with tobacco companies to make the market operate above ground.

That having been said, the next question is how do we go about designing an objective function for government to operate with the tobacco companies? In my view, the government/tobacco industry dialogue and partnership: 1) needs to focus on minimizing the illicit, non-regulated market. In other words, high quality tobacco products must be readily available at a reasonable price to attract consumers to purchase tobacco from tobacco companies rather than from smugglers or other illegal dealers. 2) recognizing the partnership model and understanding the negative consequences of tobacco use, focus on how we can reduce smoking prevalence. 3) positive incentives (carrots) need to be used as well as negative incentives (sticks) to bring about the desired policy goals.

Quite simply we have a consumption problem with respect to tobacco. Growing tobacco doesn't hurt anyone, nor does buying and selling tobacco. Even international trade in tobacco is little different than international trade in anything else. But consuming tobacco is where the harm occurs. So, the issues surrounding tobacco are not a matter of production or trade; they are exclusively a matter of consumption.

Direct cures for direct problems are the answer: A consumption solution for a consumption problem. What you want to make sure you do is allow all tobacco to legally cross national boundaries as long as there is a consumption cure to the consumption problem—that could entail taxing consumption, subsidizing non-tobacco consumption, or using government spending in some way to reduce tobacco consumption. Governments should look at the cost/benefit differences in those potential programs.

This book focuses most prominently on using taxation as the solution to the tobacco consumption problem, as that is the current *modus operandi* of most governments around the world. We walk through a host of considerations that any government should consider in setting tobacco tax policy and do so in a way that I believe is clear, helpful, enlightening, and always follows sound economics. Along the way, we reaffirm a number of the common conclusions about tobacco tax policy, but also provide both new ideas and critiques of some existing orthodoxy.

Executive Summary

Excise taxes are consumption taxes applied to a specific good, such as alcohol, gasoline, or tobacco, for example. Such taxes may be a mechanism to generate revenues for the overall government budget, be intended to curb consumption (e.g., "sin" taxes on alcohol and tobacco), act as an "earmarked tax" to fund a public good (e.g., gasoline taxes often fund road maintenance and repair), or correct for a negative externality of consumption (e.g., fat taxes on fatty foods)—or any combination of the four.

Adam Smith laid the groundwork for taxing consumable goods, with an excise tax on such goods seen as the most market-neutral tax—guaranteeing government revenue without increasing the natural wage rate of laborers. The premise of this assertion is that if goods like tobacco, rum, or sugar become too expensive, then consumers can simply cut them out of their budget, as they are not necessities.

Over the subsequent centuries, a number of economists have expanded upon Smith's theories. The additional research, along with years of practical experience, has cemented tobacco as one of the most frequent targets of tax increases, on both public health and public finance grounds. While the levying of excise taxes is theoretically substantiated for generating government tax revenues with minimum market distortions, as well as correcting for externalities, there are numerous theoretical and practical issues to consider when introducing or increasing excise taxes.

In addition to the traditional theoretical considerations for excise taxation, there is also a growing political push for international tobacco taxation (i.e., additional tobacco taxes administered globally by an international body), as well as international tobacco tax harmonization (i.e., international guidelines for structuring tobacco taxation). While there may be mounting pressure for international taxation or harmonization, at present there is scant theoretical rationale for either. As the theory and practical experiences make clear, countries need to retain control of their own fiscal policy because one size does not fit all. There are vast differences in policy objectives and priorities, social and economic circumstances, and existing industry and excise tax structures across the globe. Because there are upper limits to the size of tax increases and how high the tax levels on tobacco products can be at the national level, countries need to retain their fiscal sovereignty to determine the optimal excise tax structure and level on tobacco products to meet their national government objectives.

Given recent discussions on international tobacco taxation, it remains of interest to find a way to objectively compare tax levels across countries. Broadly three approaches exist: comparing tax incidence, expressing taxes as a percentage of the retail consumer price; comparing monetary tax levels, in a common currency per pack of cigarettes; or comparing tax levels taking into account domestic income levels. Our study shows that this last approach, which takes into account the domestic affordability of tobacco products, is the most sensible for public policy benchmarking purposes.

In general, governments levy excise taxes on tobacco to achieve fiscal and public health objectives. In order to evaluate both objectives, it is first necessary to review the elasticity of tobacco demand. From there, fiscal revenue and public health goals will be discussed in context of the Laffer Curve (fiscal) and the Bhagwati Theorems (public health). Other theoretical concerns, such as affordability, regressivity, illicit trade, and the excise tax structure are also considered in this book. Of course, no analysis would be complete without an overview of the practical aspects of excise taxation—each of these topics are highlighted below.

I. ELASTICITY OF DEMAND

In order for policymakers to assess the impact of tax policy on various government objectives—raising tax revenues, public health, employment, and so on—it is critical to have a working understanding of several relevant micro-economic concepts, such as price elasticity of demand, cross-price elasticity of demand, and income elasticity of demand. Each form of elasticity plays a crucial role for identifying the demand characteristics of tobacco consumption, which in turn will help policymakers to formulate the best system of taxation on tobacco products.

Many publications on tobacco taxes are based on the conventional wisdom that the price elasticity of tobacco products is between -0.3 and -0.5, which implies that tax increases can generate the double dividend of increasing tax revenues and reducing smoking incidence at the same time. Although this appears to be a correct assessment in many cases, there are also increasingly examples of much higher price elasticities, indicating that tax policies may need to be adjusted to achieve the desired policy outcome.

For these reasons, it is vital for policymakers to understand how demand is measured in order to interpret the precise meaning of the price elasticity. First, governments need to properly measure the number of smokers and the amount that those smokers smoke. Next, four separate price elasticity measurements should be estimated: the elasticity of aggregate tax-paid demand (to assess the impact of tax and price changes on tax revenues), the elasticity of aggregate consumption (to assess the impact on illicit trade and cross-border sales), and the elasticity of both smoking prevalence and smoking intensity (to understand the impact of tax and price changes on individual smoking behavior). Based on our research, in general, countries don't have in place a systematic survey to measure all relevant elasticities and how they evolve over time, even though these are fundamental parameters to establish a well-founded tax policy for public health and tax revenue purposes.

II. LAFFER CURVE

The Laffer Curve illustrates the relationship between tax rates and government tax revenues, and provides an explanation for why this relationship is not always positive. Broadly speaking, changes in tax rates have two effects on revenues: arithmetic and economic. Arithmetically, if tax rates increase, tax revenues per dollar of tax base will similarly increase. Economically, however, higher tax rates will discourage consumption and encourage switching to lower taxed substitute products or illicit tobacco products—thereby *decreasing* the tax base. The arithmetic effect and economic effect are opposing forces—therefore, when the two are combined, the consequences of the change in tax rates on total tax revenues are no longer quite so obvious.

The price elasticity of tobacco demand will impact the shape of the Laffer Curve and the revenue maximizing tax rate: the more elastic, the lower the revenue maximizing tax rate will be, as consumers will be more sensitive to price increases. Most of the time, when tobacco tax rates are increased, government tax revenues increase, as well. However, there are increasingly examples of countries whose tax rates have entered the so-called "prohibitive range" of the Laffer Curve. Within the EU Cyprus, Denmark, Germany, Greece, Ireland, Latvia, Portugal, Sweden and the United Kingdom have experienced multiple yearly declines in tobacco tax revenue over the decade to 2012, while Malaysia, Norway and Singapore have reached the upper limits on tobacco tax increases. A number of states within the United States have at times found themselves in or bumping up against the prohibitive range of the Laffer Curve, meaning tax revenue would only fall with further tax increases and tax revenues could actually increase by lowering tax rates.

Additionally, it is important to bear in mind that the tax rate at which government revenues are *maximized* (the highest point on the Laffer Curve) is not automatically the point at which tax policy is *optimized*. If for instance the illicit tobacco trade and its impact on crime, or the regressive impact of excise taxes on lower income individuals are serious concerns, these may be reasons to enact tax rates below the revenue-maximizing level. Conversely, if the objective of reducing tobacco consumption for public health reasons is seen as the primary objective, tax rates may correspondingly need to be above the revenue-maximizing point (constrained by the illicit trade potential). The optimal tax rate from a revenue perspective is thus not automatically equal to the optimal tax rate from a broader policy perspective.

III. UNINTENDED CONSEQUENCES OF TOBACCO TAXATION—BHAGWATI THEOREMS

In many instances, governments use economic policies in order to achieve non-economic outcomes that are welfare improving rather than technically efficient. The taxation of tobacco is an example of this—governments typically intervene in the Pareto-optimal free market in order to pursue their non-economic objective of reducing tobacco consumption.

Jagdish Bhagwati is a world-renowned international trade theorist whose work on the optimization of economic policy while accounting for non-economic objectives, such as reducing consumption of certain products (e.g., for health reasons), is particularly relevant to tobacco taxation. Bhagwati addresses three potential policies in order to constrain consumption levels—a production or factor tax-cum-subsidy, a tariff, or a consumption tax-cum-subsidy. Although policy interventions are rarely economically efficient, when the policymaker has non-economic objectives, the Bhagwati Theorems can be used to analyze and rank different policy decisions in order to minimize the cost to the overall economy and reduce the distortionary impacts on the market.

The consequences of choosing a sub-optimal policy can be dire—Bhagwati notes that pursuing the wrong economic policy can result in a peculiar situation where economic growth can potentially lead to a country being worse off than it was prior to growth, a situation he coined as "immiserizing growth". Therefore, if the economic target is to constrain consumption, then the available policy options are to: a) tax the targeted behavior, b) subsidize desirable behavior, or c) spend money to reduce the targeted behavior in some way. Any other policy response has the potential of creating unintended consequences far worse than the problem that needs to be solved.

Bhagwati concludes that the optimal government intervention policy in order to curb consumption of a particular good is a tax policy, as consumption taxes directly impact consumption levels, which is the non-economic objective. Accordingly tobacco taxation is, in principle, a good policy instrument to reduce tobacco consumption, but it has to be managed and structured carefully.

IV. TAX AND INCOME DISTRIBUTION

As one of Adam Smith's four maxims of taxation, equity continues to be a crucial consideration for policymakers to ensure that tobacco taxes are not regressive—that is that the tax burden does not disproportionately fall onto individuals in lower income brackets. For tobacco excise tax policy, this especially becomes a concern if the prevalence of smoking is higher for lower income individuals and if the price elasticity of tobacco demand is less elastic for lower income individuals. Such a case is particularly problematic since increases in excise taxes can further diminish the standards of living for individuals in lower income brackets—the choice may come down to forgoing proper nutrition in order to maintain current tobacco consumption.

For a comprehensive evaluation of taxes on income distribution, one should look at the overall impact of all taxes and subsidies on individual consumers. Domestic structures of direct and indirect taxes, as well as social security systems, are further examples of unique, country specific characteristics, as a result of which tobacco tax policy will need to be tailored to individual country circumstances. An internationally harmonized tax approach is likely to exacerbate issues of equity and regressivity in individual countries.

V. EXCISE TAX AND ILLICIT TRADE IN TOBACCO PRODUCTS

When a good becomes too expensive, consumers may discontinue or reduce its consumption, reduce the consumption of other goods in order to continue consuming the highly taxed product, or turn to illicit tobacco products. Taxes thus create a financial opportunity for illicit trade, but this is not a sufficient condition in and of itself. The potential profits for smugglers (and savings for consumers) from illicit trade must be weighed against other factors. Consequently, it isn't just high tax rates that indicate whether illicit trade activity will be a problem, but rather high tax rates coupled with other factors such as affordability, level of corruption, effectiveness of enforcement, and cultural and societal reasons.

VI. TAX STRUCTURE

Excise taxes come in two main forms—specific and *ad valorem*. A specific excise tax is a fixed monetary amount per unit of tobacco product (e.g. pack, weight, carton, piece), whereas an *ad valorem* excise tax is a percentage tax on the price of each unit. In both instances, however, there is a wedge created between the amount paid by consumers and received by producers. The consumer will face prices that are higher than what the producer will receive for the good, and the government collects this difference as tax revenue.

Around the world, there is a remarkable variation of excise tax structures in place for cigarettes and other tobacco products. Governments tailor these systems to meet certain domestic policy objectives, but clearly some of these objectives evolve over time, and will be different from country to country. Many countries design their excise structure to primarily reduce smoking prevalence, and implement a fully specific structure that does not encourage consumers to shift consumption to lower taxed products, thus maximizing the impact of tax increases on the average consumer price. Other countries want to balance their objectives, and also give priority to protecting employment, for instance, by applying lower taxes to hand-made tobacco products to promote this goal. Still other nations are concerned about the regressive impact of tobacco taxes on low income smokers and therefore see a policy need for lower taxed fine-cut tobacco. These are just some of the examples of how domestic policy considerations translate into a certain type of excise tax structure.

On the more general discussion of specific versus *ad valorem* taxes, there is a global trend towards more specific systems, as tax revenue and public health objectives have started to dominate other public policy considerations (e.g., income distribution, employment, protecting domestic producers). From a public finance and public health perspective, specific taxes are clearly preferred over *ad valorem* taxes. Specific taxes offer a more stable and controllable source of tax revenue, for instance because government income does not depend on consumer brand choice trends. If public health is an important objective for policymakers, then a specific excise is also highly encouraged since it is based on the number of units sold, which implies that the tax burden is equal per unit (i.e., if all cigarettes are equally bad, tax them all the same). Given that a specific excise tax equalizes the tax burden across all cigarettes, it is more likely that the consumption of cigarettes will fall following a tax increase because consumers will not be able to offset a tax increase by down-trading to lower taxed cigarettes.

VII. TOBACCO TAX SYSTEM: PRACTICALITIES

At the individual country level, there are four key elements that must be correctly in place for an efficient and effective tobacco excise tax system. Firstly, clear and precise tobacco product category definitions are required, in particular if countries wish to apply different tax levels to different tobacco products. Without proper product definitions government tax revenue will be lost as "loophole products" are likely to be launched—products that technically fall in a lower-taxed category, but are seen by consumers as adequate substitutes of a higher-taxed category. Moreover, these product definitions need be amended and updated over time in response to new product developments.

Secondly, correct excise tax structures are required to ensure that similar tobacco products are treated on an equal basis. From a government tax revenue standpoint, the excise tax structure should support stable and predictable collections and ensure, as much as realistically possible, that excise tax increases translate into government tax revenue increases. While there are a vast array of tax structures applied across the globe, from a pure tax revenue point of view, specific tax structures ensure that all similar tobacco products will pay the same amount of excise tax, while at the same time specific taxes reduce the incentive for consumers to down trade to lower taxed products—as well as reduce the tax revenue losses if they do trade down.

Thirdly, the correct excise tax level must be applied to each tobacco category. While on average the price elasticities for cigarettes and other tobacco products are low, this can change over time, particularly in response to relatively large tax increases or changes in macroeconomic factors. As many countries have experienced, the Laffer Curve also applies to tobacco taxation. When tax levels become too high, consumers will reduce consumption, down-trade to lower-taxed products, and switch to non-taxed, illicit tobacco products. Accordingly, after a certain point, further tax increases will not result in commensurate increases in government tax revenues. Governments must also keep in mind that the tax bearing capacity of tobacco products will vary from one tobacco category to the next, for instance because of production cost differences, and the tax levels applied on each category need to be calibrated accordingly.

Finally, the excise tax system needs to be supported by good tax administration and collection systems. The tax administration and collection systems should facilitate the efficient collection of the excise tax revenue by the customs and excise officials and should not be unnecessarily burdensome on the manufacturers or importers. A proper legal framework that provides a balance between the rights of taxpayers and the powers of the tax agency should be in place. Overall, the tax administration system should be as simple as possible to expedite efficient payment of tobacco taxes by all manufacturers and importers.

PART I
General Principles of Excise Taxation

Tobacco and Taxation

General Principles of Excise Taxation

I. ECONOMIC THEORY OF TAXATION

Excise taxation is the practice of applying a unique tax to a specific good or service, such as alcohol, gasoline, airline tickets, or tobacco, for example. Such taxes may be a mechanism to generate revenues for the overall government budget, be intended to curb consumption (e.g., "sin" taxes on alcohol and tobacco), act as an "earmarked tax" to fund a public good (gasoline taxes often fund road maintenance and repair), or correct for a negative externality of consumption (e.g., carbon taxes on air transportation)—or any combination of the four. Excise taxes may either distort or correct consumer preferences, and are a uniquely targeted tool by which consumption may be affected.

A. Review of the History of Excise Taxation

Prior to discussing the structure, design, and administration of excise taxes, this book will first examine the origins of excise taxation, as well as the relevant underlying economic principles.

The practice of excise taxation to collect government tax revenue can be traced as far back as the Han dynasty in China and to the Mauryan period in India,[1] but it was Adam Smith's *Wealth of Nations*[2] that laid the groundwork for taxing consumable goods. Excise taxes were seen as the most market-neutral taxes, guaranteeing government revenue without increasing the natural wage rate of laborers.[3] The premise of this assertion is that if goods like tobacco, rum, or sugar become too expensive, then consumers will simply cut it out of their budget, as it is not a necessity.

Smith's opinion was that taxes should not be higher than necessary and should not reach a point of encouraging evasion.[4] The government should neutrally collect the minimum required revenues needed to sustain itself—this is the central premise of Smith's efficiency maxim on taxation. Smith also addressed three other maxims with respect to taxation—equality, transparency, and convenience. Equality, as Smith defined it, is the notion that each individual "ought to contribute towards the support of the government…in proportion to the revenue which they respectively enjoy under the protection of the state". Smith noted the importance of taxes being both transparent and convenient in order to minimize uncertainty, because uncertainty "encourages the insolence and favours the corruption of an order of men who are naturally unpopular". Taxes should be convenient in that the consumer pays them "by little and little, as he has occasion to buy the goods".

In the early 19th century, English political economist David Ricardo expanded on Smith's theories to account for substitution effects; during the same period, French economist Jules Dupuit developed the notion that there is a break point in taxation or a point where taxation becomes excessive in his 1844 essay "On the Measurement of Utility from Public Works."[5] While the argument was not entirely new, Dupuit was the first to distinctly identify two ranges in a certain tax rate that were divided by an optimal tax level. Dupuit noted that, "If a tax is gradually increased from zero up to the point where it becomes prohibitive, its yield is at first nil, then increases by small stages until it reaches a maximum, after which point it gradually declines until it becomes zero again."[6] This idea of taxes being raised to the point of diminishing revenues was previously alluded to in Smith's *Wealth of Nations*[7] and in Alexander Hamilton's *The Federalist Papers*.[8]

In the early 20th century, Frank Ramsey proposed in his article, "A Contribution to the Theory of Taxation" (1927)[9] that taxes on consumption products should be formulated in a way that minimizes any reduction of utility. In his analysis, he finds that consumption taxes should be inversely related to the price elasticity of demand for the underlying product.[10]

In other words, if a good is inelastic, i.e., not very sensitive to price change, Ramsey would argue that it is a prime candidate for higher taxation, as increasing the price of that good will fail to reduce demand by a proportional amount. Ramsey theorized that by taxing inelastic or low price elasticity goods at a higher rate, distortion to consumer choice is minimized—that is, the distribution of expenditure over different goods is closest to the original market equilibrium prior to imposing the tax. This book will further discuss the Ramsey Rule, including its shortcomings, in a later section.

The theory of optimal taxation was later expanded into the realm of macroeconomics via the Laffer Curve.[11] The Laffer Curve illustrates the point at which taxes become so high that tax revenue begins to decline: otherwise known as the Prohibitive Range of the curve. The Laffer Curve was employed in discussion of income tax rates, but the idea is also broadly applicable to discussions on excise taxation.

The basic idea behind the relationship between tax rates and tax revenues is that, broadly speaking, changes in tax rates have two effects on revenues: arithmetic and economic. Arithmetically, if tax rates decline, tax revenues per dollar of tax base will similarly decrease. Economically, however, lower tax rates further incentivize labor, output, consumption, and employment—thereby increasing the tax base. (Raising tax rates has the opposite economic effect by penalizing participation in the taxed activities.) The arithmetic effect and economic effect are opposing forces and, therefore, when the two are combined, the consequences of the change in tax rates on total tax revenues are no longer quite so obvious. For example, if the government increases the excise tax rate by 10 percent, this does not imply that government tax revenue will also increase by 10 percent. If excise tax rates are already high, the additional 10 percent might discourage taxed consumption enough that tax revenues would not increase by 10 percent since some consumers may choose to purchase less as a result.

Tax revenue responses to a tax rate change will depend upon many factors: the tax system in place, the time period being considered, the ease of moving into underground or untaxed activities, the level of tax rates already in place, how long these tax structures and tax rates have been in place, the prevalence of legal and accounting-driven tax loopholes, the characteristics of the supply factors, and the interaction between supply and demand. If the existing tax rate is too high—in the "Prohibitive Range" shown below in Figure 1—then a tax-rate cut would result in increased tax revenues. In this particular case, the positive economic effect of the tax cut would outweigh the arithmetic effect of the tax cut.[12]

Figure 1

The Laffer Curve

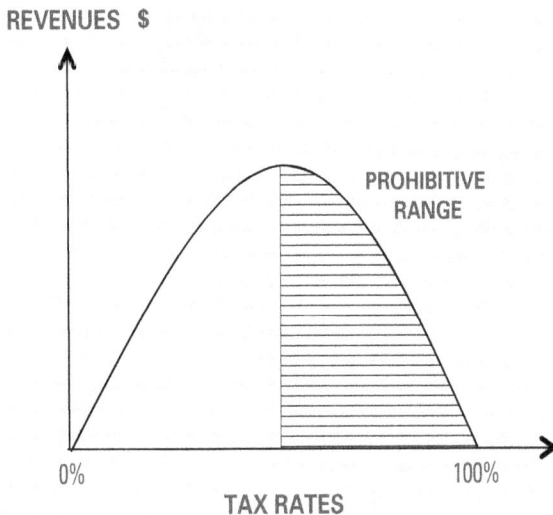

Our discussion so far was limited to introducing taxes to generate government revenue. However, other policy objectives have also been proposed, such as correcting for externalities, which was originally put forth by Arthur Pigou.[13] Externalities are the costs imposed upon or benefits conferred to others, which should be taken into account by the consumer of a particular good. Optimally, according to Pigou, activities with negative externalities (e.g. causing health care costs or environmental damage) should be taxed in order to more accurately represent the true costs of such an activity—and to discourage its prevalence.

Conversely, activities that produce positive externalities can be seen as valuable to society and as such, should be rewarded with subsidies—such as vaccines, or flu shots. Not only do these lower an individual's chances of becoming ill, they also provide a degree of "herd immunity": because if one is unlikely to contract measles (due to having received a vaccine), then others are less likely to contract measles as well, even if someone hasn't been vaccinated. These taxes are called "Pigouvian taxes", and are typically set equal to the marginal social damage (or benefit) of the underlying action.[14] Unfortunately, while the optimal level of a Pigouvian tax does exist in theory, it's nearly impossible to determine this in practice— as it requires an exact calculation for the marginal social cost of the negative externality.

The Pigouvian tradition was widely accepted until 1960, when Ronald Coase demonstrated that the optimal solution is to allow the individuals generating externalities to bargain with the individuals who are impacted by the externality.[15] This eventually led to Buchanan and Stubblebine demonstrating that voluntary negotiation between the relevant parties yields a Pareto optimum solution (one in which no one can be made better off without making someone else worse off), whereas the Pigouvian tax does not.[16] Furthermore, the effectiveness of a Pigouvian tax can also be impacted by the market structure, as Pigou's original results rely on a perfectly competitive market framework. Specifically, Pigouvian taxes lead to market distortions in the presence of both oligopoly[17] and monopoly structures,[18] as these make it nearly impossible to estimate ideal tax levels.

Recent Developments in Excise Taxation

Modern advances in economics have led to the development of more sophisticated models, which are better able to analyze the effects of excise tax increases on consumption. Without going into too much detail, such models include the following:

- The log-log model (where both dependent and independent variables are expressed in logarithmic terms), which directly estimates (constant) price and income elasticities of demand. However, the problem of implying constant elasticities is that it is generally inappropriate,[19] as will be further discussed in Section II;

- The "myopic addiction" model, a dynamic demand-based model describing short-sighted addictive behavior (used to describe consumers who completely ignore the future while making current consumption decisions);

- The "rational addiction" model, where consumption of an addictive good increases both the future utility of consuming that same good (due to addiction), as well as the costs of discontinuing use.[20]

Importantly, the rational addiction model predicts that the current consumption of addictive goods will respond to future prices—that is, if future tax increases are expected on addictive goods, then consumers will reduce their consumption of such products, as higher prices imply higher lifetime costs associated with consumption. An important theoretical implication of this model is that long run price elasticity of demand exceeds short run price elasticity of demand—in other words, the model theorizes that a price increase will have a bigger impact on consumption in the long run compared to the short term impact.

More recently, Gruber and Koszegi have expanded the rational addiction approach by allowing for consumers' time inconsistent preferences,[21] a term that describes consumers' behavior when their consumption preference changes over time. Consider, for example, New Years' resolutions: I resolve to exercise every day, but I have discontinued this resolution by March. Because what I expected to prefer in March (i.e., exercising) differed from what I actually preferred (i.e., not exercising), I can be said to have time inconsistent preferences.

Applying their model to tobacco taxation, Gruber and Koszegi find that the optimal tax per pack of cigarettes in the U.S. ranges from $0.40 to $14.66, depending on the value of several parameters which model the time inconsistency of consumers (parameters that they do not measure, but assume).[22] To compare, the average combined federal and state excise tax per pack on cigarettes in the U.S. was $2.22 in 2012. The large estimated range for the optimal tax per pack of cigarettes calculated by Gruber and Koszegi is due to the absence of reliable estimates for inputs such as the long-run discount factor, the hyperbolic short-run discount factor, and the relationship between current demand for cigarettes and past smoking. This wide range is very unpractical for policymakers—in fact, this range covers the full variation of tax rates implemented in the USA from Missouri, with the lowest total tax rate of $1.18 ($1.01 federal taxes, $0.17 state taxes), to New York City, which has the highest combined federal, state and local tax rate, at $6.86 per pack of cigarettes as of 2012.[23]

While Gruber and Koszegi's models make an interesting academic exercise, the wide range of potential optimal tax levels mean they are not particularly useful for policymakers, due to the intrinsic uncertainty in the model's parameters.

In conclusion, while the levying of excise taxes is theoretically substantiated for generating government tax revenues with minimum market distortions, as well as correcting for externalities, merely establishing the theoretically optimal tax level isn't sufficient, as there are a plethora of practical issues with its implementation.

B. The Economic Principles of Taxation

The standard theory of public finance contends that taxation is necessary in order to finance public expenditures since the market fails to provide certain public goods. To determine whether the appropriate tax system is being administered,[24] the following five criteria are used to evaluate excise taxes: (1) economic efficiency, (2) administrative costs, (3) flexibility, (4) political responsibility or accountability and (5) equity.[25] The fifth criterion, equity, requires its own section in order to fully discuss the consequences that tobacco excise taxes have on issues surrounding equity. The material on equity is presented in Section V.

1. ECONOMIC EFFICIENCY

The concept of an economically efficient tax system can be described as a tax system that disturbs the least the efficient allocation of resources. Since individuals optimize their utility based on their preferences and on the real cost of goods and services, introducing a tax will always, to some extent, distort consumer choice in that it changes their bundle of goods and services, which affects the overall allocation of resources.

i. Deadweight Loss

Deadweight loss is the term given to a loss of economic efficiency when the equilibrium for a good or service is not Pareto optimal—that is, due to the presence of market distortions, some mutually beneficial transactions are not occurring (resulting in a net loss of welfare). Deadweight loss may also be referred to as "excess burden" or "allocative inefficiency".

Consider a hypothetical example, where there is a market for bicycles: consumers are given the option to purchase a bicycle at the market price of $100. If bicycles are taxed by 20 percent (raising the price from $100 to $120), some consumers who would have purchased a bicycle at $100 will choose not to do so at a price of $120—their net loss of utility would be considered a deadweight loss. Conversely, if bicycles are instead *subsidized* by 20 percent (decreasing the price from $100 to $80), some consumers will purchase a bicycle, even though their benefit is less than the true cost of $100 per bicycle. This unnecessary expense results in similar deadweight loss, as resources are not being allocated efficiently.

Furthermore, consider a slightly different scenario, where a consumer has the option to consume either wine or beer, with the consumer preferring beer over wine. If the two goods are priced equally, the consumer will choose that which he prefers—however, if an additional tax is levied on beer, the consumer may choose to drink wine instead. In this scenario, the net loss of utility (from consuming the less-preferred good) would also be considered deadweight loss.

Deadweight loss is one of the primary criteria for evaluating taxation efficiency—if the benefits generated from public expenditure programs (funded by the excise tax revenues) are greater than the combined costs associated with the deadweight loss and the administration of the excise tax, then the excise tax system is said to be efficient.

Of course, there are degrees of "efficiency"—tax systems that reduce the deadweight loss or the administrative costs are considered more efficient because fewer distortionary effects are created. Therefore, the criterion to be used to measure efficiency is whether the deadweight loss is as small as possible for the required revenues to be generated. In order to measure the deadweight loss from an excise tax, it is first necessary to estimate the shift in consumption resulting from a shift in price—otherwise known as price elasticity of demand.[26] The less responsive consumption is to changes in price (i.e., the more inelastic the good), the smaller the deadweight loss—as the percentage change in the quantity demanded will be less than the percentage change in the price increase. However, this approach neglects to account for the fact that consumers will have to decrease their consumption of other goods and services to stay within their budget, which also reduces their overall utility. Furthermore, long run estimates of the price elasticity of demand tend to be more elastic than short run estimates, which will result in higher deadweight loss over time.

It is also important to note that an excise tax in general is less efficient than a broad-based tax on all consumption goods—broad-based taxes do not discern between goods, thus making substitution between goods impossible as a means of avoiding taxation. That is, the most efficient tax system is the lowest possible tax rate on the broadest possible tax base. Excise taxes, however, target particular goods (and thus have a smaller tax base), making it possible for consumers to substitute the taxed good for the untaxed good—reducing government tax revenues. Therefore, excise taxes will be less efficient and will have a larger deadweight loss relative to broad-based taxes. Although broad consumption taxes (such as sales tax or VAT) are preferred over excise taxes, if excise taxes are used, then taxing all tobacco products (and close substitutes) at the same rate will help restore some efficiency that would be lost under a differential tax system, where some tobacco products are taxed higher than others.

When assessing whether tobacco excise tax increases would be efficient, the policymaker must be aware of the following: (1) the effects of increasing tobacco excise taxes with respect to other goods and services (i.e., distorting the quantity demanded), (2) the long run price elasticity of tobacco demand, and, (3) the size of the illicit market. Given that the long run price elasticity of tobacco demand is estimated to be more elastic[27] and that the illicit market for tobacco products is a concern in many countries,[28] increasing tobacco taxes may well reduce efficiency due to higher deadweight loss and relatively small increases in tobacco excise tax revenue. In fact, additional increases may push tobacco excises into the "Prohibitive Range" on the curve, which would very clearly indicate that the tax system is inefficient.[29]

ii. Are Tobacco Taxes Effective at Meeting Public Health Goals?

The fact that tobacco products have a negative price elasticity, which means that tax and price increases are expected to reduce the quantity consumed, is not sufficient to conclude that tax and price measures are necessarily effective as a public health tool.

First, there is the topic of illicit trade. Price increases will reduce the demand for tax-paid product (i.e., there is a negative price elasticity of demand), but consumers may instead buy illicit products, as a result of which overall tobacco consumption may remain stable or decline less compared to tax-paid product (i.e. price elasticity of consumption may be closer to zero compared to price elasticity of demand).

Second, many studies focus on predicting an overall reduction in the cigarette market as a result of tax and price increases. However, from a public health perspective it may make a difference whether this reduction in market size is achieved as a result of a decline in smoking prevalence (percentage of people smoking), a reduction in smoking rate (daily number of cigarettes per smoker), or a combination of these two factors.

Third, cigarettes are far from homogenous since they differ in quality, size, and tar and nicotine levels. In fact, results from Evans and Farrelly (1998)[30] and by Farrelly et al (2004)[31] find that following a tax increase, smokers will adapt their consumption by switching to cigarettes yielding more tar and nicotine. These results, in part, are built on the theoretical foundation laid out by Harris (1980),[32] who established a theoretical framework to account for smokers' change in behavior under higher excise taxes.

In other words, the conclusion that tax and price increases reduce overall tobacco consumption may be correct (provided illicit trade plays no role), but this does not necessarily imply a reduction in the harm caused by smoking to the individual or population.

2. ADMINISTRATIVE COSTS

Although excise taxation usually provides a steady stream of tax revenue to the government, policymakers must weigh those revenue funds against the costs of administering the tax. There are direct costs associated with administering excise taxes, which are mainly the government's costs of collecting and enforcing the tax system, such as infrastructure (buildings), labor, computers, etc. Furthermore, there are indirect costs, which are borne by tax payers; these include the compliance costs of time (i.e., filling out forms, record keeping) and of additional labor (i.e., hiring accountants and tax lawyers). Additionally, complex tax systems are more costly than simpler systems, usually due to special provisions. For instance, in the case of tobacco, complexity can arise when governments apply different systems of excise taxes based on certain characteristics (i.e., roll-your-own versus cigarettes, weight or length differentiation, *ad valorem* versus specific tax system, etc.).

Although measuring the cost of administering tobacco excise taxes would be useful, there is a lack of data on the topic. However, given the growing presence of the illicit trade of tobacco, it is likely that the administrative costs associated with enforcement and compliance are increasing. For instance, the UK government reported £69 million in expenditure on tackling tobacco smuggling in 2011/2012.[33]

3. FLEXIBILITY

Ideally, the tax system, whether the tax is on consumption or income, should be flexible (although rarely is in practice)—it accommodates changes in economic circumstances by automatically adjusting with the business cycle, such that lower rates are used during recessions to offset the decline in consumer income.[34] Furthermore, the appropriate tax system should allow for swift changes in the tax rate. If a tax change comes too late, it may exacerbate, rather than ameliorate, existing economic conditions; by the time the change takes effect, the economic climate may have already shifted, making the new tax rate inefficient and detrimental to further economic growth.

Excise taxes (and indirect taxes in general) are not particularly flexible with respect to business cycles, since excise tax rates do not fluctuate with the cycle.[35] Australia has now started to link tobacco tax increases to wage growth (average weekly earnings)[36]—thus linking tobacco taxes to the business cycle to some extent, although only in one direction: up. When wages decline, for instance during a recession, the law in place will not reduce the excise tax level accordingly. Compared to other taxes, such as income or corporate taxes, excise taxes tend to be relatively easy to adjust, and many countries use excise taxes as a convenient last minute fiscal tool to finalize the government budget. This "flexibility" may mean that excise taxes are "overused" and set at very high levels compared to other tax categories simply because they are the most easy to adjust and often most acceptable, politically, to increase. But this flexibility tends to go only one way—rare are the examples where government reduces excise taxes.

Recent trends in tobacco excise taxation have focused on establishing internationally agreed upon guidelines for the taxation of tobacco products, which would greatly reduce the flexibility to adjust tax rates from a domestic perspective. Furthermore, an international excise tax level or rate could be detrimental to many economies given that each country faces its own set of economic and political issues and characteristics.

4. POLITICAL RESPONSIBILITY OR ACCOUNTABILITY

The political responsibility or accountability criterion relates to the notion that tax systems should be designed such that there is transparency with respect to who bears the tax burden and to the uses of the tax funds—taxpayers should be made aware of the tax and what it is funding. Many indirect taxes fail to meet these requirements since, more often than not, taxpayers are unaware of where the true tax burden lies and the amount of tax revenue that is allocated toward the general revenue fund versus the amount that is directed toward specific aims or the cost of administering the tax.[37]

To illustrate this lack of consumer awareness, Table 1 shows the results of a recent survey asking 1,023 Argentinean adults what percentage of the retail selling price of a pack of cigarettes do they think goes to the government as tax.[38] As Table 1 demonstrates, neither the general public, nor adult smokers themselves, are very much aware of the current excise tax level, as the average tax incidence in Argentina is 69 percent. The average response among smokers was 43 percent for the average tax incidence on a pack of cigarettes, while 78 percent of all smokers believe the average tax incidence is below the 60 percent mark.

Table 1

	TOTAL / N=1023	SMOKER / N=311
0-10	9%	10%
11-20	13%	15%
21-30	18%	17%
31-40	12%	10%
41-50	15%	16%
51-60	11%	10%
61-70	9%	9%
71-80	8%	7%
81-90	3%	4%
91-100	3%	2%
UNSURE	0%	0%
MEAN	43.7	42.7
MEDIAN	40.0	40.0

II. ELASTICITY OF DEMAND: PRICE, CROSS-PRICE AND INCOME

In order for policymakers to assess the impact of their tax policy on various government objectives—raising tax revenues, public health, employment, and so on—it is critical to have a working understanding of several relevant micro-economic concepts, such as price elasticity of demand, cross price elasticity of demand, and income elasticity of demand. Each form of elasticity plays a crucial role for identifying the demand characteristics of tobacco consumption, which in turn will help policymakers formulate the best system of taxation on tobacco products.

A. Price Elasticity of Demand

The price elasticity of demand, which measures the change in quantity demanded in response to a given change in price, is a critical measure for policymakers to consider when determining the optimal taxation level. This section will cover relevant topics concerning tobacco taxation with respect to the price elasticity of demand.

1. ECONOMIC EXPLANATION OF THE PRICE ELASTICITY OF DEMAND

The price elasticity of demand measures the percentage change in the quantity of the good demanded for a given percentage change in the price of that good. For example, if a 10 percent price increase leads to a 10 percent decline in the quantity of that good demanded, then the price elasticity of demand would be -1, which is defined as "unit elastic". If, however, a 10 percent price increase leads to *less than* a 10 percent decline in the quantity demanded, then the elasticity of demand would be more than -1 (e.g., -0.5), which is inelastic. When a good is inelastic, the demand for the product is relatively insensitive to its price changes. Lastly, if a 10 percent price increase leads to a *greater than* 10 percent decline in the quantity demanded, then the price elasticity of demand would be *less than* -1 (e.g., -2), which is elastic. When a good is elastic, then a percentage increase in the price would lead to a relatively larger percentage decrease in the quantity demanded.

It is important to note, that when economists refer to a good or service as being "more" elastic or having a "larger" elasticity, even though on the number scale it is smaller, it is based upon how large the quantity response is, not based upon the mathematically larger number (e.g., -3 is "more" elastic but mathematically smaller than -0.5). In other words, when it comes to elasticities, "larger" or "smaller" is based upon the absolute values of the measured elasticities, which are very rarely positive numbers.

Calculating the price elasticity of demand for a product requires the following inputs: initial price (P_0), initial quantity demanded (Q_0), new price (P_1), and new quantity demanded (Q_1). Some hypothetical prices and quantities are given below in Table 2, which will then be used to demonstrate the calculation for the price elasticity of demand.

Table 2

Hypothetical Price and Quantity Data

Initial Price P_0	$2
Initial Quantity Demanded Q_0	15
New Price P_1	$3
New Quantity Demanded Q_1	10

The equation for calculating the price elasticity of demand is simply the percent change in quantity demanded over the percent change in price[39]—formally:

$$Price\ Elasticity\ of\ Demand = \frac{dQ/Q}{dP/P} = \frac{\%\Delta Q}{\%\Delta P} = \frac{[(Q_1 - Q_0)/Q_0]}{[(P_1 - P_0)/P_0]}$$

Plugging in the numbers from Table 2, the price elasticity of demand is the following:

$$Price\ Elasticity\ of\ Demand = \frac{[(10 - 15)/15]}{[(3 - 2)/2]} = -0.67$$

Therefore, in the example above, a 50 percent price increase (i.e., going from $2 to $3) will reduce quantity demanded by 33.3 percent, which corresponds to a price elasticity of demand of -0.67, indicating an inelastic price elasticity of demand (since the percent change in quantity demand is less than the percent change in price).

2. PRICE ELASTICITY OF TOBACCO DEMAND AND THE INCOME EFFECT

The price elasticity of demand is the result of two effects of a price increase: the income effect and the substitution effect. The income effect occurs because a change of the price of a product (e.g., a price increase) leads to consumers experiencing a resultant change in the real purchasing power of their incomes. To illustrate, if the price per pack of cigarettes is $5.50 prior to a tax increase, and a consumer smokes a pack a day, then his or her annual expenditure on cigarettes is $2,007.50. Assuming this consumer's income is $35,000 annually, then the amount spent on cigarettes constitutes 5.74 percent of the consumer's income. Suppose there is a 10 percent price increase (due to a tax increase), which brings the new cost per pack to $6.05. Using the same consumer information, the amount spent on cigarettes annually will increase from $2,007.50 to $2,208.25, accounting for 6.31 percent of the consumer's income. The consumer will now have $200.75 less to spend annually, either on cigarettes or on other goods and services, which is effectively a reduction in real purchasing power. The impact of this reduction in purchasing power on the consumption of cigarettes is what we refer to as the income effect component of the price elasticity of demand.

3. PRICE ELASTICITY OF TOBACCO DEMAND AND THE SUBSTITUTION EFFECT

In addition to the income effect of a higher tax/price on products, there is also a substitution effect. The substitution effect occurs when the relative price of a good, compared to all other goods, changes when its price changes. For example, if the price of Coca-Cola rises and consumers are indifferent between Coca-Cola, Pepsi-Cola, and Sprite, then Coca-Cola consumers will shift to Pepsi-Cola and Sprite, as both are now relatively cheaper. Generally speaking, the larger the number of substitutes available and the more homogenous those products, the larger the substitution effect will be on the own-price elasticity of demand—and, consequently, the more price elastic the good will be with respect to its own price. While the substitution effect and the cross-price elasticity of demand are related, the substitution effect measures the change in the quantity demanded that is due to other goods becoming either more or less attractive from the change in relative price, while holding utility constant. Therefore, the substitution effect for normal goods implies that own price increases will always decrease the quantity demanded. The cross-price elasticity of demand is specifically measured with respect to two goods and does not consider the net effect of the relative price changes between all goods. In the context of tobacco, if there is a tax increase on cigarettes, but not on other forms of tobacco (e.g., roll your own, cigarillos, cigars, etc.), then some consumers will switch from cigarettes to the other forms of tobacco, as these are now relatively cheaper. Of course, this assumes that consumers are somewhat indifferent between the different forms of tobacco.

The substitution effect among tobacco products has often been ignored by the literature. Of the studies that do exist, the scope is often limited to the cross-price elasticity of demand rather than the overall substitution effect. However, results do indicate that changes in the relative prices of tobacco products can induce substitution toward the relatively cheaper products.[40] Although the cross-price elasticity of demand is not a complete picture of the substitution effect, the two concepts are related. Therefore, further studies are reviewed in subsection B on the "Cross Price Elasticity of Demand".

While the substitution effect may not be particularly well represented in the research, it has been indirectly addressed by reports focusing on the problem of illicit trade. For example, one of the influences on Ireland's high estimate for the elasticity of demand is due to consumers substituting untaxed cigarettes[41] in lieu of taxed cigarettes.[42] In fact, it is estimated that in 2011, untaxed cigarettes accounted for about 20 percent of total cigarettes consumed in Ireland.[43] The same trend is also present in the E.U. as a whole, where consumption of both untaxed cigarettes and "other tobacco products"[44] increased in 2012.[45] In fact, sales for the other tobacco products category increased 6.8 percent from 2011 to 2012, while taxed cigarette consumption decreased by 5.7 percent over the same period in the E.U.[46]

As far as policymakers are concerned, ignoring the potential for substitution effects can lead to undesirable economic outcomes: if policymakers increase excise taxation on cigarettes, but not on other tobacco products, consumers have the option to substitute the relatively more expensive cigarettes for other relatively cheaper and lower taxed tobacco products. In addition, failing to consider substitution effects leads to an incomplete understanding of consumer demand dynamics, hence of what can be appropriate policies and their actual impact.

The tax structure, a topic that we will discuss in more detail further in this book, also plays an important role in this context. If the tax system is fully *ad valorem*, lower price products will pay a lower tax amount. Moreover, with an *ad valorem* tax, any change in retail price is amplified by the tax itself—as shown below in Table 3, if cigarettes are subject to a 50 percent *ad valorem* tax, low price cigarettes (retail price: $3.00) will pay an excise tax of $1.50 per pack, while premium cigarettes (retail price: $5.00) will pay $2.50. Under *ad valorem* tax systems, if there is either a tax increase or decline in consumer income levels, consumers have a greater financial incentive to down-trade, as lower priced products will have a larger price advantage for consumers (because these products have both a lower pre-tax price as well as paying less excise tax). Moreover, with *ad valorem* tax, if the retail price of premium brands is reduced from $5.00 per pack to $4.00 per pack, the excise tax amount declines by $0.50 per pack—in effect, the *ad valorem* tax subsidizes any retail price reduction.

Table 3

Excise Tax Breakdown
Illustration of *Ad valorem* and Specific Excise Tax

$ per Pack	*Ad valorem* Excise Tax 50 percent on retail price		Specific Excise Tax $2 per pack	
	Low-Price Cigarettes	Premium Cigarettes	Low-Price Cigarettes	Premium Cigarettes
Retail price	$3.00	$5.00	$3.64	$4.38
VAT - 20%*	$0.60	$1.00	$0.73	$0.88
Excise tax	$1.50	$2.50	$2.00	$2.00
Total tax	$2.10	$3.50	$2.73	$2.88
Pre-tax price	$0.90	$1.50	$0.90	$1.50

*Note: The effective VAT rate is 20% of the retail price, indicating that the nominal, or statutory, VAT rate is 25%

Conversely, with a "specific" excise tax system, all cigarettes are taxed equally—lessening the incentive to substitute to lower priced products. Furthermore, under a fully specific tax system, a reduction in retail price will not reduce the amount of tax paid.

Since the rationale behind excise taxation on tobacco products is usually to increase government tax revenue, as well as achieve a health goal (i.e., reducing tobacco consumption and therefore, tobacco related illnesses), the substitution effect can potentially undermine both policy objectives. Consequently, this must be accounted for when considering excise tax options.[47]

This book will further address these cases of income effects and substitution effects, as they will help explain the variation of price elasticities of demand across different countries.

4.   MEASUREMENTS OF THE PRICE ELASTICITY OF TOBACCO DEMAND

Chaloupka and Warner (1999) survey the economic literature and find that the price elasticity of cigarette demand estimates range from -0.14 to -1.23, with most studies falling in a range from -0.3 to -0.5.[48]   For high income countries, the range of the estimates falls between -0.25 to -0.5, with a large cluster around -0.4.[49]   In general, the studies reviewed by Chaloupka and Warner (1999) use varying specifications, econometric techniques, and measurements of key variables, but do tend to control for income and other factors, such as advertising. One limitation is that many of the studies do not consider the substitution effect between cigarettes and other tobacco products.

Furthermore, policymakers should exercise caution when using these general estimates from Chaloupka and Warner (1999)—illicit sales may or may not be included, depending on how the demand function is characterized. If the demand function is estimated based on tax paid (i.e., non-illicit) sales of tobacco products (this is a common estimate as tax paid sales data are easily available), then the price elasticity refers to the tax-paid sales only. For instance, if the elasticity measured in this way is -0.5, then a 10 percent price increase is estimated to cause a 5 percent drop in tax paid sales.

This estimate is, of course, highly relevant for the finance authorities, as tax paid sales generate tax revenues. For the health authorities, however, the price elasticity of demand only gives part of the story—a 5 percent drop in tax paid sales does not necessarily denote a 5 percent drop in total tobacco consumption. If consumers are shifting towards untaxed cigarettes or other tobacco products instead, the price elasticity of total consumption could be significantly smaller than -0.5 (e.g., -0.2).

There is empirical evidence that suggests accounting for the illicit tobacco market is important. Using aggregate tax revenue data, Reidy and Walsh (2011)[50] estimate a price elasticity of demand for taxed cigarettes in Ireland to be -3.6, several times larger than previous estimates. Their conclusion is not that Irish consumers are unusually price sensitive, but that contraband, counterfeit, or otherwise-illicit cigarettes are being substituted for their legal counterparts. In fact, the share of cigarette consumption that is represented by contraband and counterfeit cigarettes is approximately 19.1 percent in 2012 for Ireland, which provides further evidence that the illicit market is impacting the price elasticity of demand estimates.[51] Results for the U.K. from 1982 to 2009 also point at very elastic demand, although not as high as in Ireland, with a price elasticity of demand for taxed cigarettes ranging from -0.92 to -1.17.[52] Therefore, policymakers should be careful when considering the price elasticity of cigarette demand—higher estimates may not imply cessation induced by price increases, but rather the substitution effect.

There are still more reasons that careful attention needs to be paid to the estimate of the price elasticity of demand. Although on average researchers estimate the price elasticity of demand at -0.4 for high-income countries, it varies by country as well as over time. In fact, particular cases demonstrate a very large deviation from this average. The price elasticity is also not constant over time and tends to change in different economic climates. For example, the recent financial crisis has stifled economic growth in many European countries (particularly Greece, Portugal, Italy, and Spain) and has reduced the real purchasing power of consumers in those countries, especially in light of the high unemployment rates. Therefore, the price elasticity of demand is likely more elastic during this recessionary period (due to the income effect), than during a more prosperous economic environment.

While most studies focus on developed countries, it is important to also consider the price elasticities of demand for low and middle income countries, where demand tends to be more sensitive to price (with typical estimates for price elasticity being approximately double the -0.4 estimate for high-income countries).[53] Similarly, elasticity of demand is higher over longer time horizons because time allows people to adapt to changing circumstances and develop new habits.

Table 4 provides a comprehensive overview of estimated price elasticities for cigarette demand from key research articles comparing different countries and time horizons—and, while it tends to be inelastic, the degree of elasticity varies significantly across countries, studies, and time periods. Furthermore, this variation is not specific to developing nations, but generalizes to higher income countries as well—indicating that tobacco tax policy needs to be uniquely adapted to fit each individual country.

Table 4

Global Price Elasticity of Cigarette Demand Estimates

Countries	Average	Range		Number of Studies
High-Income Countries	-0.461	-0.14	-1.23	6
Argentina	-0.265	-	-	1
Bolivia	-0.85	-	-	1
Brazil	-0.36	-0.11	-0.8	2
Bulgaria	-0.8	-	-	1
Canada	-0.25	-0.11	-0.31	2
Chile	-0.33	-0.21	-0.45	1
China (Sichuan province)	-0.65	-0.47	-0.8	2
China	-0.41	-0.007	-0.84	7
Egypt	-0.545	-0.27	-0.82	1
Estonia	-0.32	-	-	1
Europe	-0.70	-0.40	-1	1
India	-0.56	-0.18	-0.85	2
Indonesia	-0.53	-0.32	-0.61	3
Ireland**	-1.105	-0.29	-3.6	7
Malaysia	-0.419	-0.077	-0.76	1
Maldives	-1	-	-	1
Myanmar	-1.619	-	-	1
Morocco	-1.025	-0.51	-1.54	1
Nepal	-0.886	-	-	1
Papua New Guinea	-0.71	-	-	1
Philippines	-0.87	-	-	1
Russia	-0.227	-0.02	-0.628	2
South Africa	-1.01	-0.59	-1.79	3
Spain	-0.38	-0.12	-0.84	2
Sri Lanka	-0.53	-0.227	-0.908	2
Thailand	-0.384	-0.09	-0.67	3
Turkey	-0.32	-0.169	-0.41	2
Ukraine	-0.39	-0.3	-0.48	2
United Kingdom**	-0.65	-0.25	-1.17	3
United States	-0.32	-0.092	-0.49	5
Uruguay	-0.445	-0.34	-0.55	1
Zimbabwe	-0.85	-	-	1

*Complete details of each study are available in the Appendix I.
**Both Ireland and the United Kingdom have two studies each that measure the price elasticity of tobacco demand, rather than strictly cigarettes. Refer to the appendix for further information.

5. THE STABILITY OF PRICE ELASTICITY OF DEMAND ESTIMATES

Many factors can affect the stability of the price elasticity estimates—different price points (location on the demand curve), time
horizon (short run versus long run), the method of measuring demand, and availability of close substitutes. Each is discussed in turn
below.

i. Price Point Impact

Even with a linear demand curve, price elasticity for any product
(including tobacco) varies as the price for that product varies. Demand tends to be relatively inelastic at lower price levels (due to
smaller income effects), but grows more elastic as price increases.
Consider Table 5 and Figure 2 below, which illustrate this effect: at
lower price levels, demand is price-inelastic, while at higher price
levels, this effect reverses completely. The source of this change in
the price elasticity of demand along a linear demand curve is due to
the arithmetic properties in the price elasticity of demand calculations as can be seen in the table.

Table 5

Price Elasticity of Demand at Different Price Levels

	Price Effect	Quantity Demanded		Price Elasticity of Demand	
Price	% Change in Price	Quantity Demanded	% Change in Quantity Demanded		
$1	-	8	-	-	-
$2	100.00%	7	-12.50%	(-12.5/100) =	-0.13
$3	50.00%	6	-14.30%	(-14.3/50) =	-0.29
$4	33.30%	5	16.70%	(-16.7/33.3) =	-0.5
$5	25.00%	4	-20.00%	(-20.0/25.0) =	-0.8
$6	20.00%	3	-25.00%	(-25.0/20.0) =	-1.25
$7	16.70%	2	-33.30%	(-33.3/16.7) =	-2
$8	14.30%	1	-50.00%	(-50.0/14.3) =	-3.5

Figure 2

Price Elasticity of Demand at Different Price Points

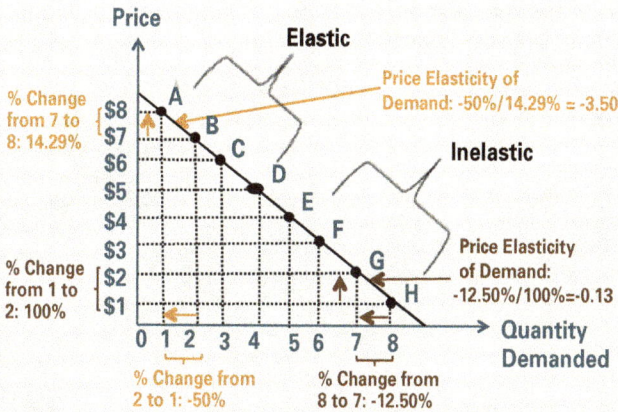

ii. Time Horizon

Not only does the price elasticity of demand change at different price points along the demand curve, but the price elasticity also changes over time. In the short run, the price elasticity of demand is normally less elastic than in the long run; consumers can compensate for a higher price in the short term by drawing down savings or consuming less of other goods.

A compelling explanation for time-inconsistent elasticities of demand is habit formation.[54] Given consumption "habits", a sharp, sudden decrease in consumption of one of these goods is much more painful than a more gradual decline. As such, if there is a permanent price increase, consumers may adjust their consumption over time, rather than all at once[55]—leading to "sticky"[56] short-run consumption and greater long-run price elasticity.

In economics, "short-run" implies that at least one factor is fixed, such as wages or capital; "long run" implies that every factor is flexible—prices can fluctuate, wages can adjust, and expectations shift accordingly. In the long run then, a price increase (which reduces real purchasing power) will motivate consumers to substitute consumption—either by replacing a more expensive product with a cheaper one, reducing or eliminating consumption entirely. Figure 3 demonstrates this concept, with D_{SR} representing short-run demand (which is less price-elastic), and D_{LR} representing long-run demand (which is more price-elastic). Comparing the slopes of the two demand curves, it is clear that a change in price will result in much greater change in own quantity demanded in the long-run versus the short-run.

Figure 3

Demand Curves Over Different Time Horizons

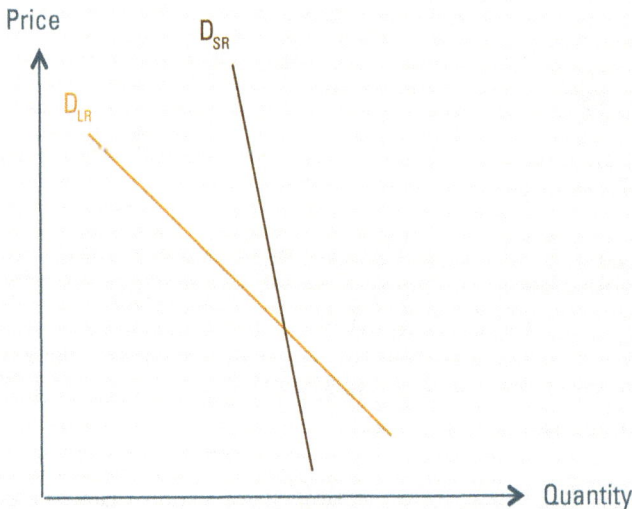

The empirical evidence is consistent with this theory: meta-analysis returned median point estimates of -0.40 for short run price elasticity, compared with -0.44 for long run price elasticity.[57] Chaloupka, Hu, Warner, Jacobs, and Yurekli (2000)[58] find in their survey that many academic papers estimate a long run elasticity that is double that of the short run elasticity when using an economic model of addiction. Using Canadian data, Gospodinov and Irvine (2005) find that the long run price elasticity is -0.31 for cigarettes, in contrast to their short run estimate of -0.11,[59] indicating that a 10 percent increase in cigarette prices yields a decrease in the quantity demanded for cigarettes of 3.1 percent in the long run, versus a 1.1 percent decrease in the short run. Meanwhile, Hu and Mao (2000) use Chinese cigarette consumption data from 1980 to 1996 and find that the short run elasticity at their sample mean is -0.35, while the long run price elasticity of demand at their sample mean is -0.66.[60]

For policymakers, understanding these implications is crucial. While increasing taxes on tobacco may increase government tax revenue initially, over time, consumers will likely adjust their behavior to compensate for the increased tax burden, which may reduce or offset the initial government tax revenue increase.

iii. Method of Measuring Demand (Demand Specification)

When discussing the price elasticity of tobacco demand, it is important to understand the manner in which demand is measured, as this will characterize the specific meaning of the estimated price elasticity.

Aggregate time series data are frequently employed, such as the total quantity of cigarettes legally sold in a country. The resulting elasticity of demand is very relevant for finance officials, as it helps to predict total legal sales (and thus government tax revenues)—yet if the objective is to predict the public health impact, this measure of elasticity may be much less relevant, for instance because total sales may grow or decline as a result of demographic changes. This factor can be properly accounted for by measuring demand as per capita sales, thereby controlling for population changes. Additionally, measuring the price elasticity of demand based on legal sales can be misleading in that declines in legal cigarette consumption do not necessarily imply a reduction (or cessation) in smoking, but could actually be due to substitution with other legal or illicit products.

An estimated price elasticity of -0.5, for example, indicates that a 10 percent price increase reduces average per capita sales by 5 percent, but it does not reveal whether this is due to a 5 percent reduction in the *number* of smokers, or a 5 percent reduction in the *amount smoked*, with the absolute number of smokers remaining constant. From a public health point of view, these outcomes are not likely to be equally preferable. Furthermore, this type of measure also fails to account for illicit, cross-border, and duty-free cigarette sales—as well as non-cigarette tobacco sales—all of which influence measurements for price elasticity of demand.[61] To measure the price elasticity of consumption, all of these other forms of tobacco consumption need to be included in the demand equation.[62]

Many other studies instead are based on data collected at the individual or household level, e.g., based on interviews or surveys. Assuming consumers accurately disclose their smoking habits, micro-level data allow us to distinguish between a shift in smoking prevalence (percentage of people smoking) versus smoking intensity (daily number of cigarettes consumed), as well as capturing any relevant substitution effects. The caveat to this, however, is that micro-data are much more difficult and expensive to obtain, and can be less reliable, as they rely on honest and accurate reporting by individual participants.

Meta-analysis of individual microeconomic panel data (data gathered over time and across geographical locations) yield more inelastic estimates for price elasticity of cigarette demand,[63] consistent with the increased substitution of non-taxed (illicit or illegal) tobacco products discussed previously. More generally, the same meta-analysis reported mean price elasticity of demand of -0.48, but with a rather large standard deviation (0.43). As would be expected, the range of estimates is similarly large, varying between -3.12 and 1.41—suggesting variation in price elasticity of demand is not only large, but country-dependent as well. This reinforces the idea that supposed outliers are likely not outliers at all, and considerable attention should be given to obtaining precise estimates for individual countries, rather than using the oft-cited estimate of -0.4.

In addition to the manner in which the data were gathered, modeling also plays a role in the variation of elasticity estimates. The "almost ideal demand system" allows the price elasticity of tobacco demand to be estimated in a way which accounts for consumers changing their preferences and habits over time,[64] which tends to produce more elastic estimates for price elasticity of cigarette demand.[65] The almost ideal demand system helps account for consumers who stop smoking following an excise tax increase, but may not follow through with that decision over time.

For policymakers, understanding how demand is measured is thus vital in order to interpret the precise meaning of the price elasticity. Four separate price elasticity measurements should be considered: the elasticity of aggregate tax-paid demand (to estimate the impact of tax and price changes on tax revenues), the elasticity of aggregate consumption (to estimate the impact on illicit trade and cross-border sales), and the elasticity of both smoking prevalence and smoking intensity (to understand the impact of tax and price changes on individual smoking behavior). Based on our research, we are not aware of any country having in place a systematic survey to measure all relevant elasticities and how they evolve over time, even though these are fundamental parameters to establish a well-founded tax policy for public health and tax revenue purposes.

iv. Availability of Close Substitutes

As with any good, the presence of close substitutes will increase the price elasticity of demand for tobacco. The intuition behind this is simple: if there are two easily-interchangeable goods (A and B), and if A becomes more expensive relative to B (due to higher taxes being imposed on good A, but not good B, for example), then consumers are incentivized to switch from good A to good B. This isn't a purely theoretical exercise—depending on consumer preferences, if cigarettes and cigarillos are subject to different tax rates, efforts to reduce the incidence of tobacco consumption by targeting only one of these products may be much less effective than anticipated. The more substitutes there are for cigarettes, the more elastic the demand for cigarettes will be, as consumers switch to alternative products rather than reducing tobacco consumption.

The following table illustrates how the price elasticity varies both with the level of prices (the "income effect", or "affordability")[66] as well as with the availability of substitutes. As explained by footnote 66, higher values of PRI indicate reduced affordability. As observed in Table 6, countries that face relatively elastic price demand for tax paid cigarettes (i.e., the UK and Ireland), tend to have reduced cigarette affordability, and either a large share of other tobacco products consumed (UK) or a large share of non-domestic consumption (Ireland).

Table 6

Price Elasticity in Select Countries, in Relation to Affordability
and the Availability of Substitutes

Country	Price Elasticity of Tax Paid Cigarettes Demand	Affordability of Tax Paid Cigarettes	Share of Non-Domestic Product (%) Legal	Illicit	Share of Other Tobacco Products (%)
Japan	-0.26	1.2 %	0 %		0 %
Singapore	-0.58	1.9 %	25.6 %		5.2 %
France	-0.74	1.9 %	5.3 %	15.8 %	19.0 %
UK	-1.05	3.1 %	2.7 %	10.1 %	15.5 %
Ireland	-3.6	2.6 %	9.9 %	17.8 %	6.1 %

*Source: Source: Price elasticity estimates for Japan, Singapore, and France are PMI estimates, based on latest available data. Price elasticity estimate for the UK is from the 2010 HMRC report, "Econometric Analysis of Cigarette Consumption in the UK". Price elasticity estimate for Ireland is from the 2011 MoF report, "Economics of Tobacco: Modelling the Market for Cigarettes in Ireland". Illicit trade estimates are from the 2013 KPMG report, "Project Star: 2012 Results".

Interestingly, alcoholic beverages have been shown to have some substitutability with tobacco products—the price elasticity for cigarettes is larger (more elastic) when cigarette demand is estimated jointly with alcohol demand.[67] This particular topic will be further discussed in Subsection B, which details the cross-price elasticity of demand relationship between tobacco products.

6. THE CHALLENGES OF ACCURATELY ESTIMATING THE PRICE ELASTICITY OF TOBACCO DEMAND

One challenge in estimating the price elasticity of tobacco demand relates to parameter identification and simultaneity when using aggregated data:[68] price and quantity data, typically assumed to reflect movement along the demand curve (Figure 4), may be indicative of simultaneous movement of both the supply and demand curves instead (Figure 5).

Figure 4

Price Elasticity of Demand - Identification Problem 1

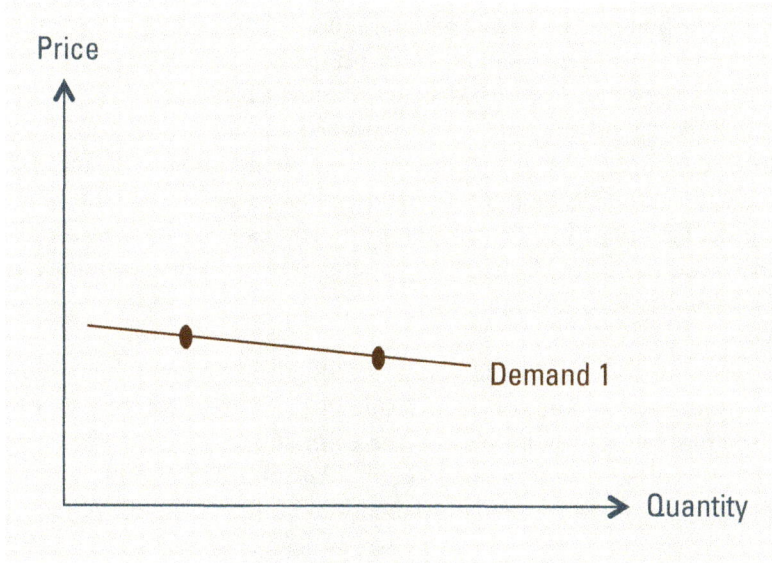

Figure 5

Price Elasticity of Demand - Identification Problem 2

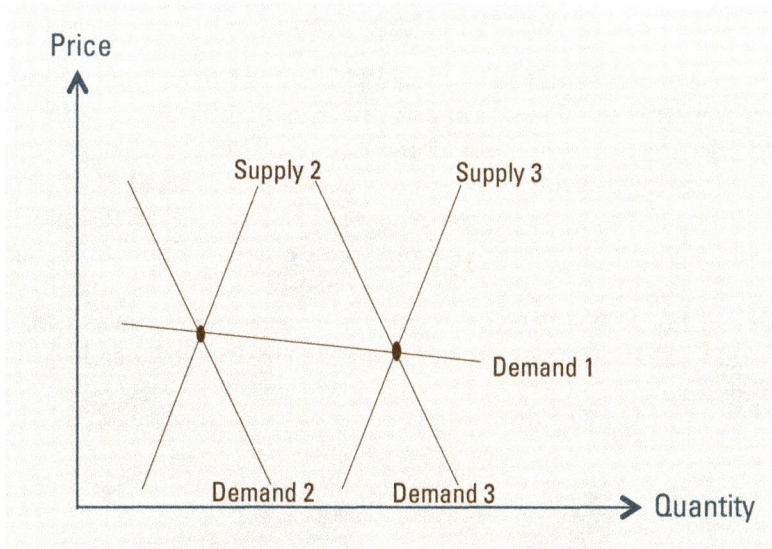

In Figure 4, the two points that are depicted represent two points obtained from price and quantity data, which are then connected to form a possible demand curve. In the literature surrounding the price elasticity of tobacco demand, Figure 4 depicts the price elasticity of demand—i.e., mapping demand by connecting two points of data. However, as Figure 5 displays, Figure 4 is not the only potential outcome—if the data points gathered are not actually obtained from demand curve 1, but instead from demand curve 2 and 3,[69] then the price elasticity of demand estimates will be greatly inaccurate. Ignoring this identification problem can lead to biased estimates for the price elasticity of demand, which, in turn, can lead to faulty policy recommendations.

Correcting for simultaneity is quite difficult, however. In fact, in many cases, the solutions can result in the same problems as the simultaneity, mainly by biasing the estimates, especially when analyzing across different countries.[70] An alternate approach is to implement an instrumental variable (IV) in lieu of the price,[71] such as cigarette taxes. However, if there is very little variability in the data, this methodology will not provide reasonable estimates—and, even with a high level of variability, such variation must stem from otherwise homogenous products to be useful to IV estimation e.g., if price variation is due to underlying product differences, such as length, production size, type, or quality, IV estimation will not be effective.

Despite these shortcomings, some U.S. studies have implemented econometric techniques to improve the simultaneity bias of estimated price elasticities of demand. Interestingly, after correcting for the simultaneity bias, the price elasticity of cigarette demand was found to be as elastic as -0.71 when using U.S. data from 1955 to 1990— much higher than the often quoted price elasticity estimate of -0.4 for developed countries.[72] In a more recent study using U.S. data from 1961 to 2002, the price elasticities of cigarette demand prior to and following a correction for simultaneity was -0.21 and -0.41, respectively.[73]

B. Cross-Price Elasticity of Demand

Consumption decisions aren't made in a vacuum—in addition to being influenced by the price of the specific good under consideration, the relative price of potential substitute goods factor in as well. For policymakers, it is important to consider the potential impact of shifts in tobacco price on the consumption of other goods, and vice-versa.

1. ECONOMIC EXPLANATION OF THE CROSS-PRICE ELASTICITY OF DEMAND

The change in the quantity demanded for a product not only depends on price and income, but can also depend on the change in the price of another good. Mathematically:

$$Cross - Price\ Elasticity\ of\ Demand = \frac{Percent\ change\ in\ quantity\ demanded\ of\ product\ A}{Percent\ change\ in\ price\ of\ product\ B}$$

$$Cross - Price\ Elasticity\ of\ Demand = \frac{(P_{b1} + P_{b2})}{(Q_{a1} + Q_{a2})} * \frac{(\Delta Q_a)}{(\Delta P_b)} = \frac{\partial Q_a}{\partial P_b} * \frac{P_b}{Q_a}$$

The cross-elasticity of demand measures this concept by calculating the percentage change in quantity demand of good A, given a percentage change in the price of good B.

If the increase in the price of good B is associated with an increase in demand for good A, then the two goods are considered substitutes—and the cross price elasticity of demand will be positive. For example, if consumers find that Pepsi-Cola and Coca-Cola products are substitutable, then an increase in the price of Pepsi-Cola, keeping everything else unchanged, will result in an increase in the quantity demanded for Coca-Cola. This essentially implies that as the price of one good increases, consumers are more likely to substitute the cheaper alternative good for the relatively more expensive good. The more willing consumers are to substitute between two goods, the larger the cross-price elasticity between the two products.

Conversely, if an increase in the price of good A is associated with a reduction in demand for good B, then the cross price elasticity of demand will be negative. Goods that display this sort of relationship are considered complementary goods, such as hot dogs and mustard, or tea and sugar. If the price of hot dogs increases, we would expect a decrease in the demand for mustard, as the two goods are frequently consumed together.

Lastly, if the cross-elasticity of demand is zero, then the two goods are considered completely independent of each other. For example, we would not expect that an increase in the price of tea (good A) would have an immediate impact on the quantity demanded for sneakers (good B), or vice versa. Broad estimates for cross-price elasticities tend to be a bit tricky, however: when income is held constant, there will tend to be a bias toward positive estimates for the cross price elasticity of demand, due to the substitution effect (as a specific product becomes more expensive, alternate forms of consumption are preferred). Conversely, when relative prices are held constant, negative estimates of cross-price elasticity are more common, due to the income effect (as income increases, consumption increases for all goods). In the short run, incomes are typically assumed to be stationary—and, accordingly, for a price increase in a price inelastic product, individuals will tend to change their consumption patterns for all goods and services in order to offset the increased expenditure for the inelastic products.

2. APPLICATION OF THE CROSS-PRICE ELASTICITY OF DEMAND TO TOBACCO PRODUCTS

As prices increase for one type of tobacco, we would expect demand for other forms of tobacco to increase proportionately, as different types of tobacco products are generally considered substitutes and have positive cross price elasticities of demand. Unfortunately, relative to the price elasticity of demand, there is far less analysis in the economics literature on the cross-price elasticity of demand for different tobacco products,[74] yet there is some evidence that estimates are positive and statistically significantly different from zero, at least when using U.S. data.[75] In fact, cigars[76] and other forms of smoking tobacco have a positive estimate for the cross elasticity of demand with cigarettes in both the short and long run, suggesting that cigars and cigarettes are substitutes. However, as Table 7 indicates, Da Pra and Arnade's results find that cigarettes and chewing tobacco are complementary goods in both the short and long run. (Estimates highlighted in dark blue indicate a complementary relationship, while estimates highlighted in light blue indicate that the two goods are substitutes.)[77]

Table 7

Cross-Price Elasticities of Demand for Various Tobacco Products Using U.S. Data[78]

	Cigarettes	Cigars	Chewing Tobacco	Smoking Tobacco
Short Run				
Cigarette Price	-1	0.4	-0.4	1.8
Cigar Price	0.01	-0.5	-0.5	-1.2
Chewing Tobacco Price	-0.02	-0.7	0.1	-1.1
Smoking Tobacco Price	0.01	-0.2	-0.1	-0.6
Long Run				
Cigarette Price	-1.02	0.98	-0.32	1.6
Cigar Price	0.1	0.12	-0.33	-1.06
Chewing Tobacco Price	-0.16	-1.58	-0.21	-0.98
Smoking Tobacco Price	0.08	-0.54	-0.11	-0.61

In a more recent study using data from New Zealand, roll-your-own tobacco was frequently substituted for cigarettes over the period 1991 to 2011.[79] The results indicate that a 1 percent increase in the price of manufactured cigarettes corresponds to a 0.87 percent increase in the demand for roll-your-own products.[80] Additionally, pipe and hand-rolling tobacco are both substitutes to cigarettes in Finland—a 10 percent increase in real cigarette prices will increase pipe and hand-rolling consumption by 17.3 percent.[81] Interestingly, a study using UK data found that a 10 percent increase in the price of duty-paid cigarettes increased the total demand for smuggled tobacco by 4.5 percent to 15 percent, depending on the model specification.[82]

In a study analyzing price differentials and ratios in the Netherlands from 1985 to 1995, the authors found the following: (1) that a 10 percent increase in the price difference between manufactured cigarettes and hand rolled cigarettes decreased manufactured cigarette consumption by 6 percent; and, (2) for every 10 percent decrease in the ratio between manufactured and hand rolled cigarette prices,[83] hand rolled cigarette consumption fell by -10.3 percent.[84] These results from the Netherlands imply that the prices of hand rolled cigarettes must be kept on par with manufactured cigarettes in order to prevent substitution.

It is important to analyze the cross elasticity of demand across different countries; consumers in different regions may be more or less likely to substitute cigarettes with other forms of tobacco. If different forms of tobacco are highly substitutable (i.e., they have cross-elasticity of demand that is large and positive), specifically-targeted policy measured may be less effective than anticipated.

3. APPLICATION OF THE CROSS-PRICE ELASTICITY OF DEMAND BETWEEN TOBACCO PRODUCTS AND ALCOHOL PRODUCTS

In addition to the cross elasticity of demand for different tobacco products, it is natural to also consider the cross elasticity of demand between tobacco and alcohol, as they may be consumed together (complementary goods), or in place of each other (substitute goods). We are interested in analyzing the effect on alcohol demand given increasing tobacco prices, as well as the effect on tobacco demand from increasing alcohol prices. Such analysis is especially important fiscally in countries that also legislate excise taxes on alcohol purchases.

Using Canadian data, an increase in cigarette prices was found to have a negative effect on beer consumption, with a cross price elasticity of -0.10[85]—indicating the two goods are complementary.[86] Using data from Sweden, the cross-price elasticity for the two goods was estimated at 0.79, suggesting that in this country, cigarettes and alcohol are substitutes, rather than complements (as a reminder, a cross-price elasticity of 0.79 indicates a 1 percentage increase in tobacco prices will yield a 0.79 percent increase in alcohol consumption).[87] A change in tobacco consumption in response to an increase in the price of alcohol was considered as well, and, interestingly, the estimate for cross-price elasticity came in at -0.31. This suggests that, if the goal for policymakers is to reduce tobacco consumption, it could be effective to increase alcohol taxes as well.

Table 8

Cross-Price Elasticities Estimates for Alcohol and Tobacco

Countries/ Authors	Data/Year	Cross-Price Elasticity (Alcohol Response to Price Change in Tobacco)	Cross-Price Elasticity (Tobacco Response to Price Change in Alcohol)
Canada Gruber, Sen, Stabile (2003)	Canadian Survey of Family Expenditure quartile data 1982-1998	-0.1	NA
Italy Pierani, Tiezzi (2009)	Time series data 1960-2002	-0.18	-0.39
Spain Jimenez, Labeaga (1994)	Cross section of individual data Spanish Family Expenditure Survey 1980-1981	NA	-0.78
Sweden Bask, Melkersson (2004)	Aggregate annual time series 1955-1999	0.79	-0.31
UK Jones (1989)	Aggregate quarterly data 1964-1983	-0.46	-0.46
U.S. Goel, Morey (1995)	Pooled data 1959-1982	0.33	0.1
U.S. Decker, Schwartz (2000)	Individual data 1985-1993 from Behavior Risk Factor Surveillance System	0.5	-0.14

The results summarized in Table 8 demonstrate the internationally inconsistent relationship between tobacco and alcohol, indicating the need for careful consideration when determining tax levels on a country by country basis. In both the U.S. and Sweden, the data indicate tobacco and alcohol tend to be viewed as substitutes, in which case policymakers should consider increasing taxes on both products if they wish to reduce overall consumption of both goods. In Canada, Italy, and the UK, the two are complementary goods instead, which means that increasing the tax of one product can be a way to reduce consumption for both. This highlights the need for country specific measurement of cross-price elasticities as well as country specific tax policy decisions to reflect these differences in market realities between countries.

C. Income Elasticity of Demand

Income elasticity of demand—the change in consumption result-ing from a change in income—is another relevant factor for policy-makers to consider. This section addresses both the basic economic theory underlying this concept, as well as its application to tobacco products.

1. ECONOMIC EXPLANATION OF THE INCOME ELASTICITY OF DEMAND

Income elasticity of demand describes the percentage change in de-mand resulting from a percentage change in income.

$$Income\ Elasticity\ of\ Demand = \frac{Percent\ change\ in\ demand}{Percent\ change\ in\ income}$$

$$Income\ Elasticity\ of\ Demand = \frac{(Y_1 + Y_2)}{(Q_1 + Q_2)} * \frac{(\Delta Q)}{(\Delta Y)} = \frac{\partial Q}{\partial Y} * \frac{Y}{Q}$$

Importantly, we are most interested in relative (rather than absolute) income—e.g., if a consumer's income doubles, but so do the prices on all of his consumption goods, the consumer is no better or worse off than before. If, however, prices increase—either for all goods, or even just one[88]—without a corresponding increase in income, the consumer is worse off than before—the same as if he or she had income dropped while prices remained constant. Similar to the price elasticity of demand, if a 1 percent increase in income yields a 2 percent increase in demand for a product, then the income elasticity of demand is 2.

A positive income elasticity of demand indicates that the product is a so-called "normal" good, demand increases in response to income increasing, whereas a negative income elasticity of demand indicates the product is a so-called "inferior" good, demand decreases in response to income increasing. If the income elasticity of demand is positive, there are several different potential classifications of goods, dependent on their specific value, refer to Table 9. Goods with income elasticities greater than 1 are "luxury" goods, as their demand increases proportionately more than the percentage change in income. Conversely, goods with income elasticity between 0 and 1 are "necessities", as the percentage change in quantity demanded is positive, but proportionately smaller than the change in income. Lastly, goods with income elasticity of 0 are "sticky", as the quantity demanded is rigid and independent from income.

Table 9

Income Elasticity of Demand

Sign of Income Elasticity of Demand Estimate	Value of Income Elasticity of Demand Estimate	Direction of Percentage Change in Quantity Demanded (Given a Positive Percentage Change in Income)	Size of Percentage Change in Quantity Demanded Relative to Percentage Change in Income	Type of Good	Example of Goods
Positive	Greater than 1	An Increase	Proportionately Larger	Luxury (Normal)	Private Jets, Yachts, Jewelry
Positive	1	An Increase	Equal	Unitary (Normal)	No concrete example
Positive	Between 0 and 1	An Increase	Proportionately Smaller	Necessity (Normal)	Basic Food, Clothing
Zero	0	No Change	Not Applicable	Sticky	Salt
Negative	Less than 0	A Decrease	Not Applicable	Inferior	Margarine, Public Transportation, Canned Soup, Fast Food

Similar to price elasticity, income elasticity of demand is likewise non-constant over a range of income levels. For example, a bicycle might be a normal good for one person (middle income brackets), a luxury good for another person (lower income brackets), and finally, an inferior good for a third person (higher income brackets).

Furthermore, if consumer preferences shift over time, the income elasticity of demand for any affected product will shift as well. For example, while tobacco was once considered a luxury good, shifting attitudes towards tobacco have led to similar shifts in its income elasticity.

2. APPLICATION OF THE INCOME ELASTICITY OF DEMAND TO TOBACCO PRODUCTS

Unlike the price elasticity of demand for tobacco products (which is generally considered inelastic), the estimates for the income elasticity of demand for tobacco products vary.

Although the mean estimate for the income elasticity of demand for cigarettes is 0.42 i.e., a normal, necessity good, it varies from -0.80 (an inferior good) to 3.03 (a luxury good), depending on the country.[89,90] Furthermore, the income elasticity of demand for cigarettes tends to be between 0.13 to 0.19 lower for short run estimates relative to long run estimates, indicating that income elasticity changes over different time horizons i.e., consumption habits are more flexible in the long run, as discussed previously.

Income elasticity of demand has been estimated at 1.25 in Canada,[91] indicating tobacco is a luxury good—however, in the U.K., income elasticity was estimated at 0.3,[92] indicating tobacco is viewed as a necessity good.

In addition to this evidence that the income elasticity depends on the geography, there is also evidence that income elasticities evolve over time within a country. In the U.S., between 1944 and 2004, tobacco went from being a normal to an inferior good[93]— and further research indicates this transition took place sometime between the 1970s and 1980s.[94]

It is also likely that the income elasticity of demand is different for different tobacco products. A fine cigar would be expected to be a luxury good, whereas fine-cut tobacco to hand-roll cigarettes is more likely a necessity normal good or perhaps an inferior good. In New Zealand, the evidence suggests that hand-roll tobacco is an inferior good, at least over the period of 1991 to 2011—a 1 percent increase in average weekly income corresponds to a 0.8 percent decline in hand-roll tobacco demand.[95] Similarly, the income elasticity of pipe and hand-rolling tobacco demand in Finland ranges from -0.836 to -1.257 over the period from 1960 to 2002; in the Netherlands, this estimate ranges from -0.485 to -0.690 over the period of 1980 to 2009—both countries' results vary based on the model specification and indicate that pipe and hand-roll tobacco are inferior products.[96]

Policymakers should be aware of the income elasticity of demand in their country when formulating their tax policy. Even in countries where tobacco consumption is income-inelastic i.e., a normal, necessity good, declines in income imply a decline in tobacco demand. During economic recessions and periods of high unemployment—when incomes are under pressure—one should expect declines in tobacco demand which will negatively impact government excise tax revenues. In fact, Spain experienced this during the most recent financial crisis, particularly from 2009 to 2012 as Table 10 demonstrates. Over this period, real GDP growth[97] contracted annually (less 2011),[98] while the release for consumption of cigarettes declined by -32 percent over these four years.[99] As such, government excise tax revenues from cigarettes began to slow down, until 2011, when they actually contracted from the previous year and continued to do so in 2012.[100] From 2009 to 2012, government excise tax revenues fell by -5.7 percent.

Table 10

Spain's GDP, Cigarette Government Excise Tax Revenue, and Consumption—In Euros

Year	Cigarette Excise Tax Revenue (in millions)	Cigarette Excise Tax Revenue (% Change from Previous Year)	Release for Consumption of Cigarettes (in 1000 pieces)	Release for Consumption of Cigarettes (% Change from Previous Year)	GDP (Annual % Growth Rate, Constant)	Inflation (Annual % Change)
2002	5,144.87	-	88,600,500	-	2.7	3.06
2003	5,537.12	7.62	93,711,449	5.77	3.1	3.04
2004	5,836.32	5.40	95,305,513	1.70	3.3	3.04
2005	6,150.76	5.39	92,699,536	-2.73	3.6	3.37
2006	6,414.59	4.29	90,097,578	-2.81	4.1	3.52
2007	7,169.73	11.77	89,102,765	-1.10	3.5	2.78
2008	7,371.30	2.81	90,288,827	1.33	0.9	4.08
2009	7,452.83	1.11	81,356,510	-9.89	-3.8	-0.29
2010	7,681.34	3.07	72,430,751	-10.97	-0.2	1.80
2011	7,390.57	-3.79	60,260,720	-16.80	0.1	3.20
2012	7,027.65	-4.91	55,065,569	-8.62	-1.6	2.45

Alternatively, if the income elasticity of tobacco demand is negative, wealthier individuals are expected to consume fewer tobacco products compared to poorer individuals, and both groups would consume less as their incomes increase. Conversely, when the income elasticity of tobacco demand is above 1 (i.e., tobacco is a luxury good), then wealthier individuals will not only consume more tobacco products relative to poorer individuals, they will also have a higher share of income that is spent on tobacco.[101] Generally speaking, in countries where the income elasticity is positive, growth in tobacco consumption and incomes are positively correlated. From a public health perspective, linking tobacco taxes to income growth could provide reductions in tobacco consumption in such cases.

Clearly, the data indicate that it is not possible to make global generalizations with regard to the income elasticity of tobacco products (Table 11)—instead, income elasticity should be assessed on a country-by-country basis, to best determine optimal tobacco tax policy within each country.

Table 11

Estimates of the Income Elasticities for Tobacco Demand

Countries	Authors	Data/Year	Income Elasticity Tobacco
High Income Countries	Sayginsoy, Yurekli (2010)	Time series data, multiple periods collected from multiple sources	0.37
High Income Countries	Gallet, List (2003)	Meta-analysis	-0.80 to 3.03, mean at 0.42
China	Gale, Huang (2007)	2002 - 2003	0.36 to 1.03
Canada	Gospodinov, Irvine (2005)	Quarterly 1972Q1-2000Q4	1.25 (long run)
Europe	Townsend (1988)	1986-1988	0.5
Italy	Gallus et al. (2003)	1970 - 2000	0.1
Spain	Fernandez et al. (2004)	1965 - 2000	0.42
U.K.	Andrews, Franke (1991)	Meta-analysis	0.4
U.K.	Duffy (2006)	Quarterly aggregate time series data 1964Q2-2002Q3	0.3
U.S.	Hamilton (1972)	Cross section 1954 and 1965	0.726 to 0.821
U.S.	Andrews, Franke (1991)	Meta-analysis	0.5
U.S.	Cheng and Kenkel (2010)	Cross sectional time series 1944 to 2004	-0.286 to -0.047

III. GOVERNMENT REVENUE OBJECTIVES

A. Ramsey Rule

Around the world, excise taxes on products such as alcohol, pet-rol, and tobacco are an important source of revenue, with excises in OECD countries representing typically between 2.72 percent and 18.31 percent of total government revenues as of 2012 see Table 12.[102] The ease and perceived low cost of excise tax collection for the state has always been a practical advantage of selecting these products for revenue purposes,[103] certainly compared to direct taxes (such as income tax)—these products were taxed long before public health or environmental concerns played a role in tax policy formulation.

Table 12

Excise Tax Revenue as a Percentage of Total Tax Revenue (in percent by year)

Country	2000	2001	2002	2003	2004	2005	2006	2007	2008	2009	2010	2011	2012
Australia	9.21	9.40	9.07	8.50	8.19	7.64	7.36	6.97	7.42	7.60	7.42	6.74	
Austria	5.98	5.84	6.06	6.24	6.36	6.26	5.94	5.81	5.58	5.62	5.65	5.79	5.59
Belgium	5.05	4.86	4.93	5.11	5.29	5.28	4.93	4.83	4.57	4.85	4.92	4.71	4.55
Canada	4.72	4.93	5.42	5.52	5.34	4.94	4.62	4.44	4.45	4.65	4.73	4.46	4.31
Chile	10.33	10.72	10.49	9.98	8.62	7.76	6.26	6.31	5.93	7.52	7.20	6.80	6.96
Czech Republic	9.25	9.19	8.90	9.11	9.35	9.83	10.03	10.16	10.11	10.81	10.75	11.21	11.16
Denmark	10.36	10.41	10.69	10.27	10.11	9.67	9.73	9.51	8.86	8.31	8.60	8.65	8.57
Estonia	9.59	10.83	10.45	10.05	11.88	11.99	11.10	11.42	10.38	14.12	12.66	13.59	13.97
Finland	8.99	9.10	9.31	9.66	9.03	8.63	8.40	7.79	7.73	7.97	8.27	8.88	8.85
France	6.19	5.98	6.35	6.15	6.02	5.67	5.53	5.31	5.26	5.56	5.50	5.48	5.39
Germany	7.46	8.07	8.51	8.95	8.62	8.37	7.96	7.28	7.04	7.18	7.03	6.88	6.47
Greece	9.00	9.42	8.71	8.71	8.48	8.19	7.90	7.93	7.20	8.45	10.56	11.76	
Hungary	10.38	9.83	9.77	9.93	9.80	9.70	10.25	9.62	9.42	9.51	9.19	9.29	9.37
Iceland	9.27	7.85	8.50	9.07	8.84	9.19	9.00	8.63	7.43	7.87	8.65	8.57	8.57
Ireland	13.49	12.17	12.48	11.78	11.24	10.87	10.00	10.09	10.49	10.70	10.35	10.14	
Israel	3.52	3.47	3.96	4.32	4.39	4.49	4.64	4.55	5.15	5.61	5.86	5.60	5.60
Italy	6.26	5.96	5.70	5.87	5.60	5.56	5.31	4.90	4.58	4.92	4.86	4.97	5.43
Japan	7.23	7.24	7.46	7.63	7.40	6.94	6.65	6.41	6.23	6.67	6.51	6.44	
Korea	13.32	15.09	13.44	13.03	12.74	12.00	10.98	10.78	10.41	9.32	10.66	7.94	8.33
Luxembourg	12.03	10.95	11.60	11.82	12.95	11.79	11.11	10.50	10.31	9.75	9.40	9.50	9.12
Mexico	8.49	10.58	12.61	9.33	6.17	3.32	2.24	2.35	2.38	3.37	3.50	3.34	
Netherlands	8.29	8.46	8.21	8.35	8.65	8.52	8.55	7.97	8.00	8.13	8.02	7.85	
New Zealand	5.40	5.49	5.33	4.79	4.21	3.88	2.74	2.54	2.63	2.84	2.85	2.77	2.72
Norway	8.69	8.25	8.35	8.41	8.06	7.41	7.10	7.18	6.62	7.17	7.04	6.58	6.30
Poland	11.15	11.39	11.97	12.61	13.16	12.71	11.85	11.99	12.98	11.94	13.26	12.77	
Portugal	11.46	12.14	12.40	12.33	12.66	12.14	12.08	10.80	10.05	10.28	10.50	9.52	8.89
Slovak Republic	9.14	8.22	8.87	9.44	10.48	11.62	9.81	11.99	9.18	9.65	10.36	10.07	9.70
Slovenia	8.39	9.28	9.33	9.19	9.35	9.03	8.98	9.18	9.55	11.46	11.49	11.56	12.40
Spain	7.51	7.24	7.19	7.18	6.87	6.39	5.94	5.83	6.26	6.79	6.62	6.41	6.24
Sweden	6.03	6.34	6.71	6.62	6.31	6.10	5.84	5.73	5.80	6.17	6.04	5.80	5.69
Switzerland	5.48	5.52	5.13	5.41	5.54	5.37	5.22	4.84	5.09	4.94	5.13	4.78	4.63
Turkey	11.72	11.16	16.04	19.16	19.64	21.17	19.85	19.26	18.17	18.59	19.90	17.77	18.31
UK	10.50	9.92	10.06	9.72	9.41	8.78	8.14	8.01	8.07	9.16	8.89	8.52	8.61
U.S.	3.72	3.86	4.23	4.25	4.07	3.86	3.70	3.52	3.55	4.20	4.06	3.94	3.91

Although practicality may have been an initial incentive for the introduction of excise taxes, economic theories were eventually developed that provided additional justification, with the Ramsey Rule, arguing that, for inelastic products, the government could impose a relatively high tax rate without being a source of market distortion (creating an inefficient allocation of resources). Unfortunately, however, increasing taxes on inelastic goods still distorts consumer choice—although the quantity demanded for the inelastic good is relatively stable in response to price increases, consumers will reduce their consumption of other goods as a result of lower relative income. This also has fiscal implications: increasing the tax on one good may increase the own tax revenue for that good, but the tax revenue for other goods may decline as a result, as the consumption of these goods will have also declined. This illustrates one of the main limitations of implementing the Ramsey Rule in practice.

A further point to be made about the Ramsey Rule is that it assumes the product tax is independent of the factors of production—that is, that a consumption tax only impacts consumers, not producers. However, as a shift in consumption works its way through the economy, it leads to a price change for these other goods, which shifts the price of factors of production, which shifts the supply and demand curves. If, for example, a tax increase leads to a decline in quantity demanded (which requires a shift in the supply curve to maintain equilibrium), the firm's revenues decline—causing the firm to lower costs, typically in the form of wages. Consequently, a product tax may act indirectly as a factor tax; with respect to tobacco (as these products are generally inelastic), excise taxation often acts as factor taxes in other industries, as consumers reduce their consumption of alternative goods and services.

A third issue stems from the large number of inelastic goods—which are the best candidates for excise taxation? Price elasticity of demand for gasoline is estimated to be between -0.33 and -0.47,[104] and the median price elasticity of demand for alcohol -0.535, with beer even less price sensitive than other alcoholic beverages, see Table 13 on the following page.[105] Eggs, cereals, and dairy have price elasticities of demand of -0.27, -0.60, and -0.65, respectively[106]—should each of these be subject to excise taxation as well? Given the broad range of goods that appear to have low price elasticity of demand estimates, the Ramsey Rule fails to provide a practicable indication of which goods should be subject to excise taxation and which ones should not. As Cnossen notes: "*the price elasticity of tobacco demand is not so low that significantly higher-than-average tax rates are warranted on inverse elasticity grounds.*"[107]

Table 13

Price Elasticities Estimates for Food, Beverage, and Oil Demand

Product Category	Mean Price Elasticity			
	U.S.[108]	U.K.[109]	China[110]	India[111]
Food away from home	-0.81 (-0.23 to -1.76)	-	-	-
Soft drinks	-0.79 (-0.13 to -3.18)	-0.37 (-0.06 to -1.28)	-	-
Isotonic, sport drinks	-2.44 (-1.01 to -3.87)	-	-	-
Juice	-0.76 (-0.33 to -1.77)	-	-	-
Beef	-0.75 (-0.29 to -1.42)	-0.69 (-0.43 to -0.96)	-0.38 -	
Pork	-0.72 (-0.17 to -1.23)	-	-1.125 (-1.59 to -0.66)	
Fruit	-0.7 (-0.16 to -3.02)	-0.29 (-0.10 to -0.48)	-0.91 (-0.94 to -0.88)	-0.917* (-0.928 to -0.893)
Poultry	-0.68 (-0.16 to -2.72)	-	-0.89 (-1.28 to -0.5)	
Dairy	-0.65 (-0.19 to -1.16)	-0.36 (-0.15 to -0.56)	-	-
Cereals	-0.6 (-0.07 to -1.67)	-0.4 (-0.20 to -0.61)	-0.265* (-0.37 to -0.16)	-0.031 (-0.309 to -0.127)
Milk	-0.59 (-0.02 to -1.68)	-	-	-1.035 (-1.076 to -0.820)
Vegetables	-0.58 (-0.21 to -1.11)	-0.66 (-0.53 to -0.79)	-0.455 (-0.48 to -0.43)	-0.917* (-0.928 to -0.893)
Fish	-0.5 (-0.05 to -1.41)	-0.8 (-0.49 to -1.10)	-0.51 (-0.67 to -0.35)	-0.82* (-0.908 to -0.779)
Fats/oils	-0.48 (-0.14 to -1.00)	-0.75 (-0.53 to -0.98)	-0.495 (-0.58 to -0.41)	-0.377 (-0.476 to -0.332)
Cheese	-0.44 (-0.01 to -1.95)	-0.35 (-0.10 to -0.60)	-	-
Sweets/sugar	-0.34 (-0.05 to -1.00)	-0.79 (-0.53 to -1.05)	-	-0.010 (-0.083 to -0.036)
Eggs	-0.27 (-0.06 to -1.28)	-0.28 (-0.56 to 0.00)	-1.36 (-1.81 to -0.91)	-0.82* (-0.908 to -0.779)
Alcohol	-0.18 to -0.86 (Short Run) -0.26 to -1.27 (Long Run)	-0.56 (Beer) -0.90 (Wine) -0.75 (Spirits)	Near 0 (Beer) -0.12 (Liquor)	-1.032 (Rural) -0.867 (Urban)
Gasoline	-0.061 (Short Run) -0.453 (Long Run)	-0.068 (Short Run) -0.182 (Long Run)	-0.35 (-0.497 to -0.196)	-0.264 (-0.319 to -0.209)

*Denotes the following for each country:
China: Cereals elasticity estimate is based on grains
India: Fruit and Vegetables are estimated together, therefore have the same estimate. Fish and Eggs are also estimated together along with "Meat", and are estimated using a different price elasticity model.

B. Laffer Curve

The Laffer Curve illustrates the relationship between tax rates and government tax revenues, and provides an explanation for why this relationship is not always positive. At times, increases in the tax rate may actually result in a decline in government tax revenues, and, as such, the Laffer Curve is an important conceptual tool for policymakers formulating tax policies. While originally developed and popularized in the context of income tax rates, this same concept may also be applied in other areas, such as excise taxation.

1. BASIC ECONOMIC EXPLANATION OF THE LAFFER CURVE

As discussed previously, the Laffer Curve describes the relationship between tax rates and tax revenues. Broadly speaking, changes in tax rates have two effects on revenues: arithmetic and economic. Arithmetically, if tax rates decline, tax revenues per dollar of tax base will similarly decrease. Economically, however, lower tax rates further incentivize labor, output, employment, and consumption, thereby *increasing* the tax base. Raising tax rates has the opposite economic effect by penalizing participation in the taxed activities. The arithmetic effect and economic effect are opposing forces therefore, when the two are combined, the consequences of the change in tax rates on total tax revenues are no longer quite so obvious.

Revisiting Figure 6, at a tax rate of 0 percent, the government will not collect any tax revenues, no matter the size of the tax base. Similarly, with a tax rate of 100 percent, the government is also not able to collect tax revenues since no individual would be willing to work for an after-tax wage of zero. Likewise, no cigarette manufacturer would be willing to operate if 100 percent of every sale was collected as tax revenue. Between these two extremes, there are two different scenarios that will collect the same amount of tax revenue: a high tax rate on a small tax base, and a low tax rate on a large tax base. The latter structure is more efficient, generating fewer distortions in the market.

Figure 6

The Laffer Curve

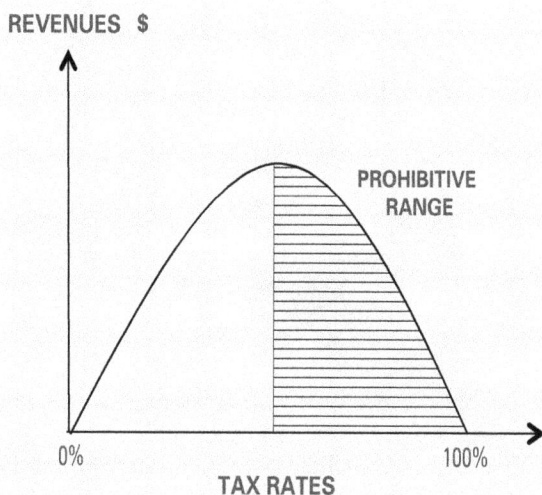

The Laffer Curve does not automatically indicate whether a reduction in tax rates will lead to an increase in tax revenues—only that it is possible for such an interaction to occur. If tax rates are past the peak on the curve in Figure 6 (i.e., in the Prohibitive Range), a tax cut will generate higher tax revenues, that is, the economic effect of the tax cut outweighs the arithmetic effect.

The price elasticity of tobacco demand will impact the shape of the Laffer Curve and revenue maximizing tax rate: if elastic, then the revenue maximizing tax rate will be lower, as consumers will be more sensitive to price increases; if inelastic, the revenue maximizing tax rate will be higher, refer to Figure 7. To further illustrate, if demand is more elastic, (the lighter curve in Figure 7) consumers will respond to price increases by decreasing their consumption much more than they would for a good with much more inelastic demand (the darker curve in Figure 7) and, as such, the revenue-maximizing tax rate will be lower for more elastic goods than it is for more inelastic goods.

Figure 7

Laffer Curves for Inelastic and Elastic Price Elasticities of Demand

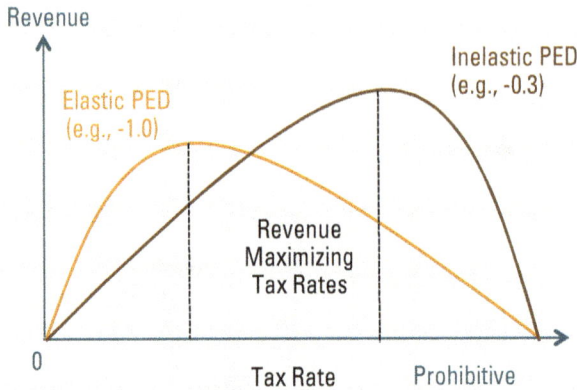

Additionally, it is important to bear in mind that the tax rate at which government revenues are *maximized* (the highest point on the Laffer Curve) is not automatically the point at which tax policy is *optimized*. If, for instance, illicit trade and its impact on crime, or the regressive impact of excise taxes on lower incomes are serious concerns, these may be reasons to enact tax rates below the revenue maximizing level. Conversely, if the objective of reducing tobacco consumption for public health reasons is seen as the sole objective, tax rates may correspondingly be above the revenue maximizing point. The optimal tax rate from a revenue perspective is thus not automatically equal to the optimal tax rate from a broader policy perspective.

As discussed earlier, tax revenue responses to a tax rate change rely on a series of factors: the relative size of the tax increase, the tax system in place, the time period being considered, the ease of transitioning into illicit or illegal alternatives, the level of tax rates already in place, the prevalence of legal enforcement loopholes, and the proclivities of the productive factors.

2. THE LAFFER CURVE APPLIED TO THE TAXATION OF TOBACCO

Most of the time, when tobacco tax rates are increased, tax revenues for the government increase, as well. However, there are growing examples of countries whose tax rates have entered the Prohibitive Range of the Laffer Curve. Latvia and Lithuania are two such examples, as can be seen in Figure 8 on the following page. When joining the European Union, both countries were required to increase cigarette tax levels substantially—from about €10 per 1000 cigarettes when they joined the EU, to the €60 per 1000 cigarette level as was then the EU minimum norm.[112] Initially, tax revenues increased in both countries, but eventually consumers started to shift to buy illicit product instead and, as a result, government tax revenues started to decline. As can be seen in Figure 8, Lithuania's revenue maximizing excise yield occurs at approximately €38 per 1000 cigarettes, versus approximately €55 per 1000 cigarettes for Latvia.[113]

Figure 8

Laffer Curves for Lithuania and Latvia

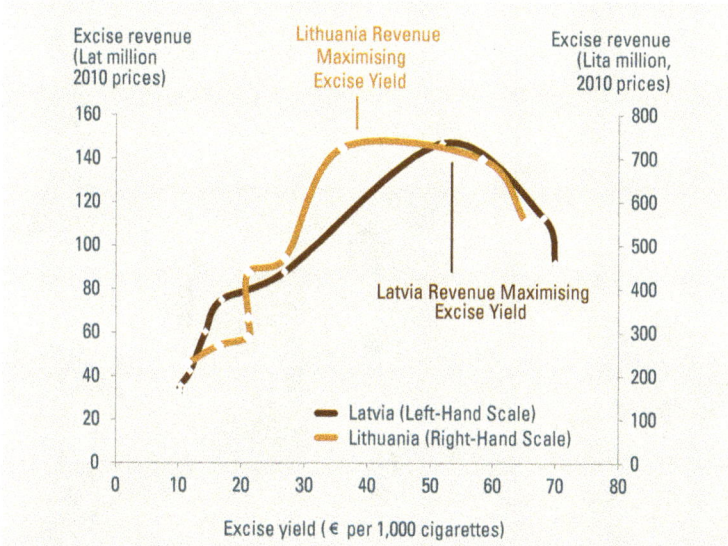

Source: International Tax & Investment Center (2012), The Impact of Imposing a Global Excise Target for Cigarettes: Experience from the EU Accession Countries; Oxford Economics and Industry Data

Latvia and Lithuania both have below-average income levels when compared with the rest of the EU, and, as such, are unable to support EU level excise taxation. These results illustrate the challenge to establish regional excise tax rates, due to the international variation in economic fundamentals and, as such, determining a universal optimum for excise taxation is an impossibility.

These are not the only countries where excise revenues started to decline—it has become a more common phenomenon particularly in the EU. Over the past 10 years or since joining the EU, 25 out of the 27 EU countries have experienced yearly declines in revenue from taxes on manufactured tobacco on at least on one occasion (Table 14). Nine countries, namely: Cyprus, Denmark, Germany, Greece, Ireland, Latvia, Portugal, Sweden, and the United Kingdom experience three or more yearly declines in tobacco tax revenue based on data from the EC DG TaxUD Data. Romania and Slovenia were the only countries not to experienced a decline in revenues from tobacco. This suggests that many countries in the EU currently apply excise levels that are close to the revenue maximizing level.

Table 14

Revenue from Taxes on Manufactured Tobacco Other than VAT

in mio EUR		2002	2003	2004	2005	2006
AUSTRIA	AT	1,296.9	1,328.7	1,317.9	1,339.7	1,408.5
% ch.			2.5%	-0.8%	1.7%	5.1%
BELGIUM	BE	1,255.0	1,617.0	1,640.8	1,657.0	1,727.2
% ch.			28.8%	1.5%	1.0%	4.2%
BULGARIA	BG					
% ch.						
CYPRUS	CY			144.7	134.6	185.1
% ch.					-7.0%	37.6%
CZECH REP.	CZ			664.4	837.5	1,110.6
% ch.					26.1%	32.6%
DENMARK	DK	1,032.3	1,032.9	945.1	967.1	988.0
% ch.			0.1%	-8.5%	2.3%	2.2%
ESTONIA	EE			58.7	76.4	77.1
% ch.					30.2%	1.0%
FINLAND	FI	592.6	584.8	593.1	600.5	617.5
% ch.			-1.3%	1.4%	1.2%	2.8%
FRANCE	FR	8,629.0	8,828.0	9,244.0	9,851.0	9,437.0
% ch.			2.3%	4.7%	6.6%	-4.2%
GERMANY	DE	13,758.0	14,094.8	13,631.3	14,247.1	14,374.5
% ch.			2.4%	-3.3%	4.5%	0.9%
GREECE	GR	2,127.0	2,248.0	2,241.0	2,257.0	2,415.5
% ch.			5.7%	-0.3%	0.7%	7.0%
HUNGARY	HU			703.8	706.8	858.7
% ch.					0.4%	21.5%
IRELAND	IE	1,140.0	1,157.0	1,058.0	1,079.5	1,103.3
% ch.			1.5%	-8.6%	2.0%	2.2%
ITALY	IT	7,854.0	8,061.0	8,713.0	8,998.0	9,723.3
% ch.			2.6%	8.1%	3.3%	8.1%
LATVIA	LV			40.9	62.3	82.6
% ch.					52.3%	32.5%
LITHUANIA	LT			62.8	74.8	102.1
% ch.					19.1%	36.5%
LUXEMBOURG	LU	406.5	467.7	568.1	598.1	485.6
% ch.			15.1%	21.5%	5.3%	-18.8%
MALTA	MT			59.3	62.4	64.5
% ch.					5.1%	3.4%
NETHERLANDS	NL	1,805.1	1,848.2	2,120.4	1,866.6	2,175.0
% ch.			2.4%	14.7%	-12.0%	16.5%
POLAND	PL				2,408.3	2,909.1
% ch.						20.8%
PORTUGAL	PT	1,159.7	1,224.0	1,027.0	1,322.7	1,426.9
% ch.			5.5%	-16.1%	28.8%	7.9%
ROMANIA	RO					
% ch.						
SLOVAKIA	SK			188.8	289.6	301.9
% ch.					53.4%	4.3%
SLOVENIA	SI			226.6	247.8	291.0
% ch.					9.4%	17.4%
SPAIN	ES	5,226.0	5,621.0	5,936.0	6,267.0	6,527.1
% ch.			7.6%	5.6%	5.6%	4.1%
SWEDEN	SE	815.0	787.1	763.7	771.3	810.1
% ch.			-3.4%	-3.0%	1.0%	5.0%
UNITED KINGDOM	UK	12,958.8	12,299.1	11,477.8	11,428.2	11,666.4
% ch.			-5.1%	-6.7%	-0.4%	2.1%
Total			60,055.87	61,199.82	63,427.51	68,153.61	70,871.36

Source: EC DG TaxUD - Excise Duty Tables (Tax receipts - Manufactured tobacco)

2007	2008	2009	2010	2011	2012
1,446.2	1,424.5	1,457.6	1,502.0	1,575.0	1,620.8
2.7%	-1.5%	2.3%	3.0%	4.9%	2.9%
1,820.2	1,756.1	1,787.3	1,986.8	1,644.1	1,922.1
5.4%	-3.5%	1.8%	11.2%	-17.3%	16.9%
688.6	876.9	904.0	777.3	1,380.0	1,189.4
	27.3%	3.1%	-14.0%	77.5%	-13.8%
191.0	202.3	195.9	198.7	221.2	212.0
3.2%	5.9%	-3.1%	1.4%	11.3%	-4.2%
1,707.4	1,422.6	1,405.6	1,615.7	1,792.2	1,842.9
53.7%	-16.7%	-1.2%	14.9%	10.9%	2.8%
971.9	966.6	990.4	1,105.0	1,004.3	1,100.7
-1.6%	-0.5%	2.5%	11.6%	-9.1%	9.6%
97.5	97.2	133.4	114.7	144.5	158.2
26.3%	-0.3%	37.3%	-14.1%	26.1%	9.5%
616.6	622.3	681.6	691.1	732.6	746.8
-0.1%	0.9%	9.5%	1.4%	6.0%	1.9%
9,380.0	9,550.4	9,894.5	10,358.7	10,943.3	11,135.4
-0.6%	1.8%	3.6%	4.7%	5.6%	1.8%
14,247.6	13,513.1	13,355.7	13,477.6	14,403.7	14,130.4
-0.9%	-5.2%	-1.2%	0.9%	6.9%	-1.9%
2,581.3	2,516.2	2,566.2	2,913.0	3,044.5	2,707.0
6.9%	-2.5%	2.0%	13.5%	4.5%	-11.1%
1,011.9	1,074.7	1,137.2	925.2	1,034.9	1,105.1
17.8%	6.2%	5.8%	-18.6%	11.8%	6.8%
1,192.1	1,146.0	1,216.5	1,159.6	1,126.1	1,072.3
8.0%	-3.9%	6.1%	-4.7%	-2.9%	-4.8%
10,051.8	10,388.0	10,495.6	10,621.5	10,934.2	10,921.9
3.4%	3.3%	1.0%	1.2%	2.9%	-0.1%
106.3	205.5	160.9	129.7	149.7	149.5
28.7%	93.3%	-21.7%	-19.4%	15.5%	-0.1%
118.0	198.2	199.9	160.5	186.4	202.3
15.5%	67.9%	0.9%	-19.7%	16.2%	8.5%
500.5	517.4	478.2	488.4	524.0	538.0
3.1%	3.4%	-7.6%	2.1%	7.3%	2.7%
58.7	62.1	64.8	70.0	71.0	75.3
-9.1%	5.9%	4.4%	8.0%	1.4%	6.1%
2,202.9	2,277.8	2,318.0	2,407.0	2,525.0	2,502.0
1.3%	3.4%	1.8%	3.8%	4.9%	-0.9%
3,521.6	3,737.6	3,856.5	4,249.7	4,082.9	4,561.8
21.1%	6.1%	3.2%	10.2%	-3.9%	11.7%
1,224.7	1,295.9	1,140.0	1,428.7	1,446.7	1,353.6
-14.2%	5.8%	-12.0%	25.3%	1.3%	-6.4%
918.7	1,081.2	1,261.5	1,345.3	1,531.3	1,741.9
	17.7%	16.7%	6.6%	13.8%	13.8%
685.8	388.5	507.3	613.5	627.5	640.4
127.1%	-43.4%	30.6%	20.9%	2.3%	2.1%
300.6	342.8	362.5	391.0	429.3	442.3
3.3%	14.0%	5.8%	7.9%	9.8%	3.0%
7,301.2	7,585.9	7,641.1	8,023.2	7,849.5	7,644.6
11.9%	3.9%	0.7%	5.0%	-2.2%	-2.6%
902.2	845.9	787.2	852.0	1,008.1	1,024.5
11.4%	-6.2%	-6.9%	8.2%	18.3%	1.6%
11,952.5	11,022.5	9,134.9	10,152.6	11,049.4	11,915.2
2.5%	-7.8%	-17.1%	11.1%	8.8%	7.8%
75,800.94	75,119.89	74,135.14	77,758.96	81,463.52	82,656.75

IV. PUBLIC HEALTH OBJECTIVES

A. Pigou

An additional argument for excise taxes is that of externalities—that the price of a good may not be reflective of the full costs of its consumption. Automobiles, for example, generate pollution when operated—and these costs are inflicted on the population as a whole, not just those who drive. As such, automobiles (or better: petrol) would be a strong candidate for a "Pigouvian tax",[114] one designed to correct for the presence of any negative externalities and their associated market failures.

Unfortunately, the efficiency of the Pigouvian framework requires a perfectly competitive market, a theoretical construct rarely observed in practice, especially in relation to tobacco markets. In the presence of monopolies, oligopolies, or imperfect competition, Pigouvian taxation generates market distortion, which may result in under-production, increased prices, or reduced employment. Furthermore, government intervention via taxation may not be the most efficient system to correct for externalities,[115] and may be more appropriate as a last resort, after bargaining fails at the individual level. [116] The government can also correct for externalities by other means than a Pigouvian tax, such as by regulatory policies.

Tobacco products are typically viewed as prime candidates for a Pigouvian tax, due to the health consequences of their consumption. Net externalities generated from smoking have been estimated at $0.15 per pack of cigarettes in 1986,[117] ($0.32 in 2013 dollars), and were updated in 1995 to $0.33 ($0.49 in 2013 dollars)[118]—both of which are below the federal and state excise tax in place at the time ($0.76 in 2001, equivalent to $1.00 in 2013).[119]

Alternatively, governments can opt for a regulatory based approach. For instance, by banning smoking from public places, the external costs of secondhand smoke are reduced or eliminated as a result of this regulatory measure, taking away the need to introduce a Pigouvian tax to address this aspect. Similarly, if insurers can differentiate between smokers and non-smokers, the health care costs of tobacco use can be accurately reflected in insurance premiums, taking away the need to address external costs through excise taxes. Of course, such a solution is not applicable in countries with socialized health care.

Based on these principles, within the U.S., there would seem to be no justification to increase the excise tax level on tobacco, as the existing tax level already exceeds the estimated external costs, and non-tax solutions to reduce consumption, such as public smoking bans and the ability of insurers to charge different rates based on smoking practice, are in effect as well.

B. Bhagwati Theorems and Unintended Consequences of Tobacco Taxation

Jagdish Bhagwati is a world renowned international trade theorist whose work on the optimization of economic policy while accounting for non-economic objectives, such as reducing consumption of certain products e.g., for health reasons, is particularly relevant for this book. Bhagwati addresses three potential policies in order to constrain consumption levels; a production or factor tax-cum-subsidy, a tariff, or a consumption tax-cum-subsidy.[120]

Since subsidies are essentially negative taxes, this book will therefore focus on taxes. A production tax is levied on firms, which causes the prices producers face to increase and as a result, the production of the taxed good will decline, causing the relative price for the taxed good to increase.[121] Production taxes generally come in the form of taxes on labor or on capital, since both increase producer prices. Social security taxes function as a labor tax, while corporate taxes and property taxes function as taxes on capital. Labor taxes vary across countries, with countries such as Afghanistan and Bangladesh imposing no labor tax (as a percentage of commercial profits using 2012 data), to countries such as Russia, Italy, and France imposing a tax on labor as high as 41.2 percent, 43.4 percent, and 51.7 percent of salaries, respectively.[122]

A tariff is a tax imposed on imported goods, thus raising the price of imported goods relative to domestically produced goods to domestic consumers and to producers if the good is an input of production.

Tariff rates also vary across different countries; in 2011, the weight mean tariff rate across all products was as low as 0 percent for Switzerland, and as high as 21.8 percent for Iran.[123]

When used to protect domestic industry, a tariff can generate market distortions and cause efficiency loss since it can lead to over-capacity in the domestic production of the importable good. It is therefore important for policymakers to exercise caution when imposing tariffs on imported goods, as implementing a tariff without sound economic reason can lead to unintended consequences.

The 2002 U.S. steel tariff is an example of a bad tariff policy decision since it was mainly implemented to protect U.S. producers of steel, rather than to correct for a trade imbalance.[124] The tariff on imported steel products ranged from 8 percent to 30 percent, based on the type of steel product.[125] As a result, steel consuming manufacturers, that is, U.S. producers who rely on steel as an input of production, could no longer effectively compete on the international market due to the high steel prices, therefore losing customers and being forced to lay off laborers.[126] In fact, 224,400 jobs were lost in 2002 in the metal manufacturing, machinery and equipment manufacturing, and transportation equipment and parts manufacturing sectors.[127]

Finally, as its name indicates, consumption taxes are levied on goods or services, and are paid by the consumer. Consumption taxes will increase the relative price of the taxed good to consumers, which can be used as a tool to correct for a consumption problem. Value added taxes, commodity taxes, retail sales taxes, and excise taxes are all examples of consumer taxes. As a percentage of total tax revenue, the taxes on goods and services vary by country from 0.3 percent in Kuwait, to 56.3 percent in Turkey using data from 2011.[128]

From the three options described above to constrain consumption levels, the policy that is least optimal is the production or factor tax-cum-subsidy policy because it does not directly apply to the non-economic objective of the government; it is a producer solution to a consumer problem, which makes it relatively ineffective. The second least optimal policy intervention is that of a tariff—again, this does not directly impact the objective to constrain consumption; instead it affects the levels of trade by increasing the price of the foreign good relative to the domestic good. The most optimal government intervention policy in order to curb consumption of a particular good is a tax policy, as consumption taxes directly impacts consumption levels, which is the non-economic objective.[129]

The consequences of choosing a sub-optimal policy can be dire— Bhagwati notes that pursuing the wrong economic policy can result in a peculiar situation where economic growth can potentially lead to a country being worse off than it was prior to the policy action being introduced, a situation he coined as "immiserizing growth".[130] Therefore, if the economic target is to constrain consumption, then policies such as production or factor taxes and tariffs should be avoided.

In many instances, governments use economic policies in order to achieve non-economic outcomes that are welfare improving rather than technically efficient.[131] The taxation of tobacco is an example of this, as governments typically intervene in the Pareto-optimal free market in order to pursue non-economic objectives of reducing tobacco consumption. Although policy interventions are rarely economically efficient, when the policymaker has non-economic objectives, the Bhagwati Theorems can be used to analyze and rank different policy decisions in order to minimize the cost to the overall economy and reduce the distortionary impacts on the market.[132] As previously emphasized, since the non-economic policy of the government for tobacco is often to reduce the consumption of tobacco products, the Bhagwati Theorems advocate that the most direct and cost efficient way to constrain the consumption of tobacco is through a consumption response, rather than via a trade or production response.

In order to achieve a consumption response, the government can choose among the following options:
1. Tax the targeted behavior;
2. Subsidize desirable behavior; or,
3. Spend money to reduce the targeted behavior in some way.

Traditionally, taxing the targeted behavior has been the policy measure many governments have pursued to bring about a consumption response. Governments tend to favor taxing certain consumption products (as an indirect way of taxing the targeted behavior) since it can generate government tax revenue (assuming the tax level is not set too high), whereas the other two options require additional spending on the government's part. Products that have been specifically taxed in order to reduce consumption include alcohol, gasoline, firearms, gambling licenses, and, of course, tobacco. However, taxes on products such as soda and "junk" food are quickly becoming the center of political discussions as candidates for excise taxation, especially in countries that face a severe obesity problem, such as Mexico and the U.S.

Although the latter two consumption response options alone are not discussed by Bhagwati, they do merit some attention since they are valid policy measures. The government could subsidize desirable behavior by offering payments to individuals to incentivize the encouraged behavior, thus promoting the government's non-economic goal. For instance, in the context of reducing tobacco consumption, the government could subsidize quitting tobacco use via payments to former smokers to no longer smoke. Of course, there is the cost of administering this sort of a subsidy (as there is for administrative taxation or other negative policies), since some evidence would need to be documented that individuals have indeed stopped consuming tobacco products.

The third policy option involves the government using funds to reduce the targeted behavior. This could be accomplished through public service ads, offering information via technology or through pamphlets, or funding programs that focus on reducing the targeted behavior. With tobacco products, this could involve the government spending funds on programs directed toward tobacco cessation, such as funding programs that disseminate health information or that provide cessation tools.

Rather than choosing among these three options, policymakers could instead use a combination of these three fiscal policies in order to accomplish their non-economic goals.

The Importance of Considering the Economic Tax Incidence and Tax Burden

In considering excise tax structure, it is also important for policy-makers to consider the economic tax incidence[133] and burden, that is, where the tax is placed versus who really feels the effect of the tax. Although Bhagwati recommends a consumption solution to a consumption problem, it is not clear that 100 percent of the tax burden will fall on consumers—hence why discussion of the economic tax incidence and tax burden is crucial.

The economic tax incidence accounts for the own-market economic effects of the tax—this would be the same as the tax statute if tobacco demand was perfectly price-inelastic. Given perfect price inelasticity, a price increase would yield no change in the quantity demanded, and, consequently, tobacco supply would not be impacted. If demand is not perfectly inelastic, however, tax incidence diverges from the tax statute—an increase in price leads to a decrease in quantity demanded, and suppliers of tobacco respond to the decreases in the quantity demanded by decreasing output. As a result, the demand for inputs used to produce tobacco also decline.

In contrast, the tax burden considers the revenue effects on other markets and can paint a more complete picture of the results of tax increases. Knowing on whom a tax is placed doesn't mean that entity actually bears the burden of the tax. In truth what happens is that in any tax structure those factors of production that are either unable or unwilling to vary their work effort in response to price changes will always bear the lion's share of the burden of taxation. In more technical terms, the greater the factor's supply elasticity the smaller will be its burden from a given tax no matter where that tax is placed. And conversely the less elastic a factor's supply elasticity the greater will be that factor's burden no matter where the tax incidence is placed.

In addition to tax incidence and burden it is also true that the further away from optimal taxation an economy tax structure is the greater will be the damage done by any absolute amount of taxation.

In extreme circumstances where the tax on a factor is already in or close to the prohibitive range of the Laffer Curve, any additional increase in that tax, by definition, will elicit large withdrawals of that factor from the productive economy. Again, if the tax were already in the prohibitive range, the large loss of productive services of that factor would more than offset the tax increase and result in less tax revenue. The end result would be a whole lot of damage to the economy and little if any additional tax receipts.

Additionally, given a tax increase and assuming tobacco demand is inelastic, consumers have less income to spend on other goods and services. This, in turn, impacts the market for other goods and services vis-à-vis the quantity demanded, the output, and the market clearing price. Therefore, even in the extreme case of perfectly inelastic tobacco demand, the tax burden will never be the same as the tax statute.

As this book has documented, the price elasticity of tobacco demand is not constant and is not completely insensitive to price changes. As such, some reduction in tobacco demand will occur for a given price increase, which can also indirectly shift the burden onto other industries or factors. For instance, once the reduction of tobacco output becomes significantly large enough, resources will be reallocated from tobacco production to other industries, displacing tobacco laborers (or their wages) and affecting the markets of these other industries, which will now face more supply, reducing the market price *ceteris paribus*. Ideally, the excise tax would be passed onto the consumer in the form of higher prices since it is a tax on consumption rather than on factors; however, this is not always the case, as suppliers may absorb some of the cost through reductions in the factors of production. As such, policymakers should be aware of these dynamic effects to fully understand how tax changes in one market spill over to others.

We could go on in rather technical detail, but the important point to bear in mind is that just because consumers literally pay the excise tax does not mean they are the only ones affected by the tax. Governments must keep this in mind as they set policy, or else unintended consequences are bound to transpire.

V. HOUSEHOLD INCOME EFFECTS

A. Affordability: Theoretical Considerations

Affordability is an important consideration for anticipating total revenues, even with very price-inelastic goods. When a good becomes too expensive, consumers may discontinue its consumption, or turn to illicit products, or instead reduce the consumption of other goods in order to continue consuming the highly taxed product. Taxes create a financial opportunity for illicit trade, but this is not a sufficient condition in and of itself. The potential profits for smugglers (and savings for consumers) from illicit trade must be weighed against the likelihood and consequences of enforcement. Consequently, it is not just high tax rates that indicate whether illicit trade activity will be a problem, but rather high tax rates coupled with low affordability and enforcement.

1. THE FOUNDATION OF AFFORDABILITY ANALYSIS: PRICE AND INCOME

Affordability is an important aspect of taxation policy, particularly as it provides a method for comparing price and tax levels internationally. In order to properly analyze the economics of affordability on an international scale, it is first necessary to discuss the two components of affordability—price and income. Global prices, even when expressed in a common currency,[134] diverge from one another due to taxes, transport costs, tariffs, and other trade barriers. Income, on the other hand, is the consumption constraint (one can't consume more than what is earned and saved) and provides a scale to determine how low or high prices are to different consumers—$100 is a relatively smaller sum of money for an individual with an income of $500,000 compared to an individual with an income of $50,000. Affordability plays a large role in the likelihood of tobacco smuggling, since high taxes alone do not necessarily imply larger incentives for illicit trade. In fact, it is both the tax and affordability components that determine the likelihood of smuggling and other illicit trade activities, as illustrated in Figure 15 on the following page.

Table 15

Likelihood of Illicit Trade

	Relatively Unaffordable	Relatively Affordable
High Taxation	High	Moderate
Low Taxation	Moderate	Low

The discussion in this section provides the theoretical foundation in order to better understand these concepts of price and income, and how they relate to affordability and the taxation on tobacco.

i. Price Theory—Law of One Price, the Big Mac Index, and PPP

Given the option between two identical goods, consumers will prefer the cheaper of the two (all else held equal). If the prices of these goods are different in different places, there exists the possibility for arbitrage—buying where prices are low, and selling where prices are high. Indeed, this is largely the basis on which international trade has flourished, and these behaviors are the fundamental basis for price theory.

Law of One Price

The law of one price is an important concept for not only linking price levels in different countries to their exchange rates, but also for understanding affordability given price deviations across different countries. In a theoretically ideal world, where transportation costs, tax differences, and barriers to trade do not exist, the law of one price states that identical goods should sell for the same price in different countries when their prices are expressed in a common currency. For example, if the U.S. dollar per British pound exchange rate is $1.50 per pound, then a shirt that sells for $30 in New York City will have to sell for £20 in London. Any deviations from the law of one price should be quickly arbitraged away.

Consider from the previous example that the exchange rate is now $1.45 per pound, which means that an individual could purchase the same shirt as before in London by converting $29 into £20 via the foreign exchange market. Therefore, the dollar price of the shirt in London is now $29, rather than $30. However, assume that the price for the shirt remains $30 in New York City. In the theoretically ideal world, U.S. importers and British exporters will be incentivized to buy shirts in London and ship and sell them in New York City. As a result, prices for the shirt in London will rise given the increase of the quantity demanded, while the price will decline in New York City given the increase of the quantity supplied. This continues until the price of the shirt is equalized in both locations.

The law of one price can be summarized formally by the following equation: $P^i_{US} = (E_{\$/£}) \times (P^i_{UK})$, where P^i_{US} is the U.S. dollar price of good i when it is sold in the U.S., $E_{\$/£}$ is the exchange rate represented as the amount of U.S. dollars required to purchase 1 British pound, and P^i_{UK} is the British pound price of good i when it is sold in the U.K. The formal representation of the law of one price is important to understand, as it will provide the foundation for PPP.

The law of one price is important for understanding affordability across different countries. For instance, assuming incomes are identical in both countries, if a pack of cigarettes is $6 in Minnesota, and the exchange rate between the U.S. dollar and Canadian dollar is 0.95 i.e., it takes 0.95 U.S. cents to buy 1 Canadian dollar, then the law of one price states that the price per pack of cigarettes in Canada should be about CAD$6.32. If the price is actually CAD$6.10, then cigarettes are more affordable in Canada, thus the incentive to cross the border and purchase cigarettes is high (for individuals living in Minnesota). If the price is higher than CAD$6.32, then the converse is true, Canadians are incentivized to purchase cigarettes in Minnesota, where they are more affordable.

Competitive forces should then equalize prices, in theory, according to the law of one price. If the prices do not equalize, then usually the cost of transport and retailing (excluding taxes) are thought to explain the price gap. However, with cigarettes, the value of the product relative to the weight of the product is high, implying that transportation costs are not a large contribution to any price differences.[135] Likewise, retailing costs for cigarettes are thought to be low when excluding taxes, which indicate that retailing costs do not provide a large contribution to price gaps. Therefore, the variations of cigarette prices across different countries are most likely due to variations in taxes.

Given that taxes are generally thought to drive cigarette price wedges across different countries, and the fact that legislation typically requires that taxes are paid in the destination country, thereby prohibiting traders to arbitrage on tax differences (indeed—this is smuggling!), the law of one price will likely not hold in the case of tobacco products. As a result, the divergence from the law of one price due to different cigarette tax policies will help explain one aspect of the variation of affordability across the globe (other aspects being differences in income and regulatory barriers to trade).

The Big Mac Index

Perhaps the most well-known application of the law of one price is the Big Mac Index, which was introduced by the *Economist* magazine in 1986. Since Big Macs are sold across the world and are consistent in terms of their recipe, one would expect that the dollar prices of a Big Mac would be similar across the different countries. If the dollar price of a Big Mac deviates across different countries, then foreign currencies are thought to be under or overvalued relative to the U.S. dollar—overtime the price for an identical good like the Big Mac should, in theory, equalize via the competitive market mechanism discussed in the previous subsection. For example, in July 2013, the average price of a Big Mac in the U.S. was $4.56 while the average price in Norway for a Big Mac was $7.51.[136] This indicates that the Norwegian Kroner was overvalued by nearly 65 percent relative to the U.S. dollar at that time.[137] Therefore, the exchange rate that would result in a Big Mac costing the same in the U.S. as Norway would be 10.10, rather than the actual rate of the time, which was 6.13.[138] Of course, these deviations in price can also be attributed to other factors, such as transportation costs, government regulations, product differentiation i.e., few substitutes exist in some markets, allowing McDonald's to price to market in certain locations, labor costs, rental costs, etc, and let's not forget that in practice arbitrage will not work for Big Mac's, as they are rapidly perishable goods.

As a law of one price exercise, Lal and Scollo (2002) calculate the dollar price of cigarettes relative to the price of a Big Mac.[139] In countries with high cigarette prices, the expectation is that one Big Mac equates to fewer cigarettes, holding all else equal. However, there is no reason to expect high Big Mac prices to be correlated to high cigarette prices. In Table 16 below, the results from Lal and Scollo's 2002 study are reproduced, where the trend of higher cigarette prices corresponds to a lower amount of cigarettes is observed.[140] The table also shows that the relation between tax incidence and price (expressed both as a percent of retail sales price, as well as the cost of cigarettes in relation to the cost of a Big Mac), is not so clear-cut. For instance, the tax incidence in Britain, Denmark and Portugal seem broadly comparable, but lead to very different price levels, both nominally and in Big Mac equivalents. This indicates that tax incidence is probably not a good benchmark to compare fiscal policies internationally.

Table 16

Cigarette Prices, Cigarette Taxes, and the Big Mac Index of Cigarettes

Country	Price of 20 Cigarettes (USD)	Total Tax Incidence (percent)	Cigarettes per Big Mac
Britain*	$6.33	79.5	9
Ireland*	$4.46	79	12
USA*‡	$4.30	27.7	12
Australia*	$4.02	68.9	9
Singapore**	$3.99	53	9
Hong Kong*	$3.97	52	7
New Zealand*	$3.88	74.5	10
Canada	$3.80	71.1	11
Denmark*	$3.77	81.7	17
Sweden*	$3.64	70.5	15
Finland*	$3.53	79	15
France*	$2.76	75.5	20
Germany*	$2.76	68.9	18
Belgium*	$2.63	73.8	21
Netherlands*	$2.56	73	19
Austria*	$2.37	73.7	20
Japan**	$2.18	61	19
Luxemburg*	$1.94	67.7	30
Italy*	$1.93	74.7	24
Greece*	$1.79	72.8	22
Spain*	$1.66	71.2	28
Portugal*	$1.63	80.7	26
Malaysia**	$1.21	34	22
South Korea**	$1.02	68	50
Poland**	$0.92	69	32
Taiwan**	$0.91	44	45
Thailand**	$0.80	56	32
Brazil**	$0.57	75	50
Philippines**	$0.44	41	59
Indonesia**	$0.43	48	86
Average	**$2.54**	**65.50**	**24.97**

Based on the most popular price category.
*Sources: *Smoking and Health Action Foundation; **Ash UK.*
†Sales weighted average (reflects 17 June 2002 increase); ‡average of highest (New York) and lowest (Kentucky).

Absolute and Relative PPP

Purchasing power parity, or PPP, is often used when analyzing international prices in a common currency and is commonly used in studies, rather than exchange rates, to convert local currency prices into a common price. Using PPP accounts for the variation in the costs of living, but it is important to note that adjusting based on PPP does not account for variations in income since it is a price measure.

Absolute PPP is an economic theory that states that the exchange rate between two countries is equal to the ratio of the countries' price levels, where the price level is defined as the monetary value of a reference basket of goods and services.[141] Absolute PPP differs from the law of one price in that it uses the overall price level of a country, rather than the price for a single good or service.

To understand absolute PPP, assume that country A's price level increases. The increase of the price level implies that the purchasing power of country A will decrease, since consumers now require more money to purchase the same reference basket of goods and services. As a result of the decreased purchasing power, country A's currency will undergo a proportional currency depreciation against other currencies.

To formalize, using the U.S. and the U.K. as an example, absolute PPP can be expressed as the following equation to predict the dollar-pound exchange rate: $E_{\$/£} = P_{US}/P_{UK}$, where P_{US} is the U.S. dollar price of a reference basket sold in the U.S. and P_{UK} is the British pound price of the same reference basket sold in the U.K. For example, if the reference basket costs $100 in the U.S. and £80 in the U.K., then absolute PPP states that the exchange rate between the dollar and pound is $1.25 per 1 pound. If prices double in the U.S., that is if the reference basket now costs $200, then the absolute PPP implied exchange rate would be $2.50 per 1 pound, which is a depreciation of the U.S. dollar relative to the British pound.

Rearranging the equation above yields an important interpretation of absolute PPP, which states that price levels across all countries are equal when measured in a common currency: $P_{US} = E_{\$/£} \times P_{UK}$. This is the case since the right hand side of the equation represents the dollar price of the reference basket in the U.K., which must be equal to the dollar price of the same basket in the U.S if absolute PPP holds. Therefore, at the prevailing exchange rate, absolute PPP holds that every currency's domestic purchasing power is the same as its foreign purchasing power.

Relative PPP is a weaker statement than what is implied by absolute PPP as relative PPP states that changes in price levels across different countries are always equal, at least over time. Therefore relative PPP between the U.S. and the U.K. can be written as the following:

$$E_{\$/£,t}/E_{\$/£,t-1} = \left(P_{US,t}/P_{US,t-1}\right)\Big/\left(P_{UK,t}/P_{UK,t-1}\right)$$

where t is the time period and $t-1$ is the time period preceding t. Since the measures developed by national statistical agencies for consumer prices are generally reported as indexes relative to a base year, absolute PPP cannot be calculated since the overall price level is not reported. However, it is easy to calculate relative PPP from published consumer prices, which is often why empirical studies rely on relative PPP despite it being a weaker statement compared to absolute PPP. Even still, the reference basket of goods and services is often not identical in each country, leading to some mismeasurement of relative PPP. Understanding these concepts of PPP will prove useful when analyzing affordability, as there is evidence of a positive relationship between national incomes and price levels.

Blecher and van Walbeek (2008) review the PPP concept to study affordability. They find that the price of cigarettes is three to four times more expensive in developed countries relative to developing countries in absolute terms. However, when using PPP, they find that cigarettes are less than twice as expensive in developed countries compared to developing countries.[142] In other words, comparing absolute prices is not meaningful, as we need to put the price of tobacco in the context of the general prices level within a country. Furthermore, as we will see later, price (whether absolute or relative) in itself is in any case not a good measure of affordability since it does not account for varying levels of income, which is the next topic for discussion.

ii. Defining Income: Broad Versus Narrow, Income Distribution, and the Gini Coefficient

In order to provide a comprehensive analysis of affordability, it is necessary to also discuss income because it allows policymakers to compare international prices as they relate to various income levels. The economic definition of income is carefully constructed, as this book will address in this subsection. Furthermore, there are different measures of income, and each method has different implications when calculating affordability. These theoretical issues are the focus of this subsection, with practical concerns being reserved for Part II of this book.

Income from an Economic Perspective

Measurements of household income and expenditure are surprisingly contentious among economists, and there exist several more metrics for such data than one might expect. Fortunately, however, they tend to be broadly divisible into two categories, and the relative merits of each group are widely acknowledged.

Microeconomic measurements, such as the Current Population Survey (CPS) or Consumer Expenditure (CE), tend to give a very representative view of income distributions, which can be especially useful if income distributions tend to be subject to large skew or dispersion. Unfortunately, there are corresponding disadvantages as well: micro data doesn't effectively capture non-cash sources of income, such as employers covering a portion of health insurance costs, or matching pension contributions, which have become an increasing component of household income in developed countries.[143] Furthermore, as micro data tends to be self-reporting (i.e., consumer surveys), use of micro data is intrinsically less accurate than macro data; consumers tend to accurately report large static or infrequent purchase, such as rent, utilities, or vehicle expenditures, but are much less reliable for "sin" consumption (e.g., cigarettes or alcohol) and small, frequent purchases, such as food or clothing.

Conversely, macroeconomic measurements, such as per capita GDP or National Income & Product Accounts (NIPAs), tend to be more accurate (as they do not rely on individual reporting) and more complete (as they more accurately capture non-wage income). Additionally, GDP per capita is attractive in that it is easier to obtain a comparable measurement across different countries, as it is far less sensitive to each country's tax and welfare policies. Furthermore, the methodology for calculating GDP per capita is well established, making it an ideal candidate to compare average income or living standards across different countries. Unfortunately, unlike microeconomic measurements, per capita GDP ignores income distribution since GDP per capita is an average, if the distribution of income is heavily skewed, then the overall income picture it represents is not accurate. Similarly, countries with a heavy export component in GDP may find per capita GDP an inaccurate or inappropriate measure of household income, as high exports tend to correlate with more skewed income distributions. In general, whether narrower, microeconomic or broader, macroeconomic measurements are chosen for income, the measurement should account for both cash and non-cash forms of welfare for a more complete representation.

Income Distribution: Inequality, the Gini Coefficient, and Constructing Lorenz Curves

Although GDP per capita is a useful measure of income, it can give the wrong picture when comparing two countries with very different income distributions. The more unequal the income distribution is, the more necessary it is to know the incomes of smokers in order to develop tax policy accordingly. Therefore, when examining issues concerning affordability and economic equity, it is helpful to divide the population into income quintiles, as illustrated in Table 17.

Table 17

2011 U.S. Census Bureau: Income, Poverty, and Health Insurance Coverage in the United States

	Total	Lowest fifth (Low Income)	Second fifth (Lower Middle Income)	Middle fifth (Middle Income)	Fourth fifth (Higher Middle Income)	Highest fifth (High Income)	Top 5 percent
Number of Households (in 1000s)	121,084	24,217	24,217	24,217	24,217	24,217	6,057
Lower Quintile Boundary (in $)	0	0	20,260	38,515	62,434	101,577	186,000

Another approach to map income distribution is to construct a Lorenz curve, three of which are provided in Figure 9 on the following page. A Lorenz curve maps the cumulative share of individuals, ordered by income from lowest to highest along the x-axis, against the cumulative share of income (y-axis). For example, in Figure 9, when considering the solid black Lorenz curve for the bottom 15 percent of all households, the share of total income earned from that segment is about 5 percent. The dotted black Lorenz curve represents an even less equal distribution- in that example, the bottom 15 percent of households earn roughly 2 percent of total income. The straight, diagonal blue line represents perfect equality, since each individual would then earn the same income—that is, the bottom 15 percent of all households earn 15 percent of the total income.

Figure 9

Lorenz Curve

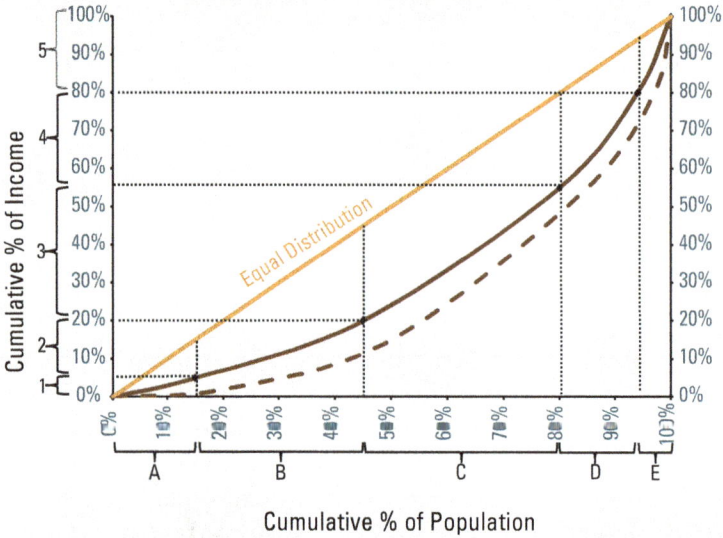

A concept related to the Lorenz curve, is the Gini coefficient of inequality, which measures the degree of inequality by comparing the area between the Lorenz curve and the line of equality with the total area under the line of equality. Essentially, the Gini coefficient measures the degree that an economy's income distribution deviates from a perfectly equal distribution. The Gini coefficient ranges from 0 to 1, where 0 represents complete equality and where 1 represents complete inequality i.e., one household holds all income, refer to Figure 10.

Figure 10

Lorenz Curves with Gini Coefficient

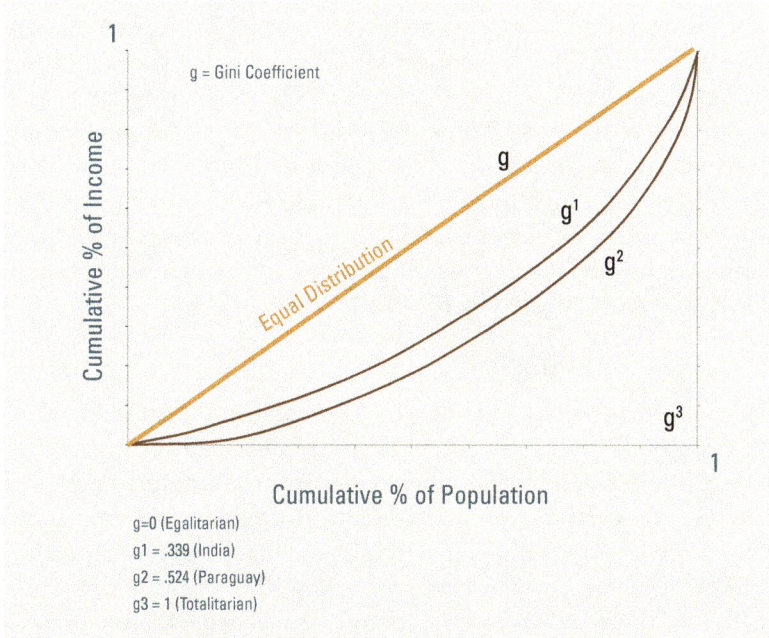

g = Gini Coefficient

Cumulative % of Income

Equal Distribution

g

g¹

g²

g³

Cumulative % of Population

g=0 (Egalitarian)
g1 = .339 (India)
g2 = .524 (Paraguay)
g3 = 1 (Totalitarian)

The Gini coefficient becomes an important estimate when comparing the impact excise tax increases will have on a country's population. Gini coefficient values closer to 1 will indicate high inequality, which therefore implies that an increase in excise tax rates could be particularly damaging to low income individuals who consume the targeted product, as their after-tax income distribution will be negatively affected.

This is especially relevant in relation to excise taxation of inferior goods,[144] which are disproportionately consumed by the poor. Excise taxes on price inelastic, inferior goods tend to be regressive—that is, the tax burden falls more heavily on lower income consumers. Further issues relating to regressivity are addressed in Subsection B.

In lieu of obtaining estimates for both the income and price elasticities of tobacco demand, policymakers can analyze the smoking prevalence for each income bracket in order to determine which segments of the population would be most impacted by tobacco excise tax increases. In fact, in a study conducted by Franks et al (2007),[145] the results indicate that the smoking prevalence gap between different income brackets has increased from 1984 to 1996, the proportion of smokers in the lowest income bracket was 27.7 percent while the same figure was 23.9 percent for all other income brackets. However, this gap widened over the period 1997 to 2004, as the lowest income figure grew to 28.6 percent while the higher income group declined to 21.6 percent; thus, the difference in smoking prevalence between low and high incomes increased from 3.8 percent points to 7 percent points.[146] Therefore, tax increases on tobacco products may further distort the distribution of income, as lower income consumers may be most affected by tobacco excise increases.

2. DEFINING AND MEASURING AFFORDABILITY

For policymakers, accounting for affordability is essential when developing tobacco excise tax policies, as simultaneous interaction between prices and income directly impact consumption decisions. Failing to properly consider affordability can lead to policies that fail to meet excise tax revenue expectations and that incentivize the illicit trade of tobacco. In the next subsections, the measures of affordability are discussed from a theoretical perspective—these measures include (1) the price relative to income, (2) the minutes of labor required to purchase a pack of cigarettes; and, (3) the percentage of daily income required to purchase a pack of cigarettes.

i. The Price Relative to Income (PRI)

Developed by Blecher and van Walbeek[147] in 2004, price relative to income (PRI) is a broad affordability measure that determines the percentage of GDP per capita needed to purchase 100 packs of cigarettes (with increased PRI indicate lower cigarette affordability). PRI can be expressed as the following equation, where RSP_{Pack} is the retail sales price per pack of 20 cigarettes and $GDP_{capita,nom}$ is the nominal GDP per capita:[148]

$$PRI = RSP_{Pack} * 100 / GDP_{capita,nom}$$

When examining price relative to income, it is important to consider what price is being used for the analysis. The relative merits of several different approaches are outlined briefly in Table 18.

Table 18

Relative Merits of Various Cigarette Price Measures

Pricing Metric	Advantages	Disadvantages
Marlboro	Standard product across countries.	May not be representative of the market as a whole.
Most Sold	Reflects the price of the product which has the highest volume within a country.	Variation in product specification (e.g., length) among different brands may misrepresent true consumption and affordability.
Cheapest Legal Cigarettes	From a public policy perspective, this is the most relevant price benchmark, as the cheapest legal cigarette both indicates the lowest tax level paid as well as the cigarettes with the highest affordability, which is relevant for public health	Specific brand varies widely by country. Doesn't consider non-cigarette tobacco consumption (such as bidis in India); may skew PRI upwards.
Weighted Average Price (WAP)	Most representative reference point for the total cigarette category; not brand dependent; will accurately reflect price movements as well as consumer up or down-trading.	May be difficult to measure, as it requires sales volume information per price point. Products are rarely directly comparable, and may present additional difficulties identifying true consumption and affordability.

The Blecher and van Walbeek PRI analysis considered the price of either Marlboro (or its closest equivalent) and the most popular local brand of cigarettes, with the cheapest pack being chosen for analysis.[149] Furthermore, the retail outlet was also accounted for— whether the cigarettes were sold in a high-volume supermarket or a mid-price retail outlet.

While adjustment for exchange rates is not needed for a PRI measurement, if particular countries experience hyperinflation, then the data for cigarette prices may not align well with GDP. As a result, countries with hyperinflation may require some data adjustments for comparison purposes, or may need to be excluded completely if the data are too volatile. Also, as previously mentioned, although

GDP per capita has the appealing feature of data availability, it fails to consider the distribution of incomes within an economy. As such, PRI may inaccurately measure affordability in the presences of high income inequality. Therefore, it is important for policymakers to ensure the accuracy of PRI by first obtaining an estimate of the Gini coefficient—as the Gini coefficient moves away from 0 and approaches 1, the degree of income inequality is worse. Prior to introducing policy changes that increase the price of cigarettes, policymakers should consider measuring PRI for the lower income brackets to prevent the income gap from further widening. This is especially true for countries where the smoking prevalence is higher in lower income brackets relative to higher income brackets.

ii. The Minutes of Labor Required to Purchase a Pack of Cigarettes

Similar to PRI, the amount of labor required to purchase cigarettes is a measure of affordability, and a relevant reference for policymakers and consumers alike. Minutes of labor required to purchase a pack of cigarettes is a useful metric, as it provides a more micro, "day to day" glimpse into consumer's purchasing decisions.

Calculating the weighted average of net hourly wages from a UBS survey conducted every three years[150] and the cigarette price data from the cost of living survey conducted by the EIU,[151] Guindon et al. compute the average number of working minutes needed to buy either a pack of Marlboro cigarettes (or an international equivalent) or a pack of local brand cigarettes for the average earner in the UBS survey.[152] As such, cigarettes are less affordable as the minutes required to purchase one pack of cigarettes increases. The minutes of labor required to purchase a pack of cigarettes can be formalized by the following equation:

$$Minutes\ of\ Labor_{pack} = (RSP_{Pack} / Wage_{weighted\ average,\ (net\ hourly,\ 12\ occupations)}) * 60$$

In contrast to the broad affordability measure, PRI, the minutes of labor method, as applied by Guindon et al., is much narrower since it uses net hourly earnings across 12 occupations rather than GDP per capita.[153] It should be noted that the UBS data is less representative of average earnings within a country since the data is collected from cities alone, which tend to be commercial centers where wages are often higher relative to wages in rural areas. Furthermore, although some of the occupations in the UBS survey are unskilled, a disproportionate amount of the occupations are in fact skilled, which likely does not represent the countries as a whole, especially developing countries. In countries where wages differ significantly between rural and urban areas, and where the population does not match the same composition of skilled to unskilled workers as UBS, estimates for affordability based on the data from the UBS survey will be biased toward cigarettes appearing more affordable than they really are.

iii. The Percentage of Daily Income Required to Purchase a Pack of Cigarettes

The percentage of daily income required to purchase a pack of cigarettes was developed by Kan as a measurement of cigarette affordability that accounted for income distribution within the UBS[154] survey data.[155] Rather than considering the weighted average of net earnings, Kan instead focuses on the average of the seven least-paid net daily wage occupations of the UBS survey, which highlights the affordability of cigarettes for lower income households.[156] Cigarette prices are constructed in the same manner for all three affordability measures—that is, through EIU's data on the international cost of living. As the percentage of daily income required to purchase a pack of cigarettes rises, the less affordable cigarettes are for the seven least-paid occupations surveyed by UBS. Kan's affordability measurement can be specified as the following equation:

$$Percentage\ of\ Daily\ Income_{pack} = (RSP_{Pack}\ /\ Wage_{average,\ net\ daily,\ 7\ least-paid\ occupations}) * 100$$

Although Kan's focus on the seven least-paid occupations in the UBS survey helped to eliminate some bias due to income disparities, many of the same problems remain as a result of the narrowness of the UBS survey data. As previously discussed with Guindon's minutes of labor estimate, the income measure likely contains measurement bias due to the gap between rural and urban wages, as well as the overstated presence of skilled to unskilled workers in the UBS survey. As such, the concern of overestimating the affordability of cigarettes remains present in Kan's affordability measure.

iv. Measuring Affordability over Time

The methodologies above provide estimates for one particular snap-shot in time, rather than a dynamic measurement of affordability trends over time. The compounded growth rate of the cigarette affordability estimate is one method to analyze cigarette affordability trends over time,[157] but may be invalid in the presence of outliers (fortunately, there are relatively simple econometric solutions if this is a concern).

Even simpler, Guindon et al.[158] analyze the trend of cigarette affordability by considering the annual real percentage changes in cigarette prices, along with the annual changes in minutes of labor required to purchase one pack of cigarettes, which controls for changes in income levels as well.

B. Tobacco Excise Taxes and Regressivity

As one of Adam Smith's four maxims of taxation, equity continues to be a crucial consideration for policymakers to ensure that the tax burden does not disproportionately fall onto individuals in the lower income brackets.[159] The key indication of whether a tax policy is "fair" is whether the overall net effect of the tax shifts the income distribution toward equality. If the tax burden falls mostly on higher income individuals, then the after-tax income of those individuals moves closer to the after-tax income of poorer individuals, or using the information from the previous subsection, a tax that falls heavily on higher income individuals will imply that the Gini coefficient is moving closer to zero, which is total equality. The converse is also true, a tax that burdens the lower income brackets disproportionately, and thus, further reduces relative after-tax income, will indicate that the Gini coefficient is moving toward one, which is total inequality.

As the after-tax income gap increases between poorer and wealthier segments of the population due to a disproportionately burdensome tax, the tax is said to be regressive since it increases in the degree of inequality i.e., Gini coefficient moves toward one. In any case, as Stiglitz notes, a regressive tax occurs when lower income individuals pay a higher percentage of income toward the tax relative to higher income individuals.[160] For tobacco excise tax policy, this becomes a concern if the prevalence of smoking is higher for lower income individuals and if the price elasticity of tobacco demand is inelastic for lower income individuals. This becomes especially problematic because increases in excise taxes can further diminish the standards of living for individuals in lower income brackets—the choice may come down to forgoing proper nutrition in order to maintain current tobacco consumption, which is certainly not an outcome policymakers would attempt to achieve.

In general, regressivity does impact countries differently due to smoking prevalence variations not only among the different income distributions within countries, but across different countries as well. For instance, Peck observes the following: (1) in developed countries, the smoking prevalence of lower income groups is higher than the smoking prevalence of higher income brackets; and, (2) the overall smoking prevalence is higher in developing countries relative to developed countries, but tobacco consumption also tends to rise in response to income increases in developing countries.[161] Therefore, issues of regressivity can be both domestic (i.e., higher smoking prevalence among lower income brackets within a country) and international (i.e., higher smoking prevalence in developing countries relative to developed countries) in nature. Due to these unique, country based characteristics, tobacco tax policy will need to be tailored to individual country circumstances, as an internationally harmonized tax approach is likely to have negative effects upon equity and regressivity in individual countries. The remainder of this subsection will discuss how to determine whether an excise tax is regressive, as well as the theoretical considerations for a tax's marginal value.

1. DETERMINING WHETHER A TAX IS REGRESSIVE

There are two aspects of equity when reviewing taxes—horizontal and vertical equity. Horizontal equity compares whether the amount of tax paid is the same for every individual in a given income group. For example, if two people earn $20,000 annually and each pays the same amount in taxes, then the tax is horizontally equitable. Tobacco taxes are horizontally equitable when a large proportion of the income group consumes tobacco. In most countries, a majority of the population does not smoke. Therefore, tobacco taxes are not horizontally equitable, as smokers pay the tax and non-smokers don't.

A tax is vertically equitable when individuals in different income groups are equally burdened by the tax, which implies that as income rises, the monetary amount of the tax paid also increases.[162] Tobacco taxes tend to be vertically inequitable when the smoking prevalence in lower income groups is relatively higher and/or when the daily smoking rate does not increase in proportion with income. Both of these conditions are usually the case, as we can also see from the fact that in many countries, the income elasticity of tobacco products is smaller than 1.

Therefore, tobacco taxation breaks both rules of vertical and horizontal equity. This may not be a major policy issue as long as tax levels are modest compared to income levels, but as countries have increased taxes on tobacco substantially over recent decades, equity issues will require more attention of policy makers.

To determine whether a tax is regressive, it is necessary to analyze how the ratio changes as income changes. Formally, the amount of tax as a share of income for each individual is represented as the following ratio, where t is the unit tax, Q is the quantity of tobacco purchased, and I is individual income:[163]

$$Amount\ of\ Tobacco\ Excise\ Tax\ Paid\ as\ a\ Share\ of\ Income = t * Q\ /\ I$$

To demonstrate the amount of tax paid as a share of income, assume the annual consumption of tobacco is 100 packs of cigarettes and that there are two individuals' incomes to consider—Joe's annual income of $10,000 and Fred's annual income of $20,000. Prior to a specific excise tax of $2 levied on a per pack of cigarettes basis, the specific excise tax was $1 per pack, indicating a $1 tax increase. The resulting shares of income required to pay the tax on 100 packs of cigarettes is summarized below in Table 19. These results indicate that Joe's income share increases by 1 percent after the excise tax increase, while Fred's income share increases by only 0.5 percent after the excise tax increase, thus implying that the excise tax is regressive. Assuming that both Joe and Fred have similar preferences, the excise tax on cigarettes will be regressive since Joe will require a greater proportion of his income to pay the tax.

Table 19

Income Share Required to Pay Tax on 100 Packs of Cigarettes

	Joe	Fred
Annual Income (in $)	10,000	20,000
Quantity of Cigarette Packs Demanded	100	100
Old Specific Excise Tax ($, Levied Per Pack of Cigarettes)	1	1
New Specific Excise Tax ($, Levied Per Pack of Cigarettes)	2	2
Old Tax Income Share (percent, Per 100 Packs of Cigarettes)	1	0.5
New Tax Income Share (percent, Per 100 Packs of Cigarettes)	2	1

Generally, if the ratio shown on the previous page between the amount of taxes paid versus income shrinks as income increases, then the excise tax is regressive since the amount of the excise tax paid declines as income rises. This occurs when the implied income elasticity of tobacco demand is between zero and one, which indicates that tobacco is a normal necessity good.[164] In this scenario, two key points are implied: (1) that the income share of tobacco taxes paid is decreasing as income increases (i.e., the tax is regressive); and, (2) that the total monetary amount of tobacco taxes paid increases as income rises (i.e., the tax is progressive).

The second argument, that tobacco consumption is more income-elastic at lower income levels, and therefore tobacco taxation is progressive, while technically accurate, misrepresents the axiomatic intent of progressive taxation. Even though lower income consumers are spending less money on tobacco products, they *are not* better off as a result of such a tax increase. To illustrate, imagine you have a strict $100 budget with which to purchase groceries. You make your purchasing decisions, and, having spent exactly $100, you leave the store with your basket of goods—however, as you leave, you're given the option to exchange your existing basket for a new, alternative basket of goods. If you exchange your existing basket for this new basket, by definition, the new basket must be worth more than $100—otherwise, you would have chosen those same goods initially. Similarly, if the price of any good in the basket increases, the consumer must reduce consumption of at least one good in the basket, making them intrinsically worse off. From a welfare perspective, price increases *cannot* improve a consumer's utility; labeling cigarette excise taxation as progressive artificially ignores the welfare damage caused by its implementation.

Related to vertical equity, progressive taxation reflects the fundamental belief that the tax burden should be directly related to income and that those with lower incomes should bear less of the costs of taxation. Ignoring the welfare loss by those who have been priced out of the market due to higher cigarette prices (indicated by higher income elasticity of demand) belies the true costs of such a tax: while the monetary costs may be progressive, the welfare costs are strongly regressive. If the income elasticity of tobacco demand is less than zero, which implies that a percentage increase in income yields a percentage decrease in tobacco demand, then tobacco taxes are regressive, at least on average, and cause further distortions to the income distribution.

The analysis above ignores the fact that many taxes other than tobacco taxes exist in the economy, and while the tobacco tax burden may be regressive, it does not imply that the total tax burden is regressive.[165] In fact, taxes that disproportionately fall on higher income brackets will potentially offset the tobacco tax burden on lower income brackets. As Peck observes, *"the tax system can be adjusted in order to ameliorate the burden of tobacco taxes…for example, offset the impact of higher tobacco excise taxes by lowering a tax on kerosene, so long as the pattern of kerosene use is similar to patterns of tobacco use"*.[166]

Despite the fact that general equilibrium effects are often ignored, empirical evidence from the U.S. and from New York in 2010-2011 suggests that cigarette excise taxes tend to be regressive.[167] Although the percentage of income spent on cigarettes for smokers is 8.8 percent overall in the U.S., for smokers earning less than $30,000 annually, this percentage is 14.2 percent overall.[168] This disparity is even more pronounced when comparing data from New York state, which has the highest cigarette excise tax ($4.35), where smokers spend 12 percent of their income overall and 23.6 percent for smokers earning less than $30,000 (Figure 11).[169]

Figure 11

Percentage of Annual Household Income Spent on Cigarettes, Overall and by Income in the United States and New York[170]

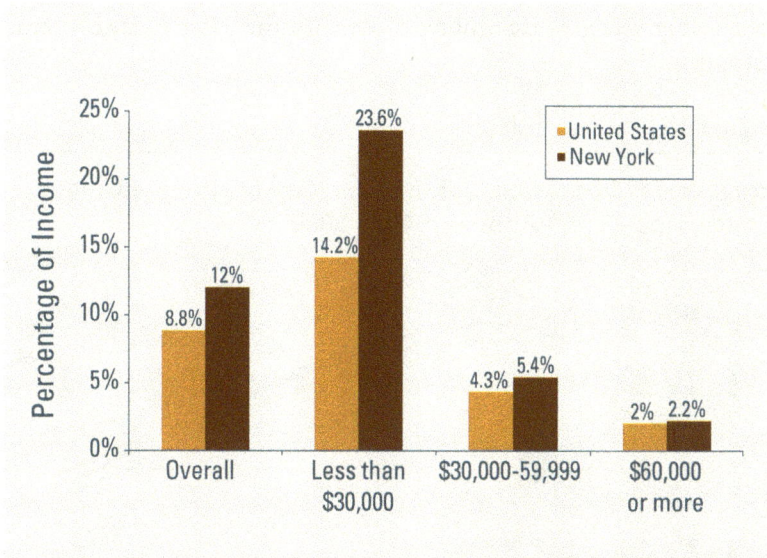

Additionally, U.S. data suggests that smoking prevalence has a very strong correlation with both education and income (which tend to be correlated themselves), and is the primary reason tobacco taxation tends to be regressive. For example, in 1995, U.S. smoking rates for college graduates (13.8 percent) are less than half the rate of either high school graduates (28.1 percent) or those who did not graduate from high school (28.2 percent). Similarly, smoking prevalence for those with incomes below $15,000 is significantly higher than for those with incomes above $50,000 (28.8 percent and 17.2 percent, respectively).[171]

Furthermore, the gap seems to be widening: in 1940, smoking prevalence for all education levels hovered close to 40 percent (ranging from 35.8 percent for those with less than a high school degree, to 40.8 percent for those with some college education).[172] By 2000, however, there was a clear relationship between educational achievement and smoking prevalence: college graduates now had smoking prevalence rates of 14.2 percent, while each other group had rates between 25 percent and 30 percent, refer to Figure 12.[173] Repeatedly, the prevalence of current smoking in the U.S. has been shown to be greatest among persons in—and independently associated with—working class jobs, low educational level, and low income.[174] Attempts to quit showed no socioeconomic gradient, while success in quitting was greatest among those with the most socioeconomic resources.[175]

Figure 12

Prevalence of Smoking by Education Category in the United States, Age 25 and Above, 1940 to 2000[176]

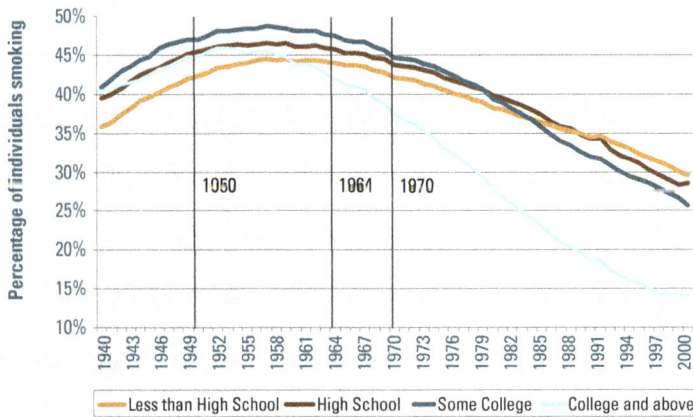

Note: From smoking histories constructed from the 1978, 1979, 1980, 1983, 1985, 1987, 1988, 1990, 1991, 1992, 1994, 1995, 1997, 1998, 1999 and 2000 National Health Interview Surveys. The information about the dangers of smoking diffused gradually: 1950, consensus in medical journals, 1964, first Surgeon General's Report, 1970, clear health warning on packages.

Source: http://www.aeaeb.org/assa/2006

2. THEORETICAL CONSIDERATIONS FOR DETERMINING A TAX'S MARGINAL VALUE

Although the discussion of average regressivity is important, analysis is incomplete without also considering the marginal impact of taxation shifts i.e., accounting for price elasticity of tobacco demand. While the example of Joe and Fred highlighted regressivity with respect to income in Subsection 1, it assumed consumer preferences, and therefore price elasticity of demand, for both individuals were identical and constant—which both theory and practice suggest is largely unrealistic. For example, assume that Joe pays $200 in tobacco taxes and still earns $10,000 annually, while Fred pays $300 in tobacco taxes and still earns $20,000 annually. Therefore, Joe pays 2 percent of his income in tobacco taxes while Fred only pays 1.5 percent, suggesting that tobacco taxes are regressive on average, see Table 20 below.

Table 20

	Joe	Fred
Income	$10,000	$20,000
Price Elasticity of Demand	-1	-1
Total Cigarette Taxes Paid	$200	$300
(As a Percentage of Income)	2.0%	1.5%
Verdict	Regressive	

However, suppose that the price elasticity of demand for Joe and Fred are no longer identical. For example, Joe will reduce his consumption of tobacco products so that he continues to pay $200 in tobacco taxes, regardless of the impact on his tobacco consumption, and Fred will maintain his current consumption of tobacco products, regardless of price increases. If the government imposes a 10 percent increase on tobacco excise taxes, Fred will now pay $330 in tobacco taxes to maintain his level of tobacco consumption, but Joe will continue to pay $200 by reducing his consumption. Therefore, the change in taxes paid has increased for the wealthier individual, Fred, while the change in taxes paid for Joe is zero, see Table 21 below.

Table 21

	Joe	Fred
Income	$10,000	$20,000
Price Elasticity of Demand	-1.0	0.0
Total Cigarette Taxes Paid	$200	$330
(As a Result of Tax Increases)	$0	$30
Tax as a Percentage of Income	2.0%	1.6%
Marginal Tax Paid (as a percentage of income)	0%	0.15%
Verdict	Progressive	

As a result, regressivity on the margin is reduced since Fred's proportion of taxes paid relative to income has increased. This example illustrates that a tax increase can distort consumer choice—Joe is forced to decrease his tobacco consumption, while Fred is not. However, while this example of a "progressive" excise tax increase is correct in the mathematical sense, it is not correct in the spirit of the definition as it describes a situation where a tax increase prices some lower incomes out of the market such that those individuals pay zero tax. Furthermore, given that many smokers do have inelastic demand preferences, a majority of these smokers will not only continue smoking, but will also pay more in excise taxes as a consequence. If smokers tend to be in the lower income brackets, such as evidenced in Figure 13, then excise tax increases will be regressive.

Even though a cigarette tax itself may be regressive, a common argument is that a cigarette tax *increase* will be a progressive measure; due to an assumed more elastic cigarette demand among lower income groups, a price increase is thought to result in those groups discontinuing tobacco consumption at higher rates, such that the majority of tax revenue comes from higher-income individuals. Empirical evidence based on the U.S. doesn't support this conclusion, as increases in tobacco prices are becoming less and less of an effective policy tool,[177] and are now beginning to impose a disproportionate burden on lower-income consumers.[178] The study from Franks et al (2007) finds that the smoking prevalence gap between the lowest income bracket and all other income brackets has increased to 7 percent, while the average cigarette pack price increased (due mainly to federal and state excise tax increases) from $2.24 (1984 to 1996) to $3.67 (1997 to 2004) in the U.S., which is nearly a 64 percent increase (Figure 13).[179] The rise in U.S. cigarette excise taxes along with the growing smoking prevalence gap implies that cigarette taxes have become more regressive in the U.S.[180]

Figure 13

Proportion of Smokers, by Cigarette Price, Income Quartile, and Year: United States[181]

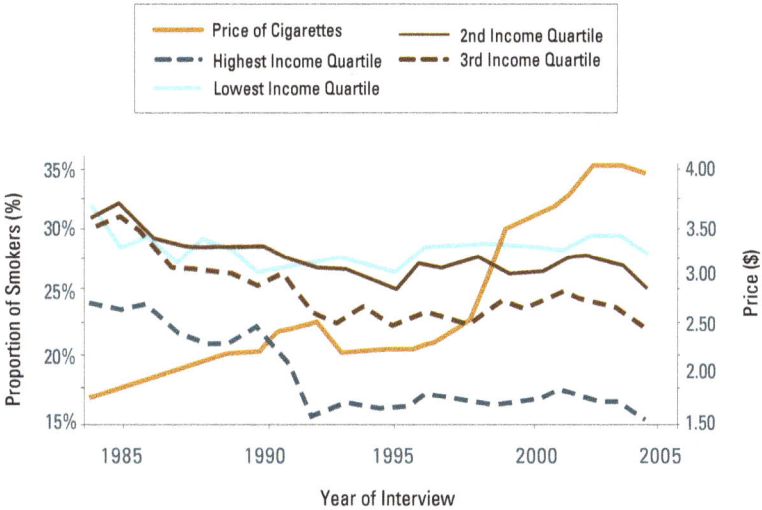

Note: From smoking histories constructed from the 1978, 1979, 1980, 1983, 1985, 1987, 1988, 1990, 1991, 1992, 1994, 1995, 1997, 1998, 1999 and 2000 National Health Interview Surveys. The information about the dangers of smoking diffused gradually: 1950,

Additionally, among low-, middle-, and high-income groups in the U.S., total cigarette price elasticity has been estimated at -0.37, -0.35, and -0.20, respectively—not *nearly* sufficient dispersion to result in the type of tax progressivity typically described.[182] Furthermore, in the same income groups, taxes absorb 1.9 percent of income for the median smoker in the lowest income tercile, 0.7 percent in the middle income tercile, and 0.3 percent in the high income tercile;[183] the higher prevalence of cigarette smoking among the low income smokers dwarfs the effect of their somewhat greater price sensitivity. These results also imply that the share of income going to cigarette taxes in 2003 rose by 2.5 percent, 1.1 percent, and 0.6 percent for low, middle, and high income smokers, respectively, as a result of a $1 per pack increase (in 1997 dollars).[184] Cigarette tax increases are neither progressive nor a movement toward progressivity; policymakers, even those who are paternalistic, must acknowledge that high cigarette taxes could curtail other factors that support health, such as safe housing and nutritious food, for smokers and their families.

Furthermore, empirical evidence using data from New York State supports the claim that excise tax increases are indeed regressive.[185] As illustrated in Figure 14, between 2003–2004 and 2010–2011, the percentage of smokers' incomes spent on cigarettes increased from 6.4 percent to 12 percent overall, and from 11.6 percent to 23.6 percent for smokers with incomes less than $30,000, as the state excise tax increased from $1.50 to $4.35.[186] As tobacco taxes represent the majority of the price of cigarettes, the increasingly regressive effect is clear.

Figure 14

Percentage of Annual Household Income Spent on Cigarettes, Overall and by Income in New York[187]

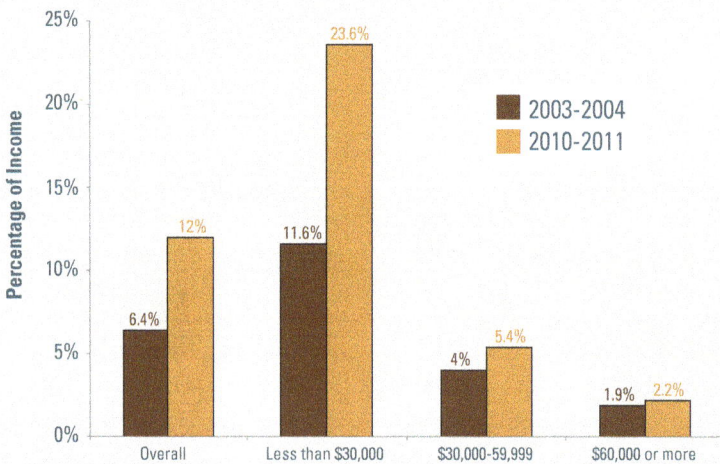

This trend, while decidedly restricted to developed countries, is not limited to the U.S.: in France, between 2000 and 2007, smoking decreased by 22 percent among executive managers and professionals, by 11 percent among manual workers, and did not decrease among the unemployed; the falling-off of smoking initiation for manual workers occurred later and was less marked than it was among executive managers and professionals.[188] In fact, in 2005, 15 percent of French smokers devoted at least 20 percent of their equivalized household income to the purchase of cigarettes, versus only 5 percent in 2000. As stated by Peretti-Watel et al., *"it is therefore likely that the increase in cigarette price contributes to pauperizing a fringe of the smoker population...in other words, increasing the cigarette price could accentuate social inequalities"*.[189]

Canadian data further demonstrate that smoking prevalence declines as education increases and that tax increases likely disadvantage low socioeconomic groups in comparison to high socioeconomic groups.[190] In India, the price elasticity for bidis was found to be the highest in richest quintile (-0.511) and lowest in the poorest quintile (-0.247), while, for cigarettes, the lowest elasticity was in the middle quintile (-0.082)[191] and highest in the richest quintile (-0.280) – which indicates that tax increases will be more effective in reducing smoking among higher incomes, such that tax increases in India have a regressive impact.[192]

In order to understand the impact of regressivity with respect to tobacco taxes, policymakers must estimate the price elasticity of tobacco demand for different income brackets of the population. The more inelastic the price elasticity of tobacco demand is for lower income consumers relative to higher income consumers, the more regressive tax increases will be on the margin since the change in taxes paid for lower income consumers will be larger than for their higher income counterparts.

i. Theoretical Considerations for Indexing Tobacco Excise Tax Increases to the Growth in Wages

Another interesting aspect of tobacco excise tax policy, as it relates to affordability and regressivity, is recent discussion to index specific excise tax increases to the growth in wages (generally, average wages), rather than to consumer price indices. In order to prevent the erosion of specific excise taxes in real terms over time, policymakers often index specific levels to CPI. Rather than pegging specific excise tax increases to CPI, policymakers with both fiscal and public health objectives may instead opt to index excise tax increases to wages, especially if wages grow faster than prices, as Australia has recently done.

From an affordability standpoint, assuming no other excise tax hikes are introduced, increases indexed to wages rather than prices would keep tobacco affordability constant within a country. However, while indexing to wages preserves a certain level of affordability within a country, it is important to remember that relative affordability vis-à-vis other countries, especially bordering nations, is a crucial policy consideration in order to avoid spurring illicit trade and cross border shopping.

Indexing tobacco excise tax increases to wage growth may have different effects on different income groups, depending on the measure of wages that is used. Furthermore, wages vary dramatically not only across different sectors, but within sectors. Therefore, the average wage growth may in fact further disadvantage poorer consumers.

VI. STRUCTURE OF TAXATION

Excise taxes come in two main forms—specific and *ad valorem*.[193] A specific excise tax is a fixed monetary amount per unit (e.g., pack, weight, carton, piece) of tobacco products, whereas an *ad valorem* excise tax is a percentage tax on the price of each unit.[194] In both cases, however, there is a wedge created between the amount paid by consumers and received by producers. The consumer will face prices that are higher than what the producer will receive for the good, and the government collects this difference as tax revenue.

A. Illustrating Government Tax Revenue with Supply and Demand Under a Specific Excise System

Figure 15 (below) demonstrates the government's tax revenue under a specific tax. Prior to the introduction of a tax, the market is in equilibrium i.e., supply equals demand at Point A, where equilibrium price and quantity are Price 1 and Quantity 1, respectively. Once the tax is introduced, the price consumers must pay is Price 2, whereas the price suppliers receive is Price 3. Since the quantity demanded falls when price rises, producers must sell their goods at the price for the new level of quantity demanded, which is at Point C. The government's tax revenue is calculated by multiplying quantity sold (Quantity 2 in this case) by the tax received per good (which is Price 2 minus Price 3)—the striped rectangle in Figure 15 thus represents the government's tax revenue.

Figure 15

Government Tax Revenue

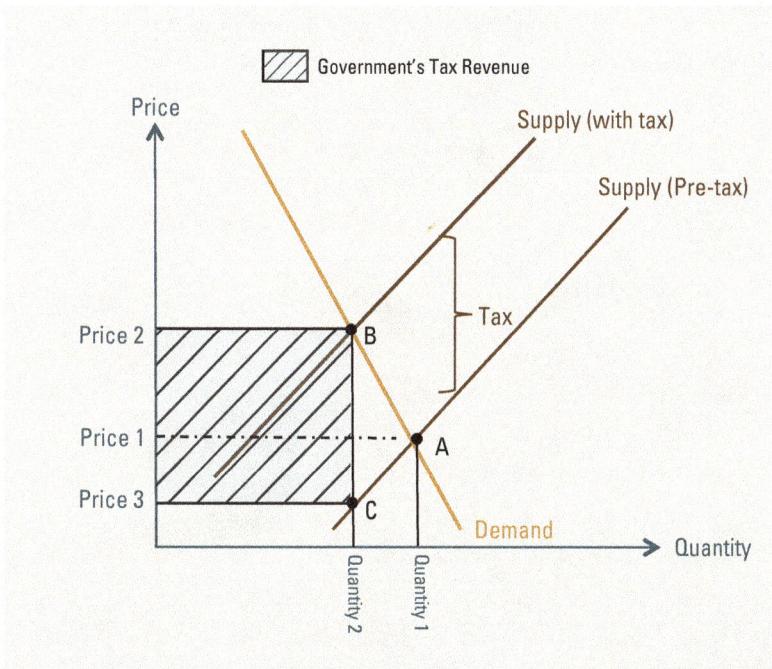

B. Illustrating Government Tax Revenue with Supply and Demand Under an *Ad valorem* Excise System

Because an *ad valorem* tax is a percentage tax on the price of each unit, it does not shift the supply curve upward in a uniform way; rather, an *ad valorem* tax will impose a pivotal shift in the supply curve, which is demonstrated in Figure 16 on the next page. As before, Point A in Figure 16 is the initial market equilibrium. After an *ad valorem* tax is imposed, the price consumers must now pay is Price 2, which reduces the quantity demand to Quantity 2—this is summarized at Point B. The price that suppliers will receive is Price 3, since that is the price that corresponds with the new quantity demand at Quantity 2 (represented by Point C). As before, the striped rectangle represents the government's tax revenue—in this case, from an *ad valorem* tax. These illustrations are of course highly theoretical, and apply to a situation of a homogeneous product – i.e., where all cigarettes are identical and sold at the same price.[195]

Figure 16

Government *Ad valorem* Tax Revenue

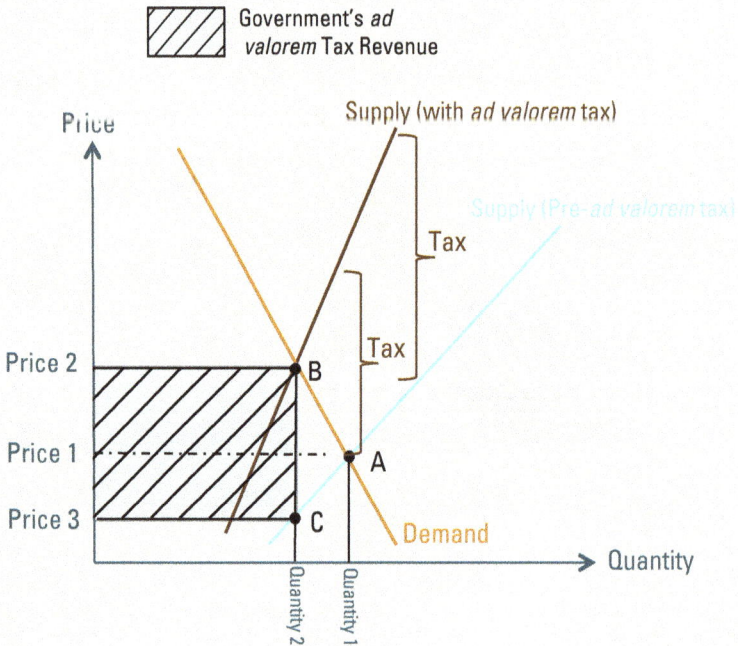

C. Comparison of the Specific and *Ad valorem* Excise Taxes

In reality, tobacco products are not homogeneous goods, all sold at the same price. Cigarettes and other tobacco products are available in different price and quality categories, and this reality needs to be considered when comparing the advantages and disadvantages of different tax structures.

There are many factors that policymakers must consider when choosing between a specific excise and an *ad valorem* excise. Broadly speaking, these factors can either pertain to the economic climate or to the overall goals of policymakers. Addressing the economic climate first, in countries where both current inflation and expected inflation are high, policymakers should consider an *ad valorem* excise tax structure since it will not need to be regularly adjusted for inflation (again, assuming the price of the taxed commodity follows inflation), or alternatively implement a specific excise tax that is automatically linked to the Consumer Price Index, thereby adjusting the tax for inflation. If tax administration is problematic (which can be the case in countries that lack sufficient funding and government infrastructure), then a specific excise tax policy should be pursued since it is far easier to evaluate the quantity of products than the value of the product.

Turning now to the public policy objectives of policymakers, specific taxes are clearly preferred over *ad valorem* taxes for a variety of reasons. From a government tax revenue perspective, specific taxes offer a more stable and controllable source of tax revenue, as government income does not depend on prices set by manufacturers or depend on consumer brand choice trends—as all cigarettes pay the same amount. If public health is an important objective for policymakers, then a specific excise is highly encouraged since they are based on the number of units sold, which implies that the tax burden is equal per unit. Given that a specific excise tax equalizes the tax burden across all cigarettes, it is more likely that the consumption of cigarettes will fall following a tax increase because consumers will not be able to offset a tax increase by down-trading to lower taxed cigarettes. In other words, consumer prices for cigarettes under a specific tax will rise equally across all cigarettes, whereas a tax increase under an *ad valorem* tax system will result in larger price increases for expensive brands compared to lower priced brands. Table 22 summarizes the main differences between the specific tax and the *ad valorem* tax.

Table 22

Comparison of the Specific Tax and the *Ad valorem* Tax Systems

Topic	Specific	*Ad valorem*
Tax Base	Per unit of product (number of cigarettes)	By value of the product (price)
Impact on Price Gap (Price difference between low and high priced cigarettes)	Maintains the price gap in monetary terms; reduces the price gap in percentage terms	Increases the price gap in monetary terms, and maintains the price gap in percentage terms
Government Tax Revenue under High Inflation	Maintained when adjusted by CPI	Maintained, no need to adjust based on CPI[196]
Ease of Tax Administration	Relatively easy; only the volume of the products needs to be determined	More challenging, the government monitors and audits retail or ex-factory prices continuously to assure that the correct amount of taxes is collected
Impact on Retail Price	Leads to overall higher prices, especially for cheaper products	Leads to lower prices; the tax system encourages manufacturers to focus competitive efforts on lower priced products that pay less tax

D. Alternate Excise Tax Structures

As previously mentioned, excise taxation can take structures other than specific excises or *ad valorem* excises. In fact, only very few countries in the world have implemented a pure specific or *ad valorem* system. Many countries have tiered systems, where the cigarette category is subdivided into a number of subcategories, each with its own set of tax rates. And very often, countries combine *ad valorem* and specific taxes in a number of ways. How these systems work in practice, and why countries have implemented such systems to address particular domestic concerns or objectives, is described in Part II.

VII. EARMARKING

A. Economic Explanation of Earmarking Taxes

An earmarked tax allocates a part or all of its tax revenue for spending on a specified government project or public service.[197] Perhaps the most distinctive characteristic of an earmarked tax is that it is implemented in order to protect certain expenditures from the regular political and government budget process—at least in theory. Earmarked taxes operate much like a user fee if the tax is levied to cover the cost of the benefits supplied, or much like a Pigouvian tax if the tax is levied to cover the costs associated with negative externalities.

The relationship between the tax source and the project it funds can be either strong or weak. If it is strong, then all or most of the tax revenue generated goes toward funding that particular expenditure, and that expenditure does not receive significant financing from other sources.[198] For example, in certain countries, residents pay a monthly sewage fee, which is based on the volume of water they use, in which case the beneficiaries are the individuals paying the earmarked tax. A weak relationship, on the other hand, implies that only part of the tax revenues are designated to the specific expenditure, for example when excise taxes on alcohol finance, in part, general education programs. The relationship with the earmarked tax and the expenditure fund is especially weak when the activity is supplemented by revenues from other sources.[199]

Secondly, earmarking can be either specific or broad according to the types of activity on which the tax funds are spent. Under specific earmarking, funds are directed toward a particular service that is usually provided by a public organization, such as highway infrastructure maintenance. On the other hand, broad earmarking assigns the funds toward more general purposes, such as general healthcare. Furthermore, earmarking can be classified as either direct or indirect: a direct earmarked tax is levied in addition to any existing taxes (i.e., in addition to excise taxes) to fund a particular purpose, whereas an indirect earmarked tax earmarks a portion of the revenues from an already existing tax (such as an excise tax) in order to fund a particular purpose.

The general argument for placing an earmarked tax on a private good (i.e., a good that owners can prevent others from using) is to fund a public good (i.e., a good that is non-excludable). For example, it is not uncommon for governments to levy an earmarked tax in the form of an excise on a product, such as gasoline (which is a private good), as a close approximation for charging for road usage (which is a public good). The funds generated from the earmarked tax on gasoline then go into maintaining roads and highway infrastructures. However, in this example, the individuals taxed are those using and benefiting from the good or services provided. Earmarked taxes can also be levied on products, such as alcohol (again, as an excise), where the tax revenues are then directed to fund social programs that benefit individuals other than those who were taxed. In this respect, an earmarked tax functions much like a transfer payment from one group of individuals to another. As this book will further address in this section, earmarked taxes on tobacco products often fall into this second category.

Economists and public finance experts tend to have a negative view on the practice of tax earmarking.[200] As Deran points out, earmarking can lead to the misallocation of resources, where too much funding is given to activities designated for earmarked tax revenues and too little is given to other projects.[201] Furthermore, earmarking can hinder efficient budgetary control, encroach on the discretion of the legislative and executive branches, and lead to budgets that are inflexible and rigid.

These conclusions are further validated by McCleary, who finds that, "*there are certainly grounds for skepticism*" about earmarked taxes since they carry their "*own set of potential problems*", especially when questions are raised about

> "*the adequacy of resources to meet sectoral needs, the adequacy of the institution designated to carry out the earmarked activity, lack of control or scrutiny over expenditure priorities or administrative outlays, and possible conflicts with the government's ability to raise resources for the general budget or with other government policies.*"[202]

Put simply, activities funded by earmarked taxes will only by accident receive the "right" amount of budget – as the earmarked tax will typically either generate more than objectively required (in which case the government is wasting resources) or not enough.

Despite these challenges, there are cases that may justify earmarking. For instance, proponents of earmarking argue that earmarked taxes can potentially protect high-priority programs, as well as dodge administrative and bureaucratic inefficiencies.[203] But these same ends can also be achieved through the normal budgetary process and with the oversight of the Finance Minister.

Experience suggests that taxes are best organized within a government's general tax framework, with revenues and expenditures both overseen by the normal legislative or parliamentary assessment of public spending priorities.[204]

B. Application of Earmarking Taxes to Tobacco Products

Although earmarking has many economic arguments against it, the earmarking of taxes, and in particular tobacco taxes, is often seen as a politically attractive proposal. In order to fund tobacco control policies, governments (such as the U.S., Canada, Finland, Korea, and Portugal) began earmarking part of tobacco tax revenue in the late 1980s.[205] There is little evidence as to how strong the linkage is between tobacco tax revenue and public expenditure or how much of these earmarked funds are actually spent on the dedicated activities. As Keen points out, *"the need to establish better links between the pain of paying taxes and the enjoyment of public spending remains nonetheless an important point"*.[206]

Advocates of earmarked tobacco taxes argue that the earmarked funds can go toward policies that include disseminating information on tobacco to the public, counter-advertising tobacco products, funding healthcare costs, research, preventing youth tobacco use, funding access to cessation services, and reducing secondhand smoke exposure.[207] Additionally, earmarked tax funds are often cited as a tool to correct for the regressivity of a tax increase by designating those funds toward providing smoking cessation products for individuals in lower income brackets.[208] All of these government spending options, however, can also be achieved through the ordinary government budget process.

Most earmarked tobacco taxes around the world fund broad programs that are not related to reducing tobacco consumption, in which case the individuals paying the tax will not be the main beneficiaries of these funds. For example, in South Korea, earmarked tax revenues collected from alcohol and tobacco products are directed toward general education, despite the fact that there is no relationship between the consumption of these products and the demand for education—prompting Bird and Jun to draw the conclusion that these earmarked tax policies lack economic rationale.[209] As a result of weak or soft earmarking, the transparency diminishes with respect to the true cost of public expenditure programs. Even more problematic, is that soft earmarking obscures any signals from the earmarked tax about public demand for the funded services provided by the expenditure programs.

As previously mentioned, earmarked taxes introduce rigidity into the budget decision making process since they prevent the government from reallocating funds in response to changes that may occur in the need or demand for public services. That is, earmarking can prevent policymakers from efficiently allocating funds based on priorities. In countries such as South Korea, where earmarked tax revenues account for almost 30 percent of total government tax revenues, the rigidity of earmarked funds could become cumbersome given that so much of the government revenue funds are not directly managed by the government.[210] For a comprehensive overview of global earmarking practices, please refer to Part II on earmarked tobacco taxes. Lastly, to the extent that countries have different earmarking policies, a tax increase to satisfy international harmonization requirements will have disparate effects across countries.

VIII. INTERNATIONAL TAXATION AND HARMONIZATION

A. Structuring the Institutional Frameworks

1. CENTRALIZED AND DECENTRALIZED GOVERNMENT SYSTEMS

One of the primary purposes of any government is to facilitate the efficient allocation of an economy's resources, by providing a distribution mechanism for wealth or public goods that the competitive market does not generate.[211] Oftentimes, the distribution mechanism is via a tax, in which one individual pays a compulsory amount to the government, who then either provides a transfer payment to another individual or provides a public good or service. The government can either take on a centralized or decentralized structure: when decisions on resource allocation and distribution are concentrated within a single agency, the system is said to be centralized.[212] Conversely, a decentralized system is characterized by having many agencies that carry out the decision making process, which permits regional or local governments to absorb certain responsibilities of the central government. Historically, the precedent has been to centralize the government, since it was assumed that local governments could not handle the technical and administrative responsibility. Over the past several decades, however, this trend has reversed as local governments have become better equipped and less dependent on guidance from the central government.[213]

Decentralization within a country can be on the political level, as well as the fiscal level. For instance, Scandinavian countries tend to be politically decentralized while also being fiscally centralized, while Germany for instance, is fiscally decentralized.[214] In general, federal states tend to have some level of decentralization with respect to tax administration, while unitary states tend to administer taxes centrally.[215] It is possible, however, for the decentralized government to administer taxes on behalf of the central government, and vice versa. Furthermore, whether the central government and local municipalities can independently tax the same base, otherwise known as tax base sharing, is important as well—in countries where only the central government has the authority, a fiscal imbalance between the local and central government can occur. Additionally, not every tax necessarily follows the same administrative framework—certain taxes may be administered in a different format from others.

There is also varying degrees of decentralization—for example, fiscal decentralization can either entail revenue sharing with the central government or taxing autonomy.[216] With respect to the fiscal institutional framework, there are four structures to consider, as introduced by Martinez-Vazquez and Timofeev (2005) and summarized in Table 23 below.

Table 23

Centralized Versus Decentralized Tax Administrations

	Type of Tax Administration	Tax Administration Independence	Shared Tax Administration**	Shared Tax Base	Tax Coordination	Case Studies
Single Centralized Tax Authority	Centralized	-	-	-	-	Unitary states: Sweden, Italy
Independent Tax Authorities at Different Levels of Government	Both	Independent	No	Some-times	Not Generally	Federal states: Australia*, Brazil*, U.S.*
Mixed Models of Tax Administration	Both	Mixed	Yes	Yes	Sometimes	Federal states: Canada*, Spain, Switzerland
Fully Decentralized Tax Authorities	Decentralized	-	-	-	-	Rare: Germany*, former Soviet Union, China (pre-1994 Reform)

Country Notes
Australia: It is illegal in Australia to share the tax base. Canada: Canada has tax coordination with both centralized and decentralized governments. Brazil: The central government and decentralized govern-ments share the tax base. US: The central government and decentralized governments share the tax base. Germany: The central government develops policy and financing, while decentralized governments are responsible for administering policies and revenue assignment.
The question of whether tax administration is shared really asks whether some decentralized taxes are administered centrally, and vice versa.

The institutional framework chosen for tax administrations in partic-ular countries is motivated by economic, political, as well as historical factors—economic and political factors are explained and summarized below. While theoretical support exists for both levels of institutions, ultimately, each country should determine the appropriate system giv-en its unique economic, political, and socioeconomic characteristics rather than applying these general theoretical considerations uniform-ly, see Table 24 on the following page.

Table 24

Economic and Political Factors for Tax Framework

Factor Category	Factor	Framework that Best Accommodates That Factor	Rationale	Study
Economic	Economies of Scale	Centralized	Central bureaucracies likely function closer to the technical production frontier, thus provide public goods and services more efficiently	Prud'homme (1995)[217]
		Centralized	Centralized tax administration likely has a lower average cost given its ability to invest in better technology and more qualified or trained staff.	Mikesell (2003)[218]
	Allocative and Tax Efficiency	Decentralized	Decentralized governments account for different local preferences and demand for local public goods and services, thus better achieving allocative efficiency.	Musgrave (1983)[219]; Oates (1972)[220]; Tiebout (1956)[221]
		Decentralized	Decentralized governments are likely to administer taxes quicker, thus are also able to distribute their revenue toward public expenditures sooner.	Mikesell (2003)[222]
		Decentralized	Decentralized tax administration avoids the problem of having to implement a national tax at the local level, since it designs and administers the tax structure with the local peculiarities in mind.	Mikesell (2003)[223]
	Government Incentives and Competitiveness	Decentralized	Decentralized governments are incentivized to engage in horizontal and vertical competition in order to earn citizen approval. Horizontal competition occurs between local governments, usually via taxation; while vertical competition arises as local governments keeps checks on the central government.	Breton (1996)[224]; Salmon (1987)[225]; Weingast (1995)[226]
		Decentralized	Decentralized governments are closer to its constituents, therefore more incentivized to provide better quality.	Inman and Rubinfeld (1997)[227]; World bank (1997)[228]
	Macroeconomic Stability	Centralized	Decentralization can work when properly planned for, but it falls apart when expenditure responsibilities exceed revenue resources (thus service levels decline or local governments require more loans) and when revenues exceed expenditure responsibilities (reduces incentive for local governments to efficiently mobilize revenue). Macroeconomic stability is compromised when local governments cannot meet debt obligations and are forced to go bankrupt.	Tanzi (1996)[229]; Wildasin (1997)[230]; Prud'homme (1995)[231]
		Either	Decentralization fails due to bad incentives and design, rather than any inherent issues to the system itself. For instance, when centralized governments decentralize in order to pass off fiscal imbalances from the central government, these imbalances are then observed locally rather than centrally (thus making decentralization to appear destabilizing).	Spahn (1997a)[232]; Spahn (1997b)[233]; Wallich (1994)[234]

Table 24 (cont.)

Economic and Political Factors for Tax Framework

Factor Category	Factor	Framework that Best Accommo-dates That Factor	Rationale	Study
Economic (cont.)	Redistribution	Centralized	Central governments are more effective at redistribution.	Musgrave (1983)[235]
		Centralized	Central governments are able to better redistribute wealth from wealthier regions to poorer regions. Thereby avoiding the localization of wealth, regional disparities, and the potential bias of local elites.	Prud'homme (1995)[236] ; Wilensky (1974)[237] ; Inman and Rubinfeld (1997)[238]
	Resource Mobility	Centralized	Central government has better resource mobility to provide better public service delivery, financing, and redistribution.	Buchanan and Wagner (1971)[239]
	Tax Enforcement and Compliance	Centralized	Generally, centralized governments can better ensure standardized tax enforcement, taxpayer monitoring, and can more easily handle large national and global businesses as well as legal litigation.	Mikesell (2003)[240]
		Decentralized	Decentralized governments have more incentives to ensure that proper care is taken to collect and enforce its taxes, especially with respect to individuals who are taxable in multiple jurisdictions.	Mikesell (2003)[241]
		Decentralized	Decentralized governments are likely to be more successful to ensure taxpayer compliance in regions where taxes and paying taxes are a relatively new concept.	Burgess and Stern (1993)[242]
Political	Good Governance	Centralized	Centralized governments are more likely to be consistent in their treatment toward taxpayers, regardless of where the taxable activities occur. Corruption is less likely to be an issue since tax authority employees can be rotated frequently.	Mikesell (2003)[243]
	Regional Autonomy	Decentralized	There is a political rationale for decentralization in order to accommodate pressure for regional autonomy, which could otherwise lead to internal conflict in a country.	Litvack, Ahmad, Bird (1998)[244]
	Political Accountability	Centralized	Tax authorities not only tend to have more discretion in decentralized governments, but they may be more likely to face pressure from local interest groups.	Prud'homme (1995)[245]
		Decentralized	In a decentralized system, it is easier for taxpayers to hold the tax authority accountable since taxes and tax expenditures are easier to observe on the local level.	Mikesell (2003)[246]

Broadly speaking, a decentralized tax system tends to excel when there is a high degree of regional variability, as its intrinsic flexibility allows for a much greater degree of legal customization and provincial autonomy. These advantages are further accentuated when a strong central government and institutions of law already exist, such that a more dispersed tax framework can "piggyback" on preexisting governmental authority and enforcement policies. Tax-specific policies will still need to be enacted, but they will benefit from an established culture of legal compliance. Where a decentralized tax system tends to falter, however, is in the absence of such established governance—such a system tends to struggle with issues of stability, corruption, lack of enforcement and efficiency, primarily when those issues are already present to some degree.

Conversely, a centralized tax system tends to thrive in regions where firm governmental control is less established, as each centralized institution has the authority (and weight) of the full government behind it. Such a system is also able to take advantage of economies of scale, allowing for lower marginal and average costs for instituting and enforcing a given tax framework; the costs of compliance and enforcement tend to be similarly reduced as well. As mentioned previously, centralized tax framework tends to have an advantage in terms of macroeconomic stability and reduced corruption, as well as both resource mobility and wealth redistribution (by virtue of having a wider tax base from which to draw).

In terms of tobacco taxation, there is no individual tax framework that is universally ideal—both centralized and decentralized systems have their advantages, and the unique circumstances of individual countries dictate the most appropriate policy. As such, insistence from international organizations about the "right" way to institute tobacco taxation is misleading, counterproductive, and potentially damaging as well.

2.   A THEORETICAL INTRODUCTION TO INTERNATIONAL TAXES

The discussion of tax administration, comparing centralized versus decentralized at the national level, has recently shifted to focus on tax administration at the international level. The key feature of international taxation is that the tax is levied at the international level, by some form of an international authority or institution, in order to allocate resources globally. Theoretically, the international organization would annually review its budget and decide how to distribute the funds collected through the international tax. This differs from international efforts to coordinate or harmonize national taxes, which is primarily done to reduce competitive distortion between countries and to avoid undesirable behavior that arises, in part, from tax differentials (i.e., illicit market activity, tax evasion, and tax avoidance). The coordination of international taxes is far less extreme since it doesn't necessarily encroach on national sovereignty and it allows national governments, whose constituents are the taxpayers, to retain the tax revenues.[247] The coordination and harmonization of taxes will be further addressed shortly.

The case for international taxation relies on many of the theoretical justifications used to support centralized taxation—mainly that international taxes can be used to correct international market failures (i.e., externalities),[248] provide more predictable revenue flows for expenditure projects since they are compulsory, and redistribute resources such that income distribution is more equitable across countries.[249] Specifically, international taxes have been proposed mainly in the context of global environmental concerns and financing development; therefore, the economics literature has thus focused on international taxes from this perspective. Despite the fact that international taxes were proposed to correct global problems, numerous concerns have been well-documented—such issues include *"the amounts they are likely to raise, the difficulties in administering them, the technical problems involved and the political viability of the proposals."*[250]

Administering international taxes is difficult in the sense that there is currently no comprehensive or effective international finance system or fiscal body—there is no form of a centralized world government that can vote on international taxes, let alone levy or collect international taxes, or impose fines for evasion.[251] Even the international institutions that exist for development are not suitable for administering international taxes since too many agencies overlap with one another (i.e., multiplicity) and do not use a standardized, international approach to finance development.[252] Additionally, using the existing international institutions to administer an international tax is problematic in that it places significant resources in unelected international bureaucracies.[253]

Theoretically, for an international tax to work, a global treaty is needed that clearly defines the tax base, the tax rate, the method of collecting the tax, the distribution of revenues, the penalties for violation, the guidelines for establishing an international fiscal body, and the protocol for reviewing the treaty after a specified period.[254] Furthermore, this global treaty would need to address whether it would establish a uniform policy across each country, or allow some deviations[255] such as allowing for minimum and maximum tax rates, flexibility of tax rates, and differential tax rates between countries. However, at this point, the global treaty then becomes more or less a harmonization of national taxes across the world rather than an international tax. Additionally, at the very least, an international tax must meet the same economic criteria that apply to the imposition of national taxes[256] —this point will be further addressed in following subsections.

Nevertheless, even with global approval of an international system of taxation, the design is hard to implement since issues arise over the *"compensation and appropriate distribution of revenues across nations."*[257]

Another design issue arises in that an international tax must be coordinated with the equivalent domestic tax, otherwise significant tax differentials form and can result in production, consumption, or labor distortions.[258] Furthermore, an international tax system requires compliance from every country; without it, country competitiveness becomes distorted by non-compliant countries evading taxes. As such, international taxes could be very expensive to administer, given the costs of compliance and enforcement.

Although some proposals are aimed at avoiding the difficulties of international tax collection by "decentralizing" tax collection (vis-à-vis leaving tax collection to the individual countries), the problem then becomes that countries have little incentive to dedicate scarce resources to ensure effective international tax collection since tax revenues generally do not proportionately accrue to the countries tasked with collecting taxes.[259] While this issue can be alleviated by allowing a proportion of the receipts to be kept with the authorities collecting international taxes, it cannot be eliminated completely.[260]

Additionally, an international tax will be regressive if participating governments do not offset the international tax by changes in other domestic taxes or transfers, whereas *"if the tax proceeds are used to reduce other taxes, the adverse output effects of the tax would be significantly smaller than if they are used to finance higher government outlays."*[261]

However, the remedies for avoiding tax regressivity can either lead to declining national tax revenues (if tax cuts target unproductive economic activity) or to increases in government spending (if transfer payments increase)—yet do have the (remote) possibility of having a positive impact as well, if excise taxation led to cuts in income taxation, for example.

Furthermore, national governments can never truly offset the international tax given that the distribution of international tax revenues are not necessarily proportional to the amount of tax paid by that country—thus implying domestic taxpayers are to be burdened regardless of national policies to offset international taxes. To explain this, first consider why national governments can, at times, offset the cost of a domestic tax—which is mainly because the national government retains (or loses) the tax revenues spurred by a change in domestic tax.[262]

International taxes, however, are directed to and released at the discretion of the international fiscal body. As such, without having access to the accrued international tax revenues to offset the international taxes, there is no direct link between revenues paid and services received, violating the principle tenant of effective and efficient taxation.

Perhaps the largest obstacle to international taxation is the political feasibility—mainly, the issue of national sovereignty. The concern over international taxes stems from the potential formation of a world government, which differs from the intergovernmental, international organization of sovereign countries, such as the UN.[263] A world government would essentially encroach upon national sovereignty such that countries would no longer have the sole jurisdiction to levy taxes upon their citizens.[264] Although some proposals have suggested removing the compulsory aspect of an international tax in order to make it more politically feasible,[265] this potentially incentivizes regulatory or tax-based arbitrage (from a production standpoint) and illicit or illegal purchasing (from a consumption standpoint).

As noted earlier, international taxes have been proposed in the context of financing development.[266] However, these proposals differ from an international tax in that they are essentially earmarked—the revenues from an international tax would theoretically be reviewed and distributed annually by the international fiscal body rather than earmarked to a particular development expenditure program. The same problems facing earmarked taxes at the national level would not only be amplified at the international level, but would also introduce further political complications as a result. Such political complications that could stem from an international earmarked tax are similar to those confronted by other fiscal development institutions, such as the IMF and World Bank. Both institutions have received criticism for not allowing input from aid-receiving countries and for tying development assistance to stringent conditions. It is likely that the governments administering the earmarked international tax would insist on having a disproportionate influence regarding how the funds are spent.

Similar to the national level, earmarked international taxes may not generate additional aid, but rather, crowd out and simply replace existing aid—this is difficult to prevent, as there is little assurance that countries would set their budget independently of their international tax payments.[267] At the same time, there will be negative effects of increased taxation in general if countries don't account for the new tax (and thus reduce existing taxes). In theory, international taxes to aid development can only work effectively if the income effects[268] outweigh the costs associated with the burden and administration of the tax.[269]

However, even when this condition holds, there is little theoretical justification for earmarking international taxes for development when there is little conceptual link between international taxes and development aid.[270]

In fact, efforts to provide development assistance would be better spent on improving the necessary infrastructure to effectively mobilize and distribute coordinated aid rather than designing international taxes.[271]

As theory has found, the cooperative setting of coordinating development assistance always generates more development aid than the non-cooperative setting, such as an international tax.[272] This should come as no surprise after considering Bhagwati's theory that the best solution is the most direct one, or that a development problem needs a development solution.

3. COORDINATING OR HARMONIZING TAXES

The coordination and harmonization of taxes are both lesser extremes of bringing national tax rates together compared to an international tax. Coordinating national taxes across the world involves structuring national taxes such that the overall system works together to avoid macroeconomic distortions caused by tax differentials. Harmonization, on the other hand, is generally applied in a regional bloc (such as the EU) that is given the power to supersede national taxes in order to create a more uniform regional tax system. Partial harmonization occurs when one aspect of the tax is harmonized, such as the tax base, while full harmonization implies that both the tax base and rate are harmonized. The main difference between coordination and harmonization is that coordinating taxes leaves countries with significant control of their tax policies, while harmonizing taxes requires countries to relinquish much of that power. The overarching goal of either system, however, is to *"eliminate obstacles to cross-border trade and investment…and to protect against the erosion of their tax bases."*[273]

Unfortunately, however, this practice leads to increased rigidity and stickiness in tax and regulatory systems, preventing policy adjustments based on relevant political and economic factors; such a suppression of market forces tends to generate broad market inefficiencies and net welfare losses for those affected.

Coordinating or harmonizing taxes is often proposed in order to simplify multiple tax systems that operate in "one market" economies—that is, regions seeking to have a single, unified market (such as the EU, or individual states in the U.S.). Doing so can reduce compliance costs that can arise due to double taxation, which occurs when individuals or firms engage in taxable activities in more than one jurisdiction.[274]

As globalization continues and technology advances through e-commerce and cross-border activities, the more costly it is for individuals and firms to comply with multiple, complicated tax systems. Furthermore, facilitating taxes across different countries can favor growth and employment since differentials in taxes can distort producer prices and the cost of capital.[275]

Distortions often arise as a result of production and investment being located in areas for tax purposes rather than in areas where operations can be most efficiently conducted.[276]

At the very least, theory finds that partial harmonization benefits all countries relative to full international harmonization and often to no harmonization—assuming capital is adequately mobile.[277]

While there are some advantages to coordinating or harmonizing taxes, the process is not without its difficulties. Even partial harmonization through the tax base can be difficult to transition to due to the technical complexities,[278] such as determining the best definition, formula, and measurements of the variables.[279]

Design issues also pose a challenge, especially if unintended economic consequences are produced as a result, such as establishing a tax minimum but not a tax maximum. Establishing a tax minimum without a tax maximum can result in taxes diverging away from the minimum, especially in countries with high initial taxes, as it will be easier for those countries to increase taxes without further reducing their competitiveness since neighboring countries will be at the minimum level (rather than below it). Coordination and harmonization, regardless of the design, can also create the wrong incentive for managing public finances—governments are less likely to be as careful in its budgetary review without tax competition.[280]

Tax competition between different countries ensures, to some degree, that governments are incentivized to find ways to reduce spending in order to optimize their budgets or give tax cuts to its citizens (which may not be possible with harmonization).

Furthermore, it is necessarily true that some countries will lose competitive advantage from coordination[281] or harmonization.[282] Generally, countries with high initial taxes will benefit at the detriment of countries with lower initial taxes—this is especially true when economic structures are asymmetric across different countries.[283]

Again, these issues raise the question of why different countries should align taxes when each country faces different economic fundamentals, socioeconomic factors, sources of competitive advantage, and demand for social programs.[284]

Perhaps more problematic, at least in terms of political feasibility, is the loss of national tax autonomy that is implied by harmonization,[285] especially in binding or compulsory situations. This creates tension not only with national sovereignty, but it also limits the arsenal of effective policy tools available to handle asymmetric shocks, which occur when a supply or demand shock affects different countries uniquely.[286]

As such, since coordination is a weaker form of harmonization, it might be politically preferred if some alignment of taxes is necessary, such as in areas where economies are open with little border control.

B. Theoretical Criteria for International Taxation—Efficient Taxation and National Sovereignty

International taxation is a recent development in public debate, fueled by international organizations' efforts to advocate for either the creation of separate international taxes or the international coordination of existing taxes, which are then levied or determined by an international body. Perhaps the most notable example of international tax coordination has been the harmonization of various taxes within the EU, which was undertaken as an effort to integrate Europe into a single market, in order to avoid distortions that are spurred by differences in standards and practices. While many international organizations, such as the UN or the WHO, draw comparisons between the EU harmonization experience to recent international tax proposals, the motivations driving both efforts differ dramatically. Rather than establishing a regional market with the free movement of goods and services, recent international tax proposals are generally targeted for non-economic policy objectives, such as reducing carbon emissions or tobacco consumption. Furthermore, the levy of international taxes has been proposed as a tool for what is known as "innovative financing for development", or IFD.[287]

The only example of an international IFD tax is the airline ticket tax;[288] however, it has only been implemented by Cameroon, Chile, Congo, France, Madagascar, Mali, Mauritius, Niger, and the Republic of Korea as a specific levy on air passengers' domestic and international ticket prices to fund UNITAID.[289] However, other international taxes have been proposed, such as environmental taxes (i.e., carbon taxes) and financial transaction taxes.[290]

There are two proposals relating to international tobacco excise taxes—the first system involves setting minimum global benchmarks on tax incidences, while the second system is implemented for IFD purposes. Currently, the WHO has recommended that the international minimum on the excise tax incidence should be at least 70 percent of cigarette retail sales prices.[291] The solidarity tobacco contribution, or STC, is a WHO proposal that is designed as an international IFD tax on tobacco products, which would fund health and development projects in developing countries.[292] The focus of this subsection is to evaluate whether international taxes meet the standards and criteria of economic theory, as well as to highlight the difference between the proposed international taxes and the EU harmonization experience.

WHO Goal of 70 percent Tobacco Taxation

The World Health Organization (WHO) has recently proposed that tobacco excise taxes should constitute no less than 70 percent of the retail price of tobacco consumption. The primary goal of such high tax rates is to increase the purchase price of cigarettes, thereby causing current smokers to reduce or eliminate their tobacco consumption, as well as discouraging new smokers (especially youth) from beginning smoking in the first place. Secondarily, an increase in tobacco excise tax rates is thought to similarly increase government tobacco tax revenues, which have been proposed to be earmarked for tobacco health or education programs.

Proponents claim that such an increase in tax rates is progressive (i.e., impacting high income individuals more than low income individuals), causes no increase in illicit trade (given uniformity of implementation), and has a minimal or positive impact on inflation and employment.

There is not a consensus among economists on these points, however, and these claims are often quite contentious. The fact of the matter is that, even in the highest tax region in the world—the European Union—not even one country currently applies such high tax rate.

The Solidarity Tobacco Contribution (STC)

The STC is a new approach taken by the WHO to fund health programs in developing countries via an additional "micro-levy" on tobacco products (between $0.01 and $0.05 (USD) per pack of cigarettes). Its primary objective is to combat the emergence of new health challenges, but it is often presented in conjunction with the aforementioned goal of 70 percent tobacco taxation. Such a levy would be voluntary at the national level (although not at the individual level), and is neither meant to replace existing tobacco tax policies, nor intended to be offset by tax rate reductions elsewhere.

Similar to the 70 percent goal for tobacco taxation, such a measure is often touted as progressive, with no expected consequences for illicit trade, inflation or employment. These claims also remain contentious and controversial among economists, however.

Utilizing the principles of efficient taxation developed previously in Section I, Subsection B, this subsection will evaluate whether international taxes meet these theoretical criteria. Additionally, policymakers must also consider the theoretical implications that international taxation has on national sovereignty. Although the focus of this handbook is on the taxation of tobacco products, these theoretical concerns are just as applicable to other international tax proposals that are based on non-economic objectives.

1. REVISITING THE FIVE ECONOMIC PRINCIPLES OF TAXATION

In order to determine whether these international taxes are economically sound, the five principles of taxation are reconsidered: (1) economic efficiency; (2) administrative costs; (3) flexibility; (4) political responsibility or accountability; and, (5) equity.

i. Economic Efficiency

The criterion of economic efficiency is not met with either type of proposed international tobacco excise tax system—setting a minimum benchmark on the tobacco excise tax incidence is likely to further distort consumer choice and exacerbate the illicit trade problem, while international IFD taxes, such as the STC, are inefficient since they are prone to many of the same issues that face earmarked taxes in addition to distorting consumer choice.

The setting of a minimum tobacco excise incidence level, as well as the STC, further distorts consumer choice since the quantity demanded for other goods and services are impacted due to the general inelastic nature of tobacco products with respect to demand. Additionally, tobacco excise tax revenues will fall short of expectations over time given that the price elasticity of tobacco demand becomes more elastic in the long-run. In particular, the projects that are financed through the STC might be underfunded over time. Furthermore, the solidarity tobacco contribution cannot rely on the Pigouvian framework since the tax revenue collected is not to correct for the externalities generated from tobacco consumption; the solidarity tobacco contribution is just an earmarked redistribution.

Moreover, imposing additional international taxes on top of existing national excise taxes could aggravate the growing problem of illicit trade, which is not only an undesirable activity, but is also detrimental to governments' collection of excise tax revenues. If international tax proposals on tobacco products are implemented in countries already experiencing Laffer Curve effects, the incentive for the illicit trade increases while excise tax collection drops, thus further rendering international taxation on tobacco products as economically inefficient.

The recommendations of the WHO are driven from non-economic objectives, which have been developed without consideration for fiscal policy. The objectives of the WHO are not economic in principle, but are instead motivated by the goal to reduce global cigarette consumption (via the proposed 70 percent global benchmark for cigarette excise incidence) and to promote health and development in developing countries (via the STC). Neither policy recommendation is considered efficient vis-à-vis the Bhagwati theorems since these non-economic objectives can be better accomplished through other means. For instance, assisting countries with developing their domestic tobacco excise tax policy would be a better approach than the global benchmark, since it would take into account each country's varying income levels, illicit trade, and estimates for the price, income, and cross-price elasticities of demand, while also minimizing distortions. As mentioned previously, a uniform international benchmark which fails to account for individual characteristics (at the national level) would be both inefficient and distortionary.

The STC fails the Bhagwati criteria for efficiency, being a consumption solution to a non-consumption problem—i.e., taxing tobacco to fund third world health development goals. A better option would be a development solution to a development problem, such as reducing remittance costs (making it cheaper for foreign nationals to send money overseas) or diaspora bonds (a bond marketed to foreign nationals living abroad, who may invest for patriotic reasons). Furthermore, the STC faces the same inefficiencies as earmarked taxes, only the problems are amplified on an international scale. For example, the beneficiaries of the STC expenditures are not just individuals who are not responsible for paying the STC, they also reside in countries outside of those responsible for the STC, thus further removing any linkage between the expenditure program and the STC itself.

Additionally, the reallocation of resources would likely be inefficient in countries where the tobacco prevalence is higher in lower income brackets, since essentially the STC would redistribute money from one set of poorer consumers to another set. In fact, in a 2012 study, the authors find that, generally, IFD contributions are small, that revenues are low, that the funds are susceptible to volatility relative to traditional sources of funding, and that the *"hype around it has not translated to substantial new funding"*.[293] Furthermore, the authors warn that *"caution should be exercised when establishing new international innovative financing schemes…instead, global leaders and donors should explore more critically how the existing integrated innovative financing mechanisms can be strengthened and used effectively."*

Moreover, it is not clear that IFD tax funds raise additional money for developing countries; it is likely that these IFD funds simply replace other forms of official development assistance. As such, IFD funds are not achieving their purpose to raise additional money for development projects. Even more troubling, Rajan and Subramantan (2008) find that the link between development aid and economic growth is not established empirically after analyzing 80 developing countries from 1960 to 2000,[294] which further calls into question the efficiency and effectiveness of these IFD taxes. As Ketkar and Ratha (2008) point out, these IFD taxes are *subject to the same concerns about aid allocation, coordination, and effectiveness*.[295] A more efficient solution to address development issues is to guide developing countries toward economic freedom, rather than providing additional monetary development assistance. Other sources of financing that are more efficient, can also be implemented, such as issuing diaspora bonds or reducing remittance costs.[296]

Going back to the WHO proposed benchmark of 70 percent excise incidence—in addition to the general concern with international benchmarks—even if such a benchmark were proposed, tax incidence is definitely a poor measure of the total weight of taxation, and, as such, is a similarly poor benchmark for global policy design.[297] Tax incidence, measured as a proportion of retail sales price, ignores the total excise tax paid. For example, as Table 25 illustrates, although the excise tax yield rises by 50 percent between Scenario 1 and Scenario 2, the corresponding increase in the excise tax incidence is only 7 percentage points, demonstrating that the tax incidence alone, and therefore the global benchmark, is not indicative of the weight of taxation.[298]

Table 25

Numerical Example of the Relationship Between Excise Tax Yield and Excise Tax Incidence		
Scenario 1: Excise Tax Yield is $200	RSP ($ per 1000 Cigarettes, sum of (a.) to (c.))	360
	(a.) Pre-Tax Price ($ per 1000 Cigarettes)	100
	(b.) Excise Tax Yield ($ per 1000 Cigarettes)	200
	(c.) Tax Paid for VAT Rate @20% ($ per 1000 Cigarettes)	60=0.2*(100+200)
	Cigarette Excise Tax Incidence (percent, Excise Yield/RSP)	(200/360) = 55.56 percent excise tax incidence
Scenario 2: Excise Tax Yield Increases 50 percent to $300	RSP ($ per 1000 Cigarettes, sum of (a.) to (c.))	480
	(a.) Pre-Tax Price ($ per 1000 Cigarettes)	100
	(b.) New Excise Tax Yield ($ per 1000 Cigarettes)	300
	(c.) Tax Paid for VAT Rate @20% ($ per 1000 Cigarettes)	80=0.2*(100+300)
	Cigarette Excise Tax Incidence (percent, Excise Yield/RSP)	(300/480) = 62.50 percent excise tax incidence
Verdict: A 50% ↑ in Excise Tax Yield Leads to 7% Point ↑ in Tax Incidence - Weak Relationship		

In fact, when analyzing EU data from 2011, there is no apparent relationship between the cigarette tax incidence and excise tax yield, as illustrated in Figure 17 on the following page.[299] Ireland, for example, has the highest excise tax yield in the EU—but, due to its similarly-high VAT rate, has a tax incidence rate that is near the EU average and median. VAT rates are not universal and even within harmonized regions, such as the EU, differ across many European countries—in Hungary, the nominal VAT was 27 percent in 2013, while Luxembourg's nominal VAT was only 15 percent.[300] Higher VAT rates will imply a larger multiplicative effect on excise tax increases, further eroding any relationship between excise tax yields and incidences. In fact, the EU shifted its position on tobacco excise tax policy after realizing that a benchmark did not prevent "*the perpetuation of wide differences in rates and retail price levels*", and thus, introduced a minimum excise yield.[301]

Figure 17

2011 Cigarette Excise Tax Incidence and Excise Tax Yield in the EU

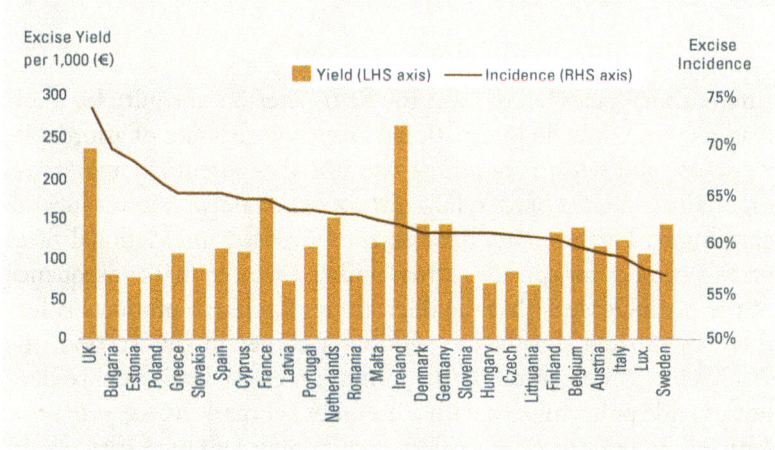

Source: European Commission (2011)

ii. Administrative Costs

The administrative costs of international taxation are, in theory, higher than similar costs for taxes issued nationally, simply due to the costs of coordinating compliance on the much larger, international scale. According to Chassin (2013), the administrative costs associated with certain international taxes are "*virtually impossible to measure, if only because it is impossible to apportion the overhead cost of the whole tax and enforcement system among specific taxes*".[302] While the French government estimates that the airline ticket tax is "marginal," the administrative and enforcement costs of an international tobacco tax or guideline would likely be higher due to the presence and incentive of the illicit trade.[303]

iii. Flexibility

International taxes by definition reduce the flexibility of individual countries to adjust such taxes, when implemented at the local level, to address changing domestic circumstances.

iv. Political Responsibility or Accountability

Currently, there is no established international fiscal body to oversee, coordinate, and collect international taxes; therefore, the criterion of political responsibility for international taxes falls short of providing an easily-identifiable government body.

v. Equity

International taxes fail to meet the final criterion of equity for a few reasons—not only do international taxes ignore issues of affordability across and within countries, they are also potentially regressive, especially if the tax burden falls disproportionately on lower income consumers. Furthermore, because the proposed international taxes on tobacco do not consider affordability, one potential consequence of the tax increase is that the illicit trade of tobacco products is further exacerbated. Lastly, as mentioned earlier in this section, the WHO recommendation on the minimum excise tax incidence does not provide policymakers with a useful benchmark, as *"very different levels of the excise yield on cigarettes can be consistent with very similar levels of tax incidence"*.[304]

2. INTERNATIONAL TAXES AND NATIONAL SOVEREIGNTY

The encroachment of each country's national sovereignty is also a compelling argument against an international tax incidence minimum or an internationally imposed tax. International taxation violates national sovereignty in two distinct ways—(1) in that an international body would have the authority to levy taxes across different countries and, (2) in that the unique economic, political, and social climates of each country would be neglected, potentially worsening any existing domestic problems in these areas. Setting a precedent for an international body to levy international taxes is particularly worrisome, as America's Revolutionary War serves as a reminder of the consequences that followed from Britain's taxation on its North American colonies, which was made up primarily of excise taxes. While in theory member states of these international bodies would govern the level and structure of an international tax, in practice the citizens of the member states would have very little control over the direction of these policies.

The second issue of national sovereignty is also important, as different countries have different views on economics, politics, and society. If this were not the case, the European tendency toward social democratic policies, and thus high overall tax burdens, would be echoed in all other countries. Instead, countries such as the U.S. or Japan have lower overall tax burdens, which reflect their differing views on social program expenditures.[305] Additionally, the combination of policies that optimizes government excise tax revenues in one country does not necessarily produce the same results in another country.

C. Harmonization

A well-known tax harmonization example is the EU, where value added tax (VAT) as well as excise taxes on alcohol, mineral oils and tobacco products are regulated by EU fiscal directives that define common product definitions, tax base, structure and minimum tax rates. The harmonization of these fiscal rules were seen as necessary to achieve *"the creation of a single integrated internal market free of restrictions on the movement of goods; the abolition of obstacles to the free movement of persons, services and capital; the institution of a system ensuring that competition in the common market is not distorted"*.[306] In particular, the abolition of border controls in the EU, without the harmonization of excise taxes, was seen as causing the system to be *"exposed to fraud and evasion"* due to the *"wide differences in excise taxation"*.[307]

In their regulations, the EU differentiated between two situations. For commercial traders, excise taxes would remain to be due in the country of destination according to the tax rates in that country of destination. By instituting a system of "excise warehouses" (the intra-EU equivalent to what customs bonded warehouses are for customs duties) and rules for "intra-EU movement of excise goods", manufacturers and traders are able to produce and trade excise goods in different EU countries, always paying the applicable excise duties in the country of destination. For commercial traders, therefore, a harmonization of excise rates was no pre-condition to make the single market work.

For private individuals, however, the EU single market implies that consumers can buy any good for personal use in any EU country, pay taxes (VAT and excise duties) at the rate of the country where the goods are sold, and bring these goods back to their home country without paying for any difference in excise duty and VAT rates. This aspect of the single market was seen as leading to the potential erosion of excise duties in high tax countries (as consumers would start to shop in low tax countries instead) and led in 1993 to the adoption of a set of excise directives for alcoholic beverages, mineral oils and tobacco products, introducing EU-wide minimum excise rates, to prevent tax revenue erosion.

For cigarettes, this initial directive established an overall minimum excise duty incidence of 57 percent of the retail sales price—leaving the EU member states some freedom in establishing the structure of taxes and of course allowing countries to exceed this minimum rate. Over time, some weaknesses were discovered of this system. With VAT rates not being harmonized across the EU (today VAT headline rates vary between 15 percent in Luxembourg and 27 percent in Hungary), the total minimum tax pressure, excise and VAT combined, would vary substantially, even if countries applied a comparable excise incidence. This could lead to a situation where a country with a high excise level in monetary terms (Euro per 1000 cigarettes), could have difficulty meeting the 57 percent minimum requirement as a result of its high VAT rate, as illustrated in Table 26.

Table 26

Numerical Example of Higher VAT Rates Leading to the Divergence of the Excise Tax Incidence

Scenario 1: VAT is 15% (EU Low)	RSP (€ per 1000 Cigarettes, sum of (a.) to (c.))	345
	(a.) Pre-Tax Price (€ per 1000 Cigarettes)	100
	(b.) Excise Tax Yield (€ per 1000 Cigarettes)	200
	(c.) Tax Paid for VAT Rate @15% (per 1000 Cigarettes)	45
	Cigarette Excise Tax Incidence (%, Excise Yield/RSP)	57.97
Scenario 2: VAT Rate is 20% (EU Medium)	RSP (€ per 1000 Cigarettes, sum of (a.) to (c.))	360
	(a.) Pre-Tax Price (€ per 1000 Cigarettes)	100
	(b.) Excise Tax Yield (€ per 1000 Cigarettes)	200
	(c.) Tax Paid for VAT Rate @20% (€ per 1000 Cigarettes)	60
	Cigarette Excise Tax Incidence (%, Excise Yield/RSP)	55.56
Scenario 3: VAT Rate is 27% (EU High)	RSP (€ per 1000 Cigarettes, sum of (a.) to (c.))	381
	(a.) Pre-Tax Price (€ per 1000 Cigarettes)	100
	(b.) Excise Tax Yield (€ per 1000 Cigarettes)	200
	(c.) Tax Paid for VAT Rate @27% (€ per 1000 Cigarettes)	81
	Cigarette Excise Tax Incidence (%, Excise Yield/RSP)	52.49

This is not a purely academic scenario either, as the case of the accession of Sweden to the EU in 1995 illustrates. The case is analyzed in detail in Section IX of Part II Suffice it to mention here, that Sweden, which at the time had a VAT rate of 25 percent, failed to meet the minimum incidence requirement despite having the fourth highest excise tax yield in the EU. Moreover, its attempts to reach the 57 percent target only resulted in a collapse of the legal market and consequent explosion of illicit trade.

To correct this issue, the EU introduced an "escape clause", whereby countries levying an excise tax exceeding (currently) €115 per thousand cigarettes did not need to meet the (percentage) minimum excise incidence rule.

A second weakness of the minimum incidence rule is that it did not necessarily guarantee a minimum monetary tax yield per thousand cigarettes—even though ultimately to stem an erosion of excise duties it was exactly this—monetary excise amount—that required a minimum threshold level. To address this point, the EU later added an additional requirement, to ensure that cigarette excise rates in member countries also meet a minimum excise yield of Euro 90 per thousand cigarettes.

Problems Encountered During Harmonization

The EU's experience with harmonization has not been without difficulty, which should be noted by policymakers when considering the global benchmark on cigarette excise tax incidence. In fact, the EU struggled to harmonize excise taxes on cigarettes since tax harmonization requires both income and price harmonization. Income harmonization is necessary to align taxes; failure to do so results in cigarette price increases that grow faster than increases in income for less wealthy countries. As such, the affordability of cigarettes declined dramatically in the Central European countries that joined the EU in 2004 and 2007, which increased the incentive for consumers to switch to illicit cigarettes. Furthermore, if the EU country borders a non-EU member, then cross-border activity is likely to happen if the non-EU member has relatively low excise duty on cigarettes.

Retail price harmonization in the EU has been impossible given that the VAT rate fluctuates across the different member countries. Since the VAT is also used in the excise tax incidence calculation, it amplifies excise tax increases on the retail sales price, which can cause countries with high tax yields to still fail to meet the EU minimum incidence requirement. As mentioned before, it is for this reason that the EU introduced an additional minimum duty, hoping in part to reduce the rate and price differentials for cigarettes across different EU countries,[308] as well as the "*growing divergence of tax burdens*".[309]

Furthermore, the EU does not set maximum excise rates, and as a result, as low tax countries increased tax rates to reach the EU minimum rates, countries that already exceeded those minimum rates also continued increasing their tax rates, as a result of which tax difference were increased, not reduced.

As an example, the gap between the highest and lowest taxed cigarettes in the EU has widened by almost €20 per 1,000 cigarettes between January 2011 and January 2014, moving from €195.47 to €215.40; that is an increase of more than 10 percent in three years.

Similarly, within the United States, there is a federal excise tax of $1.01 per pack of cigarettes[310] (which acts as an effective minimum tax rate), but each state is allowed to implement additional excise taxes as they see fit (meaning there is no effective maximum). Despite the minimum federal excise tax on cigarettes, for all other intents and purposes, cigarette taxation in the U.S. is not harmonized. In fact, state cigarette taxes per state range from a low of $0.30 per pack in Virginia, to $4.35 in New York, where the average retail price per pack of cigarettes was $10.11 in 2013.[311] Even though U.S. markets are highly homogenized in all other respects, differences in intra-U.S. tax rates have had a strong impact on tobacco sales, especially in relation to illicit trade.

In New York, between 2000 and 2010, state excise tax rates increased by $4.46, or 596 percent—with the vast majority (402 percent) of that increase taking place after 2006.[312] Between 2000 and 2008, duty paid volumes declined by 42 percent; between 1990 and 2006, the average incidence of smuggled cigarettes was 20.9 percent,[313] which had increased to 56.9 percent by 2012.[314] Similar experiences have been reported in Minnesota, where a recent tax increase raised the retail price of a pack of cigarettes by $2. While statistical data is not yet available, anecdotally, cigarette sales in the state have dropped by 27 percent for individual packs, and by 45 percent for cartons; Iowa gas stations near the state border have reported a corresponding increase in cigarette carton sales, while sales of individually purchased packs have remained relatively constant[315]—indicating a high likelihood of cross-border shopping. Furthermore, a recent $1 tax increase left Massachusetts with the second-highest cigarette tax rate in the nation ($3.51). Prior to this tax increase, cigarette smuggling into Massachusetts accounted for roughly 18 percent of total cigarette consumption; following the increase, smuggling is expected to account for 43 percent of total consumption, with the resulting increase in illicit trade costing the state 3.3 percent of total cigarette tax revenue.[316]

As noted by John D'Angelo of the Bureau of Alcohol Tobacco and Firearms (ATF), *"There is no doubt that there is a direct relationship between the increase in a state's tax and an increase in illegal trafficking."*[317] This is even more of an issue in the U.S. than other harmonized markets, as open borders between states and an absence of federal enforcement both contribute to a very high degree of illicit trade, all else held equal.

Although excise tax differentials within the U.S. have lead to revenue erosion at the state level for states combating the illicit trade, there is theoretical support for allowing states to independently set excise taxes.[318] For one, there is the seminal "Tiebout Hypothesis", which proposes that tax competition between the states is welfare enhancing.[319] Although the "Tiebout Hypothesis" has been critiqued on a theoretical level for leading to less than efficient levels of output of local, public services,[320] it continues to be implemented in the literature for *"recognizing that this competition introduces efficiency-enhancing incentives similar to the profit motives facing competitive firms"*.[321] Furthermore, empirical evidence has suggested that tax increases to fund public services have not led to more or higher quality public services.[322]

Additionally, although the U.S. is a single market, incomes vary across and within states—in 2011-2012, the median income in the U.S. was $51,058.[323] However, the gap between the states with the highest and the lowest median incomes, Maryland ($71,075) and Mississippi ($39,295) respectively, was quite large at nearly $32,000.[324] Meanwhile, the cost of living also fluctuates across the U.S., with the cheapest and most expensive states being Mississippi and Hawaii, respectively—in fact, as of 2013, Hawaii's cost of living index is over 1.75 times higher than Mississippi's.[325] Therefore, due to the absence of income and price harmonization across the U.S., harmonizing excise taxes would lead to cigarettes becoming relatively unaffordable in certain states and could potentially exacerbate the regressivity of tobacco taxation. Furthermore, allowing excise taxes to vary also permits states to express their different views on public health and to take into account the different set of socioeconomic circumstances they must face. Despite both the EU and the U.S. facing similar situations (i.e., a single market), the solutions chosen differed—the EU followed harmonization while the U.S. left state sovereignty intact. The EU experience illustrates the weakness of trying to set either a benchmark or minimum tax rate as a percentage of retail price, while the U.S. example highlights a system that can lead to fiscal revenue erosion—on both state and federal levels—it can also lead to potentially healthy tax competition. On a global scale, VAT rates and production costs vary greatly, as do local income—which, consequently, causes affordability to vary widely as well. These are issues which cannot be internationally harmonized, and attempting to homogenize tax rates in the presence of heterogeneous underlying conditions is a policy that has not seen great successes in the past.

To summarize the key points of this section,

1) Harmonization only makes sense if economic conditions are comparable;

2) If economic conditions are very different, countries or states should have sufficient liberty to set tax rates as needed;

3) If economic conditions do vary, border controls or other ways to limit cross border trade will be necessary and unavoidable; and,

4) Some degree of reasonable approximation may help reduce the incentive for cross-border sales, but then both a minima and maxima are required. Furthermore, the minima and maxima need to be defined in monetary units rather than percentage.

PART II
Practical
Considerations
for the Design of a
Tobacco Tax System

Practical Considerations for the Design of a Tobacco Tax System

I. INTRODUCTION

The design and implementation of a tobacco excise tax system requires the definition of a series of key elements that allow the authorities to determine the tax due and to collect the relative amounts. There are also a series of accessory regulations and procedures that can supplement a tobacco tax system in areas that are closely related, such as price setting and communication, licensing, interaction with other taxes and duties.

The key elements of a tobacco tax system include, at a minimum:

- A set of product definitions that determines what is subject to excise taxation and that distinguishes between different products subject to excise taxation: the "what";

- A tax structure that identifies the "tax base" or the "tax bases" on which the tax liability is based (e.g., weight; volume; number of specifically defined units), which is dependent upon defined product characteristics: the "how";

- A set of rates that determine the tax due on each product subject to excise taxation, based on its tax base: the "how much";

- The identification of the subject liable to pay the excise due: the "who";

- The determination of a "trigger" that determines when the excise tax liability emerges: the "when".

Accessory regulations can also be included to determine some key elements that affect the viability or the efficiency and effectiveness of a tobacco taxation system. These can include, amongst others:

- Rules and procedures for the collection of the amounts due and the refund of duties paid on goods lost, stolen or destroyed;

- Price registration and/or communication systems;

- Restrictions on "forestalling" practices;

Part II will describe first and foremost the key, practical elements of a tobacco tax system and analyze the impact on the tobacco market and whether or not policy objectives are achieved. The interaction between tobacco excise taxes and Value Added Tax (VAT) will also be evaluated, which will in turn introduce the concept of the tax multiplier. The accessory regulations mentioned above will also be considered, along with the resulting impact that such regulations have on the functioning of the overall tobacco tax system.

An analysis of the relationship between tax levels, affordability, and the undesired effect of excessively high taxation will then follow, supported with various examples of countries' experiences with tax increases and tax harmonization.

Finally, this book will consider the subsequent topics: earmarking taxes, tobacco as a component of inflation, international taxes, and international tax benchmarks.

II. PRODUCT DEFINITIONS

A. Overview of Tobacco Product Definitions

When governments decide to levy an excise tax on tobacco products, it is legally necessary to precisely define the taxable product in order to draw a clear boundary between what should be taxed and what should not. Furthermore, governments often apply different tax rates for different tobacco products, mainly to address different product characteristics or political needs—further highlighting the need to carefully delineate between different products.

There is a wide variety of tobacco products available to adult consumers globally. Cigarettes are by far the largest and most common category of manufactured tobacco products. In addition to cigarettes, there are many other types of tobacco products—usually referred to as "other tobacco products" or "OTP". Often these products are more traditional forms of manufactured tobacco compared to cigarettes and their popularity differs by geography.

The distinction between smoking and smokeless tobacco products is the first characteristic to categorize different tobacco products. Smoking tobacco products are consumed through the combustion of tobacco or a tobacco mixture; smokeless tobacco products, on the other hand, do not require combustion (i.e., the tobacco is not burned).

Cigarettes fall in the *smoking category* of tobacco products, along with the following:

- Cigars and cigarillos ("small cigars");

- Fine-cut tobacco for the hand-rolling (called roll-your-own, or RYO) or hand-making (called make-your-own, or MYO) of cigarettes;

- Pipe tobacco or other smoking tobacco, which is cut tobacco that is not "fine-cut", as it is generally used for pipe smoking;

- Bidis, primarily consumed in India and places where cut tobacco is rolled in a tendu tree leaf;

- Kretek cigarettes, primarily consumed in Indonesia and places where cut cloves are mixed with the cut tobacco, and then rolled into conventional cigarettes.

In contrast, *smokeless tobacco* products include the following:

- Chewing tobacco;

- Moist snuff, also known as dipping tobacco;

- Dry snuff, which is ground, nasal tobacco.

B. Different Approaches Used to Define Tobacco Products

To illustrate the different approaches that countries have taken to define tobacco products in their excise legislation, the examples of Italy, Turkey and the U.S. State of Minnesota are presented below.

1. ITALY

The tobacco excise Directive in the European Union (Directive 2011/64/EU) contains a set of definitions that cover all manufactured tobacco products that are smoked (cigarettes, cigars and cigarillos, fine-cut tobacco and other smoking tobacco). These four categories are mandatory for all EU Member States, thus leading to a harmonized approach in terms of product definitions within the EU. For smokeless tobacco products, however, no such harmonized definitions exist, and each EU Member State is free to define and tax (or not) any of such products. In the case of Italy, for instance, the tobacco excise law explicitly includes snuff and chewing tobacco, making these products subject to excise taxation.

Figure 1

Tax Classification–Approach Taken by Italy

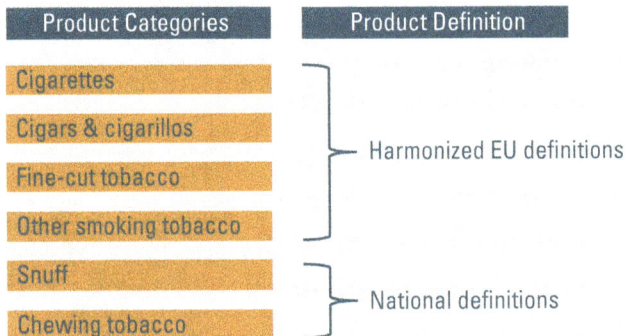

2. TURKEY

Generally speaking, there is no need for a strict match between customs classification (how products are defined and classified for import duty purposes, using the so-called "Harmonized System") and excise classification. Indeed, in the case of the EU, different cigar definitions apply for customs and excise purposes. However, as Turkey demonstrates, a strict alignment of both classification mechanisms can be achieved by using the customs classification codes from the Harmonized System ("HS Code") when defining tobacco products in the excise law, as can be seen in Figure 2 below.

Figure 2

Tax Classification–Approach Taken by Turkey

Product Categories	Product Definition - HS Code
Cigars including tobacco	2402.10.00.00.11
Cigars with loose ends	2402.10.00.00.12
Cigarillos	2402.10.00.00.19
Cigarettes	2402.20
Other (made of tobacco substitutes)	2402.90.00.00.00
Smoking tobacco	2403.10
Other less than 500g in net weight of content	2403.10.10.00.19
Other more than 500g in net weight of content	2403.10.90.00.19
Snuff and chewing tobacco	2403.99.10.00.00

3. MINNESOTA

Finally, the example of the U.S. State of Minnesota distinguishes between three tobacco categories: cigarettes, premium cigars and everything else in a general category of "tobacco products", which excludes cigars and cigarettes. At least two points of interest can be found in these definitions. First, it is quite unusual that a category be defined with reference to the wholesale prices: "*and has a wholesale price of no less than $2*", as is the case with premium cigars. Second, Minnesota was among the first jurisdiction to include electronic cigarettes, or e-cigarettes, in the tobacco excise category by broadening a product definition. By adding the words "*or derived from tobacco*" the "tobacco products" category also includes e-cigarettes because the nicotine in the e-cigarette liquid is commonly derived from raw tobacco (Figure 3).[1]

Figure 3

Tax Classification— Approach Taken by Minnesota

Product Categories	Product Definition
Cigarettes	any roll for smoking made wholly or in part of tobacco.... 1) the wrapper ....of which is made of paper.... or 2) wrapped in any substance containing tobacco,.... which,....is likely to be offered to or purchased by consumers as a cigarette,....
Premium cigar	any cigar that is....hand-rolled, has a wrapper that is made entirely from whole tobacco leaf, has a filler and binder that is made entirely of tobacco....and has a wholesale price of no less than $2.
Tobacco products	any product containing, made, or derived from tobacco that is intended for human consumption, whether chewed, smoked, absorbed, dissolved, inhaled, snorted, sniffed, or ingested by any other means....; but does not include cigarettes.... ....Except for the imposition of tax....tobacco products includes a premium cigar....

C. Tax Driven Product Innovation

As mentioned in the previous subsection, governments often apply different tax rates to different tobacco products in order to achieve specific policy objectives. For instance, cigars generally have substantially higher production costs compared to other tobacco products, and applying the same tax rates may effectively price such products out of the reach of most adult consumers. It is therefore not surprising that most governments apply substantially lower tax levels to cigars relative to cigarettes. But as can be expected, these tax differentials provide a financial incentive for manufacturers to develop products that, according to the legal definition, can be categorized as cigars—thus allowing these products to be defined in the lower tax category relative to cigarettes in spite of having similar production costs as cigarettes and remaining a close substitute of the higher taxed cigarette category.

It is therefore necessary for governments to accurately consider what the key characteristics of a product are to determine the need for a differential tax treatment and reflect them in a product definition that does not lend itself to the kind of undesirable arbitrage described above.

To illustrate the level of technical detail required by a legal definition, refer to the definitions of cigars and cigarillos that were in place in the EU until 2011. As is evident below, these definitions provide very precise limitations to the production method ("spiral wrapping"), dimensions (minimum weight), ingredients used, as well as appearance:

> *The following shall be deemed to be cigars or cigarillos if they can be smoked as they are:*
>
> *(a) "rolls of tobacco made entirely of natural tobacco;"*
>
> *(b) "rolls of tobacco with an outer wrapper of natural tobacco;"*
>
> *(c) "rolls of tobacco with a threshed blend filler and with an outer wrapper of the normal colour of a cigar covering the product in full, including, where appropriate, the filter but not, in the case of tipped cigars, the tip, and a binder, both being of reconstituted tobacco, where the unit weight, not including filter or mouthpiece, is not less than 1,2 g and where the wrapper is fitted in spiral form with an acute angle of at least 30° to the longitudinal axis of the cigar;"*
>
> *(d) "rolls of tobacco with a threshed blend filler and with an outer wrapper of the normal colour of a cigar, of reconstituted tobacco, covering the product in full, including where appropriate the filter but not, in the case of tipped cigars, the tip, where the unit weight, not including filter or mouth-piece, is not less than 2,3 g and the circumference over at least one third of the length is not less than 34 mm."*

The above definition was already a refined version of the original definition introduced in the 1990s. By introducing a minimum weight rule of 1.2 gram in paragraph (c), this definition aimed to close the so-called "filtered cigarillo" loophole (an example is shown in Figure 4 below). Filter cigarillos were designed to be a close substitute for cigarettes, but were classified as a cigarillo according to the EU's tobacco product definition and thus are taxed at the lower cigar/cigarillo tax rate.

Figure 4

Cigarillo

But as soon as this product definition was introduced, closing the original "filter cigarillo" loophole, other products were launched to continue benefitting from the low cigar tax rates. For example, the product featured in Figure 5 below, is categorized as a cigar according to item (c) above, simply because manufacturers doubled the length of the product (thus doubling the weight and meeting the "not less than 1.2 g" weight rule)—with the understanding that adult consumers would cut the product in two pieces for final consumption, therefore obtaining two pieces very similar to a manufactured cigarette. The exploitation of this loophole led to a further tightening of the EU product definitions.

There are many other examples of new tobacco products that have been launched for the purpose of exploiting a tax advantage created by existing loopholes in the legal product definitions. For example, until

Figure 5

Cigarillo classified as cigar

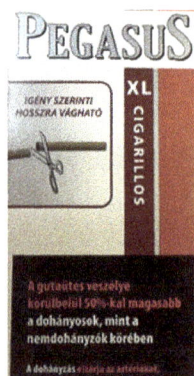

1992, the EU definition of cigarettes (applicable in all EU member States) was:

"Rolls of tobacco capable of being smoked as they are and which are not cigars or cigarillos [...] shall be deemed to be cigarettes."[2]

In 1990, "tobacco rolls" were launched in Germany. These products consisted of rolls of fine-cut tobacco wrapped in permeable paper, that were to be inserted by adult consumers into an "empty", separately sold cigarette tube in order to be smoked (see Figure 6 below). As these tobacco rolls were not *"capable of being smoked as they are"*, they were not classified as cigarettes for taxation, but instead, fell under the much lower-taxed category of fine-cut tobacco. With a significant tax and price advantage relative to cigarettes, tobacco rolls grew to 9.3 billion units sales volume by 1993 in Germany.

Figure 6

Germany - Tobacco Roll

The definition of cigarettes was therefore changed in the EU Directive in 1992 to close this tax loophole, adding (b) and (c):

"(a) rolls of tobacco capable of being smoked as they are and which are not cigars or cigarillos ....;

(b) rolls of tobacco which, by simple non-industrial handling, are inserted into cigarette-paper tubes;

(c) rolls of tobacco which, by simple non-industrial handling, are wrapped in cigarette paper."

In effect, the definition of cigarettes was broadened to include to-bacco rolls which could be made into a cigarette through a *simple non-industrial* process, thus closing this tax loophole. Germany was given a transition period until 2001 to apply the new EU cigarette definition at the national level.

Tobacco rolls were not a unique event—a review of the German tobacco market since 2000 shows the continued evolution of new products in Germany that were produced in order to take advantage of any tax gains made available by legal loopholes, especially fol-lowing significant excise tax increases on cigarettes. Such products include cigarillos without filters, eco cigarillos, tobacco portions, and tobacco rods. Over different periods, each of these products gained market share in Germany, until legislative changes were implement-ed to close these "loopholes" (see Figure 7 below). These examples demonstrate how producers and adult consumers respond to tax op-portunities created by legal loopholes in fiscal policy.

Figure 7

Evolution of German Tobacco Market Since 2000

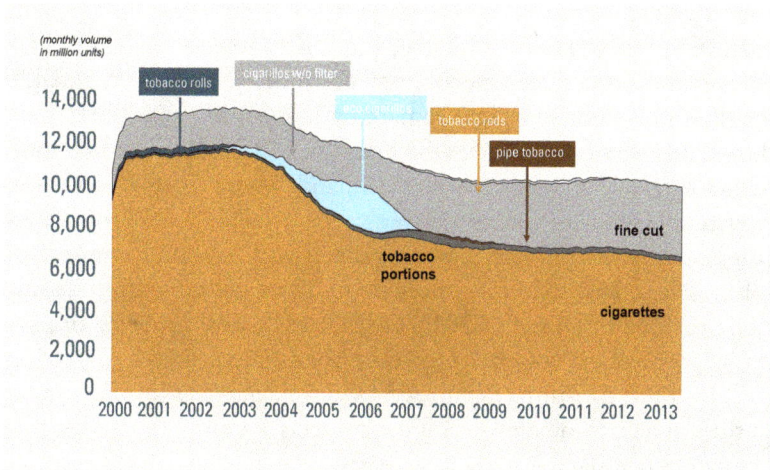

(monthly volume in million units)

Labels in chart: tobacco rolls, cigarillos w/o filter, eco-cigarettes, tobacco reds, pipe tobacco, fine cut, tobacco portions, cigarettes

Years: 2000 2001 2002 2003 2004 2005 2006 2007 2008 2009 2010 2011 2012 2013

Germany: Tax Level On Different Tobacco Products, 2013

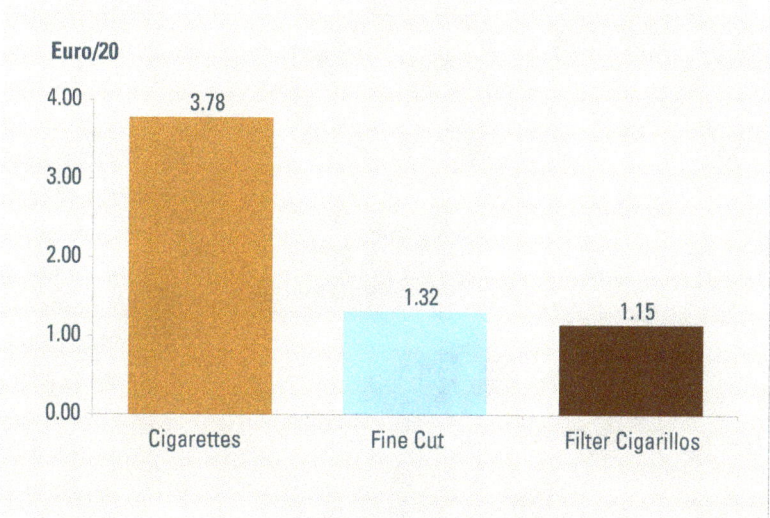

Euro/20

Cigarettes	Fine Cut	Filter Cigarillos
3.78	1.32	1.15

Source: Philip Morris International market statistics based on MSI / volume smoothened by a 12 MMA. Tax rates as of year end 2013. Fine-cut converted in to cigarettes using 0.75 g per stick conversion rate.

A further example of a tax loophole product is the so-called "party cigar". Many countries in the EU define the excise tax rate for cigars and cigarillos per unit of product, while only 4 out of 28 EU countries define the excise tax for cigars and cigarillos on a weight basis (Cyprus, Ireland, Lithuania, and UK). However, when the tax is expressed as a monetary amount per unit of a product, and the length and weight of a cigar remain undefined, it is feasible to produce extremely long cigars, which would still be taxed as one unit. This has been done for example in Poland, where cigars of 35 cm in length appeared on the market—the "party cigars". Such products consist of mixed tobacco leaves wrapped with an outer wrapper of tobacco leaf, and therefore meet point 1a of cigar/cigarillo definition provided in Directive 2011/64/EU: *"rolls of tobacco with an outer wrapper of natural tobacco"*. However, the product is not smoked as such by adult consumers, but used to make cigarettes instead—refer to the visualization below in Figure 8—thus avoiding the higher fine cut taxation.

Figure 8

Party Cigars

As a result of the undesirable incentives generated by legal loopholes, it is common to observe policymakers amend existing tobacco excise legislation in order to tighten product definitions and thus limiting a substantial tax advantage to those products for which that advantage is intended (e.g., high cost, hand-made cigars). Consequently, tobacco manufacturers then develop new products to meet new, stricter legal definitions.

Naturally, legal definitions will depend on historical precedent and on authorities' interpretation of the spirit of the law. In the EU, for instance, the current definition of cigars gives ample leeway to authorities, but will likely require legal interpretation at some point despite improving on previous definitions:

> *"For the purposes of this Directive the following shall be deemed to be cigars or cigarillos if they can be and, given their properties and normal consumer expectations, are exclusively intended to be smoked as they are."*[3]

The practical experience is, however, that large tax differentials will stimulate a continuous stream of product innovations that benefit from "loopholes" in these definitions. Therefore, policymakers must carefully consider whether it is appropriate to levy different tax levels on different tobacco products—the smaller the tax difference between product categories, the smaller the incentive for manufacturers to develop "loophole" products that "game the system".

Over the years, many countries have moved towards simplifying and harmonizing the tax rate on different tobacco categories, thus avoiding the need for extensive product definitions. Brazil, for instance, previously applied different tax levels to cigarettes packed in box and soft pack formats. As one can expect, it is not straightforward to provide a product definition that distinguishes unambiguously a "box" from a "soft" packaging. The Brazilian government then decided from a fiscal policy perspective that it did not make sense to differentiate tax levels according to the packaging of the product. In December 2011, Brazil put in place a 3 year plan to harmonize the tax rate on box and soft packs, which, indirectly, also removed the need to introduce legal definitions of these two packaging types.

But some important political and policy reasons to differentiate taxes between different tobacco product categories are likely to remain, including different production costs (and the resulting difference in "tax bearing capacity"), different employment related aspects (handmade products compared to machine made products), and potential health advantages (e.g., smokeless tobacco compared to conventional cigarettes). Therefore, the art of drafting and updating product definitions will remain a critical component in designing a tobacco excise tax system.

In summary, it is important that all tobacco products are clearly defined to prevent the opportunity to take advantage of a tax loophole, which can distort fair competition and lead to government excise tax revenue erosion. At the same time, fiscal authorities need to ensure that the excise tax gaps between different tobacco categories are not larger than justified for policy reasons, as large tax differentials are the root cause behind the proliferations of loophole products. Last, but not least, it is impossible to always foresee product innovation; governments will therefore need to be ready to adapt product definitions as the market evolves.

III. EXCISE TAX STRUCTURES

A. Overview of Tobacco Excise Tax Structures

Globally there is a vast array of different excise tax structures applied to tobacco products. These can range from simple unit specific structures, such as in Norway or the U.S. federal excise tax, where the excise tax is a fixed monetary amount per thousand cigarettes, to complex, multi-tier excise tax structures, such as Indonesia where there are 13 excise tax tiers depending on multiple factors including production method, volume of products sold and retail price.

Historically countries often applied weight based tax systems, where the tax level was simply based on the weight of the tobacco in the final product, but over time many different systems were developed, in response to the changes in the tobacco market as well as government policy objectives. Figure 9 below, demonstrates examples of tax structures applied to cigarettes around the world. More details about cigarette taxation around the world can be found in Appendix II.

Figure 9

Overview of Cigarette Tax Structures

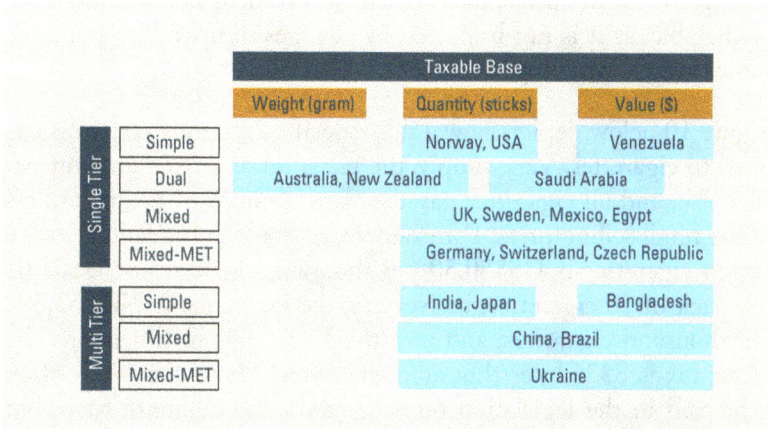

		Taxable Base		
		Weight (gram)	Quantity (sticks)	Value ($)
Single Tier	Simple		Norway, USA	Venezuela
	Dual	Australia, New Zealand		Saudi Arabia
	Mixed		UK, Sweden, Mexico, Egypt	
	Mixed-MET		Germany, Switzerland, Czech Republic	
Multi Tier	Simple		India, Japan	Bangladesh
	Mixed		China, Brazil	
	Mixed-MET		Ukraine	

First and foremost, countries must decide the taxable base on which to determine the tax. For tobacco products, typical candidates are the following specifications: the weight of tobacco, the quantity of units (e.g., cigarette sticks), the price of the product, or some combination of these variables. As new products are developed, such as electronic cigarettes, the taxable base will have to be adapted accordingly (e.g., milliliters of nicotine containing liquid).

Countries can then decide to apply a "single-tier" excise tax system, where the same rate or set of rates is applied to all products within a particular category sold on the market, or a "multi-tier" system where the market is sub-divided into several sub-categories, based on criteria such as size (e.g., cigarette length), type (e.g., filter or plain cigarettes), the price, etc., with each tier having a different excise tax.

B. Specific Excise Tax Structures

A specific excise tax is levied as a fixed monetary amount per a defined unit of product. The taxable base for the specific tax could be the weight of tobacco (weight based specific), or a specifically defined unit, e.g., one cigarette (unit based specific). A specific tax is relatively easy to administer as the tax authorities only need to know the quantity of product or weight of tobacco sold to determine the amount of tax due. With a single-tier, fully specific tax structure, all units of product within a category pay the same amount of tax irrespective of the price, making the government tax revenue more predictable, as it is not impacted by changes in price levels or consumer brand switching.

Figure 10 below depicts how a fully specific excise tax system is applied to cigarettes. Very simply, the tax is set at a fixed amount per cigarette, and all cigarettes pay the same amount of tax, regardless of the retail selling price. For example, in the U.S. the federal excise tax on cigarettes is US$50.50 per thousand cigarettes or US$1.01 per pack of 20 cigarettes; in Norway, the excise tax is NOK 2,390 per thousand cigarettes; and as a third example, in Singapore, the excise tax is S$352 per thousand cigarettes. The excise tax is often expressed in the legislation on a per thousand cigarette basis, but some countries such as the Philippines express the tax on a per pack basis, while in Australia the excise tax is expressed on a per stick basis. In the case where the tax is defined on a per pack basis, it is important that either pack content is regulated (quantity of cigarettes), and/or that the law clearly explains that the specific tax is expressed for a pack of 20 cigarettes and that other pack sizes pay the tax in a proportionate amount.

Figure 10

Fully Specific Excise Structure

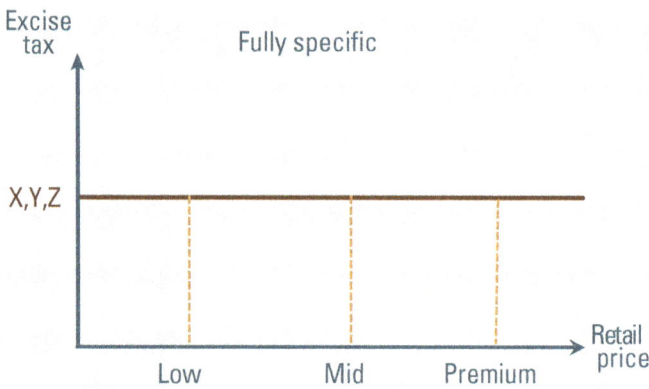

A key element that must accompany the application of a specific excise is a robust definition of what constitutes a "unit" of product. Taking the example of cigarettes, it would seem straightforward to determine what constitutes one cigarette. However, many countries today do not define the "taxable length" of a cigarette. What this implies when the tax is expressed as a monetary amount per cigarette, is that it is feasible (and this has indeed been done) to produce extremely long cigarettes (20-30 cm long) which are only subject to the excise due on one cigarette, but which consumers cut into several normal length cigarettes.

In the EU, excise tax applied on cigarettes must include two obligatory elements: a specific component in Euro applied per thousand cigarettes and an *ad valorem* element calculated based on retail selling price of pack of cigarettes (discussed later in this book). Council Directive 2011/64/EU of 21 June 2011 on the structure and rates of excise duty applied to manufactured tobacco, defines the cigarette "unit" based on the length of the tobacco rod:[4]

Article 3

1. For the purposes of this Directive cigarettes shall mean:

(a) rolls of tobacco capable of being smoked as they are and which are not cigars or cigarillos within the meaning of Article 4(1);

(b) rolls of tobacco which, by simple non-industrial handling, are inserted into cigarette-paper tubes;

(c) rolls of tobacco which, by simple non-industrial handling, are wrapped in cigarette paper.

2. A roll of tobacco referred to in paragraph 1 shall, for excise duty purposes, be considered as two cigarettes where, excluding filter or mouthpiece, it is longer than 8 cm but not longer than 11 cm, as three cigarettes where, excluding filter or mouthpiece, it is longer than 11 cm but not longer than 14 cm, and so on.

In the past, several countries taxed cigarettes through a fixed monetary amount per weight of tobacco, however this changed as manufacturing developments allowed for the production of cigarettes with less tobacco weight, which in turn reduced the tax paid per cigarette.

For instance, Australia previously applied a weight based tax on cigarettes and between 1974 and 1998 the excise amount was increased from AU$15 to AU$ 88 per kg of tobacco, an increase of 488 percent over 24 years. Over the same period the average weight of tobacco in one cigarette declined from 0.92 gram of tobacco per cigarette to 0.68 gram of tobacco per cigarette, in effect a 26 percent decline in the average weight of tobacco—see Figure 11 below.[5]

Figure 11

Tax Structure Affects Market Dynamics
Example Australia: weight based tax leads to reduced weight cigarettes

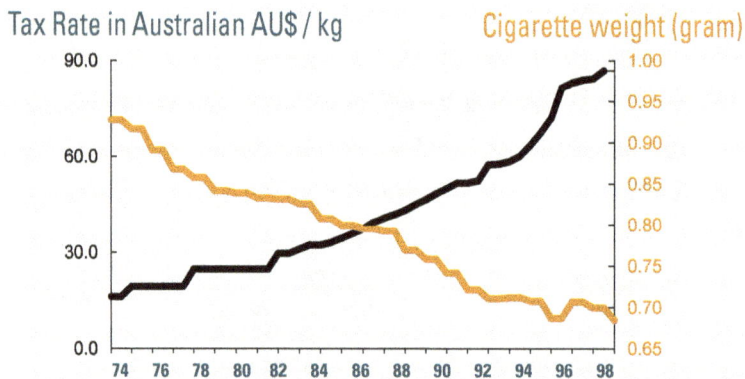

In order to address this erosion of the taxable base, the Australian tax authorities amended the existing tax system by introducing a minimum tax per cigarette. Cigarettes with a weight of less than 0.8 kg per thousand cigarettes must pay a fixed monetary excise tax on a per thousand basis, while cigarettes weighing more than 0.8 kg per thousand cigarettes continued to pay a fixed monetary tax on a per kg of tobacco weight basis as shown in Figure 12.

Figure 12

Australia Weight-Based Tax with Min. per Stick

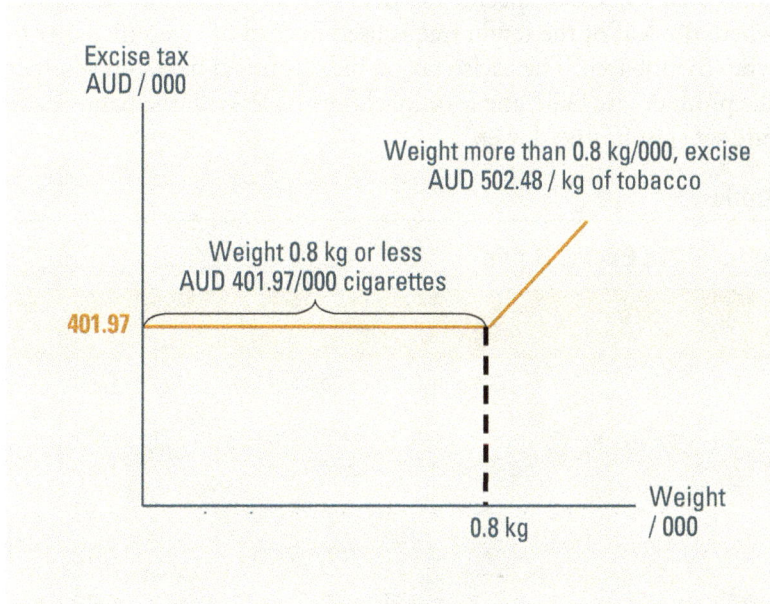

Excise tax
AUD / 000

Weight more than 0.8 kg/000, excise
AUD 502.48 / kg of tobacco

Weight 0.8 kg or less
AUD 401.97/000 cigarettes

401.97

0.8 kg

Weight
/ 000

Australia's experience demonstrates why the excise tax system on tobacco products requires adjustment in response to market changes, to remain effective. This example also introduces the concept of the minimum excise tax, which is applied in many other countries to prevent tax erosion and to provide some degree of certainty and predictability for government tax revenue. This will be discussed in more detail in Subsection E below, which is dedicated specifically to dual tax structures.

C. Multi-Tier Specific Tax Structures

A multi-tier specific tax system defines different sub-categories of a tobacco product based on certain product characteristics, each subject to a different specific tax rate. Throughout the world, a wide variety of multi-tier specific tax systems is applied.[6]

In India for example, excise tax levels vary for filter and non-filter cigarettes as well as based on the length of the cigarette, resulting in nine different excise tax tiers—see Table 1 below. In addition, India applies two separate specific tax tiers on bidis, which are cigarettes where the leaf of the tendu tree is used instead of cigarette paper to wrap the tobacco. The excise tax on bidis is tiered based on whether the products are hand-made or machine-made, with the hand-made rate set significantly lower.

Table 1

India: 2014 Excise Rates

Type of cigarette	Tier	Specific Rate (INR/'000)
Filter Cigarettes	Cigarettes of Tobacco substitutes	1,661
	Length ≤ 65 mm	669
	65 mm < Length ≤ 70 mm	1,409
	70 mm < Length ≤ 75 mm	2,027
	75 mm < Length ≤ 85 mm	2,725
	Length > 85 mm	3,290
Non filter Cigarettes	Length ≤ 60 mm	669
	60 mm < Length ≤ 65 mm	764
	65 mm < Length ≤ 70 mm	2,027
Bidis	Hand Made	13
	Machine Made	32

Another type of a tiered tax system is applied in Indonesia, where approximately 92 percent of the tobacco market is comprised of kretek cigarettes, which are cigarettes containing clove, with the remaining 8 percent comprised of conventional cigarettes.[7] Before 2007, Indonesia applied a multi-tier *ad valorem* system. It then moved to a multi-tier mixed system until 2009, when it introduced a fully specific system with 19 tiers, along with an "excise roadmap".[8] The excise roadmap foresaw a reduction to 2 tiers (1 for machine-made and 1 for hand-rolled cigarettes) by 2016, in order to support the Government's revenue, health, and employment objectives. In line with this policy direction, the number of tiers has been gradually reduced to 13 by 2013.

The current tax tiers are determined by a combination of four factors: product type (kretek or conventional cigarette); type of production (handmade or machine made); annual production volume by company; and retail price—see Table 2 below.

Table 2

Indonesia: 2014 Excise Tax Rates

	Category	Production Volume Tier	Price Tier*	Specific Rate (IDR/stick)
Hand-Rolled Kretek	Tier 1	> 2 bio.	> 749	275
			≥ 550 - 749	205
	Tier 2	> 0.3 - 2.0 bio.	> 379	130
			> 349 - 379	120
			≥ 336 - 349	110
	Tier 3	≤ 0.3 bio.	≥ 250	80
Machine Made Kretek	Tier 1	> 2 bio.	> 669	375
			≥ 631 - 669	355
	Tier 2	≤ 2.0 bio.	> 549	285
			≥ 440 - 549	245
White Cigarettes	Tier 1	> 2 bio.	> 679	380
	Tier 2	≤ 2.0 bio.	> 444	245
			≥ 345 - 444	195

* Note: Price Tier based on Banderole Price per stick

The hand-rolled kretek category has significantly higher employment levels per unit of production than machine made kretek, and the lower excise tax on the hand-rolled category in Indonesia is effectively a subsidy to maintain employment within this sector as stipulated in the law.[9] This approach in Indonesia of a lower excise tax rate on hand-rolled products is consistent with other countries, e.g., the earlier example of India, which applies lower excise on hand-rolled bidis.

As illustrated in Table 2 above, a further layer of tiers is applied to grant smaller companies a tax advantage. For cigarettes and machine made kretek, companies that produce a maximum of 2 billion units annually (volume tier 2) benefit from lower excise tax rates. For hand-rolled kretek, a third tier exists, granting further reduced rates to companies with a maximum annual production of 0.3 billion units yearly (volume tier 3).

This tax system led some companies to divide their production volumes by establishing affiliates (so-called "sister companies") with an annual production not exceeding 2 billion cigarettes to take advantage of lower excise tax rates for lower production volume tiers. In an effort to address this practice, to create a level playing field, and to safeguard excise tax revenues, the Government has issued a decree determining the criteria of what constitutes an "affiliate" relationship, whereby direct/indirect equity ownership and the use of raw materials is taken as basis. In case an affiliate relationship is determined, the production volumes of the affiliated companies will be merged to establish the appropriate excise tax category.[10] Given the large tax advantages granted to small producers, it is likely that companies will try to find new loopholes in these definitions of affiliated companies. More fundamentally, one could ask whether the excise tax system is the best government instrument to advantage smaller companies; other tax measures may be more suited to achieve that government objective.

Under a multi-tier tax system, if the tax differences between the tiers are large enough to lead to material price differences between products, there is a risk that consumers will down-trade to the lowest tax category, particularly in cases of large tax increases or of economic shocks (e.g., an economic downturn) that make consumers more sensitive to price differences.

For example, Japan has applied a two-tier fully specific tax system since 1984 with a standard specific tax on what Japan defines as "Class-A" cigarettes and a lower specific tax rate on "Class-C" cigarettes. The former accounts for over 95 percent of the cigarette market, while the latter, which is comprised of six low priced, locally produced, regional brands, accounts for the remainder of the market.[11] Until 2010 the excise tax was increased relatively moderately on both tax tiers and the market share of the low tax Class-C cig-

arettes remained stable at between 1 to 2 percent of the total cigarette market. However, in 2010, there was a 40 percent excise tax increase in both tax tiers. The tax on Class-A cigarettes increased from
¥8,744 to ¥12,244 per thousand, and the tax on Class-C cigarettes
increased from ¥4,150 to ¥5,812 per thousand cigarettes. Not only
was this a large tax increase in absolute terms, but the tax gap between the two tax tiers widened from ¥4,594 to ¥6,432 per thousand
cigarettes, creating a strong incentive for consumers to down-trade
from Class-A to Class-C cigarettes. As a matter of fact, following
this tax increase, the market share of the low tax Class-C cigarettes
almost tripled from 1.6 percent in 2010 to 4.4 percent in 2013, as
shown in Figure 13 below.

Figure 13

Japan: Excise Tax Increases and Market Share of Class-C
Cigarettes

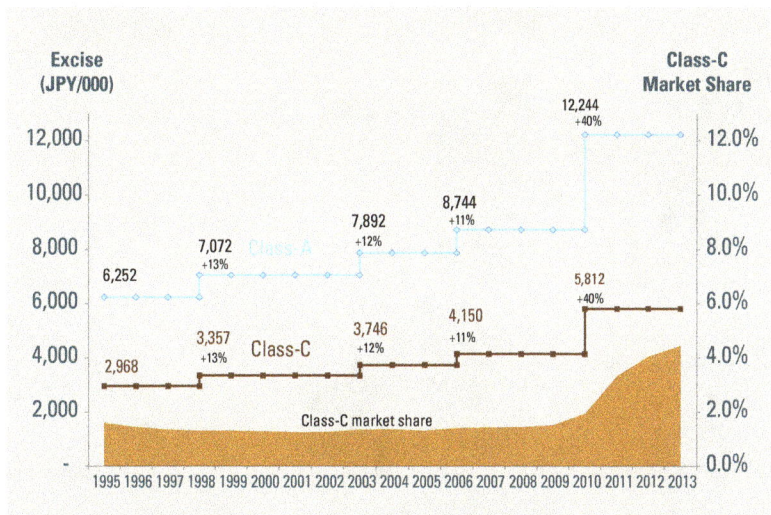

As the example above shows, when tax increases are moderate, consumers will generally not seek alternative, lower taxed products.
However, in response to large tax increases or to other changes that
affect market conditions, such as a severe economic down-turn or
rising unemployment, tax differences will drive shifts in consumption, thus eroding the excise tax base. Moreover, as the low tax tier
gains market share, it will often become increasingly difficult, from

a political point of view, to address this "tax gap"—especially given the increased commercial interests at stake. In such a situation, one possible approach, which has been used in countries such as the Philippines and Brazil, is to adopt a phased reduction in the tax gaps between tiers over a number of years, to gradually arrive at a single tax tier.

In the Philippines, the excise system consisted of 4 specific excise tiers with cigarettes tax classified on the basis of 1996 net retail prices. The new excise law that entered into force in January 2013 significantly reformed this system by gradually moving to a single tier specific of 30 Philippine pesos per pack of 20 cigarettes in 2017, with subsequent annual excise rate increases in line with projected inflation as shown in Table 3 below:

Table 3

Philippines Tax System Evolution

Tiers[1]		New tiers	Excise rates (PHP/pack)					
Net Retail Price (NRP)	Excise rates (PHP/pack)	Net Retail Price (NRP)	2013	2014	2015	2016	2017[2]	2018
NRP > 10.00 (premium)	28.3							
6.50 < NRP ≤ 10.00 (high)	12	> 11.50	25	27	28	29	30	
5.00 ≤ NRP ≤ 6.50 (mid)	7.56	≤ 11.50	12	17	21	25	30	+4 % p.a.
NRP < 5.00 (low)	2.72							
(1) Brands classification based on 1996 prices.								
(2) Single tier from 2017 onward								

While the simplification of the excise tax system in the Philippines provided a level playing field and will improve the predictability and sustainability of tobacco tax revenues, the magnitude of the initial tax increases in 2013 (between 108 percent and 341 percent) has led to market disruptions with a sharp growth of illicit trade and down trading. This tax reform will be discussed in more detail later in this book.

Figure 14 below shows which countries worldwide apply fully specific tobacco tax systems, both single and multi-tier. As can be seen, multi-tier systems are found almost exclusively in Asia and Oceania, typically in countries where traditional, locally manufactured products are popular.

Figure 14

Fully Specific Tax Structures

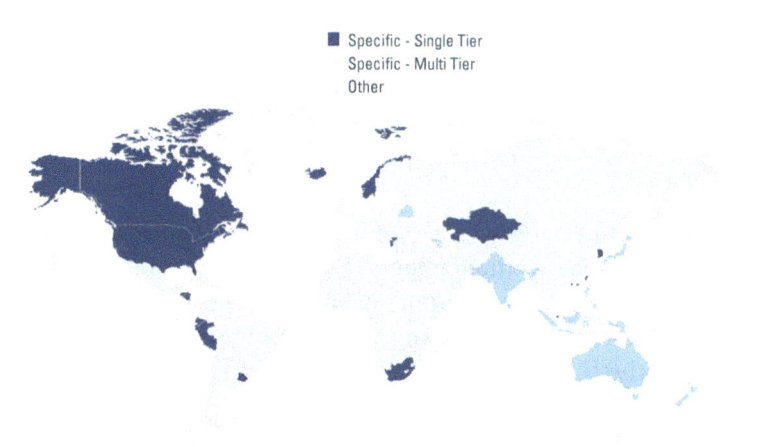

- Specific - Single Tier
- Specific - Multi Tier
- Other

D. Ad valorem excise tax structures

Under an *ad valorem* system, the excise tax is expressed as a percent of the price, whether this is the retail selling price, wholesale selling price, import price, or net ex-factory selling price.[12] The defining feature of an *ad valorem* tax system is that the excise tax amount is determined by price: premium brands pay a higher amount of excise tax and low price brands pay a lower amount of excise tax—see Figure 15 on the following page.

Figure 15

Fully *Ad valorem* Excise Tax

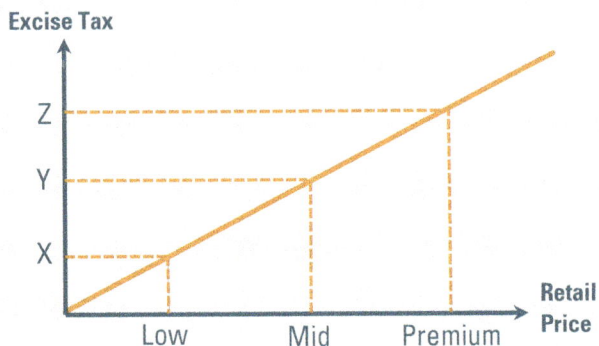

Historically, fully *ad valorem* excise tax systems were favored in countries with tobacco monopolies, as this excise system favored the usually lower priced, local monopoly brands compared to imported, more expensive, international brands. This point was highlighted in a report by the European Commission in 2008:

> *"Ad valorem duties increase absolute price differences and consequently promote cheaper brands of cigarettes. In the past ad valorem duties were applied to favour cheaper local cigarettes above more expensive international brands."[13]*

Under an *ad valorem* tax system, tax revenues will not only depend on market volumes, as in a fully specific system, but also on prices and consumer preferences between premium and cheaply priced products. If a change in prices or in the market shares of the different price segments occurs, this will affect the excise tax revenues collected by the government.

Ad valorem excise tax systems are able to generate tax revenue growth as long as cigarette prices increase regularly over time, while remaining affordable, so as not to trigger consumer down-trading to cheaper, and thus less taxed, alternatives. However, when affordability becomes an issue, e.g., during periods of economic downturn, producers will be inclined to hold prices or even reduce prices to protect their market share, and consumers will have a stronger incentive to down-trade to lower price brands, which pay less tax. In these circumstances, *ad valorem* excise systems fail to guarantee or grow government tax revenue.

In the past, when state-owned tobacco monopolies could set both tax rates and retail prices for all brands, authorities could obviously prevent price wars from occurring. Currently, however, there are only a few countries left where the state controls tobacco prices, as markets around the globe have been liberalized and state monopolies have been privatized. This has exposed the intrinsic vulnerability of the *ad valorem* excise to market dynamics and has led many governments around the world to revise their tobacco taxation systems to make them more robust to pricing and consumption dynamics by emphasizing the specific component instead of the *ad valorem* component. Irrespective of the existence of government price controls, governments do not control which brands adult consumers choose to smoke and therefore the effects of consumer brand switching on tax revenues remain a weakness of *ad valorem* excise systems.

There are several different price points within the distribution chain on which the *ad valorem* tax can be based: i) the final retail price to consumers; ii) the wholesale price; iii) the "CIF" price (referring to "Cost, Insurance, Freight", which is the reference price when a product is imported); or, iv) the net ex-factory price. As a general rule, when an *ad valorem* tax is applied to cigarettes, the price on which the tax is based should be relatively easy for the tax authorities to monitor and should be transparent, so that the correct tax is levied on all cigarette brands in a fair and transparent manner.

For example, Thailand applies a fully *ad valorem*[14] excise to cigarettes based on the net ex-factory price for domestic products and on CIF price for imported products. However, the Thai tax authorities contested the CIF value of cigarettes imported from the Philippines into Thailand claiming that the CIF value was under declared so imported products would pay less tax.[15] This international trade dispute was ultimately reviewed by a World Trade Organization Panel, which ruled in favor of the Philippines and found that the CIF values were correct, and the correct tax was being paid on imported brands. The case however clearly highlights the difficulties of using an *ad valorem* tax system especially when based on a reference price that is not easily verified and audited.

As this example shows, when there is an *ad valorem* element within the excise tax systems the authorities need to be able to monitor both the volume of cigarettes sold as well as the price at which these products are sold in order to determine the tax revenue. The large majority of countries that apply an *ad valorem* tax element use the final retail price as the tax base—compared with other options, this is the easiest one to monitor and implement. However, there are some technical aspects to consider when establishing the *ad valorem* tax based on the final retail price, namely the interaction of the tax base with VAT, a topic that will be discussed in more detail later in this book, and the fact that the final selling price must be known to the subject liable for the payment of the excise, usually the manufacturer or importer.

For example, if the *ad valorem* tax is 50 percent of the final retail selling price, assuming a final retail selling price of $5.00 per pack, then this price must be known by the manufacturer so that the correct tax (in this case $2.50 per pack) can be paid to the government. In order to make this system work, governments usually introduce legislation that the tax payer (typically manufacturer or importer) establish a maximum or fixed retail price for each of their products—to be respected by retailers when they sell the product to consumers. Without such regulations, the tobacco product could be sold at a higher price by the retailer (say $5.50 per pack) and the excise tax would not be collected on the additional price mark-up (in this case, excise would remain unpaid on $0.50, i.e., a $0.25 tax loss for the state).

As an example, Israel restructured its excise tax system to improve the tax base on which the *ad valorem* tax element was applied. Prior to 2003,[16] the *ad valorem* portion of the excise tax was applied to the "price to the consumer". However without rigorous control on the retail price, many retailers were selling cigarettes at prices that exceeded the manufacturers or importers recommended retail price, thus avoiding some of the excise tax due. To address this situation, in 2003, the *ad valorem* excise tax base was redefined to be "the common wholesale price plus 10 percent" for purposes of calculating the tax. This system worked well for a number of years, but the 10 percent markup over the wholesale price was considered arbitrary and incorrectly assumed a uniform retail trade margin. In July 2009, the Knesset amended the Purchase Tax Law by establishing the wholesale price net of tax as the basis of the *ad valorem* portion of the tax.

At the same time, the authorities took the opportunity to increase the relative size of the specific tax element which had two major benefits: first, the *ad valorem* tax base was now the wholesale price net of tax, which reduced the opportunity of avoiding tax, as this price could be verified by the invoice issued by the manufacturer or importer; second, the proportion of the total tax derived from the specific element increased, making government revenues less dependent on the *ad valorem* tax and its tax base.

In much the same way as for specific excise, the *ad valorem* excise has also been implemented within a multi-tier system, where products in different price bands are subject to different tax rates. This for instance is the case in three countries in West Africa—Ivory Coast, Burkina Faso and Mali, all part of the West African Economic and Monetary Union (also known by its French acronym, UEMOA), where multi-tier, *ad valorem* excise systems based on net ex-factory price apply. Refer to Figure 16 below.

Figure 16

Fully *Ad valorem* Tax Structures

- *ad valorem* - Single Tier
- *ad valorem* - Multi Tier
- Other

E. Dual Excise Tax Structures

The fully specific and fully *ad valorem* excise tax systems described in the previous subsections, can be combined in a dual tax structure, where either an *ad valorem* tax, or a specific tax is applied, depending on whichever results in the highest tax amount—refer to Figure 17 below. In this case, the specific tax is normally referred to as a Minimum Excise Tax (MET)—a minimum monetary amount of tax that is paid below a certain price point (the so-called "kick-in price" or KIP).

Figure 17

Dual Excise Tax Structure

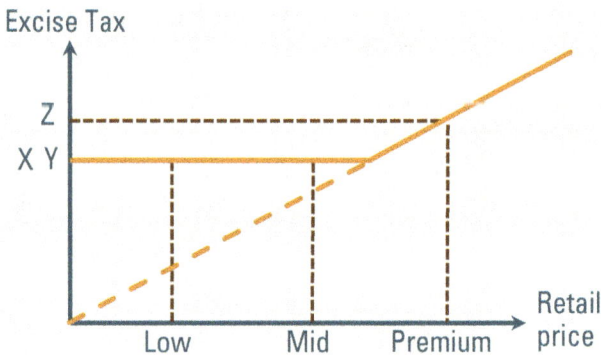

For example, under a dual tax system, the tax can be structured as 50 percent of the price but not less than US$100 per thousand cigarettes. In this example, cigarette brands priced above US$200 per thousand cigarettes pay the *ad valorem* tax, while those brands below US$200 per thousand cigarettes threshold pay the MET. In effect, the price of US$200 per thousand cigarettes is the "kick-in-price" at which the MET applies.

Although technically not an excise tax rate, a dual tax structure system is applied as a customs duty or an import tariff on cigarettes imported into the Gulf Cooperation Council (GGC), which includes Bahrain, Kuwait, Oman, Qatar, Saudi Arabia, and the United Arab Emirates. Domestic cigarette manufacturing industries are absent in these countries; therefore, all cigarettes are imported and pay an import duty instead of an excise tax.

Senegal applies a dual tax system within a multi-tier structure. Cigarettes with a net ex-factory price above Central African Franc (CFA) 250 per pack pay a tax rate of 45 percent on the net ex-factory price while cigarettes with a net ex-factory price below CFA 250 per pack pay 40 percent of the net ex-factory price—refer to Figure 18 below. Furthermore, Senegal applies two MET levels: for the top tax tier, the MET is CFA 160 per pack of 20 cigarettes while for the lower tax tier the MET is CFA 60 per pack of 20 cigarettes.

Figure 18

Dual Tax Structure

- Dual - Single Tier
- Dual - Multi Tier
- Other

F. Mixed Excise Tax Structures (With and Without MET)

The mixed excise tax structure consists of different combinations of specific and *ad valorem* excise taxes—refer to Figure 19 below, in which all products pay a specific amount of tax per unit plus an *ad valorem* tax based on the price.

Figure 19

Mixed Excise Tax Structure

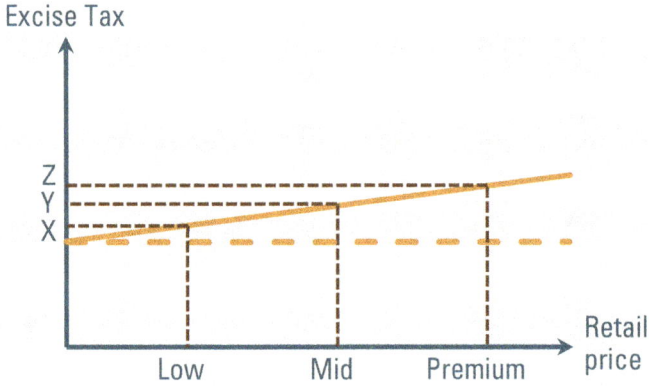

Excise Tax

Z
Y
X

Low   Mid   Premium

Retail price

Furthermore, many countries with a mixed tax structure apply an MET in which case products pay a specific amount of tax per unit plus an *ad valorem* tax based on the price, but this combination is never less than a monetary MET, see Figure 20 below.

Figure 20

Mixed Excise System with Minimum Excise Tax (MET)

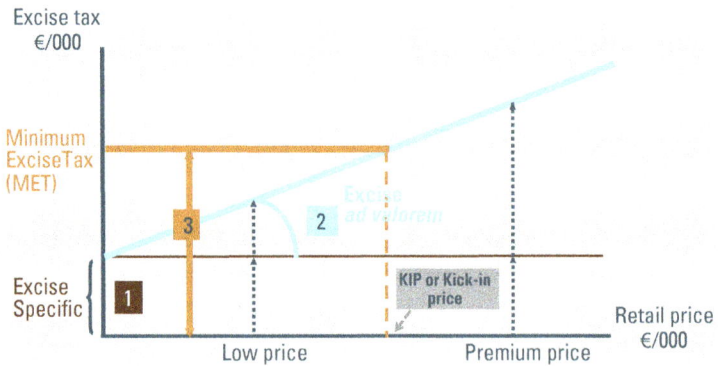

Excise tax €/000

Minimum Excise Tax (MET)

Excise ad valorem

Excise Specific

1

3

2

KIP or Kick-in price

Low price   Premium price

Retail price €/000

A mixed excise tax system is required for all the 28 EU member countries, is applied in several other major economies including China, Mexico, Russia, Turkey and Brazil, and is the most common cigarette excise system globally, as shown in Figure 21 below. As with previous tax structures there is also the possibility to create a multi-tiered mixed system; in Ukraine, for instance, a different mixed tax regime is applied to filtered versus non-filtered cigarettes.

Figure 21

Mixed Tax Structures and METs

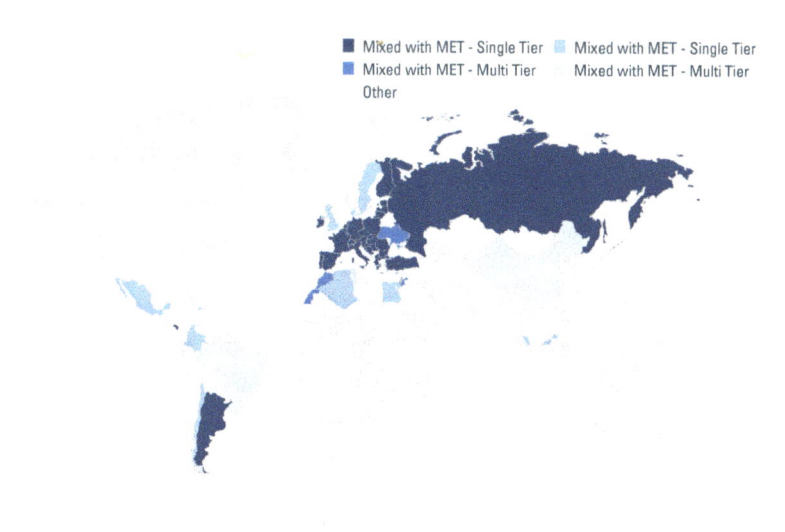

Within the mixed excise tax systems applied globally there is a wide variance in the *ad valorem* excise tax rates applied. Denmark and Sweden have the lowest *ad valorem* excise rates of 1 percent of the retail price while Turkey has the highest at 65.25 percent of the retail price, refer to Figure 22 on the following page.

Figure 22

Mixed Excise Tax Systems: *Ad valorem* Rates on Cigarettes

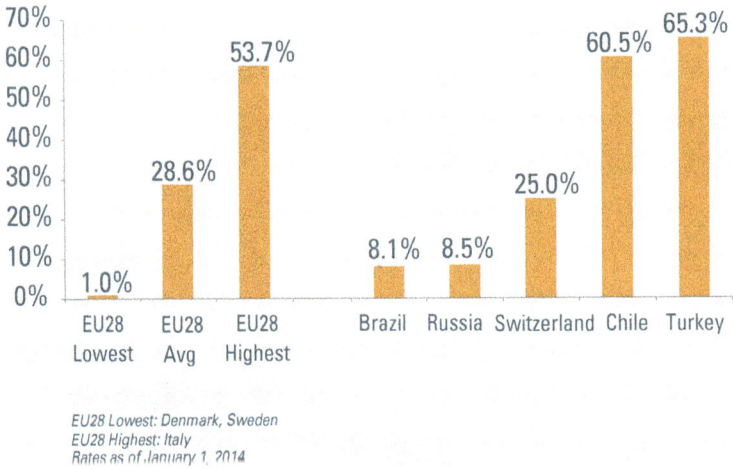

Within the EU, there has been a shift in the excise tax structures on cigarettes, as a majority of countries have reduced the *ad valorem* excise tax element on cigarettes since 2010, as is shown in Figure 23 below. In some instances, this reduction in the *ad valorem* excise rates was intended to correct for increases in the VAT rate (e.g., France, Spain, Slovakia, Cyprus), while in other cases the reduction in the *ad valorem* excise tax corresponded with increases in the specific element (e.g., Sweden, Denmark, France, Germany, Greece, the Netherlands) as countries decided to rebalance their tax structure.

Figure 23

Ad valorem Change in EU-28: January 2014 vs. January 2010

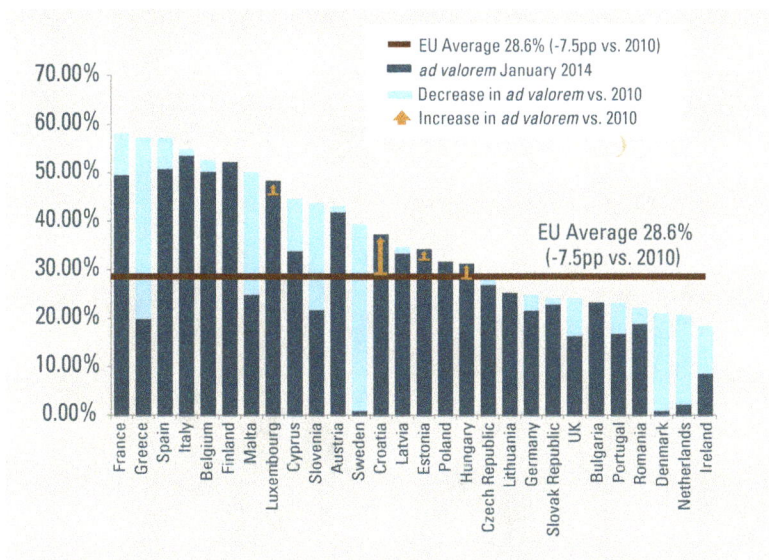

For example, in 2010, Sweden undertook a broad-reaching restructuring of its tobacco excise tax system for cigarettes by:

1. Reducing the excise tax *ad valorem* component from 39.2 percent to 1 percent of retail selling price;

2. Removing minimum excise tax altogether; and,

3. Increasing the specific component of excise tax to a level such as to effectively compensate for the removal of the minimum excise tax.

The reasoning behind such restructuring was explained by the Ministry of Finance, as follows:

> *"The tax system will become more stable following the restructuring. The minimum excise tax, as designed today, may be reduced following a potential change in MPPC i.e. if a low price brand becomes most popular in demand. Such a change will result in a lack of predictability on the cigarette market which is not preferable from a public health point of view. A tax restructuring will prevent this from happen."*[17]

As a consequence of the change in the structure of the tobacco excise tax system, as described above, government revenues from excise tax, which had been stagnant in previous years, showed a marked improvement between 2010 and 2012, as shown in Figure 24 below.[18]

Figure 24

Sweden Government Revenues from Tobacco Excise

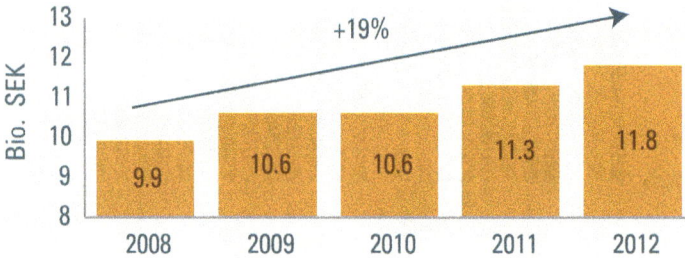

In a mixed system, the amount of excise due on a particular product depends also on the price of the product itself. This makes both government revenues and the effectiveness of the excise system as a whole dependent on producers' pricing decisions as well as consumers' behavior (e.g., down-trading). The introduction of an MET can effectively insulate government revenues from down-trading by ensuring that a certain amount of excise is always paid regardless of retail price. Moreover, an MET also increases the break-even price of tobacco products, thus protecting the effectiveness of the excise system from deflationary pressures on prices.

The effectiveness of an MET to achieve the results stated above is crucially dependent on the level at which the MET itself is set. Obviously, if the level of the MET is so low that all products on the market would pay higher excise in the standard system, the MET is not effective—much like a price floor set below the equilibrium price. There are two general ways in which the MET level can be set:

1. A nominal monetary amount per unit; or

2. A set percentage of the excise tax paid by a specific reference price point (usually the "Most Popular Price Category" (MPPC) or the "Weighted Average Price" (WAP)).

The benefit of the second option is that it automatically adjusts to changes in prices, without requiring any further legislative intervention. However, an automatic mechanism that adjusts the MET level over time (e.g., by linking it to inflation) can be implemented in the first option by governments, thus avoiding the need to frequently adjust the MET level.

For example, in the EU where a mixed excise tax system is mandatory for cigarettes, Member States are explicitly allowed to introduce an MET:

> *"Where necessary, the excise duty on cigarettes may include a minimum tax component, provided that the mixed structure of taxation and the band of the specific component of the excise duty as laid down in Article 8 is strictly respected."*[19]

At present, 25 out of 28 countries in the EU impose an MET on cigarettes, with Denmark, Sweden, and the UK being the exceptions. Out of these three countries, Sweden and Denmark have very low *ad valorem* rates (1 percent of retail selling price), rendering an MET redundant in practice.

Another country with a mixed excise tax system is Brazil. As mentioned earlier, Brazil maintained a unique and complex multi-tier tax system on cigarettes, with tax rates determined by both the cigarette length and whether the cigarettes were sold in box format, soft pack format, or both. Cigarette brands that were sold only in a soft pack format had a lower tax rate than cigarette brands that were sold in both a soft pack format and box format, resulting in a total of 6 different tax tiers.

In December 2011, the number of tax tiers was reduced from 6 to 2, distinguishing only between box and soft pack formats. At the same time, the government set out a 3 year plan to further reform the tax system from 2 tiers to a single tax tier by 2015—refer to Table 4 below. As of 2015, all cigarettes in Brazil will pay the same set of excise tax rate: R$1.30 per pack plus 9.0 percent of the retail price.

Table 4

Brazil: Excise Tax System Evolution

| Timing | Specific tax element - R$ per pack | | Ad valorem tax | Minimum retail price |
	Soft	Box	Percent of retail price	
December 2011 to April 2012	0.8	1.15	0.00%	
May 2012 to December 2012	0.9	1.2	6.00%	3
From January 2013	1.05	1.25	7.10%	3.5
From January 2014	1.2	1.3	8.10%	4
From January 2015	1.3	1.3	9.00%	4.5

As part of this tax reform Brazil also introduced a minimum retail price level for all cigarettes of R$3.00 per pack, which will increase in steps to R$4.50 per pack by 2015. This minimum price is a price-floor below which cigarettes cannot be sold—indirectly establishing a minimum tax amount per pack of cigarettes (namely the specific tax, plus the minimum retail price times the *ad valorem* rate), which is an important consideration following the introduction of the *ad valorem* tax element.

G. Excise Tax Rates on Other Tobacco Products

So far, this book has focused on the tax structure of cigarettes, but similar variations of tax structure can also be applied to other tobacco products. Furthermore, governments need to consider the appropriate level of tax on other tobacco products in comparison to cigarettes, as this too has consequences for market dynamics and excise tax revenues.

For example, in Germany, the average excise tax per pack of premium cigarettes[20] has increased from Euro 1.46 in January 2001 to Euro 3.04 in January 2013,[21] while over the same period, there has been a steady increase in the percent of the market accounted for by so-called "budget smoking" alternatives,[22] growing from 38.9 percent to 74.3 percent of the total tobacco market. The fastest growth occurred in the "smoking tobacco" category (RYO/MYO and pipe tobacco—refer to Figure 25), which increased from 9.9 percent market share to 28.9 percent market share during this period.

Figure 25

Germany: Consumer Down-Trading to Lower Taxed Alternatives

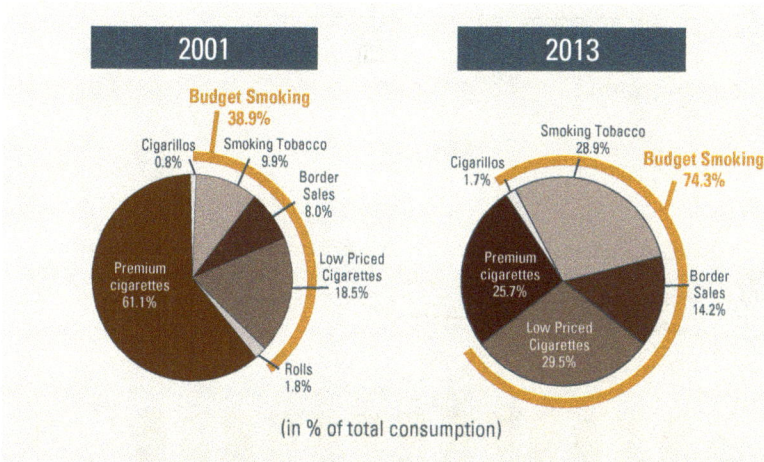

(in % of total consumption)

Source: PMG, Sales Planning & Trade Compliance , RTC, RTR, Bordersalesstudie

To optimize government revenues excise tax levels should be established in such a way that each tobacco category is taxed according to its tax bearing capacity. Establishing this "optimal" tax level for each category is not a science, rather it is more a practical policy exercise. The tax level should be set sufficiently high to generate realistic levels of government revenues but not too high as this will lead to unintended consequences (e.g., cause consumers to switch to lower taxed or illicit alternative products). The tax on an individual category should also not be set too low as this may cause a switch by consumers of higher taxed categories towards the low taxed category (unless, of course, such consumer switching is the policy intention of the government, e.g., to switch consumers towards reduced risk products).

Thailand is one example where tax differentials on different tobacco products induced consumers to switch from high taxed to low taxed products. In 2001, the excise tax gap between low priced and high priced cigarettes was Thai baht 7.1 per pack, and following several tax increases over 12 years, this gap widened to Thai baht 18.8 per pack. As a result of this tax gap widening, the low price market share increased from less than 10 percent in 2001 to approximately 57 percent of the market by 2013—refer to Figure 26 below.

Figure 26

Thailand: Effects of Tax Gap on Cigarette Market Share by Price Segment

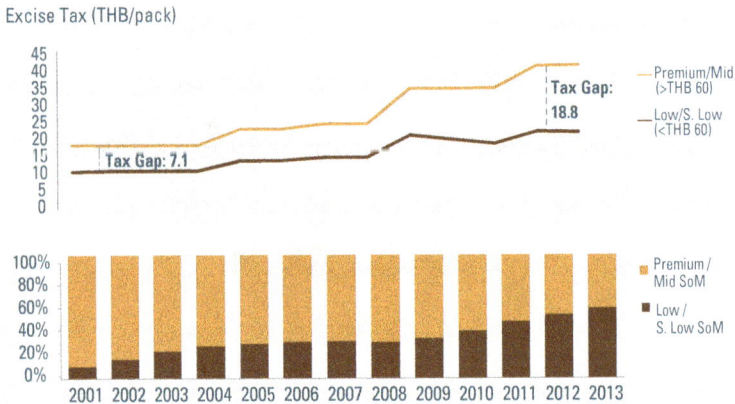

Source: Excise tax expressed on pack of 20s, calculated on MPPC per segment. PMI estimates SoM data source Nielsen

Likewise, a similar pattern emerges when the roll-your-own (RYO) category is included. The excise tax on roll-your-own is exceptionally low in Thailand—initially being held constant at the equivalent of Thai baht 0.02 per 20 hand-rolled cigarettes between 2001 and 2011, it then increased to only Thai baht 0.15 in 2012 while RYO from locally grown tobacco remains not taxed at all. As such, there is a significant tax gap between the tax paid on RYO and the tax paid on even the lowest price cigarette, as observed in Figure 27. As a result, the RYO category has steadily gained share of the total tobacco market in Thailand between 2001 and 2010, which has eroded overall government tax revenue from tobacco.

Figure 27

Thailand: Tax Gaps Between Cigarettes and RYO

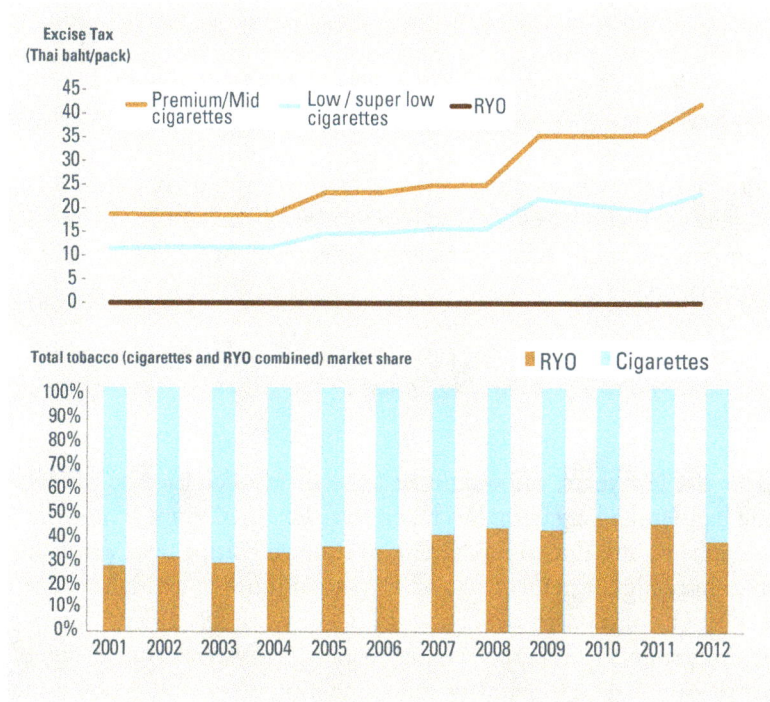

Excise tax expressed on pack of 20s. Calculations for RYO assume 0.75g per stick equivalence. SoM of RYO calculated on total tobacco market (Cigarettes and RYO).

One technical issue for governments considering the appropriate tax level on different product categories is how to best compare tax and price levels among a variety of products. For instance, how high must the tax be per kilogram of fine-cut tobacco in order to be considered equivalent to the tax on cigarettes?

There are various approaches to this topic: one approach could be to study average daily consumption, e.g., if research in a country finds that cigarette smokers consume, on average, 20 cigarettes a day, while "hand rollers" consume, on average, 15 grams of tobacco per day, then one could conclude that 1 cigarette is "equivalent" to 0.75 gram of fine-cut tobacco, and this could then become the basis for tax comparisons. A more technical approach could also be taken: if manufactured cigarettes were found to contain, on average, 0.7 gram of tobacco, then one could use this ratio as the conversion between cigarettes and fine-cut tobacco. Another suggested approach is to compare the "puff counts" of the products while consumed, which may be reasonable when comparing cigarettes with e-cigarettes, but will be of no use when considering smokeless tobacco products. Clearly, this is an area that could benefit from further research, as it is a key element for formulating an appropriate tax policy for different tobacco product categories.

In the EU, there is no official weight conversion ratio between RYO products and cigarettes, although reports published by the European Commission imply that one cigarette is equivalent to 750mg of fine-cut tobacco:

> *"A unit of product is one cigar, one cigarette, 750mg of fine-cut tobacco; and 1 g of pipe, snuff, water-pipe, snus, or chewing tobacco."*[23]

Over the last years, the weight of fine-cut tobacco used to produce one hand-rolled cigarette has fallen to as low 0.40 gram. The reduction of weight is due to product innovation, as companies include increasingly higher percentages of "expanded tobacco", which requires less weight of tobacco per cigarette stick. Figure 28 depicts a sample of the products available on the market, as well as the "claimed" conversion ratios. Obviously, reductions in conversion ratios result in substantial excise tax savings for consumers.

Figure 28

Conversion Ratio of Fine Cut vs. Cigarettes

55g for 100 cigarettes → 1 cigarette = 0.55g

100g for 180 cigarettes → 1 cigarette = 0.56g

70g for 100 cigarettes → 1 cigarette = 0.70g

70g for 120 cigarettes → 1 cigarette = 0.58g

8g for 20 cigarettes → 1 cigarette = 0.40g

Tax authorities need to continually assess developments in the tobacco market and respond with appropriate tax measures to ensure that one tobacco category does not have a significant tax advantage compared to a similar or substitutable product. This view was clearly stated in a report by the European Commission:

> *"Notwithstanding the fact that cigarettes and fine-cut tobacco have different characteristics, they are competing products and are equally harmful for health. The gap between the current level of taxation for cigarettes and fine-cut tobacco gives rise to product substitution. Between 2002 and 2006, the consumption of cigarettes decreased by more than 10 percent but, in parallel, the consumption of fine-cut tobacco increased by around 10 percent in the EU25. To address this problem, the Commission proposes a partial alignment of the minimum rate for fine-cut tobacco to the minimum rate for cigarettes."*[24]

H. Conclusions on Excise Tax Structure

Around the world, there is a remarkable variation of tax structures in place for cigarettes and other tobacco products. Governments tailor these systems to meet certain domestic policy objectives, but clearly some of these objectives change over time and will be different from country to country.

Many countries design their excise structure to reduce smoking prevalence and thus implement a fully specific excise tax structure that treats all products as equally harmful and does not encourage consumers to shift consumption to lower taxed products, as can be the case in tiered or *ad valorem* structures. Other countries balance their policy objectives by not only considering public health goals but by also prioritizing the protection of employment: for instance, by applying lower taxes to hand-made products. Again, other countries are concerned about the regressive impact of tobacco taxes on low income smokers and, therefore, see a policy need for lower taxed fine-cut tobacco.

Clearly, policy priorities will differ per country, but countries must realize that there is a close inter-relationship between excise tax levels and excise tax structures. As excise tax levels increase, any weaknesses in the excise tax structure will be exposed and exacerbated. If the tax structure allows, consumers will compensate tax increases by switching to lower tax alternative products. As a result, government tax revenue may not increase as expected, and the public health objectives will be undermined following a tax increase.

Countries thus need to continuously evaluate whether the tax structure in place addresses their policy objectives, and, as tax levels increase, the tax structure needs to be fine-tuned, e.g., by gradually approximating taxes on competing product categories to reduce down-trading.

The global trend, with respect to the excise tax structure, points towards simpler systems (no or fewer tiers), as well as systems that rely predominantly on specific tax components—i.e., either mixed systems with a relatively large specific or minimum excise tax, or fully specific systems. This development is consistent with public health objectives becoming an increasingly important topic in the tobacco tax debate, and it also reflects the increasing pressure on tobacco tax levels in many countries, which leads to a need for more stable and controllable tax structures. Two quotes from the European Commission and the IMF illustrate this thinking:

> "Specific duties reduce relative price differences and minimize the variability of prices. Consequently specific duties have an advantage from a health point of view. [....] Furthermore, as they are based on consumption volumes rather than on prices, specific duties are more stable, easier to forecast and to administer and increase the stability of tax revenues."[25]

> "If a primary purpose of the excise is to discourage tobacco consumption, a strong case can be made for specific excises that would impose the same tax per stick. Specific taxes also are easier to administer because it is only necessary to determine the physical quantity of the product taxed, and not necessary to determine its value."[26]

IV. VALUE ADDED TAX

A. Introduction

Value Added Tax (VAT) is a consumption tax paid ultimately by final consumers and collected by businesses. VAT is levied on a broad base as it applies to all or most goods and services, thus meeting neutrality conditions for businesses.[27] The purpose of VAT is to generate tax revenues for the government similar to the corporate income tax or personal income tax.

There are, in general, three categories of VAT applied within each country: (1) a standard rate that applies to the vast majority of consumer purchases; (2) a reduced rate which is applied to a limited range of goods such as: medical equipment, educational services and goods, basic foods stuffs; and, (3) a zero rate that applies to specific activities, such as hospital or medical care, or to transactions that do not fall into the scope of VAT, such as insurance or financial services. Individual countries can decide how goods are classified between the standard and preferential VAT rate, but, generally speaking, countries seek to keep the number of items receiving the preferential VAT rate to a minimum.

The tax base for VAT is the value added to a product or service, that is to say, the difference between the selling price of said good/service and the cost of the inputs used to produce it. This is technically achieved through a system of payments and credits, whereby a buyer generally pays VAT on the purchase price of a good/service, not on the value added, which is then credited back if the good/service is used as an input to produce another good/service. The new buyer will then pay the whole VAT due on the selling price of this new good and so on. As such, only the final consumer will ultimately pay VAT, while the intermediate buyers/sellers only act as agents to collect VAT for the state. More details on the collection mechanism for VAT can be found in Section VI.

B. Nominal Versus Effective VAT Rates

It is important to understand the difference between the "nominal" and the "effective" VAT rate. The nominal VAT rate, or mark-up rate, is the rate applied to the product prior to the VAT itself. The effective VAT rate, on the other hand, is the VAT expressed as a per cent of the final retail price.

In the example presented in Table 5 below, the nominal VAT rate of 25 percent is applied to the pre-VAT price, of say, 100 per unit. The final retail price to consumers, including the VAT is then 125 per unit. The effective VAT rate therefore is 25/125 or 20 percent. Likewise, if the nominal VAT rate is 20 percent, then the effective rate is 16.67 percent or (20/120).

Table 5

Nominal Versus Effective VAT Rate Calculation

Nominal VAT Rate	Effective VAT Rate
25.00%	20.00%
20.00%	16.67%
15.00%	13.04%
10.00%	9.09%
5.00%	4.76%

The Effective VAT Rate is calculated as the amount of tax paid for the nominal VAT rate divided by the retail price including VAT. For example, if the price prior to VAT is 100 and the Nominal VAT rate is 25%, the tax paid for the nominal VAT rate is 25. Therefore, the retail price including VAT is 125, indicating that the effective VAT rate=25/125=20%

It is imperative to notice that the VAT effectively works as an additional *ad valorem* component of tobacco taxation. Moreover, if the *ad valorem* excise tax is applied on the final retail selling price to the consumer, as is often the case for cigarettes, this implies that the excise tax is included in the VAT base calculation. In effect, for excisable products such as tobacco, VAT is a tax-on-a-tax, and this can have significant implications when the VAT rate is increased, as explained in more detail in Section V below.

On a global basis, the EU has the highest VAT rates, with an average effective VAT rate of 17.5 percent, while Asia has the lowest average VAT with a rate of 9.0 percent, as shown in Figure 29 on the next page. Within Asia, Hong Kong and Brunei do not apply any VAT, while Malaysia applies a sales tax to certain commodities including cigarettes. Australia, New Zealand, Pakistan, and Singapore apply a General Sales Tax, or GST.

Figure 29[28]

Average Effective VAT Rates as of January 2014

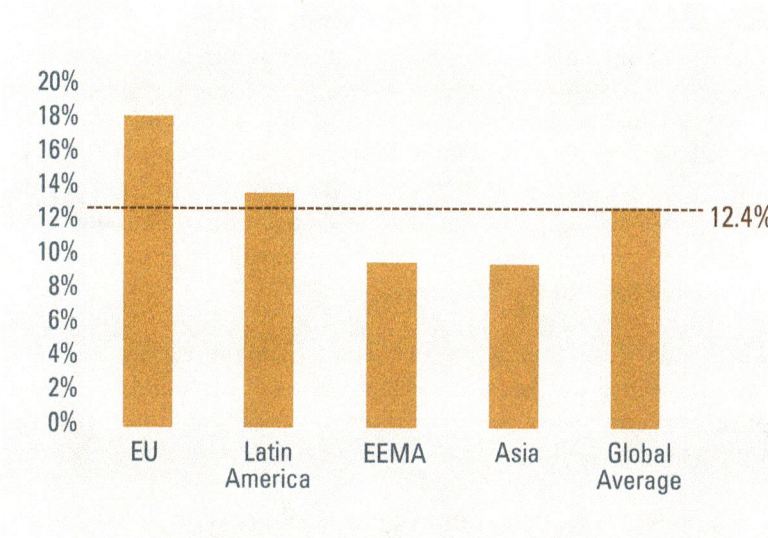

The combination of tobacco excise and VAT is often referred to as "total tax". Total tax is not only an important concept in of itself because it captures the overall tax burden imposed on tobacco products, but it is also essential for determining the dynamic adjustment of tax and retail prices to changes in the proportional (*ad valorem*) and non-proportional elements of retail selling price, as described in the following section.

V. DYNAMIC EFFECTS OF TAXATION

A. Interrelationship Between VAT and Excise Tax

As discussed in the previous section, although VAT is in theory a consumption tax levied on the value added to goods and services, in the case of excise goods, such as tobacco products, it is levied on both value added and excise tax. In other words, in the case of cigarettes, VAT is not only a tax on value added, but it is also a "tax-on-a-tax".

One key consequence then, is that for countries with an *ad valorem* excise based on the final retail selling price, an increase in the VAT rate will also result in an increase in the amount of excise tax paid, as the retail selling price will have to increase to accommodate the higher VAT. The increase in excise, in turn, will once more increase the taxable base for the VAT and so on.

The result of the interaction between *ad valorem* excise, VAT, and their respective tax bases, is a disproportional increase in the retail price of excise goods compared to non-excise good, whenever the VAT rate is increased.

Let us take for example three products all priced at $5.00, but respectively:

1. A good not subject to excise;

2. A good subject to a fully specific excise of $2.50; and,

3. A good subject to *ad valorem* excise of 50 percent of retail price (i.e., $2.50).

Let us then assume that all products are initially subject to a 20 percent nominal VAT rate, which is then increased by 1 percentage point. Table 6 below shows what happens to the retail price of the three products.[29]

Table 6

Interaction of VAT and Excise Tax

	Product 1 No Excise			Product 2 Fully Specific Excise			Product 3 *ad valorem* Excise		
VAT Rate (Nominal)	20%	21%	Increase	20%	21%	Increase	20%	21%	Increase
Pre Tax Price	($)4.17	4.17	-	($)1.67	1.67	-	($)1.67	1.67	-
Specific Excise	-	-	-	($)2.50	2.50	-			
ad valorem Excise	-	-	-	-	-	-	($)2.50	2.55	0.05
VAT	($)0.83	0.88	0.04	($)0.83	0.88	0.04	($)0.83	0.89	0.05
VAT on Pre Tax Price	($)0.83	0.88	0.04	($)0.33	0.35	0.02	($)0.33	0.35	0.02
VAT on Specific Excise	-	-	-	($)0.50	0.53	0.03	-	-	-
VAT on *ad valorem* Excise	-	-	-	-	-	-	($)0.50	0.54	0.04
Retail Price	($)5.00	5.04	0.04	($)5.00	5.04	0.04	($)5.00	5.11	0.11

As can be seen by comparing the retail price of the good subject to *ad valorem* excise to that of the other two goods after the VAT change, the increase in retail price is more than double for the good subject to *ad valorem* excise. This is due to the combined effect of the increase in VAT and the associated increase in *ad valorem* excise.

In order to avoid such distortions, some countries have adopted either formal legislation or ad-hoc changes to reduce the *ad valorem* component of excise tax rates in order to correct for the unintended interaction between VAT increases and excise tax.

As an example, in Germany the Tobacco Tax Act empowers the Ministry of Finance to adjust the tobacco tax in conjunction with a VAT increase according to the ratio below:[30]

$$\frac{100+ \text{ percentage points of previous sales tax}}{100+ \text{ percentage points of new sales tax}}$$

B. Tax Multiplier

When there is an *ad valorem* excise tax element based on the retail selling price, whether this is with a fully *ad valorem* excise tax system or a mixed excise tax system, there is a non-linear relationship between increases in the *ad valorem* excise tax rate and the final increase in the retail selling price of cigarettes—for every 1 percentage point increase in the *ad valorem* excise tax rate, the retail selling price will increase by more than 1 percentage point. This is compounded if there are other *ad valorem* tax elements, such as VAT, also applied on the retail price. An increase in the *ad valorem* excise tax rate from 60 percent to 61 percent, for example, will have a much greater impact of the final retail price than an increase in the *ad valorem* excise tax rate from 50 percent to 51 percent as demonstrated in Figure 30 below.

Clearly, taxes based on the final retail selling price can never exceed a rate of 100 percent, and as the *ad valorem* excise approaches 100 percent (minus the VAT rate, if applicable) the retail selling price will diverge to infinity.

Figure 30

Excise Incidence Increases: Non-Linear Relation with Retail Price

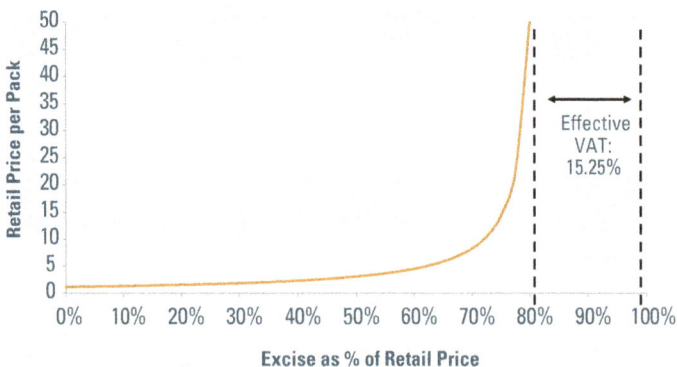

Assumes constant pre-tax value and nominal VAT of 18%

The non-linear relationship between *ad valorem* excise tax increases and retail prices can have significant effects on tobacco prices and inflation within the overall economy.

In Turkey for example, the *ad valorem* Special Consumption Tax (SCT) was increased from 58 percent to 63 percent in December 2009, and again to 65 percent in October 2011. Although the 2 percentage point increase from 63 percent to 65 percent may seem relatively small in absolute terms, given the already extremely high tax rate of 63 percent, this had such a significant impact on retail price levels that the Turkish Central Bank revised its inflation forecast upwards, explicitly identifying tobacco prices as a contributing factor—refer to the Central Bank's inflation forecast in Figure 31 on the following page. Fitch Rating—the sovereign credit rating agency—cut Turkey's long-term foreign currency rating outlook as a result. Driven by the above-target inflation rate that resulted from the unanticipated effects of the *ad valorem* tobacco tax increases, the Turkish Central Bank raised interest rates.

In 2013, following the negative inflationary consequences of the *ad valorem* excise tax increases, Turkey introduced a specific tax element of Turkish Lira 0.09 per pack of cigarettes and increased the *ad valorem* tax element by only 0.25 percent to 65.25 percent of the retail price.

Figure 31

Possible Contribution of Exchange Rate Developments and
Tax Adjustments in Tobacco Products to Annual Inflation without the CBRT's Policy Response (Percent)

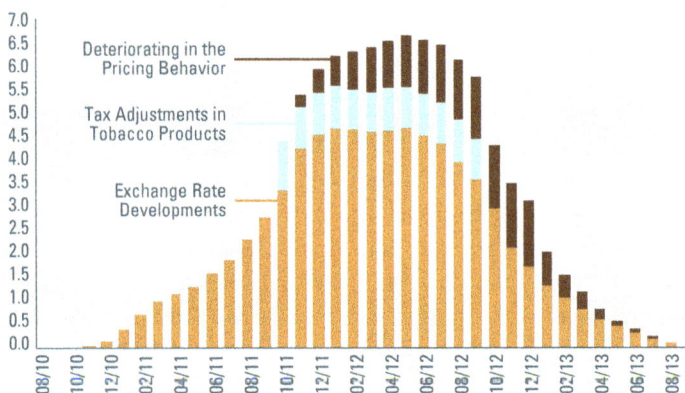

Source: Turkish Central Bank Q4 2011 Inflation report (http://www.tcmb.gov.tr/yeni/eng/)

The non-linear relationship between the *ad valorem* excise tax and
the retail price is not the only compounding factor. Other *ad valorem*
tax elements, such as VAT, General Sales Tax (GST), or retail trade
margins will also impact the retail price in non-linear terms. The
non-linear interaction between the *ad valorem* excise tax rate, VAT
rate, and the retail price is captured mathematically by the tax multiplier and can be calculated with the following formula:

$$Tax\ Multiplier = 1\ /\ (1 - VAT\ effective - ad\ valorem)$$

The tax multiplier captures the fact that when there are *ad valorem*
tax elements based on the retail price, any change in the non-proportional elements (e.g., production costs), which lead to an increase
in the retail price, will have a further knock-on effect on the retail
price because of the additional tax due on the initial increase in retail price. The higher the total *ad valorem* tax rates, the stronger this
effect, and therefore the larger the impact on the final retail price.

For example, Belgium and the Netherlands have the same effective VAT rate of 17.36 percent. However, in Belgium the *ad valorem* excise tax is 50.41 percent of the retail price, while in the Netherlands the *ad valorem* excise tax is 2.36 percent of the retail price. As a result, the tax multiplier in Belgium is 3.10 compared to 1.25 in the Netherlands. In practice, this has the following impact: suppose that the production costs for cigarettes increase by $0.25 per pack. This cost increase will then lead to a $0.31 price increase in the Netherlands (1.25 * 0.25), and a $0.78 price increase in Belgium (3.10 * 0.25). That is to say that the same increase in the production cost of cigarettes will cause the retail price in Belgium to increase by twice as much as in the Netherlands (Figure 32).

Figure 32

Tax Multiplier Effect: Belgium and Netherlands Example

$$\text{Belgium (high } ad\ valorem \text{ tax)} = \frac{1}{(1 - 17.36\% - 50.41\%)} = \text{Tax Multiplier of } 3.10$$

$$\text{Netherlands (low } ad\ valorem \text{ tax)} = \frac{1}{(1 - 17.36\% - 2.36\%)} = \text{Tax Multiplier of } 1.25$$

VI. TAX ADMINISTRATION AND COLLECTION SYSTEMS

A. Excise Collection Systems

1. TAX CREDIT TERMS AND PAYMENT TRIGGER POINTS

Excise goods during the production process, and when stored and distributed, usually fall under a "suspension arrangement", which suspends the excise tax liability until the goods are "released for consumption". Countries will typically define the release for consumption as the moment when the goods leave the production center and are distributed to retailers or, alternatively, when the products leave an excise or customs "bonded warehouse" if they were imported from another country.

From a practical point of view, however, the excise tax liability is normally triggered by a tax declaration. Tax declaration periods vary widely, from a per transaction declaration to periodic consolidated declarations (weekly/monthly/bi-monthly). A majority of countries have implemented a monthly excise tax declaration (to be filed within a predefined number of days after month-end).

Different tax credit terms (the period to pay the excise taxes declared) may apply, ranging normally from one week to 90 days. In determining credit terms, countries try to eliminate cash flow disadvantages for producers/traders for pre-financing excise taxes, which are not yet collected from sales (considering that the excise tax is a consumption tax)—refer to Table 7 below.

Table 7

Examples of Excise Tax Trigger Point and Payment Terms

Country	Tax Trigger point	Tax payment term
Bosnia	Receipt of tax stamp	Pre-payment
France	Release for consumption	5th day of the second month following release from an excise warehouse
Germany	Tax sticker removal for production	Removal from 1st to 15th of the month at the 12th of the following month, removal from the 16th to the end of the month as of the 27th of the following month (exception: Dec 1-15th at Dec. 27th)
Indonesia	Tax stamp order placement	60 days after ordering tax stamps
Israel	Release from bonded ware-house	At the time of custom clearance
Italy	Release for consumption	Month end for releases for consumption in first 15 days of the month, 15 days after month end for releases for consumption in second 15 (16) days of the month
Montenegro	Receipt of tax stamp	60 days after receipt of excise tax stamps
Turkey	Shipment (sales) from factory	15th of the month following the shipment

Source: National legislations

2. TAX STAMPS/FISCAL MARKINGS

One common way for authorities to collect excise and/or to ensure that products released for consumption have actually been subject to excise is to mandate the application of a tax stamp or other fiscal marking on the products themselves. Five classes of fiscal marking can be distinguished:

1. Tax stamp (also referred to as "banderole");

2. Fiscal sticker;

3. Price indicator;

4. Duty paid indicator; and,

5. Digital fiscal marking.

These types of fiscal markings and their workings are described below.

i. Tax stamp or banderole:

A tax stamp, or banderole, is a special stamp issued by fiscal authorities to manufacturers or importers of cigarettes—the purchase and issuance of which is the basis of paying the excise tax. In practice, only licensed manufacturers or importers are allowed to acquire tax stamps. Manufacturers generally need to arrange secure and insured transportation of the stamps to the factory, as reimbursement is not guaranteed in the case of theft or accidents.

In the production process, stamps are affixed to the packs according to national regulations, which usually require that the position of the stamps on the pack is such that when the consumer opens the pack, the stamp will be damaged (to prevent re-use of a tax stamps, for instance on counterfeit product). Stamps that are damaged in the production process or are not needed due to price or tax changes are returned to the tax authorities or destroyed under customs supervision. In these cases reimbursement of the excise tax is possible for each stamp accounted for.

Tax stamps represent the excise value or, in case of a single-stage VAT collection system, both the excise and VAT. In the case of a mixed excise system, the excise value will refer to the specific combination of stick count and retail selling price indicated on the tax stamp. There is usually no extra or separate cost for the stamp itself—this is included in the tax amount.

In case of price changes, retailers generally sell the old stock at old price (usually printed on the stamp), until they run out of stock and start selling cigarettes at the new price. In practice, this means that the actual effect of a price and tax change in the market never occurs on a single day but instead is spread out over time depending on stocks available in the distribution and retail supply chain.

For each tax change the Ministry of Finance generally specifies dates by which cigarettes with the "old tax rate" tax stamps need to be cleared from the retail trade. Additionally, there is often a limitation on the volume that can be cleared in the weeks before a tax change, which is usually related to each manufacturer's normal or average volume.

For example, Germany uses tax stamps for all tobacco categories. Each stamp indicates the respective product category, e.g., the ones for cigarettes mention "Zigaretten". Furthermore, the tax stamp indicates the fixed retail selling price and the stick count, which, in combination with the excise rates, determine the excise tax amount represented by the stamp. The small letter "P" below the price of €5.20 per pack refers to the applicable tax rates at that moment: with every change in tax rates a new series of tax stamps with a new letter is issued. See Figure 33 below.

Figure 33

Tax Stamp: Example, Germany

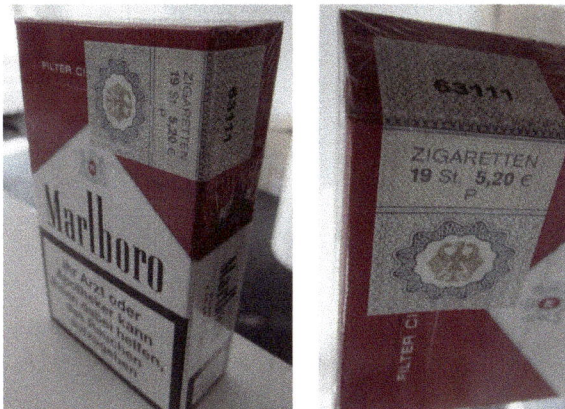

ii. Fiscal sticker

A fiscal sticker is also a special stamp issued by fiscal authorities, but it does not form the basis of any payment of excise tax. Instead, it serves to identify taxed cigarettes within a fiscal territory. Tax authorities also use it as a tax audit mechanism as it allows for comparing the quantity of stickers sent to a manufacturer with the excise duty payments from that manufacturer.

Similar to fiscal stamps, only licensed manufacturers or importers are allowed to acquire fiscal stickers from the State printing shop. The main difference with tax stamps is that the fiscal sticker does not represent a tax value. This is especially true in Italy, where the same fiscal sticker is affixed to cigarettes of any retail selling price, despite the fact that cigarettes with different retail prices will pay different excise amounts. Generally, fiscal stickers cost a certain "paper value" that is paid by the manufacturer.

Fiscal stickers are always used in combination with an administrative tax collection system, i.e., a system whereby the tax trigger point is the clearance of cigarettes from the excise warehouse in the country of final destination. In some countries fiscal stickers have the retail selling price printed on them (e.g., Portugal), but this is not the case in other countries (e.g., Spain and Italy).

As previously stated, the tax authorities also use fiscal stickers as a means to audit tax collections: the quantity of stickers sent to a manufacturer needs to match the volumes cleared from a warehouse plus the change in stock levels of finished goods and stickers. Therefore, although it is often said that these stickers have a paper value, it is also clear that an unaccounted loss of fiscal stickers may have significant monetary consequences. It is for this reason that the transport of fiscal stickers to the factory is insured for the average tax value of the cigarettes. See Figure 34 below.

Figure 34

Fiscal Sticker: Example Italy

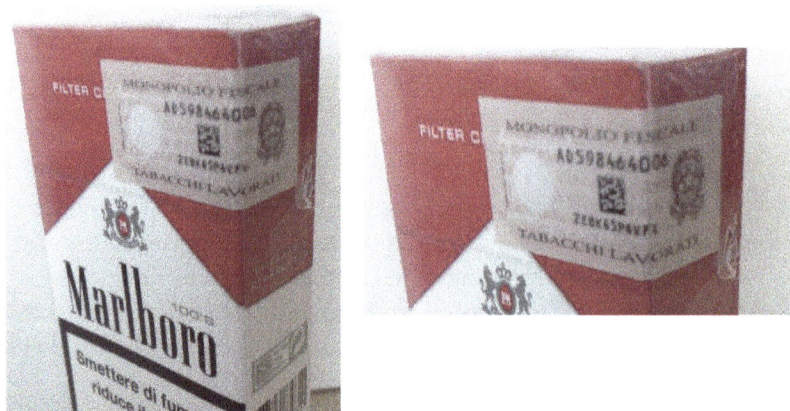

iii. Price indicator

In countries where fiscal legislation requires manufacturers or importers to establish (maximum) retail prices, there is a need to communicate these (maximum) prices to the trade and to the consumer. This can be done in various ways, such as mandatory publication in newspapers, publication of official price lists in licensed tobacconists, or price indication on the cigarette packs. Tax stamps always have a price indication; fiscal stickers sometimes do.

Some countries that have not chosen to use tax stamps or fiscal stickers nevertheless require price indication on the pack by law. In this case, manufacturers may often choose their own method of indicating the price, e.g., by printing the price directly on the pack or by putting "self-made" stickers with price indication on packs. These countries always collect taxes via a pure administrative system, e.g., based on excise warehouse clearances and company invoices, where the *ad valorem* tax amount calculated on the invoice should match the maximum retail selling price indicated on the pack.

Figure 35 below depicts cigarette packs from Switzerland, where the maximum retail selling price of CHF 8.20 per pack is directly printed on the pack.

Figure 35

Price Indicator: Example Switzerland

iv. Duty paid indicator

This is a legally required marker printed on the pack, to identify duty paid cigarettes for a specific market. Countries that do not require tax stamps, fiscal stickers, or price indication generally still require some indication on the pack to show that it is intended for duty-paid sales in their domestic market. Austria, France, and the UK are examples of this practice in the EU.

The UK tax law requires that manufacturers put the mark "UK DUTY PAID" on cigarettes sold in the UK market. Size, colors, and text of the marker are defined by law, see Figure 36 below.

Figure 36

Duty Paid Indicator: Example UK

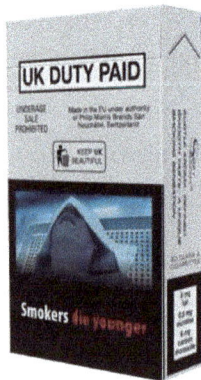

v. Digital fiscal marking

In addition to the fiscal stamps and stickers described above, new technological developments have allowed for the use of a digital fiscal marking system to enforce the collection of excise tax on tobacco products. A digital fiscal marking system could be integrated with the local excise tax collection system, allowing both global tracking and tracing of tobacco products and, at the same time, replace paper fiscal stickers. While such a digital fiscal marking system has not yet been applied in any country, the technology already exists and is being piloted in several countries, for instance Switzerland. The alphanumeric codes on the pack, as shown below in Figure 37, represent the digital tax stamp, which can authenticate the cigarette pack as a genuine, tax paid product via the internet on a secure website.[3]

Figure 37

Digital Fiscal Marking: Example Switzerland

3.   CROSS BORDER MOVEMENT OF EXCISABLE PRODUCT

With the development of free trade regions and common markets across the world over the past decades, combined with the consolidation within the tobacco industry, cigarette trade has increased across borders. As an excise tax is a tax on consumption, regulations are required to ensure that the excise is paid in the country of consumption rather than the country of production or the countries through which the cigarettes transit. This is achieved by allowing the movement of goods from one country to another under excise suspension with excise tax only paid on goods released for domestic consumption in the country of destination.

There must be a clear system of accountability for the international movement of excise goods to know which party is held responsible for excise payment in case goods traveling under duty suspension are lost or stolen.

In Europe, the 28 EU members, Norway, Switzerland, Liechtenstein, and Iceland have a common electronic system called New Computerized Transit System (NCTS), for the movement of goods under customs duty and excise suspension. This system allows for the movement of cigarettes over their respective territories without triggering import duty and excise liabilities. The system works as follows:

At the start of a shipment, the sender (consignor) enters specific data elements into the NCTS system to which authorities from both the departure and arrival country (as well as transit countries) have access. Each shipment receives a unique Movement Reference Number (MRN) which can be displayed (on paper or screen) as a barcode. This barcode is printed on documents accompanying the actual shipment. At any moment in time during transit, the barcode can be used to display the relevant details of the shipment in the NCTS system for confirming the legality and conformity of the shipment. Upon arrival at the final destination, the receiving customer (consignee) can enter the data and confirm receipt of the shipment in the NCTS system (i.e., confirming correctness/completeness of the shipment and taking over the liability for excises of the shipment).

Specifically, for the movement of excisable goods within the EU Customs Union the EU has implemented an Excise Movement Control System (EMCS)—an electronic system that allows authorities to monitor and control excise products as they move within the EU single market. The EMCS system was built on the same basic platform as NCTS with a similar modus operandi. Effective from the beginning of 2010, this electronic system has replaced a paper system.

B. VAT Collection Systems

Regarding VAT collection on tobacco, countries have two main options: multi-stage or single-stage.

A multi-stage system occurs when each party is liable for the collection of their proportion of the total VAT due in a standard supply chain of manufacturer/importer, wholesaler, and retailer. Table 8 below provides a simple demonstration on how a multi-stage VAT system is administered. The VAT paid by the consumer on the final purchase price ($22) is partially collected by the manufacturer ($20) and partially collected by the retailer ($2).

Table 8

Multi Stage VAT Collection

	In $		Input	Output	Total
Manufacturer	Net Selling Price	100			
	Tax Paid for VAT Rate of 20 percent	20		20	20
	Gross Selling Price	120			
Retailer	Purchase Price	120			
	VAT Credit		(20)		
	Adds Margin	10			
	Tax Paid for VAT Rate of 20 percent			22	2
	Gross Selling Price	132			
Consumer	Purchase Price	132			
	Tax Paid for VAT Rate of 20 percent	22			22
	Price Excluding VAT	110			

A multi-stage VAT collection system is required when the final retail selling price is not known and each agent in the distribution chain collects the VAT on their respective mark-up or value added.

A multi-stage collection system is the standard VAT collection mechanism. Nevertheless, due to the number of stakeholders in the supply chain, this system may create VAT gaps whereby countries end up with uncollected VAT, mainly related to VAT fraud or from bankruptcies and insolvencies.

When the final retail selling price is known or registered with the tax authorities, it is possible to apply a single stage VAT collection system, where the total VAT amount is collected by the manufacturer or importer and paid to the government. The rest of the supply chain does not need to reclaim or charge the VAT, as it is already accounted for in the final price to the consumer—see Table 9 below.

Table 9

Single Stage VAT Collection: Final Selling Price Known or Registered

			Total
Manufacturer	Net Selling Price	100	
	Tax Paid for VAT Rate of 20%*110	22	22
	Gross Selling Price	122	
Retailer	Purchase Price	122	
	(Does Not Reclaim VAT)		
	Adds Margin	10	
	(Does Not Charge VAT Rate of 20%)		
	Gross Selling Price	132	
Consumer	Purchase Price	132	
	Tax Paid for VAT Rate of 20%	22	22
	Price Excluding VAT	110	

The single stage VAT collection system is applied on cigarettes in Albania, Belgium, France, Greece, Hungary, Indonesia, Italy, Luxembourg, Montenegro, Malaysia, Portugal, and Thailand, as seen in Figure 38 on the following page. The advantage of a single stage VAT collection system is that it can be combined with the excise tax collection to ensure a more efficient collection system. A single stage VAT will reduce the complexity and administration requirements as there is only one point for VAT collection. The possibility of VAT fraud is thus reduced at the various intermediate stages. With tobacco products, in most instances, there are generally a small number of relatively large manufacturers or importers, so the overall control and audits of the VAT collection is much easier to administer under such a collection system.

Figure 38

VAT/GST Single and Multi Stage

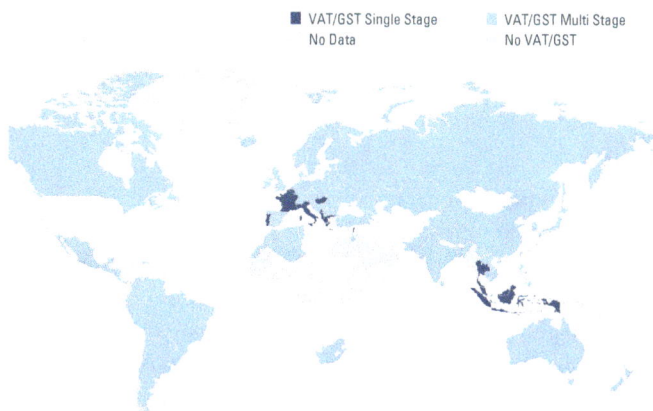

Note: In USA sales taxes set and administered at state and local level

VII. FISCAL FORESTALLING

Fiscal forestalling refers to the "release for consumption" (buildup of tax paid stock) of large volumes of cigarettes prior to an excise tax increase so that the products pay the old tax rate. Such a release can occur at the manufacturing or importer level, but also at the wholesale or retail level. In fact, to some scale, it may be driven at the consumer level, as individuals will stock-up with products in advance of an excise tax increase. From a government's perspective, forestalling will delay any excise tax increase, thus delaying the higher tax revenue returns.

In order for fiscal forestalling to occur there must be: (1) some predictability of the timing of future tax increases; (2) the tax increase must be of sufficient size to make forestalling commercially worthwhile; and, (3) no laws or regulations preventing or restricting forestalling. For governments which adopt long terms plans with predictable tax increases—unless appropriate anti-forestalling regulations are in place—fiscal forestalling can become an issue.

From the manufacturer, importer, or trade point of view, there is the potential for increased short term profitability if the products are cleared at the old tax rate and sold at a new higher retail selling price. Alternatively, the products can be sold at the old price following the tax increase by operators seeking to gain a competitive advantage. Whether the final retail selling price is or is not printed on the pack of cigarettes will determine which situation is applicable, amongst other factors.

A. Country Experiences

From the government point of view, fiscal forestalling generates an advanced collection of tax revenues as significant levels of future sales are brought forward. However, these advanced payments take place at a lower tax rate than otherwise would be the case. For example, in 1993, the United Kingdom's government introduced a new policy on tobacco taxation, called the "duty escalator", with excise duty increases set at 3 percent above forecasted inflation—this rate was increased to 5 percent above forecasted inflation in 1997. There were no regulations in place to restrict the quantity of cigarettes that could be released for consumption prior to tax increases and, as a result, significant volumes of cigarettes were cleared for tax payment in the month prior to an excise tax increase—refer to Figure 39 on the following page. In 2001, a cap on the volume of cigarettes that could be released for consumption was introduced, based on average volumes during the previous year[32] and this measure was effective in reducing fiscal forestalling—as one can observe when comparing the blue bars in Figure 39—before and after the year 2001.

Figure 39

Monthly Volume of Cigarettes Cleared for Tax Payment
(vertical lines indicate moment of tax rate change)

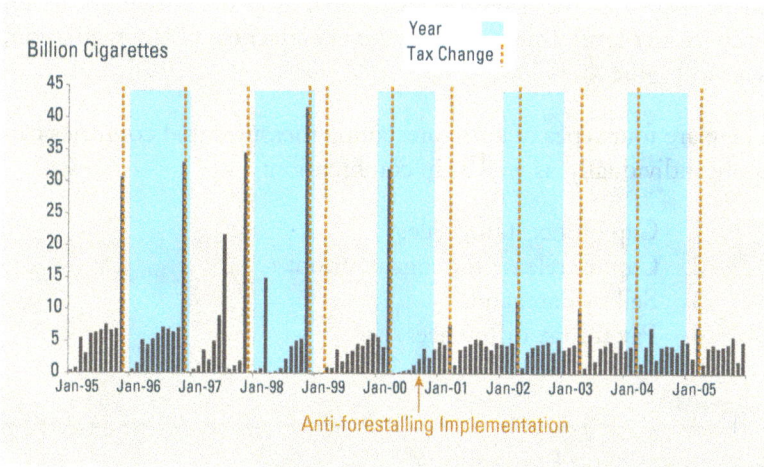

B. Anti-Forestalling Regulations

Once forestalling becomes an established practice in a country, it can be difficult to introduce effective regulations to prevent such activities. From the government's standpoint, there will be a one-off negative impact on cash flow when the regulations are initially introduced. In the first year that forestalling takes place, a government will receive more than 12 months' worth of excise tax payments within a year (assuming annual excise tax increases). In subsequent years, the government will only receive 12 months' worth of excise tax payments, *provided* forestalling is continued! Finally, if forestalling regulations are introduced, the government will experience a reversal of the cash flow benefit in that year that it had experienced in the very first year.

Effective regulations need to be tailored to the local environment, in particular reflecting the tax collection system in place, as well as the existing fiscal systems and regulations on tobacco products. At the same time, there is a trade-off between the ease of administration and the effectiveness of anti-forestalling regulations. For example, if the anti-forestalling regulations affect an early stage of the production and distribution chain, such as a cap on fiscal tax stamp sales, this will be relatively easy for the authorities to regulate and monitor as there are generally only a small number of cigarette producers or importers who purchase fiscal stamps. However, under such an anti-forestalling measure it is possible for fiscal forestalling to occur further down the distribution chain such as at the wholesale, retail, or consumer level, thus reducing the effectiveness of the regulation, refer to Figure 40 below.

There are four types of anti-forestalling measures that countries can apply, individually, as well as in combination:

1. Cap on tax stamp sales;
2. Cap on release for consumption;
3. Sell by date; and,
4. Pay for tax differences.

Figure 40

Anti-Forestalling Regulations

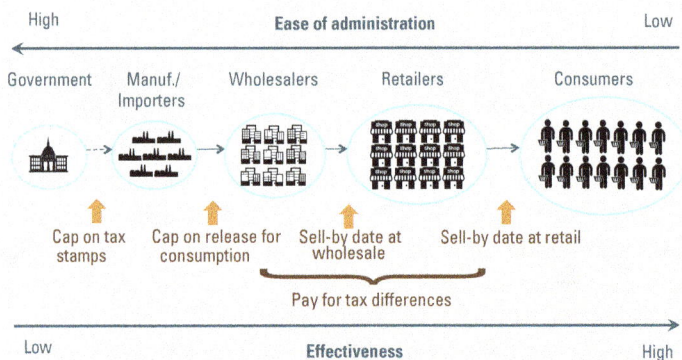

Anti-forestalling regulations for both the cap on tax stamps and the cap on release of products for consumption are generally applied by authorities restricting the quantity of tax stamps or products that can be sold in the month(s) prior to a tax increase based on a historical average. In Australia, for example, the volume of cigarettes that can be released for consumption in the month prior to a tax increase must not be greater than the average monthly sales over the previous three months.

A third form of anti-forestalling regulation is the use of a "sell-by-date". This approach can be used in countries where some form of visible marking on cigarette packs exist, making it possible to differentiate between packs taxed at the old and new tax rate. The authorities can then adopt regulations stating that cigarettes with the old tax rate can only be sold for a certain period after the tax increase. Under such a system, there has to be sufficient time to allow for the normal flow of products through the distribution chain, but not such a long timeframe that would make the regulation ineffective. Furthermore, with a sell-by-date regulation, it is necessary for the tax authorities to accept returns of unsold products so that after the cut-off date, it should be possible to return old tax paid products, which are not sold, for a tax refund.

In Indonesia, for example, a colored fiscal banderole is applied to cigarettes with the banderole price and tax rate printed on it. Every fiscal year, the color of the banderole is changed, and manufacturers are allowed to apply old banderoles on packs until the end of the first month of the fiscal year. They are permitted to sell these packs with old banderoles until the end of the fourth month of the fiscal year, after which the packs with old banderoles can be returned for a tax refund.

The fourth form of anti-forestalling regulation is "pay for tax difference". Under such regulation, some or all operators in the tobacco distribution chain—from manufacturers, importers, or through to the retailers—must fully account for their stock of tobacco products. Following an excise tax increase, they must pay for the tax difference between the old tax and the new tax rate based on their tobacco stock.

This system requires substantial administrative monitoring from the fiscal authorities as they have to be able to audit the full distribution chain to ensure the correct additional tax payment is made by each manufacturer, importer, wholesaler, and retailer. This system tends to exist in countries with a high degree of government regulation on the distribution systems on tobacco products such as Canada, Japan, and the U.S., see Figure 41 below on Japan. Figure 42 on the following page summarizes current anti-forestalling regulations.

Figure 41

Japan Tobacco Tax Laws

System in place in which government collects increased amount of excise tax based on the stock held on the effective date by the trade

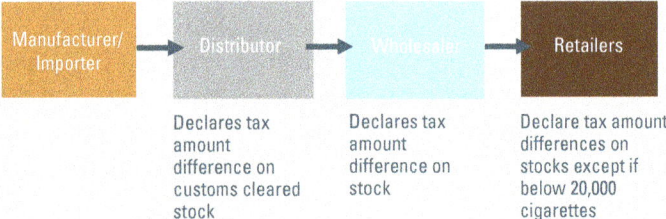

| Manufacturer/ Importer | → | Distributor | → | Wholesaler | → | Retailers |

| Declares tax amount difference on customs cleared stock | Declares tax amount difference on stock | Declare tax amount differences on stocks except if below 20,000 cigarettes |

Figure 42

Anti-Forestalling Regulations

Cap on fiscal tax stamp sales or cap on release for consumption	Sell by /Produce by date restriction	Pay for tax difference
Australia	Belgium	Albania
Belgium	Estonia	Bosnia
Bulgaria	Hungary	Croatia
Caucasus	Indonesia	Denmark
Cyprus	Netherlands	France
Denmark	Poland	Japan
Indonesia	Portugal	Kosovo
Kosovo	Slovakia	Latvia
Luxembourg		Montenegro
Malta		Serbia
Portugal		Slovenia
Russia		Lithuania
South Korea		
UK		
Ukraine		

VIII. PRICE REGULATIONS ON TOBACCO PRODUCTS

A. Retail Price Registration and Approval

From a price regulation point of view, cigarettes are highly regulated compared to many other consumer goods, with countries applying an array of rules to regulate and monitor retail prices. Historically, the tobacco industry was a state monopoly in many countries, and, as such, retail price setting of tobacco products tended to be regulated by the government. Furthermore, for countries with *ad valorem* or mixed excise tax systems, tobacco pricing directly influences government excise tax revenue, and as such, governments sought some degree of control over the retail price setting.

The simplest pricing system is to have no approval required whatsoever by the government: manufacturers or importers are free to change the price levels as and when they deem appropriate. This approach to pricing is used in countries such as Australia, Norway and the UK.

Moving up the scale in terms of regulations on retail price setting, are countries where tobacco manufacturers or importers must purchase a fiscal stamp or register the retail price of the tobacco product in advance of any changes. In many countries with price registration of tobacco products or tax stamp requirements, the frequency or speed by which retail prices can be changed is limited by law or due to practicalities. In countries where tax stamps are required, such as Germany, Netherlands, or Indonesia, and where the retail price must be printed on the tax stamp, there is a time delay caused by logistics and production between the moment of ordering the tax stamp with a new price and actually selling that product on the market. Similarly, where retail price registration is required, such as in France, Italy, and South Korea, the price registration process can take weeks or even months.

Finally, at the most restrictive end of the spectrum in terms of price approvals are countries, such as Japan and Morocco, where full government approval is required before manufacturers or importers can change cigarette retail prices. Such a system, although only applied in a limited number of countries, imposes significant government control over tobacco pricing.

B. Minimum Retail Price Regulations

In the United States, minimum cigarette price laws were initially introduced to protect tobacco retailers from predatory pricing practices by large retail outlets. These laws typically require a minimum percentage markup to be added to the wholesale price. According to a 2009 report,[33] 25 states in the U.S. apply minimum price regulations. The minimum price regulation system in the U.S. takes the form of a minimum price on a per brand basis, prohibiting retailers from selling at a loss, or below the manufacturer list price, plus various margins.

New York City introduced a price floor for cigarettes and small cigars in December 2013. This price floor is a public health measure and applies equally to all cigarettes and small cigars. It prohibits the sale of cigarettes below US$10.50 per pack. Moreover, the New York City legislation introduced the possibility that the price floor can be increased in line with the local New York-northern New Jersey-Long Island consumer price index, as per the legislative text below taken from File # Int. No. 1021-A:

> d. Price floor for cigarettes and little cigars. (1) Prohibition on the sale of cigarettes below the cigarette price floor. No person shall sell or offer for sale a package of cigarettes to a consumer for a price less than the cigarette price floor. The cigarette price floor shall be $10.50 per package of cigarettes, provided that the cigarette price floor may be modified pursuant to paragraph three of this subdivision.
>
> (2) Prohibition on the sale of little cigars below the little cigar price floor. No person shall sell or offer for sale a package of little cigars for a price less than the little cigar price floor. The little cigar price floor shall be equal to the cigarette price floor.
>
> (3) The department may modify by rule the cigarette price floor and little cigar price floor to account for changes in the New York - northern New Jersey - Long Island consumer price index, adjusted for inflation, or changes in taxes for cigarettes or little cigars.

Outside of the US, price floors or Minimum Retail Prices (MRPs) for cigarettes have been introduced in several countries over the past 10 years, including Ecuador (2004), Pakistan (2005), Canada (Quebec, 2006), Guadeloupe (2007), Kazakhstan (2007), La Reunion (2008), Vietnam (2008), Malaysia (2010), and Brazil (2011). Several EU countries (Ireland, France, Austria, and Italy) previously applied Minimum Retail Prices as well, mainly for public health purposes. However, these measures in the EU were later abandoned as the European Court of Justice ruled that they were not compatible with the EU Tobacco Excise Directives.[34]

Minimum Retail Prices (MRPs) have been introduced for a variety of policy reasons. In several countries, the main objective was to ban the sale of low priced cigarettes from a public health perspective. In other countries, there was also a tax revenue objective: if countries apply *ad valorem* excise taxes, an MRP implicitly guarantees also a minimum excise amount per pack of cigarettes. In certain countries, MRPs have also been introduced as a tool to fight against illicit trade, as cigarettes sold below the minimum price must be illegal. While the MRP can be set in absolute terms, as is the case in New York City, it is also possible to link the MRP level to the weighted average price or to the price of the most popular price category. The advantage of this linkage is that the MRP will increase automatically with the general price of cigarettes.

C. Retail Price Regulations Applying to Retailers

The price floors or minimum retail prices, as mentioned in the previous section, are an example of the regulations that primarily apply to retailers (but of course, indirectly affect manufacturers and wholesalers). But even in the absence of price floors, there are often regulations related to retail prices applying to retailers.

In countries where the excise tax system contains an *ad valorem* tax element (which uses the retail selling price as the tax base) there is need for some form of control over the retail selling price. For example, if the *ad valorem* excise tax is 50 percent of the retail selling price, the manufacturers and the governments must know the final retail price so that the correct excise tax amount is collected and paid to the government. If retailers sell the cigarettes at a higher price than already set by manufacturers, then governments will not collect the tax revenue on this additional mark-up. There are several ways to regulate retail price setting to prevent such practices. A majority of EU countries apply "fixed retail pricing", whereby the final retail price printed on the tax stamp, cigarette pack, or communicated through official price lists is the mandatory retail selling price for retailers. This system is also used outside of the EU, for instance, in Malaysia and Japan.

There are also instances where countries with a mixed tax structure apply "maximum retail pricing". The maximum price is used as the excise tax base, and manufacturers and retailers are prohibited by law to sell a pack of cigarettes above the maximum price indicated on the pack, but retailers may sell at a reduced price. Maximum price regulations thus allow for some pricing flexibility for retailers, but tax revenue is protected as the maximum price remains the tax reference base. Countries which apply maximum retail price regulations include Switzerland and Russia.

Finally, a few countries have implemented recommended price regulations, where the recommended price is used as the tax base, but the retailer can mark-up or discount from this recommended price. The UK implements such a system.

In conclusion, compared to other consumer products, the retail price setting for cigarettes is often highly regulated. This is driven primarily by three factors. First, many countries historically operated a government monopoly on the production, distribution, and sale of tobacco products, including countries such as Austria, Czech Republic, France, Greece, Italy, Korea, Morocco, Poland, Portugal, and Spain. Today, tobacco monopolies are still in place in Algeria, Belarus, China, Cuba, Egypt, Iran, Japan, Lebanon, Libya, Moldova, Tunisia, and Vietnam. Under monopoly structures, governments tend to impose a high level of control over how retail prices are set and regulated. In countries where the tobacco industry has been privatized, many of the price regulations have remained in place. The second factor influencing the high degree of regulation on cigarette retail price setting is that, in many countries, the retail price is used as a base to determine either or both excise and VAT tax payment. As such, in order to control the tax payments, governments have sought to maintain a high degree of control over the retail price setting. Finally, as a more recent development, some countries have introduced minimum pricing regulations on cigarettes, as price is considered a key tool from a public health perspective.

IX. AFFORDABILITY

For policymakers, measuring affordability is crucial for developing optimal excise tax policy both in terms of tax revenue collections and preventing cross-border and illicit tobacco products. In countries where cigarettes are relatively expensive, incentives for illicit trade are high which in turn will undermine both the government's excise tax revenues and health objectives.

A. Price Measurements

Here, we analyze cigarette affordability in nominal retail prices expressed in U.S. dollars, retail prices expressed in the purchasing power of parity (PPP), retail prices per cigarette compared to the Big Mac price index, retail prices per 100 packs of cigarettes relative to income levels or Price Relative to Income (PRI), the number of minutes of work required to purchase a pack of cigarettes, and the percentage of daily income required to purchase a pack of cigarettes. We use the UBS survey sample of countries to determine the countries included in this price analysis and compare prices for the premium, mid, and low price categories.[35] Although retail price levels alone are not sufficient for calculating affordability, they are used as starting reference.

1. RETAIL SALES PRICE IN U.S. DOLLARS

As depicted in Figure 43, there is significant variation in the retail sales price of a pack of cigarettes[36] both within countries and between countries. On average, the relative gap between different price categories is higher in lower income countries than in higher income countries—on average, the retail sales price for the cheapest brand of cigarettes is only about 44 percent the price of premium brands, versus about 63 percent in higher income countries.[37] However, higher income countries appear to have more variation in price, when comparing between countries, as the retail sales price can be as low as $0.41 per pack in the UAE and as high as $16.30 per pack in Norway.

Figure 43

Retail Sales Price US$ Per Pack of Cigarettes

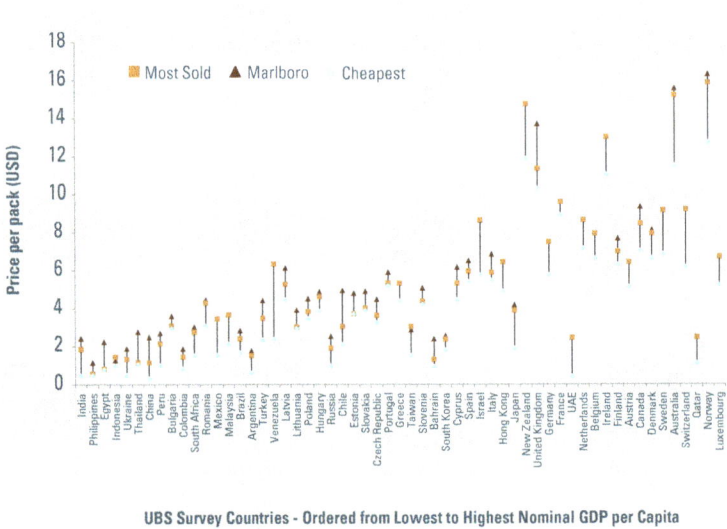

UBS Survey Countries - Ordered from Lowest to Highest Nominal GDP per Capita

Retail Sales Price data: PMI, as of January 1st, 2014
Exchange Rate data: Bloomberg, as of January 1st, 2014
Nominal GDP per capita data: Global Insight estimates for 2013, as of January 1st, 2014

However, nominal retail price levels are not the most meaningful series for international comparisons as basis economics would predict that low income countries would have low retail price levels and high income countries would have higher retail prices.

2.   RETAIL SALES PRICE IN PURCHASING POWER OF PARITY TERMS

Purchasing power parity (PPP) adjusts retail price into how many dollars are needed to purchase one dollar's worth of goods in the country at hand compared to the United States, allowing for differences in the cost of living across countries.

Figure 44 demonstrates that the retail sales prices, when converted to PPP terms, tend to have more variation across different price categories for lower income countries, and furthermore, indicates that cigarettes are relatively more expensive, using this measure, in higher income countries.[38]

Figure 44

Retail Sales Price with PPP Conversion Factor to Market Exchange Rate US$

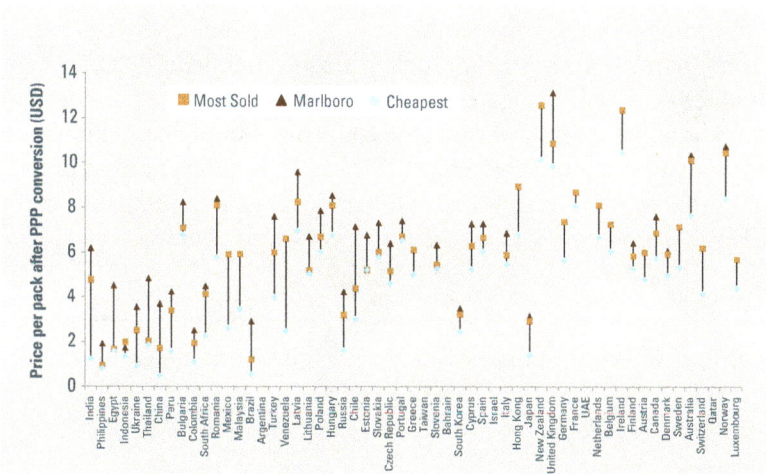

UBS Survey Countries - Ordered from Lowest to Highest Nominal GDP per Capita

Retail Sales Price data: PMI, as of January 1st, 2014
Exchange Rate data: Bloomberg, as of January 1st, 2014
PPP: World Bank, as of 2012
Nominal GDP per capita data: Global Insight estimates for 2013, as of January 1st, 2014
The following countries are excluded due to missing observations: Argentina, Bahrain, Israel, Taiwan, UAE, and Qatar

3.   THE BIG MAC INDEX OF CIGARETTE RETAIL PRICES

The Big Mac index from *The Economist* offers a unique valuation of PPP, as it relies on the McDonald's Big Mac sandwich as its reference good. The Big Mac index estimates the number of cigarettes that can be purchased with the money that would buy one Big Mac, with larger values implying that cigarettes are cheaper, relative to a Big Mac.[39]

As evidenced from Figure 45, the number of cigarettes that can be purchased with the money that buys one Big Mac is quite larger in lower income countries compared to higher income countries, particularly when considering the cheapest cigarette price. In fact, the number of the cheapest cigarettes per Big Mac is over 50 in

12 out of the 21 countries in Figure 45—whereas the ratio is never above 40 in higher income countries. As such, across the board, lower priced cigarettes tend to be relatively cheaper in low income countries, when compared with high income countries, based on the Big Mac index. For premium priced cigarettes such as Marlboro, the difference between low and high income countries is less pronounced. For instance, in higher income countries,[40] the average number of premium cigarettes per Big Mac is nearly 13, while this figure is about 23 in lower income countries—implying a difference of about 10 premium cigarettes (23-13=10). For the cheapest brand, this difference between lower and higher income countries is nearly 39 (56-17=39)!

Figure 45

Number of Cigarettes per Big Mac: Higher Income Countries

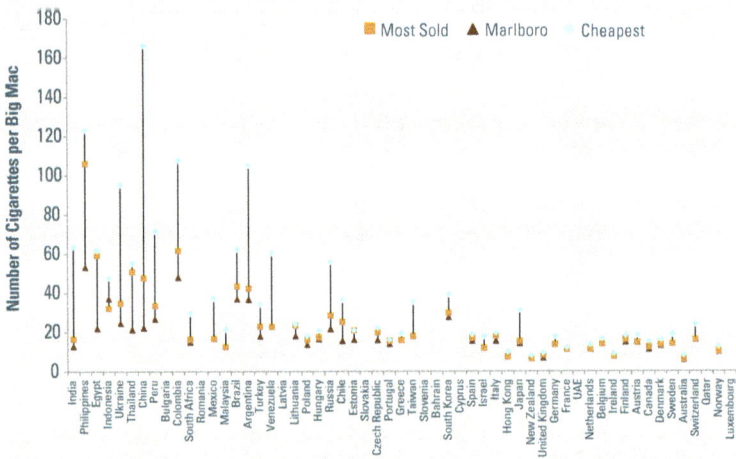

UBS Survey Countries - Ordered from Lowest to Highest Nominal GDP per Capita

Retail Sales Price data: PMI, as of January 1st, 2014
Exchange Rate data: Bloomberg, as of January 1st, 2014
Big Mac data: The Economist, as of January 2014
Nominal GDP per capita data: Global Insight estimates for 2013, as of January 1st, 2014

B. Affordability Measurements

1. PRI: PRICE RELATIVE TO INCOME

Affordability measures describe the relationship between cigarette prices and consumer income levels, which can be broadly or narrowly defined (e.g., GDP per capita versus after-tax wages). The retail sales price relative to income, or PRI, calculates the percentage of per capita nominal GDP that is required to purchase 100 packs of cigarettes.

Higher values of PRI indicate lower cigarette affordability, and, as Figure 46 demonstrates, PRI is generally higher in lower income countries, indicating that cigarettes are less affordable in low income countries compared to high income countries.

Figure 46

Price Relative to Income

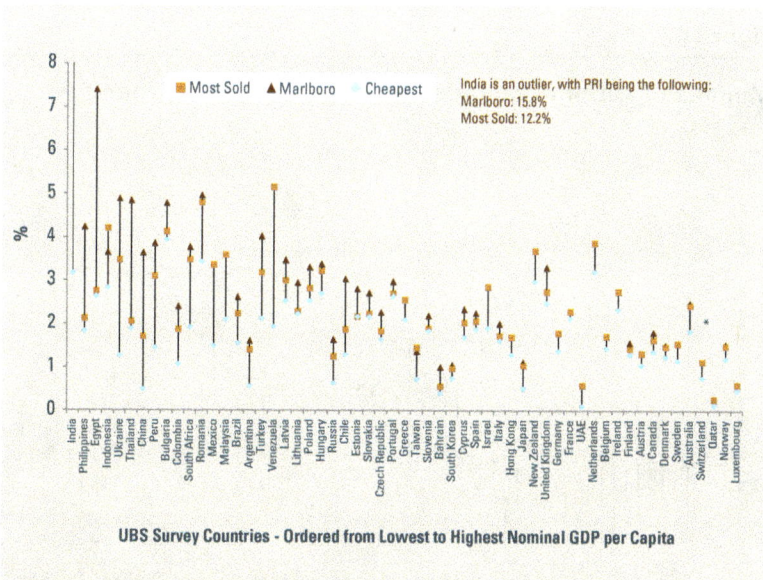

India is an outlier, with PRI being the following:
Marlboro: 15.8%
Most Sold: 12.2%

UBS Survey Countries - Ordered from Lowest to Highest Nominal GDP per Capita

Retail Sales Price data: PMI, as of January 1st, 2014
Exchange Rate data: Bloomberg, as of January 1st, 2014
Nominal GDP per capita data: Global Insight estimates for 2013, as of January 1st, 2014

2. MINUTES OF LABOR REQUIRED TO PURCHASE A PACK OF CIGARETTES

The minutes of labor required to purchase a pack of cigarettes is a measurement of domestic purchasing power—the more minutes required, the less purchasing power consumers in that country have as measured by net hourly wage (higher values implying lower affordability). As evidenced in Figure 47, the variability in the minutes of labor by cigarette prices, comparing low priced cigarettes to high priced cigarettes, tends to be higher for lower income countries. The UBS survey is only conducted every 3 years, and May 2012 is the most recently available data.[41] However, in spite of that, using price data from January 2014 should not present a major issue since real GDP does not appear to have grown as quickly as cigarette prices. In fact, when using data from the World Bank, the real GDP growth estimate for the world is 2.4 percent for 2013, versus 2.5 percent for 2012 —indicating that while wages have likely grown, it is not likely that they rose as quickly as cigarette prices.

Figure 47

Minutes of Labor Required to Purchase a Pack of Cigarettes

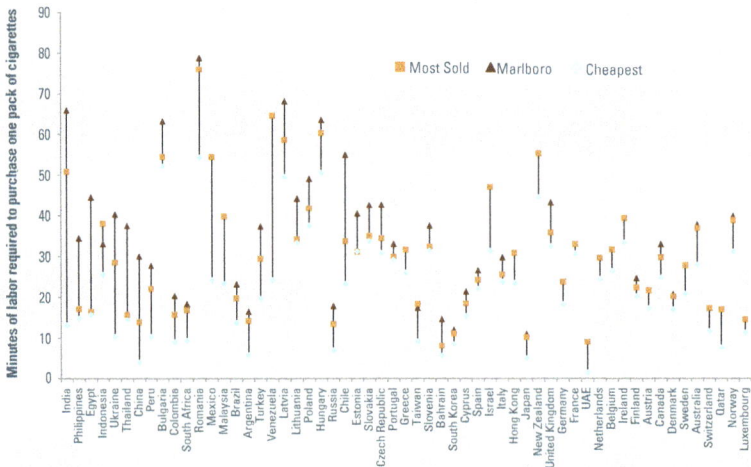

UBS Survey Countries - Ordered from Lowest to Highest Nominal GDP per Capita

Retail Sales Price data: PMI, as of January 1st, 2014
Exchange Rate data: Bloomberg, as of January 1st, 2014
Net Income data: UBS Survey, as of April 2012
Nominal GDP per capita data: Global Insight estimates for 2013, as of January 1st, 2014

3. PERCENTAGE OF DAILY INCOME REQUIRED TO PURCHASE A PACK OF CIGARETTES

Lastly, Kan's measure of affordability, the percentage of daily income required to purchase a pack of cigarettes, is interesting to policymakers not only because it provides a benchmark of affordability, but also because it captures trends in regressivity—especially as lower income groups are over-represented in regards to tobacco usage in many countries.[43]

Figure 48 and Figure 49 plot the percentage of daily income required to buy a pack, for both the 7 lowest earning occupations, and the average across all occupations. Analyzing these differences gives some indication of regressivity of cigarette prices, but the analysis is not complete without accounting for the general equilibrium or price elasticity effects of cigarette demand.[44]

Although the estimate for the percentage of daily income is based on the 7 lowest paying occupations, Figure 49 provides estimates of this variable for all occupations for comparison purposes. As Figure 48 and Figure 49 demonstrate, the variability across the different cigarette brands declines as income increases; however, for the 7 lowest earning occupations, the percentage of daily income required is much higher than when considering all occupations, suggesting that affordability not only declines in lower income countries, but also that it declines within the lower income brackets within countries.

Figure 48

Percentage of Daily Income Required to Purchase a Pack of Cigarettes: For 7 Lowest Paying Occupations

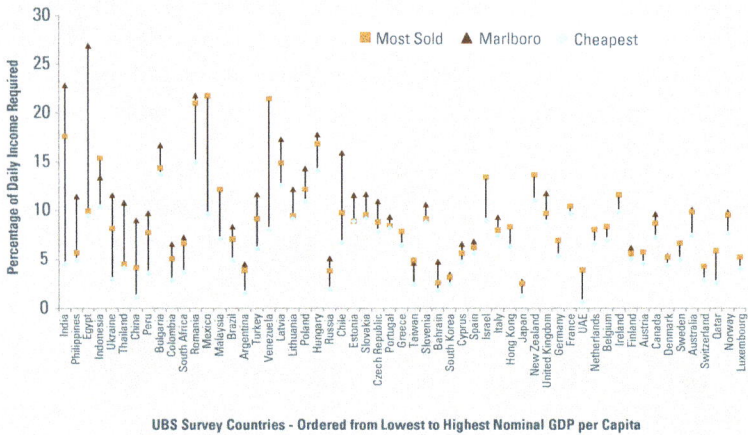

UBS Survey Countries - Ordered from Lowest to Highest Nominal GDP per Capita

Retail Sales Price data: PMI, as of January 1st, 2014   Exchange Rate data: Bloomberg, as of January 1st, 2014
Net Income data: UBS Survey, 7 Lowest Occupations, as of April 2012
Nominal GDP per capita data: Global Insight estimates for 2013, as of January 1st, 2014

Figure 49

Percentage of Daily Income Required to Purchase a Pack of Cigarettes All Occupations

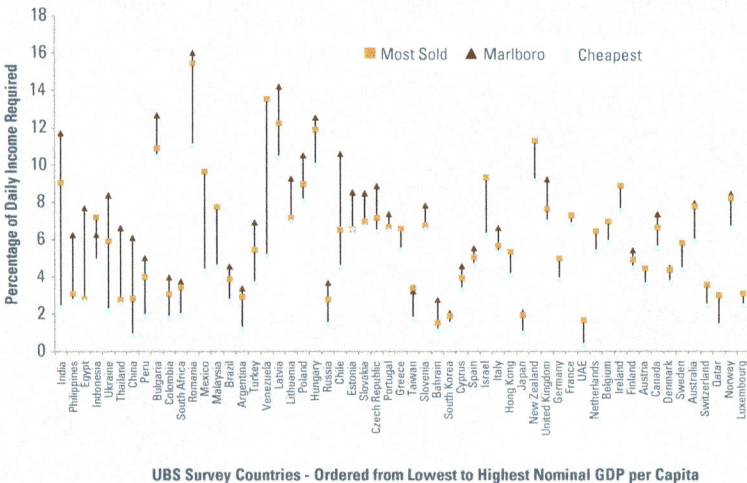

UBS Survey Countries - Ordered from Lowest to Highest Nominal GDP per Capita

Retail Sales Price data: PMI, as of January 1st, 2014   Exchange Rate data: Bloomberg, as of January 1st, 2014
Net Income data: UBS Survey, All Occupations, as of April 2012
Nominal GDP per capita data: Global Insight estimates for 2013, as of January 1st, 2014

In summary, a number of affordability measures were discussed, which, while not perfect, are better to use in practice than price measures for international comparisons as they capture the interaction between price and income. While PRI provides a useful benchmark of affordability, using nominal GDP per capita may not accurately reflect affordability in countries with high degrees of income inequality. Therefore, in countries with significant income inequality it is best to assess cigarette affordability using the percentage of daily income required to purchase a pack of cigarettes for the 7 lowest paying occupations. The main finding from our analysis is that, generally speaking, cigarettes are less affordable and price gaps are larger in low income countries compared to high income countries.

X. COUNTRY EXPERIENCES WITH EXCISE TAX INCREASES

A. Sweden's Experience with EU Excise Tax Harmonization

Sweden's accession to the EU in 1995 demonstrates the difficulty of approximating excise tax, especially without VAT harmonization. At the time of Sweden's accession, the EU imposed a minimum excise incidence on cigarettes of 57 percent as its benchmark. Sweden had the fourth highest excise tax yield in the EU at SEK 750 per 1000 cigarettes in 1995.[45] However, because of its high nominal VAT rate of 25 percent[46] and the effect of VAT on the excise tax incidence calculation (as described previously), the excise incidence in Sweden was relatively low in comparison to other EU countries, at 49.1 percent.

In an effort to meet the EU minimum excise incidence requirement, Sweden significantly increased cigarette excise taxes in 1997.[47] As a result, cigarette retail sale prices increased by 43 percent over a six-month period. Despite the fact that cigarette prices in Sweden were the highest in the EU, the excise incidence after these tax increases only reached 52.56 percent,[48] which was the lowest in the EU and well below the required EU benchmark. Additionally, cigarette retail prices in the EU only diverged further, rather than being harmonized: in 1996 the difference between the countries with the most (Denmark) and the least (Spain) expensive cigarettes was ECU 148.82 per 1000 cigarettes,[49] by 1997 this differential was ECU 166.11 per 1000 cigarettes, with Sweden as the most expensive.[50]

In response to such retail price increases, illicit trade in tobacco products increased substantially in Sweden—as Figure 50 and Figure 51 demonstrate,[51] the duty paid volume declined while the amount of cigarettes collected in seizures of illicit products rose significantly over this period. Ultimately, Sweden abandoned its policy to aim for meeting the EU minimum incidence requirements due to the concern that *"the illicit trade will remain and the fiscal erosion... will continue".*[52] The revenue lost as a result of the increased tobacco taxation has been estimated at around 900 million Swedish kroner.[53]

Figure 50

Swedish Excise Tax Yield and Duty Paid Volume

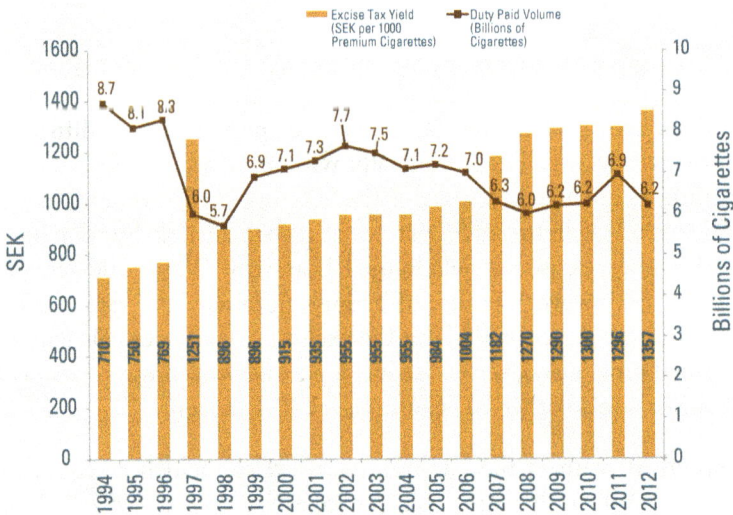

Figure 51

Swedish Seizures of Illicit Cigarettes and Government Excise Tax Revenues

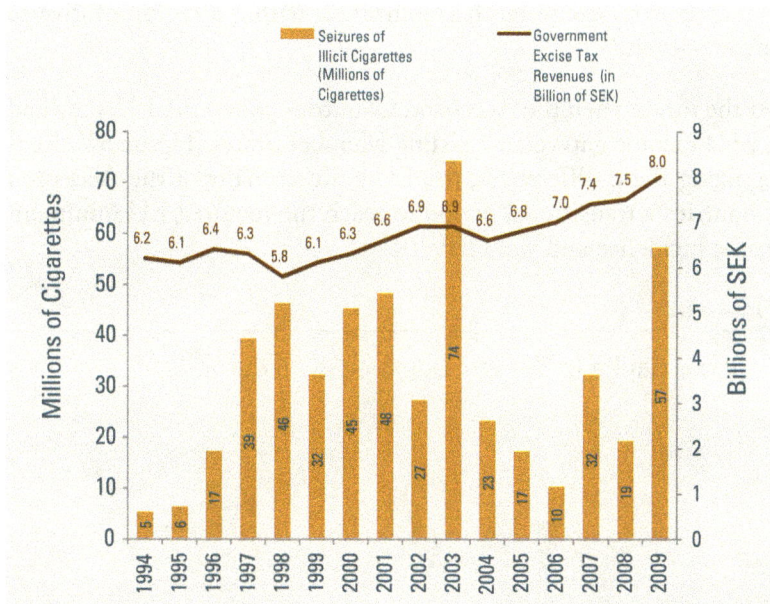

Legend:
- Seizures of Illicit Cigarettes (Millions of Cigarettes)
- Government Excise Tax Revenues (in Billion of SEK)

Left axis: Millions of Cigarettes (0–80)
Right axis: Billions of SEK (0–9)

Bar values (Seizures, Millions of Cigarettes): 1994: 5, 1995: 6, 1996: 17, 1997: 39, 1998: 46, 1999: 32, 2000: 45, 2001: 48, 2002: 27, 2003: 74, 2004: 23, 2005: 17, 2006: 10, 2007: 32, 2008: 19, 2009: 57

Government Excise Tax Revenues (Billion SEK): 6.2, 6.1, 6.4, 6.3, 5.8, 6.1, 6.3, 6.6, 6.9, 6.9, 6.6, 6.8, 7.0, 7.4, 7.5, 8.0

In response to the growing illicit trade and eroding excise tax revenues, Sweden reversed its policy, reducing excise tax rates, depending on the retail price point, by between 25 and 30 percent.[54] Following this excise tax reduction, the volume of customs seizures on
illicitly traded products declined nearly 30 percent in a one year period, from 45.6 million cigarettes in 1998, to 32 million in 1999 and
the government tobacco excise revenues started to increase again.[55]
However, the illicit trade continued to persist, as it is very hard to
eradicate once established (Figure 51). Smoking incidence remained
stable at 19 percent from 1998 to 2001, suggesting that the reduction in excise tax and prices did not increase smoking incidence,
probably because consumers simply switched back from illicit to tax
paid products.[56]

B. Accession Countries' Experience with Tax Harmonization

The experiences of the EU Accession Countries (those joining in either 2004 or 2007) is a further illustration of the difficulties that can arise from excise tax harmonization within a region of diverse income levels.[57]

At the times when the Accession Countries joined the EU, they had a wide income gap versus existing Member States (Figure 52). Recognizing these differences, the EU granted many of the Accession Countries a transitional period to reach the required EU minimum excise incidence and yield targets.

Figure 52

GDP per Capita in Europe: Constant 2005 Euros

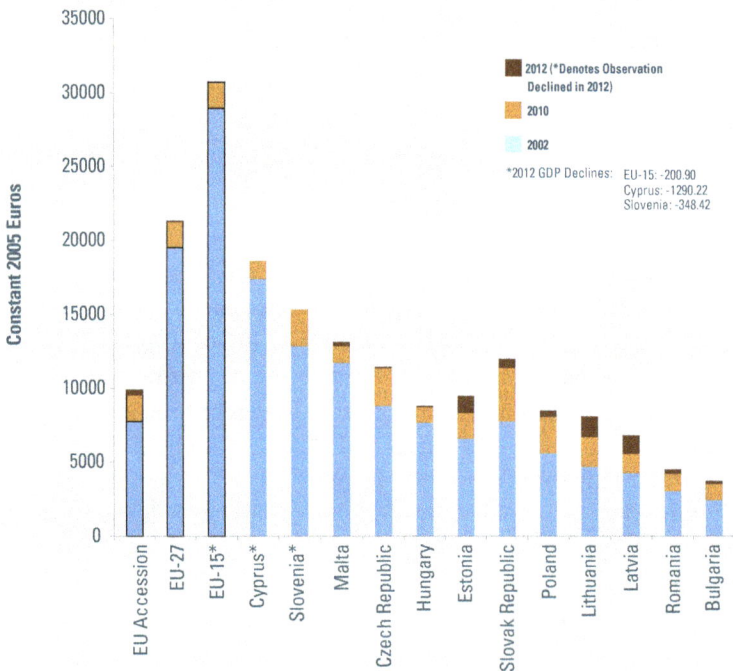

Despite the transitional period, the forced tax harmonization caused cigarette prices to grow faster than income in the Accession Countries (Figure 53) and as a result, they consistently and continually have had lower levels of affordability relative to the existing, or "old" EU countries—indicating that the harmonization policy has been regressive on both the international and within-country level (Figure 54).

Figure 53[58]

Affordability of Most Popular Price Category Cigarettes by Minutes of Labor in the EU

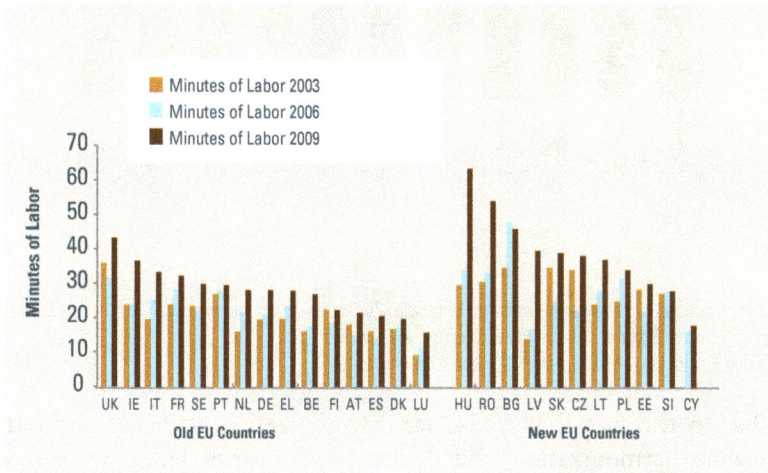

Source: Bogdanovica, I., Murray, R., McNeill, A., and J. Britton (2011), Cigarette Price, Affordability and Smoking Prevalence in the European Union.

Figure 54[59]

Proportion of Daily Disposable Income Required to Purchase a Pack of 20 MPPC cigarettes in the EU in 2002 and 2010

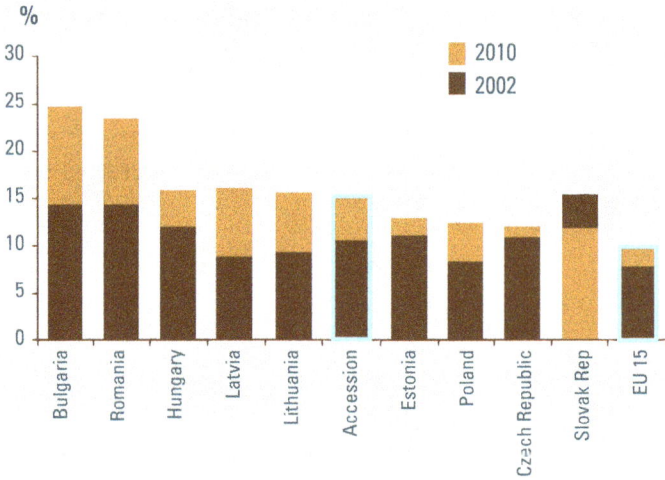

Source: International Tax & Investment Center (2012), The Impact of Imposing a Global Excise Target for Cigarettes: Experience from the EU Accession Countries
Oxford Economics/Industry data/European Commission (2011)

Due to the fact that excise tax harmonization occurred without income harmonization, the Accession Countries faced decreased cigarette affordability relative to the other EU countries, and, as a result, as many as half of them experienced an increase in the market share of the non duty-paid tobacco products, while nearly every one of them had reductions in duty-paid sales tobacco products (Figure 55).[60] In fact, Bulgaria's duty-paid cigarette sales dropped by 50 percent from 2002 to 2010, and the non duty-paid cigarettes' share of the market expanded from 15 percent in 2007 to 30 percent in 2010.[61] In Romania, non duty-paid cigarettes accounted for 10 percent of cigarette consumption in 2007 and increased to 20 percent in 2010;[62] while over the same period, Romania experienced a 30 percent drop in duty-paid cigarette sales.[63]

Figure 55[64]

Non Duty Paid Market Share in the Accession Countries in 2010

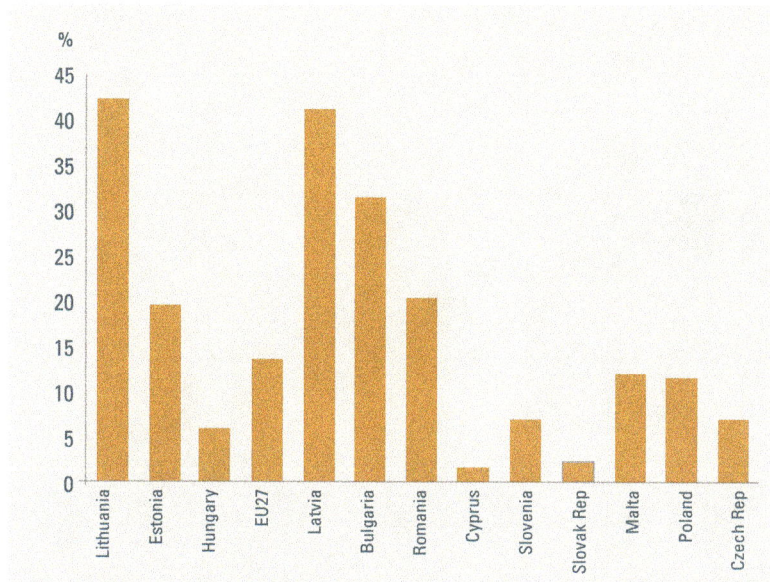

Source: KPMG (2011) Project STAR 2010

As the EU Accession Countries increased tobacco tax levels to EU standards, the tax administration policies of these countries could no longer adequately account for tax differences with non-EU neighboring countries. This led to an increase in illicit trade activity: *"[there is a] widening price gap between the accession Countries and their neighboring third countries, which renders bootlegging and smuggling more profitable."*[65] Lithuania, in particular, faced this very issue, as it shares borders with Belarus and Russia, neither of which are EU member states.

As demonstrated by Figure 56, there is significant disparity within-country as well: the regions in Lithuania that share borders with either Belarus or Russia tend to have higher non duty-paid market shares for cigarettes compared to Lithuania as a whole.[66] These local discrepancies within one country are often ignored by regional tax harmonization efforts, but can produce very damaging consequences for a country's fiscal goals if the illicit trade of cigarettes spreads within the country as a whole.

Figure 56[67]

Non Duty Paid Market Share by Region in Lithuania in 2010

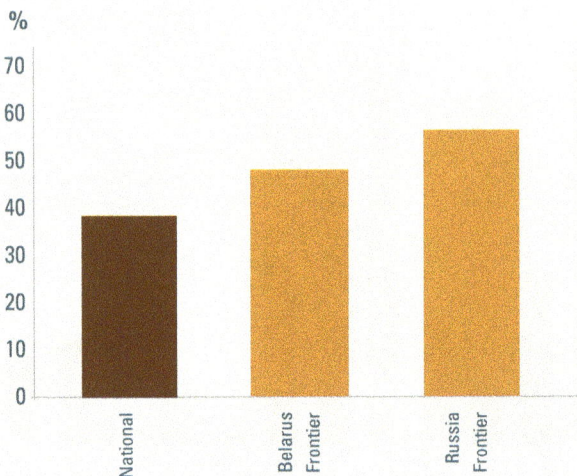

KPMG (2011) Project STAR 2010

C. Greece: Stable Policy Followed by Tax Shocks in Response to Financial Crisis

In the years 1999 to 2009, Greece applied gradual excise tax increases, which led excise tax levels and government revenues to rise by 56 percent[68] and 50 percent[69] respectively. Over the same period, duty paid volume remained relatively stable (Figure 57), while consumption of counterfeit and contraband cigarettes remained well below the EU average (3 percent versus an EU average of 8.9 percent in 2009).[70]

In 2010, the pressing need to raise revenues due to the economic crisis led the government, among other measures, to radically increase excise duties and VAT: between January and May excise tax rates were modified four times and VAT increased twice. In 2011, excise tax rates increased again twice, and a minimum excise duty for fine-cut tobacco was introduced. Finally, in January 2012, specific and minimum excise duties increased once more for both cigarettes and fine cut tobacco (Table 10).

Table 10

Greece: Excise Tax Evolution

		2/11/2009	1/1/2010	1/18/2010	3/4/2010	5/3/2010	1/1/2011	6/27/2011	11/12/2012
CIGARETTES	Ad valorem excise duty (% of RSP)	53.83%	53.83%	57.08%	58.82%	58.43%	52.45%	52.45%	52.45%
	Specific excise duty (€/1,000 cigs.)	5.51	5.88	9.48	9.88	13.71	19.66	19.66	20.37
	MET (€/1,000 cigs.)	69.00	73.60	75.60	78.00	80.40	76.32	101.76	105.48
FINE-CUT	Ad valorem excise duty (% of RSP)	59%	65%	65%	67%	69%	67%	67%	67%
	Specific excise duty (€/1,000 cigs.)*	n/a	n/a	n/a	n/a	n/a	n/a	n/a	n/a
	MET (€/1,000 cigs. equiv.)*	n/a	n/a	n/a	n/a	n/a	81.44	81.44	88.97
VAT nominal (%)		19%	19%	19%	21%	23%	23%	23%	23%

* Conversion rate: 1 cigarette = 0.75g fine-cut.

All these tax increases had a significant impact on the tobacco market:

- The adjustment in retail prices due to the increased tax burden, combined with a significant drop in consumers' purchasing power led to a sharp decline in the demand for legal cigarettes (Figure 57).

- Consumers down-traded to low price propositions.

- Consumers switched to fine cut tobacco, which until 2012 was substantially less taxed.[71]

- Illicit trade increased considerably in the market: according to KPMG, illicit trade amounted to 13.4 percent of total consumption in 2012 compared to 3.0 percent in 2009.[72]

Figure 57

Greek Cigarette Excise Tax Revenue & Duty Paid Volume

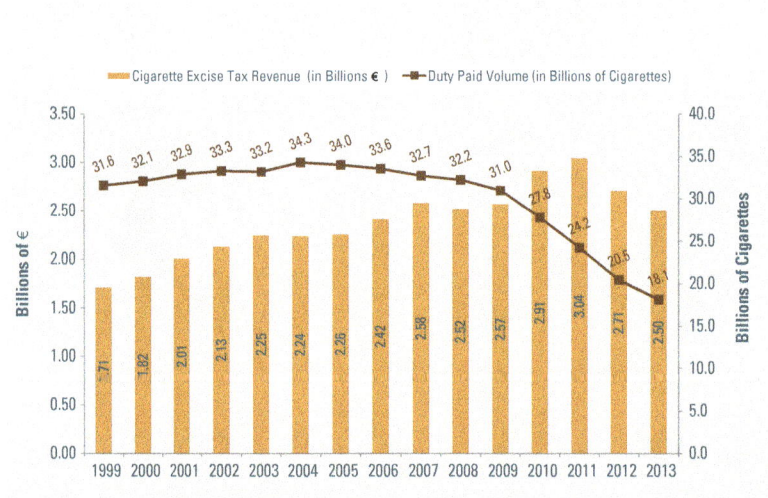

Despite the significant increases in excise duties, government revenues increased only marginally. In 2011, if one excludes the one-off effect of a reduction in payment terms (from 56 to 28 days) worth €172 million, excise tax revenues actually decreased by €39 million compared to 2010. In 2012, excise revenues decreased by a further €338 million.

The drop in Greek consumers' purchasing power, the substitution of cigarettes with fine-cut tobacco or illicit trade, and the change in market segmentation also had the effect of reducing the predictability of tax revenues (Figure 58). This effect was particularly strong, due to the high reliance of the excise system on *ad valorem* excise duty. Over the 3 year period, 2010-2012, tobacco excise revenues fell short by over € 1.5 billion.

Figure 58

Cigarette Excise Revenue Shortage vs. Budget (in Billions €)

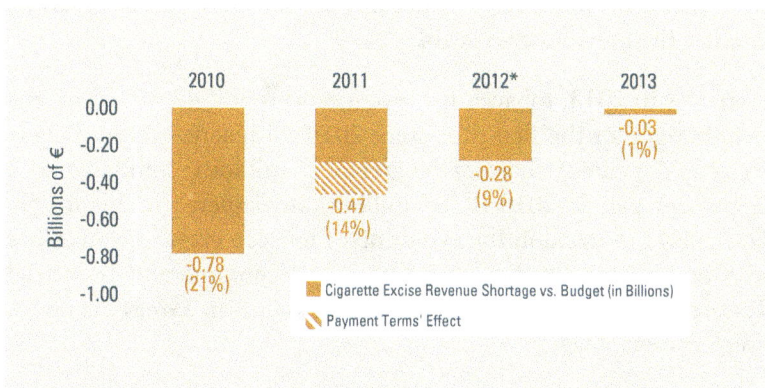

In November 2012, in order to address the decline in excise revenues and achieve greater revenue predictability, the Greek government reformed the excise tax structure on tobacco to a higher specific and a lower *ad valorem* component for cigarettes and to a fully specific system for fine-cut tobacco, while equalizing the minimum excise tax level between the two categories (Table 11).

Table 11

		October 2012	November 5th, 2012
Cigarettes	*Ad valorem* excise duty (percent of RSP)	52.45%	20.00%
	Specific excise duty (€/1,000 cigs)	20.37	80.00
	MET (€/1,000 cigs)	105.48	115.00
Fine-Cut	*Ad valorem* excise duty (percent of RSP)	67.00%	n/a
	Specific excise duty (€/1,000 cigs eq.)*	n/a	114.75
	MET (€/1,000 cigs. eq.)*	88.97	n/a

* Conversion rate: 1 cigarette = 0.75g fine-cut.

While it is still too early to assess the long term impact of the restructuring of the tobacco excise system, it can be noted that both the decline in duty paid cigarette volume and the decline in government excise revenues have noticeably slowed down in 2013, compared to the previous two years.

Moreover in 2013, tobacco tax revenues were in line with Government budget for the first time since 2010, with actual revenues falling only 1 percent short of budget (€33 million), compared to a 21 percent gap in 2010 (€783 million), as depicted in Figure 58. The change in trend in the evolution of tobacco excise revenues has been highlighted by the Foundation for Economic and Industrial Research (IOBE) in its quarterly reports about the Greek economy, which stated:

> "All categories of tax revenues, except taxes from past fiscal years, declined, due to the continuing fall of income and economic activity, with the largest deviation from the annual target observed in consumption taxes. These deviations came mostly from taxes on oil products (VAT and excise duties), while the revenues of the tobacco taxes were close to the target".[73]

D. Ireland: Excise Shocks Leading to Illicit Trade & Excise Policy Freeze

In 2000, Ireland pursued excise tax increases in order to achieve health policy objectives. Driven by the government's effort to dissuade consumers from using tobacco, excise tax yields increased by 107 percent from 1999 to 2009 (Figure 59).[74] These excise tax hikes were mainly implemented from 2000 to 2003 and from 2006 to 2009, translating into a 29 percent and 20 percent increase in the retail sale prices of cigarettes for the first and second periods, respectively.[75]

The dramatic increase in the excise yield prompted illicit trade activity so severe that government excise tax revenues hardly increased from 2001 to 2009. Despite relatively stable smoking incidence estimates between 2000 and 2009, duty paid volumes declined by 33 percent over the same period,[76] while the number of counterfeit and contraband cigarettes consumed increased to 1.44 billion by 2009,[77] accounting for 22.3 percent of total cigarette consumption that year (Figure 60).[78]

Furthermore, the Irish government's health objectives were not met, as smoking incidence did not decline following these excise tax increases; the second phase of excise tax increases (2006 to 2009) left total consumption[79] at nearly 6 billion cigarettes, virtually unchanged from duty paid volume in 2003 (Figure 60).[80] As such, the Irish Minister of Finance decided to freeze excise tax policy at the end of 2009:

> *"I have decided not to make any changes to excise on tobacco in this budget because I believe the high price is now giving rise to massive cigarette smuggling. My responsibility as Minister of Finance is to protect the tax base."*[81]

The Minister of Finance did not raise cigarette taxes for a second successive year in his 2010 Budget for the same reason.

Although the volume of counterfeit and contraband cigarettes decreased, it has continued to account for 19.1 percent of total consumption in 2012, illustrating the difficulties of eradicating illicit trade once it has become established in a market.[82]

Figure 59

Irish Excise Tax Yield and Excise Tax Revenues

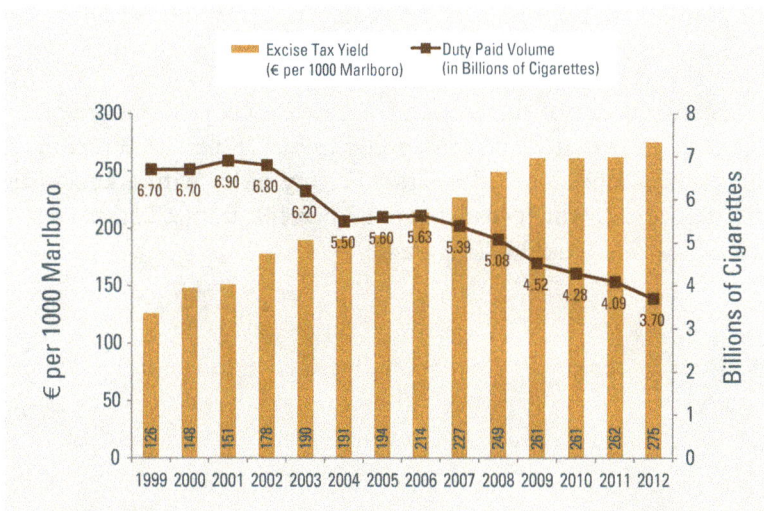

Figure 60

Irish Government Excise Tax Revenues, Total Consumption and Duty Paid Volumes

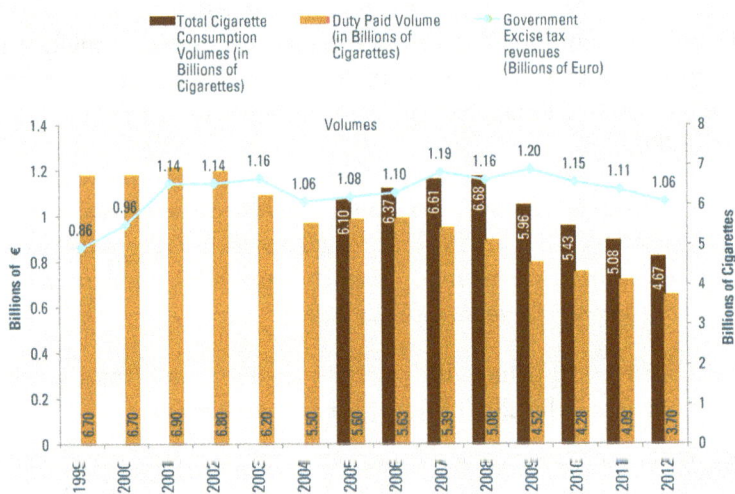

E. United Kingdom: Excise Increases Followed by Excise Policy Moderation

In the autumn of 1993, the UK implemented a "tobacco tax escalator", whereby tobacco excise taxation increased yearly by 3 percentage point above forecast RPI inflation.[83] In 1997, the escalator was increased to 5 percent above forecasted inflation.[84]

As a consequence of the escalator, the excise tax yield on premium cigarettes increased 71 percent, going from £78 per 1000 premium cigarettes in 1993 to £133 in 2000 (Figure 61),[85] with a knock-on effect on prices, which soared over 67 percent, from £2.52 per pack in 1993 to £4.22 in 2000 (Figure 62).[86]

Figure 61

UK Excise Tax Yield and Duty Paid Volume

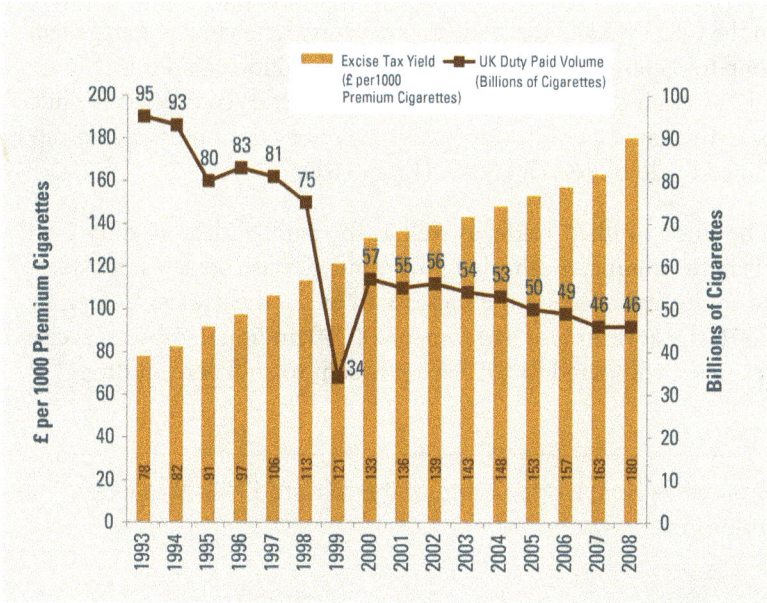

Figure 62

UK Government Excise Tax Revenues and RSP

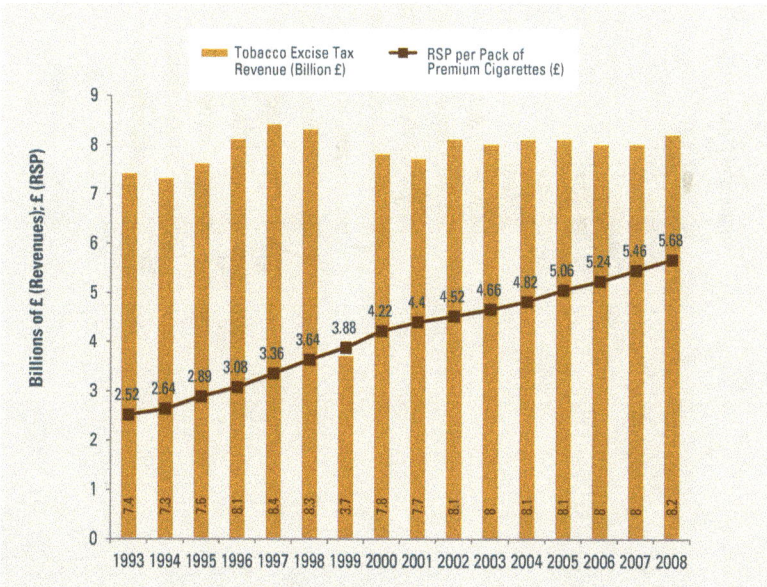

Although real GDP grew steadily from 1993 to 1999, the excise tax yield increased at a faster pace, thereby rendering cigarettes less affordable (Figure 63).[87] Consequently, illicit trade began to thrive in the UK: by 2000, the non-duty paid cigarette volume had grown four-fold compared to 1996, reaching 25 billion cigarettes (Figure 63)[88]—equivalent to 30 percent of all cigarettes consumed—while over the same period, duty-paid cigarette consumption had declined by 26 billion cigarettes (Figure 61).[89]

The surge in illicit trade, as well as the parallel drop in duty paid cigarette volume, meant that government excise tax revenues started to decrease despite the increase in excise duty rates. In fact, by 2001, the government had foregone £700 million in tobacco excise revenues, compared to 1997—equivalent to an 8 percent drop. [90,91]

Figure 63

Change in Real Excise Yield and Estimated Non Duty Paid Volumes

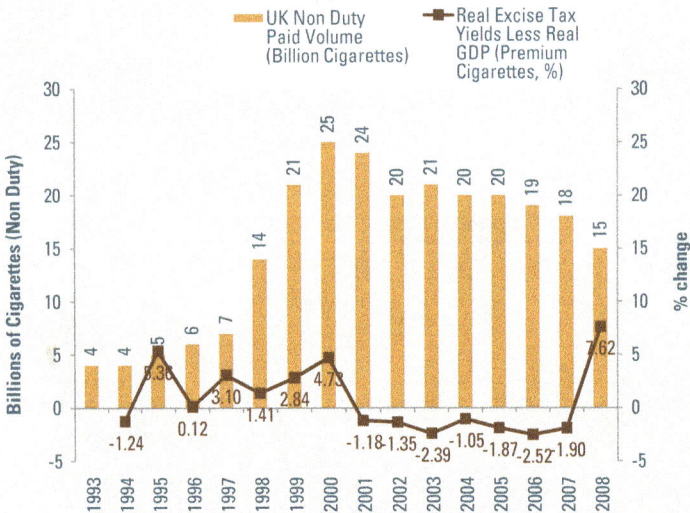

As a result of diminishing government excise tax revenues and increasing illicit trade activity, the UK reversed its course on excise tax policy in 2001 by tying future excise tax increases to forecasted inflation (removing the additional 5 percent increase that had been in place since 1997). By implementing this more moderate approach to excise taxation, government excise tax revenues stabilized at about £8.1 billion annually from 2002 to 2008 (Figure 62).[92]

As a matter of fact, following the demise of the escalator, non-duty paid volume has started to slowly decrease in the UK, presumably as a result of increased tax enforcement programs in combination with this more moderate tax increase policy. Nevertheless, smuggling and cross border shopping accounted for about £45 billion in revenue losses for the UK between fiscal year 2000 – 2001 to fiscal year 2008-2009.[93] Furthermore, combating illicit trade in the UK has been expensive, as it has required additional investments of over £917 million in 2011 alone, as well as an additional 1,200 customs employees.[94]

F. Singapore: Excise Tax Hikes Leading to a Decline in Government Revenue

1. EXCISE AND RETAIL PRICE DEVELOPMENT

Singapore applies a fully specific single tier cigarette excise tax structure on cigarettes. The government's excise tax policy between 2000 and 2005 was characterized by steep annual excise tax increases, cumulating in a 135 percent increase from SGD150 to SGD352 per 1000 cigarettes over this period.

The annual excise tax increases led to sharp retail price increases between 2000 and 2005, with the weighted average cigarette retail prices going up by 67 percent from SGD6.3 to SGD10.5 per pack of 20 cigarettes.[95] The government then changed its policy and did not increase excise tax rates between 2005 and 2013,[96] as observed in Figure 64, which led to a stabilization of prices.

Figure 64

Excise Tax Development

SGD per Thousand

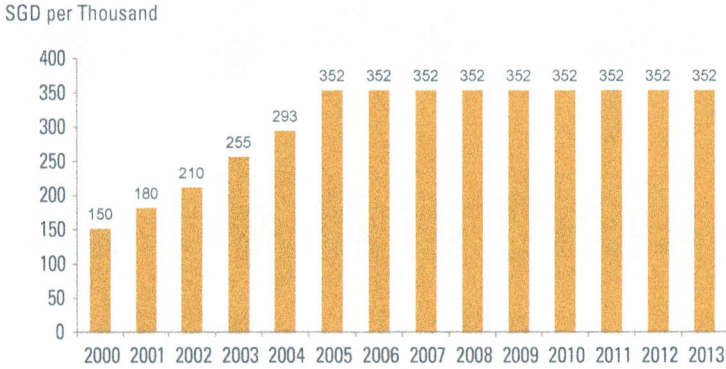

2. DUTY PAID CIGARETTE VOLUME AND GOVERNMENT EXCISE TAX REVENUE DEVELOPMENT

The duty-paid cigarette volume dropped by 43 percent from 3.2 billion cigarettes in 2000 to 1.8 billion cigarettes in 2006 and gradually recovered following the excise freeze and reached 2.7 billion cigarettes in 2013.[97]

Driven by the sharp annual excise tax increases, excise tax revenue initially rose steadily from SGD502 million in 2000 to SGD743 million in 2003, as is evidenced in Figure 65 below.[98] However, the continuous steep decline in duty-paid volume led to a drop in excise tax revenues in subsequent years, reaching a low of SGD621 million in 2006. Thereafter, following the recovery of the duty-paid volume, excise tax revenue started to rise again, reaching SGD1.0 billion in 2013 (Figure 65).

Figure 65

Duty Paid Volume and Cigarette Excise Tax Revenue

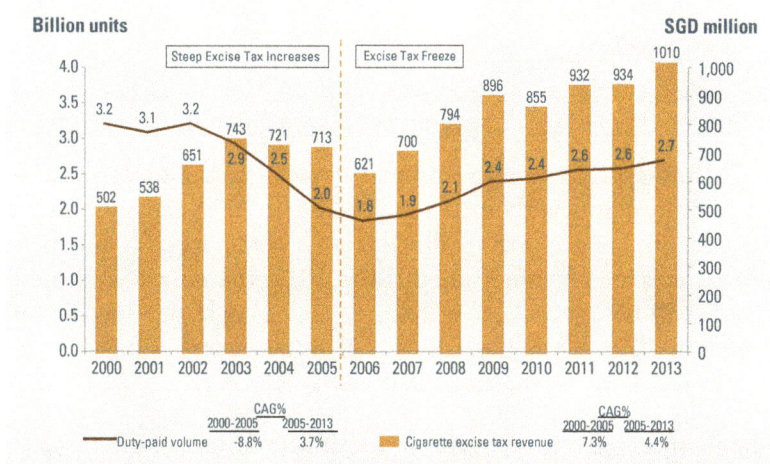

3. ILLICIT TRADE AND SMOKING INCIDENCE

The decline in duty-paid volume coincided with a marked increase in seizures by Singapore Customs, from 8 million cigarettes in 2000 to 106 million cigarettes in 2006, implying a sharp growth of illicit trade as legal cigarettes became less affordable for lower income consumers. However, smoking incidence remained essentially stable during this period, as it was 13.8 percent in 2001 and 13.6 percent in 2007,[99] indicating that the policy of steep annual excise tax increases was not effective in reducing the number of smokers, as many consumers simply switched from legal to illegal cigarettes.

In this regard, Finance Minister Lee Hsien Loong stated in his 2006 budget speech that *"I seriously considered raising tobacco duties, but have reluctantly decided against it because we are already seeing revenues declining, not because people are smoking less, but because smuggling has gone up"*. (Source: Singapore Finance Minister and Prime Minister. "Budget Statement 2006: Building on our Strengths, Creating Our Best Home." February 17th, 2006. http://app.mof.gov.sg/data/download/2006/FY2006_Budget_Statement.pdf)

However, illicit trade remains a serious concern, with an estimated illicit trade incidence of 19.6 percent of total consumption (63 million cigarettes) in 2013.[100]

This demonstrates that, notwithstanding an eight year excise freeze and robust anti-illicit trade legislation including deterrent penalties, illicit trade is extremely difficult to eradicate once established.

G. Philippines: Excise Tax Reform

1. CIGARETTE EXCISE RATE INCREASES UNDER REPUBLIC ACT 10351

In 2013, the Philippine government implemented a tobacco excise tax reform, significantly increasing the excise rates and simplifying the structure, which was modified from a 4-tier specific system to a 2-tier specific system. From 2014 to 2017, the tax rates on these 2 tiers will be approximated, resulting in a single tier specific tax system in 2017. Thereafter, the law plans automatic annual tax increases in line with projected inflation of 4 percent.

Many aspects of this tax reform are similar to tax reforms implemented in other countries; this book already mentioned the examples of Brazil and Indonesia. These countries and their tax systems are, obviously, not directly comparable, reflecting different domestic priorities. Nevertheless, the general themes of all these reforms are the simplification of the tax system, the approximation of tax rates on different products and brands, and the implementation of the reform over a number of years, through a multi-year time table.

In particular, the Philippine example stands out for the draconian magnitude of the initial tax increase. On January 1st, 2013, cigarette brands in the following categories experienced the following excise tax increases:

- Low tax tier (65 percent share of tax-paid volume): increased by 341 percent, from PHP 2.72 to PHP 12 per pack of 20 cigarettes;

- Mid tax tier (8 percent of tax-paid volume): increased by 231 percent, from PHP 7.56 to PHP 25;

- High tax tier (26 percent of tax-paid volume): increased by 108 percent, from PHP 12 to PHP 25.

On a weighted average base, the excise tax level almost tripled, increasing by 173.4 percent.[101]

2. IMPACT ON OVERALL CONSUMPTION

The massive excise tax increase led to retail price increases that ranged from 59 percent to 175 percent per pack for the most sold brands in the various price segments; however, the weighted average retail price increase was significantly less at 41.7 percent[102] due to wide scale down trading, as explained below. As a result of these price increases, the legal sales volume dropped by 15.6 percent, from 102.2 billion to 86.3 billion cigarettes between 2012 and 2013.[103] A simple, "back of the envelope" calculation suggests that the price elasticity for legal products must have been close to -0.37,[104] which is low for a developing country, but consistent with the fact that, initially, tobacco taxes and prices in the Philippines were low by international standards.[105] The drop in legal sales was largely compensated by a huge jump in illicit trade, from an estimated 6.4 billion cigarettes in 2012 (5.9 percent of total consumption) to an estimated 19.1 billion cigarettes in 2013 (18.1 percent of total consumption).[106] The largely stable overall market volume (sum of tax paid and illicit trade) is reflected in the adult smoking incidence and daily cigarette consumption figures, which remained essentially flat between 2012 and 2013 at 49 percent and 50 percent (smoking incidence), and 13.1 and 12.8 cigarettes (daily consumption), respectively.[107]

3. EXACERBATION OF DOWN-TRADING TREND

In addition to the sharp increase of illicit trade, the excise tax increase in January 2013 has led to a major shift of consumption towards the cheapest, legally available cigarettes on the market—the so-called "super low" price segment—which more than doubled from 17.1 percent market share in December 2012 to 41.3 percent market share in December 2013 (Figure 66).[108] Many consumers that previously smoked brands in the "low", "mid", and "high" price segments, compensated for the price increases by trading down to lower tax and priced cigarettes—thereby containing, to some extent, their expenditure on tobacco products.

Figure 66

Price Segment Share of Market (%)

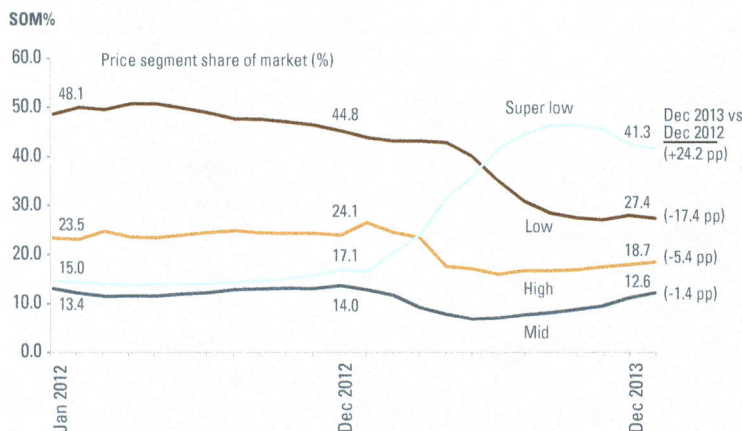

SOM%

Price segment share of market (%)

	Jan 2012	Dec 2012	Dec 2013
Super low	15.0	17.1	41.3 (+24.2 pp)
Low	48.1 / 44.8		27.4 (-17.4 pp)
High	23.5	24.1	18.7 (-5.4 pp)
Mid	13.4	14.0	12.6 (-1.4 pp)

Dec 2013 vs Dec 2012

4. IMPACT ON GOVERNMENT REVENUE

The 2013 excise tax hike more than doubled cigarette excise tax revenue, from PHP 32.9 billion to PHP 70.4 billion. However, the non-tax paid volume of 19.1 billion cigarettes is estimated to represent foregone excise revenue of PHP 12.7 billion,[109] whilst the erosion of the tax bases, as consumers shift towards lower tax products, represents foregone excise tax revenues of an estimated PHP 6.4 billion (Table 12, Table 13).

In summary, the massive average tax increase of 173.4 percent led to a significant 113.7 percent increase in excise tax revenues. But the difference between these growth rates illustrates an erosion of the tax base—both illicit trade, as well as consumer down trading—which affects tax revenue growth going forward. From a public health perspective, the tax increase seems not to have had a major impact. The data show that many consumers who could not afford to continue smoking their current brand, instead switched to lower priced legal or illegal cigarettes. With the envisaged approximation and, ultimately, harmonization of the tax rates, the scope for further down-trading will be more limited. This will remain an interesting case study to follow over the next years.

Table 12

Down-Trading Impact on Government Excise Tax Revenue

| | Tax Tier Segment | | | |
	High	Mid	Low	Total
2012* tax-paid volume % share	26.3%	8.4%	65.3%	100.0%
2013* tax-paid volume % share	24.1%		75.9%	100%
% point change	-10.5%		+10.5%	
2013 equivalent change in tax-paid volume (billion units)	-9.8		+9.8	
2013 excise tax (PHP/pack)	25		12	
2013 excise tax gain/(loss) PHP million	(12,245)		5,877	(6,367)

Source: Bureau of Internal Revenue (BIR)

Table 13

Philippine Excise Tax Reform: Summary

	2012	2013	Percent Change
Cigarette sales volume (billion cigarettes)			
- legal tax paid sales	102.2	86.3	-15.6%
- estimated Illegal Sales	6.4	19.1	198.0%
- total estimated tobacco consumption	108.7	105.5	-3.0%
Smoking Incidence	49.0%	50.0%	+2.0%
Daily cigarette consumption (number of cigarettes)	13.1	12.8	-2.3%
Excise tax revenues (PHP billion)	32.9	70.4	113.7%
Foregone excise tax revenues (PHP billion)			
- estimated revenues not collected from illicit tobacco product	1.8	12.7	610.2%
- estimated revenues impact of consumer down trading	–	6.4	
- total foregone excise tax revenue	1.8	19.1	965.5%

Source: BIR, Asia-11 Illicit Tobacco Indicator 2013 Update for the Philippines, Oxford Economics and the International Tax and Investment Center, June 2014 and Philip Morris International estimates

XI. LONG-TERM TAX PLANNING

Tobacco tax revenue is an important source of overall government tax revenues accounting for 2-3 percent of total government tax revenue in many developed countries such as Germany, Japan, Korea, Ireland, and Singapore—as shown in Figure 67 below. However, there are several countries in which tobacco taxation represents a much larger share of total tax revenues, such as France, Turkey, or Indonesia, where tobacco tax revenue accounts for 4.3 percent, 6.2 percent and 8.4 percent of total government tax revenues, respectively.

Figure 67

Tobacco Tax Revenues as a Percent of Overall Government Tax Revenues

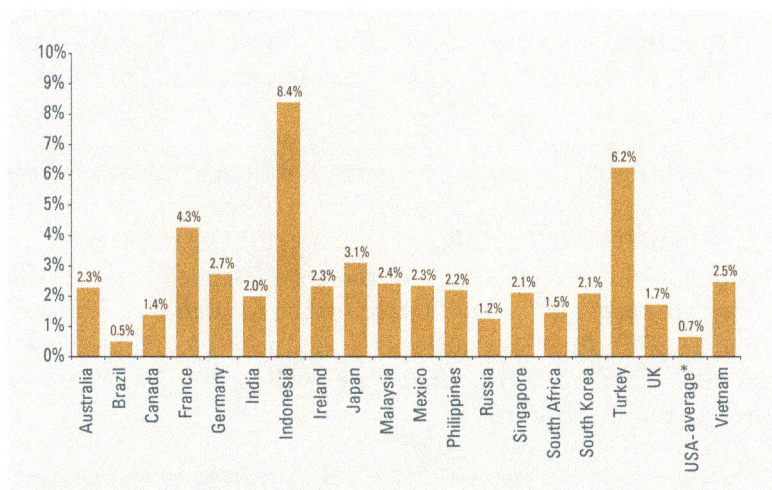

Source: Philip Morris International estimates based on local state static offices as of 2011.
U.S. data is based on Federal taxes for FY 2011- Final Monthly Report Treasury Statement and Orzechowski & Walker report on tax burden.

Given the importance of tobacco tax as a source of government tax revenue, governments need to consider carefully how and when to increase the tobacco tax levels. More and more countries are adopting a long term approach in this regard, either by implementing some form of automatic indexation, which will we discuss first, or by introducing multi-year tax plans.

When Australia amended its excise tax system on cigarettes in 1999, it introduced automatic, biannual excise tax increases linked to the Consumer Price Index (CPI). The effect of this legislation is that the specific excise tax on cigarettes increases in line with inflation twice per year—February and August—ensuring that the excise tax amount remains constant in real terms. Several other countries including Canada, Colombia, Honduras, Philippines,[113] Sweden, Turkey and the UK apply a similar approach as Australia, where excise tax rates are indexed, usually to inflation.

More recently, the Australian Government further amended the excise indexation calculations. From March 2014, the excise level is linked to the Average Weekly Ordinary Time Earnings (AWOTE) index instead of the CPI, with adjustments continuing on a biannual basis in March and September. The change from CPI to AWOTE follows recommendations from "Australia's Future Tax System Review" of 2010, which recommended that, *"Tobacco excise should be indexed to a broad measure of wages rather than CPI"*. As a result, Australia's fully specific excise will remain constant in real average earnings adjusted terms.[110]

Having in place an indexation system does not preclude countries from making further adjustments to the excise tax level, if seen necessary. In the case of Australia, for instance, the Government decided both to amend the indexation method, as described above, as well as to implement additional increases in the tobacco excise tax level. In April 2010, the Government increased tobacco excise tax by 25 percent.[111] From late 2013, tobacco taxes will increase by 12.5 percent every year until 2016.[112]

A different approach is applied in South Africa, where a fully specific excise tax system is applied on cigarettes, and additional measures are implemented to ensure that the tax is adjusted automatically over time. The way the system works is that the government has established by law that the total tax incidence must be kept at 52 percent of the retail price of the most popular price category. The nominal Value Added Tax (VAT) rate in South Africa is 14 percent, which implies that the excise tax incidence must be 39.72 percent (52 percent—(14/114)). Using the excise tax incidence of 39.72 percent and the retail price of the most popular brand, the tax authorities calculate the specific tax amount which is then applied equally to all cigarettes.

The retail price level is reviewed annually and the specific excise tax amount is increased in line with cigarette retail price increases, maintaining a constant excise incidence. For example, in 2012, the most popular (most sold) cigarette was Peter Stuyvesant, with a retail price of ZAR 26 per pack. Based on the excise tax incidence requirement of 39.72 percent, the specific excise tax was updated from ZAR 9.73 to ZAR 10.33 per pack, which is then applied equally to all cigarette brands (Table 14).

Table 14

South Africa: Excise Tax Adjustments Linked to Tobacco Price Increases

Tax Rates	Calculation	2011	2012
(A) Reference total tax incidence		52%	52%
(B) VAT – nominal rate		14%	14%
(C) Reference excise incidence	= A – (B / (1+B))	39.7%	39.7%
(D) Reference retail price (ZAR/pack)*		24.50	26.00
(E) Excise tax (ZAR/pack)	= C * D	9.73	10.33

*Reference retail price is based on most common retail price in previous calendar year.

For excise tax structures that include an *ad valorem* tax element, there is often no need for the government to amend tax rates, because retail prices increases will automatically generate a higher tax yield for tobacco products. However, many countries with mixed tax systems have adopted multi-year tax planning as a tool to increase revenue predictability. Multi-year plans are also often applied during periods of excise tax reform, to facilitate the transition from on tax system to another, as this book has illustrated with the earlier examples of the Philippines and Brazil.

Germany, for example, adopted a 5-year plan for excise tax increases on cigarettes and fine cut tobacco over the period 2011 and 2015, with the objective of gradual approximation of taxes between these two product categories. Over this period, on both cigarettes and fine cut tobacco, the specific excise element was increased gradually and the *ad valorem* excise tax rate was reduced. At the same time, Germany increased the minimum total tax on fine cut tobacco at a slightly faster rate than on cigarettes, which helped to reduce the gap between the two categories (Table 15).

Table 15

Germany: 5-year Tax Plan

Cigarettes	2010	2011	2012	2013	2014	2015
Ad valorem tax (% of RSP)	24.66%	21.94%	21.87%	21.80%	21.74%	21.69%
Specific tax (Euro / 1000 cigarettes)	82.7	90.8	92.6	94.4	96.3	98.2
Minimum Total Tax (Euro / 1000 cigarettes)	175.86	181.56	185.18	188.81	192.59	196.36
Fine Cut	2010	2011	2012	2013	2014	2015
Ad valorem tax (% of RSP)	18.57%	14.30%	14.41%	14.51%	14.63%	14.76%
Specific tax (Euro / kg)	34.06	41.65	43.31	45	46.75	48.49
Minimum Total Tax (Euro /1000 kg)	53.28*	81.63	84.89	88.2	91.63	95.04

* Minimum Excise Tax
Source: all figures are based on the Excise Tax Law as approved by the German Parliament on December 2nd, 2010. Minimum Total Tax (MTT) includes VAT and excise tax except for fine cut in 2010

As stated by the German Federal Ministry of Finance:

> *"The model will bring security in planning for public administration as well as for trade and industry."*[114]

Russia has implemented a slightly more flexible fiscal plan than Germany. In Russia, there is a 3 year rolling plan where the government legislates on tax increases for a 3 year horizon, on an annual basis (Table 16). Each year the authorities have the possibility to fine-tune the previously agreed rates, but this longer term rate setting, nevertheless, does provide greater predictability and stability on the fiscal environment.

Table 16

Russia: "Rolling" 3 Year Tax Timetable

Law	Cigarettes	2009	2010	2011	2012	2013	2014	2015
	Specific	150	180	216				
2008	*Ad valorem*	6.00%	6.50%	7.00%				
	MET	177	216	260				
	Specific		205	250	305			
2009	*Ad valorem*		6.50%	7.00%	7.50%			
	MET		250	305	375			
	Specific			280	360	460		
2010	*Ad valorem*			7.00%	7.50%	8.00%		
	MET			360	460	590		
	Specific				360 - 390	550	800	
2011	*Ad valorem*				7.50%	8.00%	8.50%	
	MET				460 – 510	730	1040	
	Specific					550	800	960
2012	*Ad valorem*					8.00%	8.50%	9.00%
	MET					730	1040	1250

Specific and Minimum Excise Tax (MET) in RUB/000, ad valorem percent of Retail Selling Price.

The map in Figure 68 below provides an overview of countries that have implemented either automatic tax indexation or have implemented multi-year tax timetables.

Figure 68

Excise Tax Long Term Plans: Indexation and Multi-year Plans

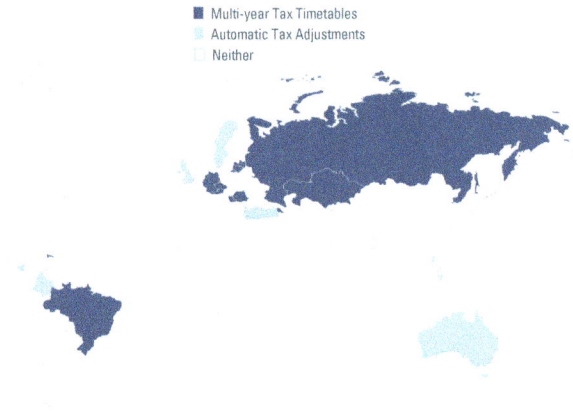

■ Multi-year Tax Timetables
▪ Automatic Tax Adjustments
▫ Neither

Note: Nicaragua uses multi-year timetables and from 2017 onwards tax indexation; Philippines will use multi – year timetables from 2018 onwards
Costa Rica, Ecuador and Honduras also have automatic tax adjustments at the time of publishing this book.

XII. EARMARKED TOBACCO TAXES

Earmarked taxes on tobacco products are implemented in 38 countries, across different regions, as displayed in Figure 69 below. Earmarked taxes can take many different forms, such as an *ad valorem* excise, a specific excise, an earmarked portion of tax revenues, and a duty on importers or exporters. Earmarked taxes can either be included or not included in tobacco excise taxes. In the first case, the earmarked tax could for instance be expressed as a fixed percentage of the excise tax revenues, to be dedicated to a specific fund. In the second case, the earmarked tax is a separate tax that comes on top of the excise tax. However, even if these earmarked taxes are not included in the calculation of the excise tax yield or incidence, the cost is passed onto consumers in one form or another.

Figure 69

Earmarking

- Earmarking included in Excise
- Earmarking not included in excise
- No earmarking.

Appendix III summarizes the global practices on tobacco tax earmarking—the important feature to notice is that there is very often a weak link between earmarked taxes and designated spending programs. Some examples of the programs funded by earmarked tobacco taxes are, for instance: student health insurance in Egypt, a man-made river project in Libya, and culture and sport in Lithuania. Overall, there seems to be no systematic order or explanation for the different approaches taken by each country to earmark tobacco taxes—in other words, there appears to be little economic linkage or pattern. Many of these earmark funded programs lack "economic rationale",[115] as they are often unrelated to the subject of the earmarked taxes, indicating that the beneficiaries of these programs are generally not the individuals paying the tax.

Another aspect of tax earmarking relates to the rigidities, and thus inefficiencies, it creates to the government budget system. In South Korea, for instance, all earmarked tax revenues (not just tobacco)[116] account for nearly 30 percent of local and central government tax revenues in 2011.[117] This implies that approximately 30 percent of the total government budget is automatically dedicated to the earmarked expenditure programs rather than facing an annual budgetary review. As a result of this rigidity, spending may become inefficient, for instance when programs and policies that do not receive earmarked funds have a greater public demand or higher returns, but remain underfunded.[118] In fact, a study commissioned by the South Korean government, recommends that earmarked tax revenues for public health promotion be directed to the general budget.[119] Generally speaking, when programs are funded by earmarked taxes, they will invariably be over- or underfunded; it will be a matter of coincidence when the taxes that are earmarked, exactly meet the program's optimal funding requirement.

XIII.   TOBACCO AS A COMPONENT OF THE CONSUMER PRICE INDEX (CPI)

A question that arises from time to time is whether tobacco products should be kept in the basket of goods and services that comprise the Consumer Price Index (CPI). Clearly, as tobacco excise taxes increase, the retail prices of tobacco products are driven up. It is sometimes argued that cigarettes and other tobacco products should be removed from the CPI so that the government could increase tobacco taxes without affecting inflation as measured by the CPI. However, from an economic point of view, this does not make sense.

As defined by international organizations:

"The consumer price index (CPI) measures the rate at which the prices of consumer goods and services are changing over time. It is a key statistic for economic and social policymaking and has substantial and wide-ranging implications for governments, businesses, and households."[120]

The CPI should be an objective, economic measure—reflecting the actual expenditure on consumer goods and services—and not become a political instrument. The CPI is a key statistic for economic and social policymaking, ranging from decisions on monetary policy to adjustments of wages, social security and other benefits to compensate for the changes in cost of living. It is also used to adjust government fees and charges, or payments in commercial contracts. The CPI is, furthermore, a key macro-economic indicator, enabling governments to formulate and assess fiscal and monetary policies, as well as trade and exchange rate policies. The public must have confidence in the integrity and objectivity in measuring this statistic by ensuring that it is representative of the goods and services actually purchased by consumers.

Recognizing the important status of the CPI, an advisory committee on the CPI in New Zealand stated:

"At the heart of a credible CPI is the concept of representational faithfulness. The basket of goods and services that are priced in a CPI should be representative of the goods and services actually used by households".[121]

The international standard reference manual on CPI states in this respect:

"All the goods and services that households willingly purchase in order to satisfy their personal needs or wants constitute consumers' expenditures and therefore fall within the scope of a CPI [....]. Particular kinds of goods or services must not be excluded because they are considered to be undesirable, harmful or objectionable. Such exclusions could be quite arbitrary and undermine the objectivity and credibility of the CPI."

It continues stating: "*if it is accepted that some goods and services may be excluded on the grounds that they are undesirable, the index is thereby exposed to actual or attempted manipulation by pressure groups.*" On the inclusion or not of indirect taxes, this reference manual states: "*All taxes on products, such as sales taxes, excise taxes and value added tax (VAT), are part of the purchasers' prices paid by consumers that should be used for CPI purposes.*"[122]

A. International Harmonization of the CPI

In 1993, the United Nations published an international standard: the "Classification of Individual Consumption According to Purpose", or COICOP. This UN classification scheme divides consumer expenditure in 12 divisions, each subdivided into groups. Tobacco has its own group (02.2) and is therefore a mandatory component for price indices based on the COICOP system.

All EU member countries, for instance, produce a Harmonised Index of Consumer Prices (HICP) based on this COICOP classification. This HICP is the mandatory, harmonized measure of inflation for all EU countries, and is used by the European Union and the European Central Bank (ECB), for instance when verifying Member States commitments with the convergence criteria for the European Monetary Union. As an example, the ECB uses HICPs as the key inflation measure for the Euro area. Tobacco is included in HICP for the Euro area with a weight of 2.4 percent (2014 data). However, different weights are applied in different countries in the Euro area to produce the national HICP, ranging from 2 percent in Spain to 8 percent in Luxembourg.[123]

B. Weight of Tobacco in the CPI

The consumer price index is generally calculated as a weighted average of the change in prices paid for goods and services consumed,

> "*The weights are meant to reflect the relative importance of the goods and services as measured by their shares in the total consumption of households. The weight attached to each good or service determines the impact that its price change will have on the overall index.*"[124]

Variances among countries in the weight assigned to a particular product, such as tobacco, therefore, reflect differences in consumption patterns as well as in relative prices. Thus, a weight of 2.40 percent for cigarettes in the United Kingdom, compared to 0.43 percent in the index for Costa Rica, indicates that a greater share of household expenditure is allocated to these products in the UK. Table 17 below provides the Tobacco weight within the CPI in selected countries:

Table 17

Tobacco Weight within the Consumer Price Index

Country	Tobacco Weight within CPI
Japan	0.51 %
Costa Rica	0.43 %
Norway	1.93 %
Australia	2.32 %
United Kingdom	2.40 %
Ireland	2.90 %

The consumer price index measures the change over time in prices of consumer goods and services acquired by households. Additionally, a wide range of governmental and commercial entities depend on the CPI to assess changes in price levels and to adjust monetary and fiscal policies, wages and benefits and assorted contractual commitments. Thus, a true and accurate reflection of price changes requires that the CPI covers all consumer goods and services of significance to the reference population, including tobacco products.

XIV. COMPARING EXCISE TAX LEVELS INTERNATIONALLY

In order to efficiently and effectively accomplish government objectives such as generating fiscal revenues or promoting public health, the optimum tax area for excise tax policy is segregated at either a national or local level given differences in economic fundamentals, socioeconomic characteristics, and political factors. However, motivated by an earlier World Bank[125] report that recommends a benchmark tax of two-thirds to four-fifths of the retail sales price of cigarettes, the WHO has continued the dialogue on global comparisons and proposes an excise tax benchmark of at least 70 percent of retail sales price of all[126] tobacco products.[127] While the benchmark rate is approximately the same in both reports, the WHO specifies that excise taxes should account for at least 70 percent of retail prices, not just total taxes. Total tax incidence differs from excise tax incidence in that the VAT or sales tax is included in the total tax incidence calculation—a distinction worth noting as countries that levy a relatively high VAT or sales tax will struggle to meet an excise tax incidence requirement versus a total tax incidence requirement. This point will be discussed in the ensuing subsection.

This section will discuss 3 different methods to compare excise tax levels internationally: (a) the excise incidence; (b) the excise yield; and, (c) affordability.[128] While these international references can provide useful insights, they should not serve as the sole measure of national excise tax policy evaluation, especially since each country has its own unique set of fiscal and public health objectives.

A. Excise Incidence

As the excise incidence will vary depending on the retail price on which it is calculated, as well as on the excise tax structure, any international comparison of excise incidence will need to be based on a reference brand or reference price point. In general, the calculation for the excise tax incidence is as follows:

$$Excise\ Incidence = Excise\ Tax\ Yield/RSP_{Reference\ Brand} \times 100$$

The first question that must be answered is how to choose the reference price point to compare excise incidence internationally in a meaningful way. In the EU, where excise incidence exists as a benchmark since 1992, initially MPPC (price of the Most Popular Price Category, or group of most sold brands) was used, later replaced by WAP (Weighted Average Price) in 2011. With some simple examples, we will demonstrate that excise incidence is not a meaningful way of comparing tobacco tax rates internationally, whatever the reference point.

Imagine we compare two countries with the same specific tax structure, the same tax level, and the same retail prices for cigarettes. The only difference is that consumers in Country A prefer premium cigarettes and consumers in Country B prefer low priced cigarettes, perhaps because incomes are lower in Country B. Therefore, as a result of these different consumer preferences, the MPPC is €10 in Country A and €6 in Country B. As can be seen in Table 18 below, if one would use the excise incidence as a tool for tax comparison, one would be led to believe that Country B applies much higher tax levels than Country A—even though tax and price levels in both countries are identical.

Table 18

Retail Selling Prices (in €)	Country A	Country B
High	10	10
Mid	8	8
Low	6	6
MPPC	10	6
Excise Tax (specific)	4	4
Excise Tax Incidence on MPPC	40%	67%

Switching the reference point to WAP does not significantly improve the situation. Imagine the same situation as before only this time the reference point will not be the price of one of the existing groups of cigarettes, but will instead be skewed towards high priced cigarettes in Country A (e.g., with a WAP of €9) and skewed towards low priced cigarettes in Country B (e.g., with a WAP of €7). Again, as illustrated in Table 19, one can see dramatic differences in the calculated excise incidence in the two countries, even though tax rates and cigarette prices are <u>identical</u>.

Table 19

Retail Selling Prices	Country A	Country B
High	10	10
Mid	8	8
Low	6	6
Weighted Average Price	9	7
Excise Tax (specific)	4	4
Excise Tax Incidence on WAP	44%	57%

The excise incidence not only fails to provide meaningful information about tax policy when making cross-country comparisons, but equally, it does not provide a good indicator of how tax policy changes over time within one country. For instance, returning to the previous example of Country A, with an excise incidence measured on WAP of 44 percent, now imagine this country suffers an economic crisis and thus consumers reduce their spending by switching to lower priced cigarettes. Alternatively, imagine this country takes some regulatory measures, such as plain packaging, which may reduce brand loyalty and lead consumers to switch towards lower priced products. In both scenarios, the weighted average price of cigarettes will decline, and the excise incidence will increase—even though from a tax and pricing perspective, <u>nothing</u> has changed. A distant observer would thus be led to believe that Country A somehow increased the excise incidence on cigarettes, as demonstrated in Table 20, even though no tax change has been taken.

Table 20

Retail Selling Prices	Before Down-trading	After Down-trading
High	10	10
Mid	8	8
Low	6	6
Weighted Average Price	9	8
Excise Tax (specific)	4	4
Excise Tax Incidence on WAP	44%	50%

These examples illustrate the fundamental issues with using the excise incidence as a basis for cross-country comparison or comparisons over time. A second issue arises from the interaction with VAT.

The calculations in Table 21 below simulate the required excise tax increase to meet a minimum excise incidence (70 percent in this example) for three countries that have the same excise tax rate to start with, but a different VAT rate in place.

Initially, the excise tax yield was €200 per 1000 cigarettes in all three countries and the Retail Selling Price gap between the high VAT and low VAT country was €51 per 1000 cigarettes. Assume then that the countries increase the excise tax in order to meet a 70 percent excise incidence benchmark. The excise tax increase that is required to meet a minimum excise incidence is significantly larger for high VAT countries—in the scenarios described in Table 21, the excise tax yield must increase by 67.5 percent for a VAT rate of 10 percent, while a VAT rate of 27 percent requires a 302.5 percent increase in the excise tax yield! Upon imposing a minimum excise tax incidence of 70 percent, the excise tax yield is now nearly 2.5 times larger for the high VAT country compared to the low VAT country and the RSP gap is about €670 per 1000 cigarettes.

These calculations demonstrate two major points about excise tax incidence: (1) the excise tax incidence does not strongly correlate with the excise tax yield—a high excise tax yield does not imply a high excise incidence; and, (2) implementing a minimum excise tax incidence requirement can move prices away from approximation. The harmonization experience of the EU demonstrates the practical issues that can arise when aiming for a minimum excise tax incidence benchmark; in fact, price differentials actually widened following EU harmonization, as was discussed earlier in this book.

Table 21

Example of Higher VAT Rates Leading to Divergence of the Excise Tax Incidence

				Excise Tax Increase Required to Reach 70% Benchmark
Country 1: VAT is 10%	RSP (€ per 1000 Cigarettes, sum of (a.) to (c.))	€ 330	€ 478.5	
	(a.) Pre-Tax Price (per 1000)	€ 100	€ 100	
	(b.) Excise Tax Yield (per 1000)	€ 200	€ 335	+ €135 or 67.5%
	(c.) Tax Paid for VAT Rate @10% (per 1000)	€ 30	€ 43.5	
	Cigarette Excise Tax Incidence (%, Excise Yield/RSP)	60.61%	70.01%	
Country 2: VAT Rate is 18.5%	RSP (€ per 1000, sum of (a.) to (c.))	€ 355.5	€ 699.15	
	(a.) Pre-Tax Price (per 1000)	€ 100	€100	
	(b.) Excise Tax Yield (per 1000)	€ 200	€490	+ €290 or 145%
	(c.) Tax Paid for VAT Rate @18.5% (per 1000)	€ 55.5	€ 109.15	
	Cigarette Excise Tax Incidence (%, Excise Yield/RSP)	56.26%	70.09%	
Country 3: VAT Rate is 27%	RSP (€ per 1000 Cigarettes, sum of (a.) to (c.))	€ 381	€ 1,149.35	
	(a.) Pre-Tax Price (per 1000)	€ 100	€100	
	(b.) Excise Tax Yield (per 1000)	€ 200	€805	+ €605 or 302.5%
	(c.) Tax Paid for VAT Rate @27% (per 1000)	€81	€244.35	
	Cigarette Excise Tax Incidence (%, Excise Yield/RSP)	52.49%	70.04%	

Based on the UBS survey countries used throughout this book, we further illustrate this point with actual data. Figure 70 below shows the excise incidence, excise yield, and VAT rate on January 2014. The correlation between the excise tax yield and incidence is not strong: correlation values are 0.56, 0.47, and 0.23 for Marlboro, the most sold brand, and the cheapest brand, respectively.[129]

Figure 70

Excise Tax Yields, Incidences, and VAT Rates

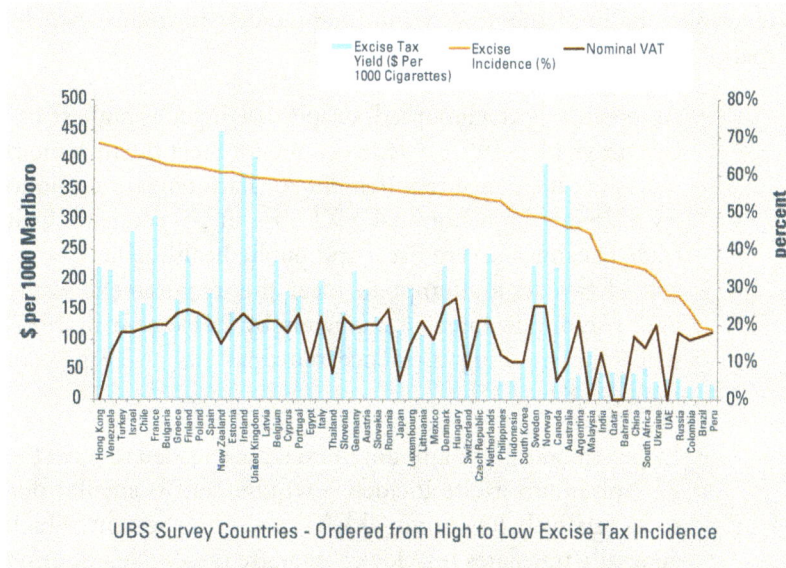

Source: Philip Morris International, Marlboro, as of January 1st, 2014
Exchange Rate Data: Bloomberg, as of January 1st, 2014

For example, Egypt and Thailand have excise incidences of 58.1 percent and 57.7 percent, respectively, which are well above the sample average of 51.4 percent. However, the excise tax yields per 1000 Marlboro cigarettes are $65 for Egypt and $81 for Thailand, which are well below the sample average of $154; while the nominal VAT rates are 10 percent and 7 percent, for Egypt and Thailand, respectively.

Furthermore, when comparing the highest excise tax incidence in the sample (Hong Kong, 68.2 percent), to Germany, Denmark, and Sweden, which have comparable excise tax yields, it is clear that the relationship between yields and incidences further erodes due to VAT differentials. In spite of having very similar excise tax yields, Germany, Denmark, and Sweden have much lower excise tax incidences relative to Hong Kong at 56.9 percent, 54.75 percent, and 48.8 percent, respectively (Figure 70). This is explained by the fact that nominal VAT rates are significantly higher than Hong Kong (0 percent), at 19 percent for Germany, and 25 percent for both Denmark and Sweden.

Although an excise incidence target has not been applied on a global scale, the EU provides a regional example of this benchmark in practice. The following case studies highlight the practical concerns and challenges of implementing a minimum excise incidence benchmark:

- As previously documented, despite having the highest excise tax yield in 1997, Sweden could not meet the minimum excise tax incidence requirement for harmonization due to its relatively high nominal VAT rate of 25 percent. Illicit trade became a severe fiscal and public health issue as a result of Sweden's attempt to meet this requirement—duty paid volume declined immediately by 28 percent in 1997, while the smoking incidence remained about 19 percent from 1998 to 2001.[130]

- In Luxembourg, the amount of excise tax needed to meet the EU minimum excise incidence requirement is smaller due to its relatively low nominal VAT rate of 15 percent, which generally translates into lower cigarette prices. Neighboring countries with higher nominal VAT rates, such as Belgium at 21 percent, tend to have higher excise tax yields and thus retail prices,[131] which can incentivize consumers to shop across the border. In fact, 63 percent of Belgium's non-domestic legal inflows were from Luxembourg in 2012.[132]

- As discussed earlier, the cigarettes tax gaps between the lowest and highest taxed EU country were not approximated, but instead widened, from €166 per 1000 cigarettes to €184 per 1000 cigarettes from 2002 to 2011. This tax divergence was driven by the imposition of the EU minimum excise incidence, which affected countries in different ways depending on the VAT rate and domestic trade margins, combined with the lack of an EU wide maximum tax level.

Therefore, with all the above in mind, the excise incidence should not be used as a benchmark to compare tobacco tax policies across countries and over time.

B. Excise Yield

The excise yield refers to the monetary amount of excise tax per 1000 cigarettes of a reference brand or price point. For countries with a single tier specific tax, the excise yield is the same as the tax rate. For countries with *ad valorem*, mixed, dual or multi-tier systems, the excise yield for international comparison purposes must be established with reference to a reference brand and price point. For instance, for countries with a mixed tax structure, the excise tax yield is represented as the following:

$$Excise\ Tax\ Yield = (RSP_{Reference\ Brand} \times ad\ valorem) + Specific$$

Also for this comparison method, one must consider which reference price to use. The EU provides an interesting insight in this regard. Currently, the EU applies a minimum excise yield benchmark of €90 per thousand cigarettes. Under the EU mixed excise tax system, the excise yield will differ by brand. However, one only needs to look at the excise yield on the cheapest cigarette to know whether a country meets this benchmark, because the *ad valorem* element implies that the excise yield on the cheapest cigarettes will be lower[133] than on all other cigarettes.

Apart from this practical reason, it makes most sense from a public policy reason to use the retail price of the cheapest cigarettes as the reference point to compared tax levels internationally. To discourage smoking, governments generally seek to reduce the affordability of cigarettes. As the cheapest cigarette is the most affordable, it is the tax level on this price category that should be the focus of the fiscal policy to discourage smoking.

If countries, as is the case in the EU, implement a regional minimum excise yield requirement, the equation above must be expressed in a common currency, such as the Euro. Although this benchmark ensures approximation such that the excise tax component of cigarette prices (for the cheapest brand) is consistent everywhere, the underlying weakness is that it relies on nominal exchange rates, which fail to account for the variation in purchasing power. In this sense, cigarettes may become relatively unaffordable in countries with weaker currencies relative to the benchmark currency used. Another potential issue is that large currency devaluations would, in turn, lead to a need to increase excise tax rates, to continue meeting the international monetary benchmark. Additionally, the minimum excise tax yield must be adjusted for the benchmark currency's inflation to ensure that the benchmark remains relevant over time.

Despite the issues outlined above, a regional minimum excise yield, as applied in the EU, ensures that the reference price cigarette is taxed the same regardless of location. From a public health or Pigouvian framework, this minimum excise yield benchmark is a positive, as cigarettes are treated as equally harmful everywhere. Moreover, with cigarettes being taxed equally in terms of the minimum monetary amount, the incentive to shop across the border may decline.[134]

The EU, the U.S., and Canada are examples of applying a minimum excise yield. In the U.S. and Canada, a federal excise tax is implemented, which functions as a minimum excise yield for the States and Provinces respectively. However, on top of the Federal excise, substantial State and Provincial excise taxes are applied to cigarettes in many cases, and there is no minimum nor maximum level agreed upon with respect to these regional excise taxes. In the EU, the minimum excise yield is currently €90 per thousand cigarettes.

Although these three examples provide case studies of the minimum excise yield in practice, it is important to recognize that all three have their own common currency (although, in the case of the EU, not applicable in all countries), eliminating the problem that currency devaluations imply automatic tax increases.

Another point to consider is the substantial differences in income within the U.S., Canada, and the EU—which is an important reason for the lack of excise tax harmonization within these geographies. However, compared to these regional income differences, the income differences at a global scale are vastly larger—illustrating the impossibility for implementing a global minimum excise yield.

Therefore, the excise yield expressed in monetary amounts is not a very useful way to judge whether a country's tobacco taxes are high or low from a public policy perspective.

C. Affordability

The final excise tax benchmark considered is affordability, which compares the excise yield against a measure of income, such as nominal GDP per capita, nominal private consumption per capita, net hourly wage, or net daily wage. The following equations formally represent the different affordability measures:

- $PRI_{GDP} = (Excise\ Tax\ Yield/Nominal\ GDP\ per\ Capita) \times 100$

- $PRI_{Consumption} = (Excise\ Tax\ Yield/Nominal\ Consumption\ per\ Capita) \times 100$

- $Minutes\ of\ Labor_{All\ Occupations} = (Excise\ Tax\ Yield/Net\ Hourly\ Wage_{All\ Occupations}) \times 60$

- $Minutes\ of\ Labor_{7\ Lowest\ Pay} = (Excise\ Tax\ Yield/Net\ Hourly\ Wage_{7\ Lowest\ Pay}) \times 60$

- $Percentage\ of\ Daily\ Income_{All\ Occupations} = (Excise\ Tax\ Yield/Net\ Daily\ Wage_{All\ Occupations}) \times 100$

- $Percentage\ of\ Daily\ Income_{7\ Lowest\ Pay} = (Excise\ Tax\ Yield/Net\ Daily\ Wage_{7\ Lowest\ Pay}) \times 100$

Consistent with the previous subsection, the recommended way to calculate the excise tax yield for these various benchmarks is based on the cheapest cigarette in each market. Also from an international perspective, when comparing the "tax level" across countries with widely differing tax structures, the lowest excise tax yield is the most transparent and meaningful.

Comparing the first two affordability benchmarks, Price Relative to Income (PRI) based on GDP or nominal consumption, the latter best reflects consumers' spending ability since savings, income taxes, and government spending are netted out of this measure. For instance, despite having the largest nominal GDP per capita in the sample of countries used in this book, which was over $112,000, Luxembourg's household final consumption as a percentage of GDP in 2012 was as low as 32 percent—implying that only about $36,000 of residents' income is spent on consumption in Luxembourg.[135] Contrast that to Australia, which has nominal GDP per capita of about $64,000 (or 57 percent of Luxembourg's), but consumed nearly $35,000— clearly nominal GDP per capita, while a very useful reference, will not capture consumer's actual spending capacity as well in countries where high private savings, a large non-resident presence in the workforce,[136] high income taxes, and large government spending programs are prevalent.

Both PRI benchmarks have the advantage that the data are easily available from the national accounts. However, as there are large differences in income equality around the world, these macro statistics may not correctly reflect the income and thus affordability among key groups from a policy perspective, e.g., low income smokers.

An affordability benchmark that measures income based on the 7 lowest paying occupations[137] is probably more appropriate if reflecting the large income differences around the world is the objective. Here, however, there is a problem with data collection. The source most commonly used for these statistics, the UBS Prices and Earnings report, does not cover all countries in the world and measures incomes only in the capitals of each country, which likely introduces a significant bias since income differences between urban and rural areas are large and vary significantly between developed and developing countries.

Considering the advantages and disadvantages of the various affordability benchmarks for excise taxes, we decided to proceed with an analysis that estimates the relationship between excise tax yields for 1000 cigarettes of the cheapest reference brand[138] with nominal private consumption per capita[139]—all data are expressed in U.S. dollar terms.[140] Additionally, both variables are transformed by the natural logarithm (ln) to ensure symmetry and due to the fact that all values are positive. In other words, the relationship that is being estimated by OLS[141] is the following model:[142]

$$\ln(Excise\ Tax\ Yield_{Per\ 1000\ Cheapest\ Cigarettes}) = b_0 + b_1 \ln(Nom\ Private\ Consumption_{Per\ Capita})$$

Using the 57 countries from the UBS survey as the sample for the regression analysis, the standard regression output is provided in Table 22 below. As such, the regression coefficient, b_1, is interpreted as an elasticity estimate: a 1 percent change in nominal private consumption per capita relates to about a 0.92 percent change in the excise tax yield. The adjusted R-squared indicates that approximately 60 percent of the variation in the excise tax yield is explained by the nominal private consumption per capita (in natural log terms of course).

Table 22

	In Excise Tax Yield (1000 Cheapest Cigarettes)
ln Nominal Private Consumption (per Capita)	0.9161*** (9.23)
Constant	-4.0554*** (-4.36)
Observations	57
Adjusted R-Squared	0.6006
t-statistics are in parentheses	
* p<0.005, ** p<0.01, *** p<0.001	

Figure 71 on the next page depicts the positive, linear correlation between the natural log of private consumption per capita and excise tax yields—as nominal consumption per capita rises, in general, the excise tax yield will also tend to be higher.[143] Observations that deviate substantially above or below from this linear trend (especially above or below the confidence intervals) indicate that the level of taxation is significantly above or below the sample, after accounting for domestic per capita consumption levels. For instance, both Romania and Slovakia have similar excise tax yields on the cheapest cigarettes (about $115 per 1000 cigarettes); however, Slovakia's nominal private consumption per capita is approximately 2 times larger. As such, Romania is well above the linear regression trend, while Slovakia much closer to this trend. In contrast, Luxembourg and Slovenia also have similar excise tax levels, but Luxembourg is well below the trend line as its per capita private consumption is more than 2.5 times larger than that of Slovenia's.

Countries that are well below the regression trend estimated in Figure 71 either indicate a low overall tax level or, alternatively, a tax structure that applies low taxes to certain brands. Consequently, countries must consider both the tax level and the tax structure in order to assess whether domestic tax policy is consistent with international practice. In the case of China and Japan, for instance, an adjustment to the tax structure, such that preferential tax treatment is eliminated, would suffice. As demonstrated by plotting the most sold brand price relative to the nominal consumption per capita (CN-MP and JP-MP, respectively) in Figure 71, shifting the tax structure in China and Japan would bring the domestic tax policies of both countries closer to international practice.

Figure 71

Regression of Excise Tax Yield on Nominal Consumption per Capita

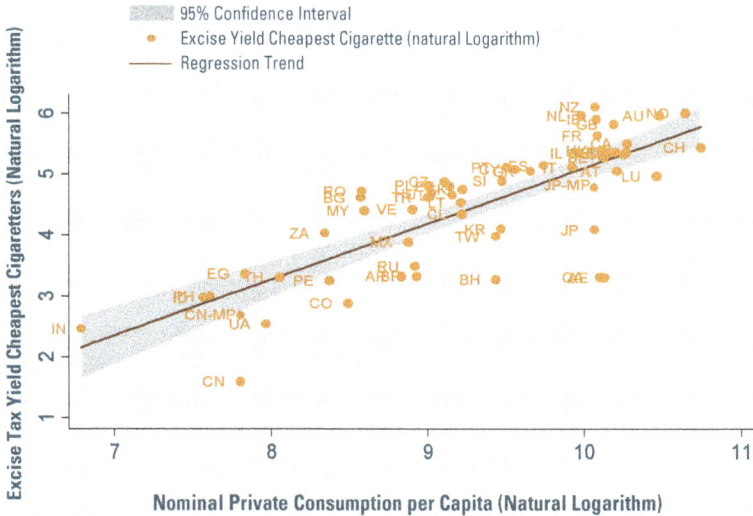

Table 23

Country	Country Code	Country	Country Code
Argentina	AR	Lithuania	LT
Australia	AU	Luxembourg	LU
Austria	AT	Malaysia	MY
Bahrain	BH	Mexico	MX
Belgium	BE	Netherlands	NL
Brazil	BR	New Zealand	NZ
Bulgaria	BG	Norway	NO
Canada	CA	Peru	PE
Chile	CL	Philippines	PH
China	CN	Poland	PL
Colombia	CO	Portugal	PT
Cyprus	CY	Qatar	QA
Czech Republic	CZ	Romania	RO
Denmark	DK	Russia	RU
Egypt	EG	Slovakia	SK
Estonia	EE	Slovenia	SI
Finland	FI	South Africa	ZA
France	FR	South Korea	KR
Germany	DE	Spain	ES
Greece	GR	Sweden	SE
Hong Kong	HK	Switzerland	CH
Hungary	HU	Taiwan	TW
India	IN	Thailand	TH
Indonesia	ID	Turkey	TR
Ireland	IE	UAE	AE
Israel	IL	Ukraine	UA
Italy	IT	United Kingdom	GB
Japan	JP	Venezuela	VE
Latvia	LV		

Additionally, countries such as New Zealand, the United Kingdom, Ireland, and Australia have exceedingly high excise tax levels in relation to private consumption per capita, and are therefore more likely to face illicit tobacco trade issues or a high proportion of tobacco consumed in the form of low tax roll-your-own. Interestingly enough, the United Kingdom, Ireland, and Australia have each become common examples of countries with a large illicit trade issue. In the United Kingdom, the 2012 share of cigarette consumption attributed to counterfeit and contraband cigarettes was 16.4 percent of the market, compared to 10.1 percent of the previous year (2011).[144] In Ireland, this figure was 19.1 percent in 2012[145]—obviously a concern in terms of government excise tax revenues.

Table 24 below estimates the excise tax yield per 1000 cheapest cigarettes, as predicted by the regression model, for the given nominal private consumption per capita input. Therefore, if the nominal private consumption per capita is $10,000, then one would normally expect an excise tax yield of about $80 per thousand cigarettes—recognizing that there may be very good reasons for an individual country to deviate from this value predicted by the regression line. Figure 72 graphs the data from Table 24, which is useful as it illustrates the regression model back in level terms, rather than in natural logarithmic transformation.

Table 24

Nominal Private Consumption Per Capita ($)	Excise Yield as Predicted by Regression Model ($ per 1000 Cigarettes)
$500	$5
$5,000	$42
$10,000	$80
$15,000	$116
$20,000	$151
$25,000	$185
$30,000	$219
$35,000	$252
$40,000	$285

Figure 72

Theoretical Log-Log Regression Trend

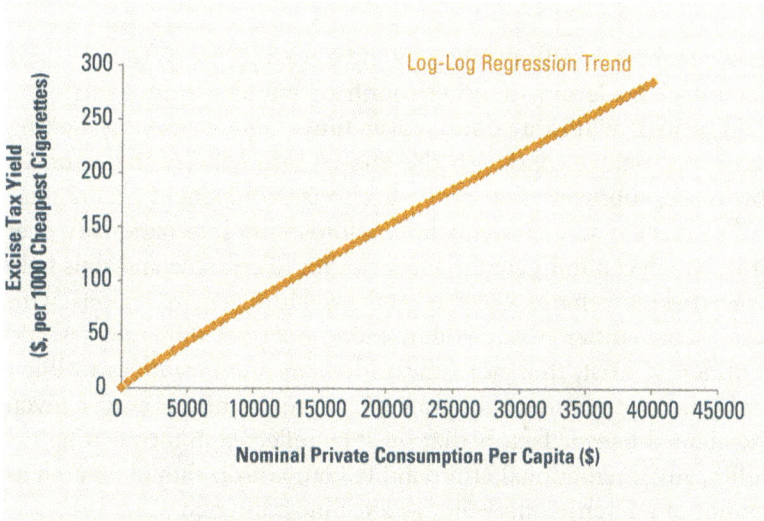

Although Figure 71 and Figure 72 are useful for analyzing international trends in excise tax yields and nominal consumption per capita, it doesn't capture regional variation due to differences in policy, socioeconomic and political factors, economic fundamentals, or market characteristics, for example.

For instance, some countries have an overall fiscal policy which puts more emphasis on direct taxes (such as Japan)—as a result, it is only normal to expect relatively lower indirect taxes, including excise taxes in these countries. This also works vice-versa. Turkey's fiscal policy mix focusses on indirect taxes—as a result, one could expect relatively high tobacco taxes.

Another point to keep in mind is that the excise yield shown in Figure 71 refers to the excise yield on the cheapest cigarette. Therefore, if a country wishes to increase tobacco tax to comparable affordability levels internationally, this may not point to an overall increase in tax levels, but rather to an adjustment of the structure. For instance, in Japan and China, the tax on the cheapest cigarettes is 1/2 and 1/3 of the tax on the most sold product, respectively. By bringing the tax on the cheapest products in line with the most sold product, both countries would move much closer to the line shown in Figure 71, which is illustrated by the two data points in the figure showing the excise yield on the most popular price category in Japan and China (JP-MP and CN-MP, respectively).

As a benchmark, affordability could be used in two ways: to assess a country's tax level with other countries, but also to pace excise tax yield growth within a country over time. For instance, by linking excise tax yield increases to the chosen affordability indicator. In this sense, approximation of the excise tax component occurs relative to income and thus equalizes affordability internationally over time, which can mitigate the incentive for illicit trade and thus help policymakers achieve fiscal objectives. However, in regions with high income differences, absolute excise and price differences would continue to exist, thus not fully addressing the incentives to illicit trade and cross-border shopping. Most importantly, however, given the many domestic factors that must be reflected in formulating tax policy, any international affordability comparison should be used as a point of reference only—not as a technocratic rule.

XV. INTERNATIONAL TAXES

International taxation, while a popular topic for theoretical discussion, tends to be much less popular in terms of implementation: at present, there exist very few examples of internationally coordinated tax policy, and *no* examples of a compulsory, centralized global tax. As discussed previously in Part I, international taxes would infringe upon national sovereignty, as well as raising issues of flexibility, accountability, and equitability—and, as such, international tax efforts have tended to be voluntary in nature.

A. Compulsory International Taxation

1. GLOBAL TAXATION

Currently, there are no instances of compulsory centralized global taxation, nor are there any such regulatory or fiscal authorities that could impose such tax. The United Nations (UN), while a large, centralized, international organization, lacks the authority to regulate or enforce tax policy in any of its member states. Furthermore, the UN does not have the ability to overrule national sovereignty, as membership (while beneficial) remains voluntary, consequently, policy impositions could not be considered "compulsory" in the strictest sense of the term. There have been various proposals to support the UN's Millennium Development Goals with some type of global taxation, but such suggestions have always been rather short-lived. A surcharge on both currency exchanges and financial transactions has been considered recently, however, criticisms of the excessively burdensome[146] nature of such taxation have prevented the movements from gaining much traction.[147]

2. REGIONAL TAXATION

The European Union is a good example of a strong regional authority, with the ability to implement tax policy in its member states. (Similar to the UN, however, such taxes are not strictly compulsory, as membership is similarly voluntary.) Presently, the EU has implemented a minimum VAT rate of 15 percent (a portion of which is remitted to the EU central budget), with individual VAT rates ranging from 15 percent in Luxembourg, to 27 percent in Hungary.[148] The primary purpose behind implementing minimum VAT levels was market harmonization—lowering or eliminating regulatory and financial barriers to intra-European trade has long been a major focus within the EU.

In addition to VAT, the EU has also harmonized to some extent excise taxation on mineral oils, alcoholic beverages, and tobacco products. The current excise tax system applied to tobacco products in the EU has evolved over 40 years to accommodate enlargement of the community from 12 member states in 1971 to 28 member states in 2014, while recognizing the diverse range of income levels and trading conditions within the single market. It comprises four key elements:

1) A harmonized set of products definitions that all EU Member States must apply. This includes: cigarettes; cigars and cigarillos; fine cut tobacco for the rolling of cigarettes; and other smoking tobacco. Member states can include other categories of tobacco products in their national legislation (e.g. smokeless tobacco).

2) A set of minimum taxation requirement by product category, determined as a minimum excise incidence; excise yield; or both (cigarettes).

3) A compulsory excise tax structure for cigarettes.

4) A set of provisions that regulate accessory processes, such as price setting, collection of excise, exemptions and refunds and reporting requirements for Member States.

For cigarettes, historically the Southern European countries applied *ad valorem* excise tax while the northern European countries applied specific tax. In 1972, it was agreed that a mixed excise tax system, consisting of one *ad valorem* excise tax element based on the final retail selling price and one specific tax element, should become the standard excise tax structure for cigarettes. At the same time, to promote greater harmonization of the excise tax structures across member countries, the share of the specific excise as a percent of the total tax (excise combined with VAT), also referred to as "specific tax ratio", was set between 5 and 55 percent—to be further harmonized over time.

In 1992, further measures were introduced in the context of the so-called Single Market, setting a minimum excise tax incidence of 57 per cent of the retail price based on the retail price of the Most Popular Price Category (MPPC). The EU tobacco tax Directives—as with most EU law—are subject to regular review. In 2002, a modification was introduced whereby countries with high excise levels in monetary terms (exceeding 95 Euro per 1000 cigarettes), would not have to respect the 57 percent excise tax incidence rule.[149] This modification was sought by Sweden, which due to its high VAT rate had difficulties meeting this minimum excise rule as discussed earlier in this book. At the same time, in view of the enlargement of the EU with 10 countries from Central and Eastern Europe joining the union, a minimum excise tax amount of Euro 60 per thousand cigarettes (to be increased to Euro 64 per thousand cigarettes as from 1 July 2006) was introduced alongside the existing tax criteria.[150] This minimum excise tax requirement forced up the tax levels in countries such as Poland, Czech Republic and Hungary and helped narrow the tax gaps with neighboring EU countries with higher cigarette tax levels. Some Accession Countries were given transitional periods of up to 10 years to meet the minimum excise tax yields on joining the EU. Note that the introduction of both monetary benchmarks, the €95 "escape clause" and the €60 "minimum excise yield", illustrate the lack of "harmonization power" provided by the existing minimum excise incidence rule, expressed as a percentage, as also discussed in the Sweden case study.[151]

While the goal of tax harmonization in the EU was to bring about the approximation of tobacco excise taxes and retail prices, excise tax yield gaps actually increased, even if only considering the "old" EU-15 countries. As Figure 73 illustrates, the excise tax yield gap between the country with the highest yield and lowest yield has risen from €166 per 1000 cigarettes to €184 per 1000 cigarettes, or by nearly 11 percent from 2002 to 2011.[152]

Figure 73[153]

Cigarette Excise Tax Gaps Between the EU 15 Countries in 2002 and 2011

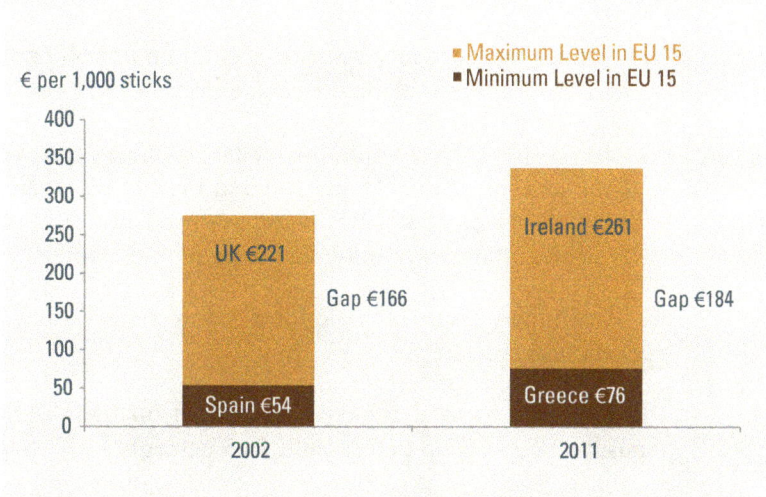

Source: European Commission (2011); International Tax & Investment Center (2012), The Impact of Imposing a Global Excise Target for Cigarettes: Experience from the EU Accession Countries

The key point cannot be stressed enough: **tax harmonization is very difficult to achieve without economic distortions, even in areas with somewhat similar income levels.** Therefore, policymakers should exercise caution when assessing the costs and benefits of excise tax harmonization. The lack of a maximum tax level was another reason why the EU tobacco tax Directives did not bring about a real approximation of tax levels. As countries with relatively low tax levels had to increase tobacco taxes to meet minimum EU requirements, EU countries with relatively high tax levels simply continued increasing tobacco taxes, resulting in an effective increase in the tax gap within the EU.

The current EU tobacco tax framework was revised again in 2010 and is set out in Directive 2011/64/EU. For cigarettes, countries must apply a specific excise tax per thousand cigarettes and must apply an *ad valorem* excise tax with the retail selling price as the tax base. In addition, countries have the option to apply a minimum excise tax (MET). Finally, all member states must apply value added tax (VAT) on cigarettes.

In addition to the excise tax structure, the EU also established requirements for excise tax levels:

- The excise tax incidence must be a minimum of 60 percent, based on the Weighted Average Price (WAP)

    o   Where the nominal excise tax amount is greater than Euro 115 per thousand cigarettes, again based on the WAP, countries need not respect this minimum excise incidence requirement.

- The minimum excise tax yield for all cigarettes is Euro 90 per thousand cigarettes

- The specific to total tax ratio, calculated on the WAP, must be between 7.5 percent and 76.5 percent

For other manufactured tobacco products, the EU allows countries more freedom with respect to tax structure: it can be specific, *ad valorem*, or a mix of specific and *ad valorem*. Furthermore, countries may apply a minimum excise tax also for these other categories. In terms of the excise tax levels, the EU has established the following minimum rates in Table 25:

Table 25

EU Requirements on Other Tobacco Products

Year	Excise Incidence (percent of WAP)	or	Excise Yield (€/kg)	Other Requirements
	Fine-cut			
2013	43%		> 47	
2015	46%		> 54	
2018	48%		> 60	
2020	50%		> 60	
	Other smoking tobacco (pipe)			
	20%		> 22	Cut width 1.5 mm
	Cigars and cigarillos			
	5%		> 12	Old "Filter cigarillos" taxed as cigarettes

Source: Directive 2010/12/EU

With respect to fine-cut tobacco, the EU has recognized that the excise tax levels on this tobacco category need to be increased to help reduce the tax gaps with cigarettes and it has taken a gradual approach to increase the minimum excise tax levels over a number of years. For "other smoking tobacco" or pipe tobacco the minimum excise tax levels are substantially lower than for fine-cut, recognizing that these are separate sub-categories of tobacco with differences in tax-bearing capacity. Finally for the cigars and cigarillos the minimum excise tax requirements are substantially lower than the other tobacco categories.

The different minimum excise tax levels required on the four EU tobacco categories highlights the need for clear product definitions in order to ensure that all products are classified correctly and pay the correct tax.

In addition to the EU, two other examples of formal coordinated tobacco tax policy are the Gulf Cooperation Council (GCC) and in the South African Customs Union (SACU).

In the GCC, the member countries apply a high level of import duties (in the absence of excise duties) at the rate of cost, insurance and freight (CIF) price on imported cigarettes, with a minimum specific import duty set in local currency, see Table 26 below.

Table 26

Tobacco Import Duty Rates in GCC Countries

Country	Duty regime	Duty rates (local currency per 1,000 cigarettes)
Bahrain	Import duty	100% of CIF, min. 10 dinar
Qatar	Import duty	100% of CIF, min. 100 riyal
Kuwait	Import duty	100% of CIF, min. 8 dinar
Oman	Import duty	100% of CIF, min. 10 rial
Saudi Arabia	Import duty	100% of CIF, min. 10 riyal
UAE	Import duty	100% of CIF, min. 100 dirham

In the Southern African Customs Union (SACU), which includes Botswana, Lesotho, Namibia, South Africa and Swaziland, there is a harmonized specific excise tax for cigarettes, currently set at 546 rand per thousand cigarettes.

B. Voluntary International Taxation

While an apparent contradiction in terms, several examples of voluntary international taxes exist—the important distinction being that they are voluntary at the national country level, rather than the individual level. Below, we describe several examples of such taxes, either already in place or being proposed. What is especially interesting is that, in addition to being international voluntary taxation, these taxes also tend to be earmarked for international programs.

1. AIR-TICKET LEVY

Since 2006, nine nations have implemented an airline ticket levy: Cameroon, Chile, Congo, France, Madagascar, Mali, Mauritius, Niger and the Republic of Korea. A surcharge (ranging from $1 to $40 per ticket) is paid to UNITAID and the International Finance Facility for Immunisation (IFFIm) to fund international health development, focusing on the eradication of HIV / AIDS, malaria, and tuberculosis.[154] While there were initial concerns that such a levy would adversely affect the French travel and tourism sector, the French National Assembly termed the tax "a French success"[155]—despite persistent criticisms of lower than anticipated revenues, deliberately opaque implementation, and rapidly increasing administrative costs. To address these claims in turn: first, the *Cour des Comptes*[156] indicated that revenues have been lower than anticipated, potentially due to similarly-underestimated price elasticity of demand for airline travel.[157] Secondly, the plurality and complexity of taxes and fees on air travel rendered the surcharge "invisible"—those paying the fee have been unaware of its existence, and unable to voice their opposition. Lastly, IFFIm's operating costs increased by 16 percent in 2007, 19 percent in 2008, and 92 percent in 2009; average remuneration per employee had increased to €160,000 in 2009, which reached €199,000 when training, representation, and travel costs were included.[158]

At the most basic level, the source of funding for the Air-ticket Levy is fundamentally disconnected from the recipients of the funds, violating one of the principle tenants of taxation efficiency, not to mention the plurality of issues discussed previously.

2. SOLIDARITY TOBACCO CONTRIBUTION

In 2009, the High Level Taskforce on Innovative Financing for Health Systems proposed the Solidarity Tobacco Contribution (STC) in order to *"expand the mandatory solidarity levy on airline tickets and explore the technical viability of other solidarity levies on tobacco and currency transactions"*.[159] Building on this idea in 2011, the WHO further recommended that a voluntary[160] STC be imposed on tobacco products for the purpose of funding international health development goals.[161] Moreover, the WHO articulates that the STC should not be designed to replace existing national excise taxes on tobacco products, but rather, should be in addition to such taxes. The suggested micro-levy is $0.01 to $0.05 per pack of cigarettes,[162] which the WHO estimates would generate at least $5.5 billion annually if all EU and G-20+ countries were to adopt this proposal.

Although furthering the cause for international health development is a laudable goal, the STC is not only an international redistribution scheme, but it would also likely further aggravate the negative consequences some countries have faced as a result of increasing excise taxes on tobacco—such as illicit trade and regressivity. Imposing a levy in countries already facing high excise tax levels, reduced affordability, and a strong illicit trade presence[163] will further worsen illicit trade conditions and will thus negatively impact government excise tax revenues.[164] Furthermore, regressivity will be exacerbated by additional excise tax increases in countries where individuals in lower income brackets are a large proportion of the smoking population. Moreover, if smokers tend to be lower income individuals, the STC will essentially redistribute what little wealth those individuals have to other lower income individuals—which is not only counterproductive, but highly regressive to those burdened by the tax.

Additionally, since the STC is essentially an international earmarked tax, it suffers from the same drawbacks of earmarked taxes in general, which is mainly the lack of relationship between the taxpayer and the service being provided,[165] as well as the rigidity it poses to government budget reviews (such as in South Korea).[166] Furthermore, internationally agreed upon taxes pose additional inflexibility and bureaucracy since changes must be approved by various national governments.

Perhaps the weakest aspect of the WHO proposal is that it not only removes billions of dollars from consumers and national governments, but it is also designed such that the beneficiaries of the tax funds are not those burdened by the tax. Furthermore, there is very little political recourse for consumers burdened by this additional tax since it is levied and managed by an international organization, which does not have to answer to the constituents of the member-states. For instance, consumers cannot vote on these international proposals or elect the governing officials of these international bodies, indicating that the spending of these proposed tax revenues will lack public oversight by the citizens contributing to the fund.

3. WHO TOBACCO EXCISE TARGET

As discussed in Part I of this book, the WHO Tobacco Tax Manual recommends that countries ensure that tobacco excise taxes represent at least 70 percent of the retail price. The recommendation of the WHO is driven from non-economic objectives, which have been developed without consideration for existing fiscal policy. In fact, the data that is used by the WHO Technical Manual shows that excise duty exceeded 70 percent of the most popular price category (MPPC) in only 9 of the 183 countries in 2008—Bulgaria, Brunei Darussalam, Cuba, Fiji, Myanmar, Poland, Seychelles, Slovakia, and Venezuela. However, based on current information, the excise incidence in Bulgaria, Myanmar, Poland, Slovakia, and Venezuela is below 70 percent, leaving only 4 countries in the world that exceed an excise incidence of 70 percent. Of these 4 countries, 3 have a population of less than half a million people (Brunei Darussalam, Fiji, and Seychelles) and 2 are isolated islands (Fiji and Seychelles).

As demonstrated in more detail in Section XIV, "Comparing Excise Tax Levels Internationally", the excise tax incidence is not an appropriate reference to use as a reference benchmark, as there is no relationship between the excise tax incidence level and the monetary amount of excise tax which a consumer must pay. Norway has a high excise tax yield of $393 per 1000 cigarettes, while the excise tax incidence is 48.3 percent. And conversely, Bulgaria has an excise tax yield of $112 per 1000 cigarettes, while its excise tax incidence is 62.6 percent—again, highlighting the fact that "one size does not fit all" when it comes to setting excise tax levels.

A major drawback of focusing solely on the excise tax incidence is that it does not take into account other taxes applied on tobacco products, such a VAT/GST, which in some countries are 0 percent, such as Hong Kong, or can be as high as 27 percent, as is the case of Hungary. These other taxes have a significant impact on the magnitudes of the retail price increases required to reach the 70 percent excise tax incidence, as recommended by the WHO, if it were ever to be adopted as a global benchmark.

Using the UBS country sample, if these countries adopted the 70 percent excise tax incidence, the average retail price would increase from $5.66 per pack to $11.71 per pack or by $6.04 per pack, an increase of 107 percent. Furthermore, the monetary gap between the retail price of the lowest and highest priced countries would increase from the current amount of $15.15 per pack between the Philippines and Norway, to $49.44 per pack if all countries adopted the 70 percent excise incidence, as suggested by the WHO and demonstrated in Table 27 below. Moreover, in Brazil given the other taxes that are applied on cigarettes, it would not be technically possible to reach the 70 percent excise tax incidence proposed by the WHO.

We already described the theoretical reasons to refrain from applying a one-size-fits-all approach to tobacco taxes, and more specifically, reasons why excise incidence is not a good way to compare taxes internationally. By simulating the impact of a global minimum excise incidence of 70%, it becomes even more clear that this WHO recommendation is far from best practice: it would lead to draconian and arbitrary tax increases in almost every country, and at the same time more than triple tax and price differences between countries, providing further incentives for illicit trade.

Table 27

Impact of 70 Percent Excise Tax Incidence

Country (lowest to highest Income)	Current situation RSP US$/pack*	70% Excise tax incidence RSP US$/pack**	RSP Increase US$/pack	%
India	2.42	9.88	7.46	309%
Philippines	1.15	2.16	1.02	88%
Egypt	2.23	3.11	0.89	40%
Indonesia	1.27	3.08	1.81	143%
Ukraine	1.88	7.19	5.31	282%
Thailand	2.75	4.42	1.67	61%
China	2.48	8.00	5.53	223%
Peru	2.68	12.02	9.34	348%
Bulgaria	3.58	5.57	1.99	55%
Colombia	1.86	4.56	2.69	144%
South Africa	3.00	8.98	5.98	199%
Romania	4.46	10.30	5.84	131%
Mexico	3.45	6.63	3.18	92%
Malaysia	3.66	7.39	3.73	102%
Brazil***	2.83	Not feasible***	-	-
Argentina	1.76	4.34	2.58	147%
Turkey	4.42	5.44	1.01	23%

Venezuela	6.36	6.87	0.51	8%
Latvia	4.29	8.03	3.74	87%
Lithuania	3.91	8.48	4.57	117%
Poland	4.51	7.77	3.26	72%
Hungary	4.87	13.37	8.50	174%
Russia	2.53	9.76	7.23	286%
Chile	4.95	6.88	1.93	39%
Estonia	4.79	8.18	3.39	71%
Slovakia	4.90	9.96	5.06	103%
Czech Rep.	4.48	10.24	5.76	129%
Portugal	5.89	12.00	6.11	104%
Greece	5.34	8.98	3.64	68%
Taiwan	2.85	6.53	3.68	129%
Slovenia	5.07	10.52	5.45	108%
Bahrain	2.39	5.09	2.70	113%
South Korea	2.55	5.12	2.56	100%
Cyprus	6.16	11.24	5.08	82%
Spain	6.51	11.06	4.56	70%
Israel	8.64	11.63	2.99	35%
Italy	6.85	13.82	6.97	102%
Hong Kong	6.45	6.83	0.38	6%
Japan	4.18	6.56	2.38	57%
New Zealand	14.75	22.93	8.18	55%
UK	13.70	24.88	11.18	82%
Germany	7.50	14.48	6.99	93%
France	9.59	14.17	4.58	48%
UAE	2.45	5.89	3.44	140%
Netherlands	8.65	18.13	9.48	110%
Belgium	7.93	15.11	7.18	90%
Ireland	13.01	24.95	11.94	92%
Finland	7.67	13.44	5.77	75%
Austria	6.44	12.77	6.33	98%
Canada	9.34	19.54	10.20	109%
Denmark	8.12	20.50	12.38	153%
Sweden	9.15	28.52	19.37	212%
Australia	15.57	33.52	17.95	115%
Switzerland	9.20	15.51	6.31	69%
Qatar	2.47	5.20	2.73	110%
Norway	16.30	51.61	35.31	217%
Luxembourg	6.71	12.54	5.83	87%
Highest	$16.30	$51.61		
Average	$5.66	$11.71	$6.04	107%
Lowest	$1.15	$2.16		
Gap: High vs Low $/pack	$15.15	$49.44		

* Based on January 2014 excise tax rates and the Retail Selling Price of Marlboro (except for Canada - Benson & Hedges); RSPs are per pack of 20 cigarettes. Exchange rates January 2014. Bloomberg
** The Retail Selling Price(RSP) under the 70 percent excise tax incidence is based solely on the assumption that the excise tax incidence increases from the current level to 70 percent and that the pre-tax price has been held constant
***Given that the current other than excise effective ad valorem rates plus VAT are already over 30 percent, a 70 percent excise rate is not feasible

XVI. CONCLUSIONS

Four key elements must be in place for an efficient and effective tobacco excise tax system. First, clear and precise tobacco product definitions are required to prevent tax loopholes. These product definitions need to be updated over time in response to product developments.

Second, robust, simple excise tax structures are required to ensure that similar tobacco products are treated on an equal basis. From a government tax revenue stance, the excise tax structure should support stable and predictable collection, while ensuring that excise tax increases translate into commensurate government tax revenue increases. While there are a vast array of tax structures applied internationally, from a pure tax revenue point of view, specific tax structures ensure that all tobacco products within a category (e.g., all cigarettes) will pay the same amount of excise tax. A tax structure that is specific, or has a large specific component, thus reduces the incentive for consumers to down-trade to lower taxed products, and isolates government revenues from pricing initiatives by tobacco companies. There is a global trend towards both simpler and more specific tax systems. The EU, for instance, has changed its excise tax Directive to increase the size of the specific tax element that member states can apply, and several EU countries have followed by changing their domestic tax system in this direction. Outside of the EU, specific excise tax structures are applied in many of the leading global economies, including the U.S., Canada, South Africa, Japan, South Korea, and Australia.

Third, the correct excise tax level must be applied to each tobacco category. In many instances, the price elasticity for cigarette demand is low, but this can change in response to large tax increases or changes in macroeconomic factors, such as rising unemployment or declining consumer income levels. As many countries have experienced, and as is supported by the Laffer Curve, there is a point at which further tax increases will not result in increases in government tax revenues. When tax levels become too high, some consumers will stop or reduce consumption, whilst others will down-trade to lower taxed products or to non-taxed illicit tobacco products. While the net effect of these tax increases may still be positive from a public health perspective, it certainly will not be positive from a tax revenue perspective, and there may well be other, more effective ways to reduce the harms from tobacco consumption.

Finally, the excise tax system needs to be supported by good tax administration and collection systems, such that the collection of the excise tax revenue by the customs officials is efficient and should not be unnecessarily burdensome on the tobacco manufacturers or importers. There should be a proper legal framework that provides a balance between the tax rights of taxpayers and the powers of the tax agency. In countries that use tax stamps or fiscal markers, these systems should not add unnecessary costs, but instead, improve tax collection in a cost effective manner. New digital fiscal marking systems are being developed, and countries may want to consider these options to modernize and improve their tax collection systems. In the same vein, countries need fair and effective anti-forestalling regulations to ensure that tax increases are passed on to consumers in a timely manner and that government tax revenues increase systematically as a result. Overall, the tax administration system should be as simple as possible in order to facilitate the efficient payment of tobacco taxes by all manufacturers and importers. In addition, the customs authorities need effective regulation, as well as the tools and resources to enforce these regulations, thus ensuring that the correct taxes are being paid by all parties concerned.

Although earmarked taxes are applied in several countries across the globe, economists, especially those in public finance, are in agreement that, fundamentally, earmarked taxes represent poor economic policy. Earmarking can lead to the misallocation of resources, where too much funding is given to activities designated to receive earmarked tax revenues and where too little funding to other, more urgently needed activities is provided. Earmarking can also hinder budget efficiency, as well as encroach upon the minister of finance's authority, who should have control over the allocation of scarce resources in order to determine the most appropriate manner to achieve national public policy.

Finally, given recent discussions on international tobacco taxation, it remains of interest to find a way to objectively compare tax levels across countries. Three commonly used approaches were investigated: (1) comparing excise tax incidence, which expresses taxes as a percentage of the consumer retail price; (2) comparing monetary excise tax levels, in a common currency per pack of cigarettes; or, (3) comparing excise tax levels, while taking into account domestic income levels.

We demonstrated that the excise tax incidence is a meaningless way of comparing tax levels internationally. A better alternative, at least for international benchmarking purposes, is a comparison of excise levels that are corrected for the differences in per capita consumption of each country. Such a measure will allow an assessment of the domestic affordability of excise taxes on tobacco products, and thus provide a reasonable point of reference (but certainly not a technocratic rule) for domestic tobacco tax policy.

Endnotes: Part I

1   Cnossen, S. (1977), *Excise Systems: A Global Study of the Selective Taxation of Goods and Services*

2   Smith, A. (1776) *The Wealth of Nations.*

3   Adam Smith's notion of the natural wage rate of laborers is approximately the wage that is equivalent to the produce of labor.

4.   Smith, A. (1776), *The Wealth of Nations.*

5   Dupuit, J. (1844), On the Measurement of Utility from Public Works

6   Dupuit, J. (1844), On the Measurement of Utility from Public Works

7   Smith, A. (1776), *The Wealth of Nations*

8   Hamilton, A. (1788), *The Federalist Papers*

9   Ramsey, F. (1927), *A Contribution to the Theory of Taxation*

10   Various elasticities of demand are discussed more in-depth in the next section, "Elasticity of Demand".

11   The story of how the Laffer Curve got its name isn't one of the Just So Stories by Rudyard Kipling. It began with a 1978 article published by Jude Wanniski in The Public Interest entitled, "Taxes, Revenues, and the 'Laffer Curve.'" As recounted by Wanniski (associate editor of the Wall Street Journal at the time), in December of 1974 he had been invited to have dinner with me (then professor at the University of

Chicago), Don Rumsfeld (chief of staff to President Gerald Ford) and Dick Cheney (Rumsfeld's deputy and my former classmate at Yale) at the Two Continents Restaurant at the Washington Hotel in Washington, D.C. (just across the street from the Treasury). While discussing President Ford's "WIN" (Whip Inflation Now) proposal for tax increases, I supposedly grabbed my napkin and a pen and sketched a curve on the napkin illustrating the trade off between tax rates and tax revenues. Wanniski named the trade off "The Laffer Curve." The Laffer Curve, by the way, was not invented by me; it has its origins way back in time. For example, the writings of 14th century Muslim philosopher Ibn Khaldun, Adam Smith, and John Maynard Keynes all make mention of the potential for lower tax receipts at higher tax rates.

12   Arthur B. Laffer, "The Laffer Curve: Past, Present and Future" Laffer Associates, January 6, 2004

13   Arthur Pigou (1920) *The Economics of Welfare*

14   Baumal, Oates (1971), *The Use of Standards and Prices for Protection of the Environment*

15   Ronald Coase (1960), *The Problem of Social Cost*

16   Buchanan, Stubblebine (1962), *Externality*

17   Davis, Whinston (1962), *Externalities, Welfare, and the Theory of Games*

18   Buchanan (1969), *External Diseconomies, Corrective Taxes, and Market Structure*

19   This is due to the fact that the price elasticity of demand often fluctuates over time as well as in the short and long run. Furthermore, the design of this model implies a positive relationship between the excise tax rate and government excise tax revenues, which is invalid; therefore, demand estimates from a double log specification should not be used as inputs when determining the optimal excise tax rate.

20   Becker, Murphy (1988), *A Theory of Rational Addiction*

21   Gruber, Koszegi (2000), *Is Addiction "Rational"? Theory and Evidence*

22   Gruber, Koszegi (2008), *A Modern Economic View of Tobacco Taxation*

23 Campaign for Tobacco-Free Kids (2013), State Cigarette Excise Tax Rates and Rankings, http://www.tobaccofreekids.org/research/factsheets/pdf/0097.pdf

24 That is, whether the tax system optimizes government tax revenue in order to finance public expenditure costs.

25 Stiglitz, J. (2000), *Economics of the Public Sector*

26 This topic is covered in depth in Section II.

27 Gallet, C. and John List (2003), *Cigarette Demand: A Meta-Analysis of Elasticities*

28 Merriman, D., Economics of Tobacco Toolkit Design and Administer Tobacco Taxes, Tool 7. Smuggling. World Bank.

29 The Laffer Curve is covered in depth in Part I, Section III.

30 Evans, Farrelly (1998) *The Compensating Behavior of Smokers: Taxes, Tar, and Nicotine*

31 Farrelly, M., Nimsch, Hyland, A., and M. Cummings (2004) The Effects of Higher Cigarette Prices on Tar and Nicotine Consumption in a Cohort of Adult Smokers

32 Harris, J. (1980), *Taxing Tar and Nicotine*

33 HM Revenue & Custom (2013), "Progress in tackling tobacco smuggling", June 6, 2013.

34 Stiglitz, J. (2000), *Economics of the Public Sector*

35 Chassin, Y. and P. Lemieux (2013), *Why New International Taxes for Development are Inefficient.*

36 Australia's Future Tax System (2009) Final Report: Detailed Analysis http://taxreview.treasury.gov.au/content/FinalReport.aspx?doc=html/Publications/Papers/Final_Report_Part_2/Chapter_e6.htm; Australian Taxation Office (2013), Excise and excise-equivalent customs duty - index tobacco excise to average weekly ordinary time earnings. https://www.ato.gov.au/General/New-legislation/In-detail/Indirect-taxes/Excise/Excise-and-excise-equivalent-customs-duty---index-tobacco-excise-to-average-weekly-ordinary-time-earnings/

37 Stiglitz, J. (2000), *Economics of the Public Sector*

38 Philip Morris International (2013), *ITS&P Barometer: Argentina 2013*

39 Since the price elasticity of demand depends on the relative change between two points rather than the change relative to the average, the "arc" price elasticity of demand is often calculated in order to eliminate this asymmetrical characteristic. However, most researchers specify demand with more advanced econometric techniques, which were reviewed in Section I.

40 Ohsfeldt RL, Boyle RG, Capilouto E. (1997) *Tobacco taxes, smoking, restrictions and tobacco use;* Tsai YW, Yang CL, Chen CS, Liu TC, Chen PF. (2005) The effect of Taiwan's tax-induced increases in cigarette prices on brand-switching and the consumption of cigarettes.

41 I.e., cigarettes purchased legally outside of Ireland and brought into the country, or cigarettes produced in or smuggled into Ireland and purchased illegally.

42 Reidy, P. and K. Walsh (2011), *Economics of Tobacco: Modelling the Market for Cigarettes in Ireland.*

43 Reidy, P. and K. Walsh (2011), *Economics of Tobacco: Modelling the Market for Cigarettes in Ireland.*

44 "Other tobacco products" include roll your own, cigarillos, cigars, etc. Many of these other tobacco products are often taxed to a lesser degree than manufactured cigarettes, inducing substitution effects.

45 KPMG (2013), Project Star 2012 Results

46 KPMG (2013), Project Star 2012 Results

47 For example, by taxing all substitutable products equally, or by applying a specific tax system within each tobacco category.

48 Chaloupka, Warner (1999), *The Economics of Smoking*

49 Chaloupka, Hu, Warner, Jacobs, and Yurekli (2000) *The Taxation of Tobacco Products*

50 Reidy, Walsh (2011) *Economics of Tobacco—Modeling the Market for Cigarettes in Ireland*

51 KPMG (2013), Project Star 2012 Results

52 Czubek, M. and S. Johal (2010), *Econometric Analysis of Cigarette Consumption in the UK*

53 Chaloupka, F., Hu, T., Warner, K., Jacobs, R., and A. Yurekli

(2000), The Taxation of Tobacco Products.

54   Officially, "convex adjustment costs".

55   In economics literature, this is referred to as "excess smoothness", as consumption is smoother (e.g., less volatile) than the Permanent Income Hypothesis would predict.

56   In economics, stickiness refers to something that is rigid or resistant to change—consumption, prices, wages, and demand for particular goods are examples where rigidity can become present.

57   Gallet, List (2003) Cigarette Demand: A Meta-Analysis of Elasticities

58   Chaloupka, F., Hu, T., Warner, K., Jacobs, R., and A. Yurekli (2000), *The Taxation of Tobacco Products.*

59   Gospodinov, Irvine (2005)) A 'Long March' Perspective on Tobacco Use in Canada

60   Hu, T. and Z. Mao (2000), Economic Analysis of Tobacco and Opinions for Tobacco Control: China Case Study

61   Wilkins, N., Yurekli, A., and T. Hu. *World Bank Economics of Tobacco Toolkit: Tool 3 Demand Analaysis. Economic Analysis of Tobacco Demand.*

62   Wilkins, N., Yurekli, A., and T. Hu. *World Bank Economics of Tobacco Toolkit: Tool 3 Demand Analaysis. Economic Analysis of Tobacco Demand.*

63   Gallet, List (2003) Cigarette Demand: A Meta-Analysis of Elasticities

64   Deaton, Muellbauer (1980) *An Almost Ideal Demand System*

65   Gallet, List (2003) Cigarette Demand: A Meta-Analysis of Elasticities

66   Affordability is measured here as PRI, or price relative to income. The price of 100 packs of cigarettes is divided by nominal GDP per capita—therefore, higher values of PRI indicate reduced affordability. Section V covers the various affordability measures in depth.

67   Gallet, List (2003) Cigarette Demand: A Meta-Analysis of Elasticities

68   Individual level data is less likely to produce potential simul-
      taneity bias since the smoking decisions of one individual will
      not affect the overall market prices for cigarettes.

69   Or if data points are obtained from other supply and demand
      curves

70   Wilkins, N., Yurekli, A., and T. Hu. *World Bank Economics of
      Tobacco Toolkit: Tool 3 Demand Analaysis. Economic Analysis of
      Tobacco Demand.*

71   An instrumental variable is simply another independent vari-
      able that is highly correlated with price (in this instance) but
      not correlated with the error terms (i.e. it won't cause simulta-
      neity).

72   Barnett, P., Keeler, T., and T. Hu (1995), *Oligopoly Structure
      and the Incidence of Cigarette Excise Taxes*

73   Huang, B., Yang, C., Hwang, M. (2004), *New Evidence on De-
      mand for Cigarettes: A Panel Data Approach.*

74   Trussler, Meschi (2011) *Review of Economic Literature on To-
      bacco*

75   Da Pra, Arnade (2009) Tobacco Product Demand, Cigarette
      Taxes, and Market Substitution

76   Da Pra and Arnade include both large cigars and cigarillos in
      their cigar category.

77   Da Pra, Arnade (2009) Tobacco Product Demand, Cigarette
      Taxes, and Market Substitution

78   This table is reproduced from Da Pra and Arnade's study. Es-
      timates highlighted in yellow indicate a complementary rela-
      tionship with cigarettes, while estimates highlighted in blue
      indicate that the two goods are substitutes.

79   Tait, P., Rutherford P., and C. Saunders (2013), Do Consum-
      ers of Manufactured Cigarettes Respond Differently to Price
      Changes Compared with their Roll-Your-Own Counterparts?
      Evidence from New Zealand.

80   Tait, P., Rutherford P., and C. Saunders (2013), Do Consum-
      ers of Manufactured Cigarettes Respond Differently to Price
      Changes Compared with their Roll-Your-Own Counterparts?
      Evidence from New Zealand.

81   Nguyen, L., Rosenqvist, G., and Pekurinen, M. (2012), Demand for Tobacco in Europe. An Econometric Analysis of 11 Countries for the PPACTE Project.

82   Cullum, P. and C. Pissarides. (2004), The Demand for Tobacco Products in the UK

83   Where manufactured cigarette price is the numerator and hand rolled cigarette price is the denominator.

84   Mindell, J. and D. Whynes (2000), Cigarette Consumption in the Netherlands 1970-1995.

85   Gruber, J., Sen, A., and M. Stabile (2003) Estimating Price Elasticities when there is Smuggling: The Sensitivity of Smoking to Price in Canada

86   No statistically significant results were found for the effect of alcohol prices on tobacco consumption.

87   Bask, Melkersson (2004) Rationally Addicted to Drinking and Smoking

88   Holding the consumption bundle constant (i.e., ignoring substitution effects).

89   The majority of studies which return positive income elasticities of demand were conducted in the U.S., but also include countries such as Finland, Taiwan, Japan, and Papua New Guinea.

90   Gallet, List (2003) Cigarette Demand: A Meta-Analysis of Elasticities

91   Gospondinov, Irvine (2005) A "Long March" Perspective on Tobacco Use in Canada

92   Duffy, M. (2006), Tobacco Consumption and Policy in the United Kingdom

93   Cheng, K.W. and D.S. Kenkel (2010), U.S. Cigarette Demand: 1944-2004

94   Hu, Wilkins, and Yurelki (2005) Economic Analysis of Tobacco Demand

95   Tait, P., Rutherford, P., and C. Saunders. (2013), Do Consumers of Manufactured Cigarettes Respond Differently to Price Changes Compared with their Roll-Your-Own Counterparts? Evidence from New Zealand.

96 Nguyen, L., Rosenqvist, G., and M. Pekurinen. (2012), Demand for Tobacco in Europe An Econometric Analysis of 11 Countries for the PPACTE Project

97 GDP is collected through the World Bank's World Development Indicators: (http://data.worldbank.org/indicator/NY.GDP.MKTP.KD.ZG/countries/1W?page=1&display=default)

98 Inflation is collected through the World Bank's World Development Indicators: (http://data.worldbank.org/indicator/FP.CPI.TOTL.ZG?display=default)

99 Release for Consumption of Cigarettes data is collected from the European Commission Releases for Consumption of Cigarettes table: (http://ec.europa.eu/taxation_customs/resources/documents/taxation/excise_duties/tobacco_products/rates/tobacco_releases_consumption.pdf)

100 Cigarette Government Tax Revenue is collected from the European Commission Excise Duty Tables on Tax Receipts for Manufactured Tobacco: (http://ec.europa.eu/taxation_customs/resources/documents/taxation/excise_duties/tobacco_products/rates/excise_duties_tobacco_en.pdf)

101 One important point should be made here however, which is that the type of tobacco products can change as income rises—poorer individuals may consume loose tobacco initially, and then switch to machine manufactured cigarettes as income rises.

102 OECD data, accessed January 9th, 2014.

103 Cnossen, S. (2005), *Theory and Practice of Excise Taxation: Smoking, Drinking, Gambling, Polluting, and Driving*

104 Puller, Greening (1999) Household Adjustment to Gasoline Price Change: An Analysis Using 9 Years of US Survey Data

105 Gallet (2007) The Demand for Alcohol: A Meta-Analysis of Elasticities

106 Andreyeva, Long (2010) The Impact of Food Prices on Consumption: A Systematic Review of Research on the Price Elasticity of Demand for Food

107 Cnossen (2006) *Tobacco Taxation in the European Union*

108 The US food and beverage data is from Andreyeva, Long

(2010) The Impact of Food Prices on Consumption: A Systematic Review of Research on the Price Elasticity of Demand for Food. Alcohol data for the US is estimated from Grossman, Chaloupka, and Sirtalan (1995) "An Empirical Analysis of Alcohol Addiction: Results from the Monitoring the Future Panels".

109 The UK food and beverage data is from Lechene, V. (2000) Chapter 6: Income and Price Elasticities of Demand for Foods Consumed in the Home, National Food Survey: 2000. Oil data is from Cooper, J. (2003) "Price Elasticity of Demand for Crude Oil: Estimates for 23 Countries". Alcohol data for the UK is estimated by Collis, J., Grayson, A., and S. Johal (2010) "Econometric Analysis of Alcohol Consumption in the UK".

110 The Chinese Food data is from Hsu, H.H., Chern,W., and F. Gale (2001) How Will Rising Income Affect the Structure of Food Demand? Chinese alcohol data is from Tian, G. and L. Feng (2011), Is the Demand for Alcoholic Beverages in Developing Countries Sensitive to Price? Evidence from China. Chinese data for gasoline is from Lin, C. and J. Zeng (2013) The Elasticity of Demand for Gasoline in China.

111 India's food estimates are from Kumar et al. (2011), "Estimation of Demand Elasticity for Food Commodities in India". Alcohol estimates for India are from John, R. (2005) Price Elasticity Estimates for Tobacco and Other Addictive Goods in India. Gasoline estimates are from Ramanathan, R. (1999) Short- and Long-Run Elasticities of Gasoline Demand in India: An Empirical Analysis using Cointegration Techniques

112 The current EU minimum level is €90 per 1000 cigarettes.

113 International Tax & Investment Center (2012), The Impact of Imposing a Global Excise Target for Cigarettes: Experience from the EU Accession Countries

114 Named for the 20th century British economist, Arthur Pigou

115 In addition to a perfectly competitive market, it also requires full knowledge of market clearing prices and the marginal social cost of the externality.

116 Ronald Coase (1960), *The Problem of Social Cost*

117 Manning, W.G. et al (1989), The Taxes of Sin: Do Smokers and Drinkers Pay Their Way?

118 Gruber, Koszegi (2002), A Theory of Government Regulation of Addictive Bads: Optimal Tax Levels and Tax Incidence for Cigarette Excise Taxation

119 Gruber (2001), Tobacco at the Crossroads: The Past and Future of Smoking Regulation in the U.S. ; Gruber, Koszegi (2002), A Theory of Government Regulation of Addictive Bads: Optimal Tax Levels and Tax Incidence for Cigarette Excise Taxation

120 Bhagwati (1969), *The Generalized Theory of Distortions and Welfare*

121 Mundell (1960), *The Pure Theory of International Trade*

122 The World Bank (2012 data), Labor Tax and Contributions (% of Commercial Profits), http://data.worldbank.org/indicator/IC.TAX.LABR.CP.ZS?order=wbapi_data_value_2012+wbapi_data_value+wbapi_data_value-first&sort=asc

123 The World Bank (2011), Tariff Rate, Applied, Weight Mean, All Products (%). This is the average of effectively applied rates weighted by the product import shares corresponding to each partner country: http://data.worldbank.org/indicator/TM.TAX.MRCH.WM.AR.ZS?order=wbapi_data_value_2011+wbapi_data_value&sort=asc

124 A trade imbalance could be created if foreign producers have a monopoly power in trade

125 Office of the U.S. Trade Representative (March 5, 2002), "Background Information"

126 Francois, Baughman for the CITAC Foundation (February 2003), The Unintended Consequences of U.S. Steel Import Tariffs: A Quantification of the Impact During 2002.

127 Bureau of Labor Statistics (2002), Covered Employment and Statistics Survey, Total Employment, Not Seasonally Adjusted

128 IMF, Government Financial Statistics Yearbook and Data Files (2011), Taxes on Goods and Services (% of Revenue). This is defined as the taxes on goods and services that include general sales and turnover or value added taxes, selective excises on goods, selective taxes on services, taxes on the use of goods or property, taxes on extraction and production of min-

erals, and profits of fiscal monopolies. http://data.worldbank.
org/indicator/GC.TAX.GSRV.RV.ZS?order=wbapi_data_
value_2011+wbapi_data_value&sort=asc

129 Bhagwati (1969), *The Generalized Theory of Distortions and
Welfare*

130 Bhagwati (1969), *The Generalized Theory of Distortions and
Welfare*

131 Technical efficiency occurs when firms are maximizing output
such that it is not possible to increase the level of output given
the same level of inputs, or produce the same level of output
but at a smaller level of inputs.

132 Bhagwati (1969), *The Generalized Theory of Distortions and
Welfare*

133 The economic tax incidence should not be confused with total
or excise tax incidence, which this book will address in subse-
quence sections. The economic tax incidence, as it relates to
this subsection, is the supply and demand effects that result in
the market for the taxed product.

134 The common currency chosen is often called the numeraire,
which is often U.S. dollars. The numeraire does not necessarily need to be a monetary currency; it could also be a good e.g.
Big Mac.

135 In fact, when using data from 1970 to 2006 for the U.S., Canada, and five OECD countries, Berka finds that the U.S. price
per kilogram weight ratio for cigarettes is nearly $100/kg,
which is quite high considering that of the 40 goods analyzed,
the average of this ratio is about $25/kg, with a median close
to $6/kg. Berka, M. (2009), Nonlinear Adjustment in Law of
One Price Deviations and Physical Characteristics of Goods

136 *The Economist* (2013), The Big Mac Index. http://www.econ-
omist.com/content/big-mac-index

137 This is calculated as the following: Percent Under or Overval-
ued=(($7.51/$4.56)-1)*100=64.69%

138 *The Economist* (2013), The Big Mac Index. http://www.econ-
omist.com/content/big-mac-index

139 Lal, A. and M. Scollo (2002), Big Mac Index of Cigarette
Affordability

140 Lal, A. and M. Scollo (2002), Big Mac Index of Cigarette Affordability

141 The price level is often thought of as a measurement for the cost of living.

142 Blecher, E. and C. van Walbeek (2008), An Analysis of Cigarette Affordability

143 Burkhauser, Richard; Larrimore, Jeff; and Simon, Kosali (2011). A "Second Opinion" on the Economic Health of the American Middle Class. http://www.nber.org/papers/w17164

144 An inferior good is one for which consumption decreases as income increases, and is characterized by negative estimates for income elasticity of demand.

145 Franks, P. et al (2007), Cigarette Prices, Smoking, and the Poor: Implications of Recent Trends

146 Franks, P. et al (2007), Cigarette Prices, Smoking, and the Poor: Implications of Recent Trends

147 Blecher, E. and C. van Walbeek (2004), An International Analysis of Cigarette Affordability

148 Median, rather than the mean, is preferred since it isn't biased by extreme values or outliers.

149 Cigarette price data is collected from the Economist Intelligence Unit (EIU), which provides data on the cost of living in about 140 cities in 93 countries.

150 The survey collects data on international prices and wages in 72 cities in 58 countries. UBS (2012), Prices and Earnings: A Comparison of Purchasing Power Around the Globe

151 The EIU, or the Economist Intelligence Unit, provides data on the cost of living in about 140 cities in 93 countries for a subscription fee.

152 Guindon, G.E., Tobin S., and D. Yach (2002), Trends and Affordability of Cigarette Prices: Ample Room for Tax Increases and Related Health Gains

153 Guindon, G.E., Tobin S., and D. Yach (2002), Trends and Affordability of Cigarette Prices: Ample Room for Tax Increases and Related Health Gains

154 UBS (2012), Prices and Earnings: A Comparison of Purchasing Power Around the Globe

155 Kan, M. (2007), Investigating Cigarette Affordability in 60 Cities Using the Cigarette Price-Daily Income Ratio

156 Kan, M. (2007), Investigating Cigarette Affordability in 60 Cities Using the Cigarette Price-Daily Income Ratio

157 The compounded growth rate is simply the following standard equation:The compounded growth rate is simply the following standard equation: $Y_t Y_t - 1 1/n - 1*100$, where Y is the affordability measurement at time t (e.g., PRI) and n is the number of time periods observed (e.g., number of years).

158 Guindon, G.E., Tobin S., and D. Yach (2002), Trends and Affordability of Cigarette Prices: Ample Room for Tax Increases and Related Health Gains

159 Smith (1776) *The Wealth of Nations.*

160 Stiglitz J. (2000), *Economics of the Public Sector.* 3rd edition.

161 Peck, R. (2011) *World Bank Economics of Tobacco Toolkit. Tool 6: Poverty. Equity Issues, Tobacco, and the Poor.*

162 This is especially true given the diminishing marginal utility of income.

163 Peck, R. (2011) *World Bank Economics of Tobacco Toolkit. Tool 6: Poverty. Equity Issues, Tobacco, and the Poor.*

164 Both sticky goods and inferior goods will also exhibit this characteristic.

165 In other words, general equilibrium effects are often not analyzed.

166 Peck, R. (2011) *World Bank Economics of Tobacco Toolkit. Tool 6: Poverty. Equity Issues, Tobacco, and the Poor,* p. 17

167 Farrelly, Matthew; Nonnemaker, James; and Watson, Kimberly (2012). The Consequences of High Cigarette Excise Taxes for Low-Income Smokers. http://www.plosone.org/article/info%3Adoi%2F10.1371%2Fjournal.pone.0043838

168 Farrelly, Matthew; Nonnemaker, James; and Watson, Kimberly (2012). The Consequences of High Cigarette Excise Taxes for Low-Income Smokers. http://www.plosone.org/article/info%3Adoi%2F10.1371%2Fjournal.pone.0043838

169 Farrelly, Matthew; Nonnemaker, James; and Watson, Kimberly (2012). The Consequences of High Cigarette Excise Taxes

for Low-Income Smokers. http://www.plosone.org/article/info%3Adoi%2F10.1371%2Fjournal.pone.0043838

170   Farrelly, Matthew; Nonnemaker, James; and Watson, Kimberly (2012). The Consequences of High Cigarette Excise Taxes for Low-Income Smokers. http://www.plosone.org/article/info%3Adoi%2F10.1371%2Fjournal.pone.0043838

171   Evans, Ringel, and Stech (1999), Tobacco Taxes and Public Policy to Discourage Smoking http://www.nber.org/chapters/c10920.pdf

172   Walque, D. (2004). Education, Information, and Smoking Decisions: Evidence from Smoking Histories, 1940-2000 https://www.aeaweb.org/assa/2006/0108_1300_0601.pdf

173   Walque, D. (2004). Education, Information, and Smoking Decisions: Evidence from Smoking Histories, 1940-2000 https://www.aeaweb.org/assa/2006/0108_1300_0601.pdf

174   Barbea, Elizabeth; Krieger, Nancy; and Soobader, Mah-Jabeen (2004). Working Class Matters: Socioeconomic Disadvantage, Race/Ethnicity, Gender, and Smoking in NHIS in 2000.

175   Barbea, Elizabeth; Krieger, Nancy; and Soobader, Mah-Jabeen (2004). Working Class Matters: Socioeconomic Disadvantage, Race/Ethnicity, Gender, and Smoking in NHIS in 2000.

176   Walque, D. (2004). Education, Information, and Smoking Decisions: Evidence from Smoking Histories, 1940-2000 https://www.aeaweb.org/assa/2006/0108_1300_0601.pdf

177   Consumption rates have plateaued for lower income consumers, despite continued real price increases in the final price of cigarette consumption.

178   Franks, P. et al (2007), Cigarette Prices, Smoking, and the Poor: Implications of Recent Trends

179   Franks, P. et al (2007), Cigarette Prices, Smoking, and the Poor: Implications of Recent Trends

180   Franks, P. et al (2007), Cigarette Prices, Smoking, and the Poor: Implications of Recent Trends

181   Franks, P. et al (2007), Cigarette Prices, Smoking, and the Poor: Implications of Recent Trends

182 Colman, Gergory and Remler, Dahlia (2008). Vertical Equity Consequences of Very High Cigarette Tax Increases: If the Poor Are the Ones Smoking, How Could Cigarette Tax Increases be Progressive?

183 Colman, Gergory and Remler, Dahlia (2008). Vertical Equity Consequences of Very High Cigarette Tax Increases: If the Poor Are the Ones Smoking, How Could Cigarette Tax Increases be Progressive?

184 Colman, Gergory and Remler, Dahlia (2008). Vertical Equity Consequences of Very High Cigarette Tax Increases: If the Poor Are the Ones Smoking, How Could Cigarette Tax Increases be Progressive?

185 Farrelly, Matthew; Nonnemaker, James; and Watson, Kimberly (2012). The Consequences of High Cigarette Excise Taxes for Low-Income Smokers. http://www.plosone.org/article/info%3Adoi%2F10.1371%2Fjournal.pone.0043838

186 Farrelly, Matthew; Nonnemaker, James; and Watson, Kimberly (2012). The Consequences of High Cigarette Excise Taxes for Low-Income Smokers. http://www.plosone.org/article/info%3Adoi%2F10.1371%2Fjournal.pone.0043838

187 Farrelly, Matthew; Nonnemaker, James; and Watson, Kimberly (2012). The Consequences of High Cigarette Excise Taxes for Low-Income Smokers. http://www.plosone.org/article/info%3Adoi%2F10.1371%2Fjournal.pone.0043838

188 Peretti-Watel et al. (2009). Cigarettes and social differentiation in France: is tobacco use increasingly concentrated among the poor?

189 Peretti-Watel et al. (2009). Cigarettes and social differentiation in France: is tobacco use increasingly concentrated among the poor? (p. 104)

190 Gospodinov, Nikolay and Irvine, Ian (2009). Tobacco Taxes and Regressivity.

191 Due to the prevalence of bidis as an alternative form of tobacco consumption in India, manufactured cigarettes serve as a form of conspicuous consumption, and, as such, one would expect high price elasticity estimates for middle-income groups.

192 Selvaraj, Sakthivel; Karan, Anup; and Srivastava, Swati (2013).

Price Elasticity of Tobacco Products among Quintile Groups in India, 2009-10

193 Although these are the two basic structures, they are not mutually exclusive, and may be combined in a number of ways. As described in more detail in Part II.

194 Yurekli, A. *World Bank Economics of Tobacco Toolkit. Tool 4: Design and Administration. Design and Administer Tobacco Taxes*

195 In the case of heterogeneous products, there would be multiple supply and demand curves, each with their own slope, intercept, and equilibria. The case of homogenous products is presented for simplicity.

196 This is of course assuming that the price of the taxed commodity (i.e. cigarettes) follows inflation. The issue of inflation with respect to tobacco excise taxes will be further addressed in later subsections.

197 Hu et al. (1988), Earmarked Tobacco Taxes: Lessons Learned

198 McCleary, W. (1989) The World Bank: Earmarking Government Revenues: Does it Work?

199 McCleary, W. (1989) The World Bank: Earmarking Government Revenues: Does it Work?

200 McCleary, W. (1989) The World Bank: Earmarking Government Revenues: Does it Work?

201 Deran (1965), Earmarking and Expenditures: A Survey and a New Test

202 McCleary, W. (1989) The World Bank: Earmarking Government Revenues: Does it Work?

203 McCleary (1991), The Earmarking of Government Revenue A Review of Some World Bank Experience

204 Keen, M. and Mooij, R. (2012) "Fiscal Devaluation" and Fiscal Consolidation: The VAT in Troubled Times

205 Yurekli, A. *World Bank Economics of Tobacco Toolkit. Tool 4: Design and Administration. Design and Administer Tobacco Taxes*

206 Keen, M. (2012) IMF Working Paper: Taxation and Development—Again

207 Yurekli, A. *World Bank Economics of Tobacco Toolkit. Tool 4: Design and Administration. Design and Administer Tobacco Taxes*

208 Yurekli, A. *World Bank Economics of Tobacco Toolkit. Tool 4: Design and Administration. Design and Administer Tobacco Taxes*

209 Bird, R. and J. Jun, (2005), Earmarking in Theory and Korean Practice

210 International Tax & Investment Center, (2013), Are Earmarked Taxes on Alcohol and Tobacco a Good Idea? Evidence from Asia

211 Stiglitz, J. (2000), *Economics of the Public Sector*

212 Stiglitz, J. (2000), *Economics of the Public Sector*

213 Mikesell, J. (2003), International experiences with administration of local taxes a review of practices and issues

214 Martinez-Vazquez, J. and A. Timofeev (2005), Choosing between Centralized and Decentralized Models of Tax Administration.

215 Martinez-Vazquez, J. and A. Timofeev (2005), Choosing between Centralized and Decentralized Models of Tax Administration.

216 Martinez-Vazquez, J. and A. Timofeev (2005), Choosing between Centralized and Decentralized Models of Tax Administration.

217 Prud'homme, R. (1995), *The Dangers of Decentralization*

218 Mikesell, J. (2003), International experiences with administration of local taxes a review of practices and issues

219 Musgrave, R. (1983), "Who Should Tax, Where, and What?" In Charles McLure, ed., Tax Assignment in Federal Countries

220 Oates, W. (1972), *Fiscal Federalism*

221 Tiebout, C. (1956), *A Pure Theory of Local Expenditures.*

222 Mikesell, J. (2003), International experiences with administration of local taxes a review of practices and issues

223 Mikesell, J. (2003), International experiences with administration of local taxes a review of practices and issues

224 Breton, A. (1996), *Competitive Governments*

225 Salmon, P. (1987) *Decentralization as an Incentive Scheme*

226 Weingast, B. (1995), The Economic Role of Political Institutions: Market-Preserving Federalism and Economic Development

227 Inman, R. and D. Rubinfeld (1997) *Rethinking Federalism*

228 World Bank (1997), World Development Report: The State in a Changing World.

229 Tanzi, V. (1996), Fiscal Federalism and Decentralization: A Review of Some Efficiency and Macroeconomic Aspects

230 Wildasin, D. (1997), Externalities and Bailouts: Hard and Soft Budget Constraints in Intergovernmental Fiscal Relations

231 Prud'homme, R. (1995), *The Dangers of Dentralization*

232 Spahn, P. (1997a) *Decentralization in Transition Economies*

233 Spahn, P. (1997b) *Decentralized Government and Macroeconomic Control*

234 Wallich, C. (1994), Russia and the Challenge of Fiscal Federalism. A Regional and Sectoral Study.'

235 Musgrave, R. (1983), "Who Should Tax, Where, and What?" In Charles McLure, ed., Tax Assignment in Federal Countries

236 Prud'homme, R. (1995), *The Dangers of Dentralization*

237 Wilensky, H. (1974), *The Welfare State and Equality: Structural and Ideological Roots of Public Expenditures*

238 Inman, R. and D. Rubinfeld (1997) *Rethinking Federalism*

239 Buchanan, J. and R. Wagner (1971), *An Efficiency Basis for Federal Fiscal Equalization*

240 Mikesell, J. (2003), International experiences with administration of local taxes a review of practices and issues

241 Mikesell, J. (2003), International experiences with administration of local taxes a review of practices and issues

242 Burgess, R. and N. Stern (1993), T*axation and Development*

243 Mikesell, J. (2003), International experiences with administration of local taxes a review of practices and issues

244 Litvack, J., Ahmad, J., and R. Bird. The World Bank (1998), Rethinking Decentralization in Developing Countries

245 Prud'homme, R. (1995), *The Dangers of Dentralization*

246 Mikesell, J. (2003), International experiences with administration of local taxes a review of practices and issues

247 This point is important since it implies that those burdened by the tax are more likely to be the beneficiaries of the tax expenditure, which is less likely under an international tax scheme.

248 Browne, M.A. (2002) Global Taxation and the United Nations: A Review of Proposals

249 Mendez, R.P. (2001), The Case for Global Taxes an Overview]

250 Sagasti, F., K. Bezanson, and F. Prada (2005), *The Future of Development Financing: Challenges, Scenarios and Strategic Choices*, p. 116

251 Working Group Chaired by J.P. Landau (2004), New International Financial Contributions for Development

252 Sagasti, F., K. Bezanson, and F. Prada (2005), *The Future of Development Financing: Challenges, Scenarios and Strategic Choices*

253 Sagasti, F., K. Bezanson, and F. Prada (2005), *The Future of Development Financing: Challenges, Scenarios and Strategic Choices*

254 Mendez, R.P. (2001), *The Case for Global Taxes an Overview*

255 Given national sovereignty issues, it is likely that a flexible policy would be adopted over a uniform policy due to political difficulties—even this may be politically infeasible.

256 Wachtel, H.M. (2000), Tobin and Other Global Taxes

257 Poterba, J. (1991), Tax Policy to Combat Global Warming: On Designing a Carbon Tax, p. 28

258 Poterba, J. (1991), Tax Policy to Combat Global Warming: On Designing a Carbon Tax

259 Keen, M. and J. Strand (2007), Indirect Taxes on International Aviation

260 Keen, M. and J. Strand (2007), Indirect Taxes on International Aviation

261 Poterba, J. (1991), Tax Policy to Combat Global Warming: On Designing a Carbon Tax, p.2

262 For example, assume that the national government increases consumption taxes, but that consumption taxes are not in the "Prohibitive Range" of the Laffer Curve; thus, ensuring

that government consumption tax revenues increases. If the national government wishes to offset this consumption tax increase to avoid regressivity, then the national government can offer tax cuts in other areas, such as labor, by using the additional tax revenues that were raised from the consumption tax increase.

263 Browne, M.A. (2002) Global Taxation and the United Nations: A Review of Proposals

264 Browne, M.A. (2002) Global Taxation and the United Nations: A Review of Proposals

265 Working Group Chaired by J.P. Landau (2004), New International Financial Contributions for Development

266 Working Group Chaired by J.P. Landau (2004), New International Financial Contributions for Development

267 Zee, H.H. (2006), A Note on Global Taxes and Aid for Development

268 For example, if the international tax facilitates aid mobilization such that it leads to global income increases by more than it would have otherwise. Or if the international tax successfully targets, and therefore reduces, activities that generate negative global externalities.

269 Zee, H.H. (2006), A Note on Global Taxes and Aid for Development

270 Zee, H.H. (2006), A Note on Global Taxes and Aid for Development

271 Zee, H.H. (2006), A Note on Global Taxes and Aid for Development

272 Zee, H.H. (2006), A Note on Global Taxes and Aid for Development

273 O'Shea, T. (2007), Tax Harmonization vs. Tax Coordination in Europe: Different Views

274 O'Shea, T. (2007), Tax Harmonization vs. Tax Coordination in Europe: Different Views

275 Kovacs, L. (2005) Tax Harmonsation versus Tax Competition in Europe

276 Sorensen, P.B. (2001) Tax Coordination in the European Union: What are the Issues?

277 Conconi, P., Perroni, C., and R. Riezman (2007) Is Partial Tax Harmonization Desirable?

278 McLure, C. E., Jr. and J. M. Weiner. (2000). Deciding Whether the European Union should Adopt Formula Apportionment of Company Income.

279 Mintz, J. M. and J. M. Weiner. (2003). Exploring Formula Apportionment for the European Union

280 Kirchgassner, G. and W.W. Pommerehne (1996), Tax Harmonization and Tax Competition in the European Union: Lessons from Switzerland

281 Brochner, J., J. Jensen, P. Svensson, P.B. Sorensen (2006) The Dilemmas of Tax Coordination in the Enlarged European Union

282 Sorensen, P.B. (2001) Tax Coordination in the European Union: What are the Issues?

283 Sorensen, P.B. (2004)) International Tax Coordination: Regionalism versus Globalism

284 McCreevy, C. (2005) Tax Harmonisation – No Thanks

285 O'Shea, T. (2010), News Analysis: Push for EU Fiscal Coordination Intensifies

286 Fourcans, A. and T. Warin (2001), Tax Harmonization versus Tax Competition in Europe: A Game Theoretical Approach

287 Chassin, Y. and P. Lemieux (2013), Why New International Taxes for Development are Inefficient.

288 UNITAID, Innovative Financing: http://www.unitaid.eu/en/how/innovative-financing

289 UNITAID is an international organization that focuses on obtaining healthcare products, such as drugs and diagnostic tools, for developing countries, as well as improving the market infrastructure for these items.

290 The concept of a financial transaction tax was introduced by economist James Tobin in 1978. Tobin's proposal, often referred to as the Tobin Tax, suggested a tax on spot currency transactions in order to reduce speculation. Tobin, J. (1978), A Proposal for International Monetary Reform.

291 WHO (2011), *WHO Technical Manual on Tobacco Tax Administration*

292 WHO (2011), The Solidarity Tobacco Contribution: A New International Health-Financing Concept Prepared by the World Health Organization.

293 Atun, R., Knaul, F.M., Akachi, Y., and J. Frenk (2012), Innovative Financing for Health: What is Truly Innovative? (p. 2048-2049).

294 Rajan, R.G. and A. Subramanian. (2008), Aid and Growth: What does the Cross-Country Evidence Really Show?

295 Ketkar, S. and D. Ratha. World Bank (2008), Innovative Financing for Development

296 Ketkar, S. and D. Ratha. World Bank (2008), Innovative Financing for Development

297 This is the metric suggested by the WHO Technical Manual on Tobacco Tax Administration (2011)

298 International Tax & Investment Center (2012), The Impact of Imposing a Global Excise Target for Cigarettes: Experience from the EU Accession Countries.

299 International Tax & Investment Center (2012), The Impact of Imposing a Global Excise Target for Cigarettes: Experience from the EU Accession Countries.

300 Philip Morris International (2013)

301 European Commission (2008), Consultation Paper on the Structure and Rates of Excise Duty Applied on Cigarettes and other Manufactured Tobacco. Quotation from section 2.2. http://ec.europa.eu/taxation_customs/resources/documents/common/consultations/tax/consultation_paper_tobacco_en.pdf

302 Chassin, Y. and P. Lemieux (2013), Why New International Taxes for Development are Inefficient.

303 Chassin, Y. and P. Lemieux (2013), Why New International Taxes for Development are Inefficient.

304 International Tax & Investment Center (2012), The Impact of Imposing a Global Excise Target for Cigarettes: Experience from the EU Accession Countries.

305 House of Commons Library (2008), *Burden of Taxation: International Comparisons*

306 Commission of the European Communities (1985), Completing the Internal Market, p.6

307 Commission of the European Communities (1985), Completing the Internal Market

308 European Council Directive (2002), Council Directive 2002/10/EC Amending Directives 92/79/EEC, 92/80/EEC and 95/59/EC as Regards the Structure and Rates of Excise Duty Applied on Manufactured Tobacco

309 Commission of the European Communities (1995), Commission Report to the Council and European Parliament on the Rates of Duty Laid Down in Council Directive 92/79/EEC

310 Campaign for Tobacco-Free Kids. State Excise and Sales Taxes per Pack of Cigarettes. https://www.tobaccofreekids.org/research/factsheets/pdf/0202.pdf

311 Campaign for Tobacco-Free Kids. State Excise and Sales Taxes per Pack of Cigarettes. https://www.tobaccofreekids.org/research/factsheets/pdf/0202.pdf

312 PMI, "Tobacco Excise Policy and Illicit Trade: Country Case Studies 2010".

313 PMI, "Tobacco Excise Policy and Illicit Trade: Country Case Studies 2010".

314 LaFaive, M. and T. Nesbit, Mackinac Center for Public Policy (2014), Cigarette Smuggling Still Rampant in Michigan, Nation. http://www.mackinac.org/19725?utm_source=Media+List&utm_campaign=2b03c09fbd-Smuggling_presser_2_17_2014&utm_medium=email&utm_term=0_272 f205f74-2b03c09fbd-259481833

315 Bennett, B. KSFY ABC (2013), Tobacco Tax has Minnesotans Driving SD to Purchase Cigarettes. http://www.ksfy.com/story/22952695/tobacco-takes-sends-minnesotans-over-the-sd-border-to-buy-cigarrettes

316 Lepiarz, J. WBUR (2013) "With Higher Cigarette Taxes, Concerns About Smuggling"

317 Bartlett, National Center for Policy Analysis (2002), Cigarette Smuggling. http://www.ncpa.org/pub/ba423

318 For a thorough review of tax competition literature, refer to Wilson, J.D. (1999), *Theories of Tax Competition*

319 Tiebout, C.M. (1956), *A Pure Theory of Local Expenditures*

320 Oates, W.E. (1972), *Fiscal Federalism*

321 Wilson, J.D. (1999), Theories of Tax Competition

322 Laffer, A.B., Moore, S., Sinquefield, R.A., Brown, T.H. (2014), *An Inquiry into the Nature and Causes of the Wealth of States. How Taxes, Energy, and Worker Freedom Change Everything.*

323 United States Census Bureau, Annual Social and Economic Supplement: Income of Households by State (Using 2 Year-Average Medians) http://www.census.gov/hhes/www/income/data/statemedian/

324 United States Census Bureau, Annual Social and Economic Supplement: Income of Households by State (Using 2 Year-Average Medians) http://www.census.gov/hhes/www/income/data/statemedian/

325 C2ER (2013), Annual Average Cost of Living

Endnotes: Part II

1   Note that nicotine can also be obtained from other plants, which would then imply that such e-cigarettes are not subject to tobacco excise.

2   Directive 79/32/EEC, Art. 3(1).

3   EU Council Directive 2011/64/EU, Article 4.1

4   Council Directive 2011/64/EU of 21 June 2011, Article 3, paragraph 2

5   Philip Morris International

6   WTO member countries are not allowed to use excise tax to discriminate against imported products, and as such, they cannot apply one level of excise to local cigarettes and another level of tax to imported products. Multi-tier systems, however, are not necessarily discriminating against imports.

7   Philip Morris International

8   Issued the Fiscal Policy Agency (BKF) under the Ministry of Finance

9   Indonesian Excise Law No. 39/2007

10 MOF Decree 131/ 2013 amending MOF Decree 1919/2010 which had first been amended by MOF Decree 78/2013

11 Japanese excise tax law, Philip Morris International

12 The net ex-factory selling price is the price of a good as it leaves the factory, and does not include any additional charges (e.g., delivery) or taxes.

13 Report from the commission to the European Parliament and the Council on the structure and rates of excise duty applied on cigarettes and other manufactured tobacco products, COM(2008) 460 final, Brussels, 16.7.2008, p.4.

14 Now with Minimum Excise Tax (MET)

15 http://www.wto.org/english/tratop_e/dispu_e/cases_e/ds371_e.htm#bkmk371abr x

16 Purchase Tax Law, 5712-1952

17 Sources: Government Budget 2012, Government proposal,Alterations of tobacco taxation due to revised Tobacco Tax Directives, http://www.sweden.gov.se/content/1/c6/14/76/20/5b861e28.pdf

18 Government's Spring Budget 2014: http://www.esv.se/PageFiles/14014/Utfallet percent20f percentc3 percentb6r percent-20statens percent20budget_ percentc3 percenta4ndrad percent2020140407.pdf

19 Directive 2011/64/EU, Art.7(4)

20 Premium brand reference is Marlboro, 20 cigarettes per pack

21 Calculation based on 19-cigarette pack, due to the change in pack sizes available on the market.

22 Budget smoking includes: smoking tobacco, tobacco rolls, cigarillos, border sales and low prices cigarettes.

23 Source: SANCO C6 TPE/ub D(2007) 360206, Reporting on tobacco product ingredients, PRACTICAL GUIDE

24 European Commission, 2008

25 European Commission, 2008

26 Curbing the Epidemic, Governments and the Economics of Tobacco Control (World Bank); "Tobacco taxation – A view from the IMF," page 87

27 OECD International VAT/GST GUIDELINES/ GUIDELINES ON NEUTRALITY

28 EEMA refers to "Eastern Europe Middle East and Africa"

29 Discrepancies in the values are due to rounding to the nearest cent.

30 Tobacco Tax Act of July 15, 2009 (Federal Official Gazette ["BGBl"], I, p. 1870), amended by Federal Statute (BGBl, I, p. 2221) of December 21, 2010.

31 For more information on digital tax stamps, see for example the website of the Digital Coding and Tracking Association, http://www.dcta-global.com/index.html

32 http://customs.hmrc.gov.uk/channelsPortalWebApp/channelsPortalWebApp.portal?_nfpb=true&_pageLabel=pageExcise_ShowContent&propertyType=document&id=HMCE_CL_000185

33 http://www.cdc.gov/mmwr/preview/mmwrhtml/mm5913a2.htm

34 For instance, ECJ case C-197/08 - Commission v France

35 UBS (2012), Prices and Earnings: A Comparison of Purchasing Power Around the Globe

36 The data are collected from Philip Morris International and measured on the first day of each quarter, and are standardized such that a pack of cigarettes comprises of 20 cigarettes.

37 Lower income countries in this sample are those countries in the bottom half of the sample when ordered according to nominal GDP per capita.

38 The following countries are excluded due to missing observations: Argentina, Bahrain, Israel, Taiwan, UAE, and Qatar

39 However, larger values do not imply any degree of affordability since income remains absent in this calculation.

40 That is, the countries in the upper half of the sample when ordered by nominal GDP per capita.

41 UBS (2012), Prices and Earnings: A Comparison of Purchasing Power Around the Globe. http://www.static-ubs.com/global/en/wealth_management/wealth_management_research/prices_earnings/_jcr_content/par/columncontrol/col1/linklist/link_0.1393999310.file/bGluay9wYXRoPS9jb-250ZW50L2RhbS91YnMvZ2xvYmFsL3dlYWx0aF9tY-W5hZ2VtZW50L3dlYWx0aF9tYW5hZ2VtZW50X3Jlc2VhcmNoL1BfTF8yMDEyX2VuLnBkZg==/P_L_2012_en.pdf

42 World Bank (2014), Global Economic Prospects

43   Kan, M. (2007), Investigating Cigarette Affordability in 60 Cities Using the Cigarette Price-Daily Income Ratio

44   Fifteen occupations are ranked by average net hour wages, and the seven lowest paying occupations in each city are grouped and averaged within the group. Data from UBS (2012), Prices and Earnings: A Comparison of Purchasing Power Around the Globe.

45   Excise Tax Yield data from Philip Morris International

46   VAT rate has remained at 25 percent in Sweden since July 1990.

47   International Tax & Investment Center (2012), The Impact of Imposing a Global Excise Target for Cigarettes: Experience from the EU Accession Countries

48   European Commission (January 1997) Excise Duty Rate Tables. https://circabc.europa.eu/sd/a/d0371627-651c-43d5-ae62-8065080c3e86/EDT percent201997 percent20Tobacco-Energy-Alcohol.pdf

49   European Commission (January 1996) Excise Duty Rate Tables. https://circabc.europa.eu/sd/a/deb0b777-4f6d-4e72-a1f7-91037db8e002/EDT-%201996-Part%20III-Tobacco.pdf

50   European Commission (January 1997) Excise Duty Rate Tables. https://circabc.europa.eu/sd/a/d0371627-651c-43d5-ae62-8065080c3e86/EDT%201997 %20Tobacco-Energy-Alcohol.pdf

51   Data on cigarette seizures is from Swedish Customs Annual Reports

52   Swedish Government Bill 1997/98:150

53   Swedish Finance Department Finanstidningen 6/11/1997

54   Philip Morris International

55   Data on cigarette seizures is from Swedish Customs Annual Reports

56   Smoking Incidence Statistics Sweden & National Institute of Public Health

57   Specifically, the Czech Republic, Cyprus, Estonia, Hungary, Latvia, Lithuania, Malta, Poland, Slovakia, Slovenia, Bulgaria, and Romania.

58 Bogdanovica, I., Murray, R., McNeill, A., and J. Britton (2011), Cigarette Price, Affordability and Smoking Prevalence in the European Union.

59 International Tax & Investment Center (2012), The Impact of Imposing a Global Excise Target for Cigarettes: Experience from the EU Accession Countries

60 KPMG (2011) Project STAR 2010

61 International Tax & Investment Center (2012), The Impact of Imposing a Global Excise Target for Cigarettes: Experience from the EU Accession Countries

62 International Tax & Investment Center (2012), The Impact of Imposing a Global Excise Target for Cigarettes: Experience from the EU Accession Countries

63 International Tax & Investment Center (2012), The Impact of Imposing a Global Excise Target for Cigarettes: Experience from the EU Accession Countries

64 International Tax & Investment Center (2012), The Impact of Imposing a Global Excise Target for Cigarettes: Experience from the EU Accession Countries

65 KPMG, (2005), "Study on the collection and interpretation of data concerning the release for consumption of cigarettes and fine-cut tobacco for the rolling of cigarettes".

66 International Tax & Investment Center (2012), The Impact of Imposing a Global Excise Target for Cigarettes: Experience from the EU Accession Countries

67 International Tax & Investment Center (2012), The Impact of Imposing a Global Excise Target for Cigarettes: Experience from the EU Accession Countries

68 EC DG TaxUD - Excise Duty Tables (Tax receipts - Manufactured tobacco)

69 EC DG TaxUD - Excise Duty Tables (Tax receipts - Manufactured tobacco)

70 KPMG (2013), Project Star 2012 Results

71 The minimum excise duty for cigarettes in 2012 was €105.48 per 1,000 sticks compared to €88.97 per 1,000 sticks equivalent for fine-cut tobacco; Conversion rate used: 1 cigarette =

0.75 gr fine-cut.

72   KPMG (2013), Project Star 2012 Results

73   Foundation for Economic and Industrial Research, *The Greek Economy: Quarterly Bulletin 03-2013*, October 2013 p 36. http://www.iobe.gr/docs/economy/en/ECO_Q3_13_REP_ENG.pdf (in English)

74   Irish Tax and Customs EIU

75   Philip Morris International

76   ITMAC

77   KPMG (2013), Project Star 2012 Results

78   KPMG (2013), Project Star 2012 Results

79   Total consumption defined as the duty paid volume in addition to counterfeit and contraband volume

80   ITMAC; KPMG (2013), Project Star 2012 Results

81   2009 Budget Speech by the Minister for Finance. http://www.fiannafail.ie/news/entry/budget-speech-by-the-minister-for-finance/

82   KPMG (2013), Project Star 2012 Results

83   Office of National Statistics

84   Office of National Statistics; Philip Morris International

85   Philip Morris International

86   Philip Morris International

87   World Bank

88   Tobacco Manufacturers Association

89   HMRC

90   The massive drop in excise revenues in 1999, to GBP 3.7 billion, was the result of forestalling activities. Anti-forestalling regulations were introduced in the UK in 2001 to address this activity; see Section VII.

91   HMRC

92   HMRC

93   HMRC: Measuring Tax Gaps

94 HMRC (2011) Tackling Tobacco Smuggling—Building on our Success

95 Source: Philip Morris International

96 The Government decided to again increase excise in 2014 from SGD 352 to SGD 388 per 1000 cigarettes.

97 Duty-paid sales volumes as per Tobacco Association of Singapore and AC Nielsen.

98 Excise revenue as per Singapore Customs Yearly Revenue Statistics and Philip Morris International.

99 Source: Health Promotion Board, National Health Survey.

100 TNS Pack Collection Study 2013.

101 Calculations based on Bureau of Internal Revenue (BIR) 2012 and 2013 withdrawals.

102 Philip Morris International estimate.

103 Legal sales volume as per BIR and Philip Morris International data.

104 Price elasticity is change in industry volume/change in weighted average retail price between 2013 and 2012

105 Following this tax increase, however, the affordability of cigarettes in the Philippines is similar to many other countries, as we will see in, "Comparing Excise Tax Levels Internationally XIV, and premium priced products are in fact relatively unaffordable.

106 Asia-11 Illicit Tobacco Indicator 2013 Update for the Philippines, Oxford Economics and the International Tax and Investment Center, June2014

107 Philip Morris International (Consumer Tracking and Segment Tracking surveys conducted in 2012 and 2013)

108 Price segments market shares based on 3 month moving averages as per BIR and Philip Morris International data.

109 *Asia-11 Illicit Tobacco Indicator 2013 Update for the Philippines,* Oxford Economics and the International Tax and Investment Center, June 2014

110 Australia's Future Tax System, Chapter E: Enhancing social

and market outcomes:http://taxreview.treasury.gov.au/content/FinalReport.aspx?doc=html/Publications/Papers/Final_Report_Part_2/Chapter_e6.htm

111 *http://www.yourhealth.gov.au/internet/yourhealth/publishing.nsf/Content/factsheet-prevention-01#.U2cKyaF--Uk*

112 *https://www.ato.gov.au/General/New-legislation/In-detail/Indirect-taxes/Excise/Excise-and-excise-equivalent-customs-duty---increase-to-tobacco-excise/*

113 The Philippines excise tax indexation will commence in 2018

114 Federal Ministry of Finance, Explanation in Excise Tax Act

115 Bird, RM, and Jun, J, (2005), "Earmarking in theory and Korean practice", International Tax Program Papers, Institute for International Business. Paper No. 0513.

116 This figure includes earmarked taxes on tobacco, alcohol, the finance industry, and the insurance industry.

117 South Korean Ministry of Finance

118 Allen, R., and D. Radev, (2006) Managing and Controlling Extrabudgetary Funds, IMF Working Paper 06/286.

119 The Nation, (2013), "Public Health Ministry vows sweeping reform", 28 March.

120 *Consumer Price Index Manual: Theory and Practice* (2004); International Labour Office, International Monetary Fund, Organization for Economic Co-operation and Development, Statistical Office of the European Communities, United Nations, World Bank; August 25, 2004

121 Consumers Price Index Revision Advisory Committee 2004; "What should the Consumers Price Index measure?", Ian Ewing, Yuong Ha, Brendan Mai, Statistics New Zealand.

122 *Consumer Price Index Manual: Theory and Practice* (2004); International Labour Office, International Monetary Fund, Organization for Economic Co-operation and Development, Statistical Office of the European Communities, United Nations, World Bank; August 25, 2004

123 Harmonised indices of consumer prices, breakdown by purpose of consumption: 1.3.2. Tobacco http://www.ecb.europa.eu/stats/prices/hicp/html/hicp_coicop_inw_022000.4.INW.en.html

124 *Consumer Price Index Manual: Theory and Practice* (2004); International Labour Office, International Monetary Fund, Organization for Economic Co-operation and Development, Statistical Office of the European Communities, United Nations, World Bank; August 25, 2004.

125 World Bank (1999), Curbing the Epidemic: Governments and the Economics of Tobacco Control

126 While it is important to administer excise taxes on other tobacco products to reduce substitution and down-trading effects, it must be done such that the different tax-bearing capacities and production costs of other tobacco products are considered.

127 World Health Organization (2011), WHO Technical Manual on Tobacco Tax Administration

128 There are a variety of affordability measures to choose from, which will be reviewed in Subsection C.

129 Correlation measures the degree to which to two variables tend to move together, with values ranging between -1 and 1 (a value of 0 indicating no statistical relationship).

130 Duty paid volume data is from Swedish Match Distribution and Tax Authority; Smoking incidence data is from Statistics Sweden & National Institute of Public Health

131 At least by definition, in order to meet EU requirements

132 KPMG (2013) Project Star 2012 Results; European Commission (July 2013), Excise Duty Tables: Tax Receipts—Manufactured Tobacco. http://ec.europa.eu/taxation_customs/resources/documents/taxation/excise_duties/tobacco_products/rates/excise_duties_tobacco_en.pdf

133 Or the same as other cigarettes, in case a country applies a Minimum Excise Tax.

134 Of course, if countries establish a tax rate that exceeds a regional minimum excise yield, such as in the EU, consumers may be tempted to cross the border for cigarettes if the price differential is wide enough.

135 Household final consumption expenditure as a percent of GDP data from the World Bank's WDI Tables. Nominal GDP per capita are 2013 estimates from Global Insight, as of January 2014.

136 In Luxembourg, only about 60 percent of the workforce is accounted for by residents—cross-border workers represent the remainder of the workforce. As such, the labor provided by non-resident workers contributes to GDP, but is not taken into account in the denominator of the ratio of GDP per capita—thus inflating GDP per capita. Refer to OECD Economic Surveys: Luxembourg. (Volume 2010/5, May 2010).

137 UBS (2012), Prices and Earnings: A Comparison of Purchasing Power Around the Globe

138 Excise tax yield data on the cheapest brand is provided by Philip Morris International, as of January 1st, 2014. The cheapest brand is used as the reference brand as it is a better price measure for affordability.

139 Nominal private consumption per capita data are 2013 estimates from Global Insight. Data includes households' expenditure on individual consumption of goods and services.

140 Exchange rate data represents the average exchange rate between the local currencies and the US dollar for 2013. Data are provided by Bloomberg.

141 OLS is ordinary least squares—a simple regression model.

142 b_0 is the intercept of the Y-axis. b_1 is the coefficient that measures the relationship between nominal private consumption per capita and the excise tax yield—it also represents the slope of the regression trend.

143 Refer to Table 23 for the list of country codes.

144 KPMG (2013) Project Star 2012 Results

145 KPMG (2013) Project Star 2012 Results

146 A tax on currency exchanges can generate inflation. A financial transactions tax would likely distort markets such that smaller firms would engage less due to higher costs (as evidenced in France), liquidity would decline, activity could shift into markets without this tax. (Chassin, Y. & P. Lemieux (2013), Why New International Taxes for Development are Inefficient)

147 Chassin, Y. & P. Lemieux (2013), Why New International Taxes for Development are Inefficient

148 http://ec.europa.eu/taxation_customs/resources/documents/taxation/vat/how_vat_works/rates/vat_rates_en.pdf

149 Directive 2002/10/EC, Art. 2.2

150 Directive 2002/10/EC, Art. 2.1

151 Directive 2010/64/EU, Art. 10.2 allows Bulgaria, Estonia, Greece, Latvia, Lithuania, Hungary, Poland and Romania a transitional period until 31 December 2017 to reach the minimum requirements.

152 International Tax & Investment Center (2012), The Impact of Imposing a Global Excise Target for Cigarettes: Experience from the EU Accession Countries

153 International Tax & Investment Center (2012), The Impact of Imposing a Global Excise Target for Cigarettes: Experience from the EU Accession Countries

154 http://www.unitaid.eu/en/impact

155 http://www.unitaid.eu/en/how/innovative-financing

156 The French government's auditors—literally, the "Audit Court".

157 Cour des comptes (2010), p. iii.

158 Cour des comptes (2010), p. 71-73

159 WHO (2011), The Solidarity Tobacco Contribution (STC) for International Health Financing. (p. 4)

160 Voluntary for the WHO's member states, not for the taxpayers burdened by such a levy.

161 WHO (2011), The Solidarity Tobacco Contribution (STC) for International Health Financing

162 Lower-middle-income countries would pay the lowest amount of $0.01, while high-income countries would pay the highest amount of $0.05 per pack of cigarettes.

163 The illicit trade is a persistent problem for many G-20+ countries, especially those countries outlined in "Country experiences with excise tax increases". Some general examples include Canada, Greece, Ireland, Sweden, the UK, and parts of the US.

164 Chassin, Y. & P. Lemieux (2013), Why New International Taxes for Development are Inefficient

165 Chassin, Y. & P. Lemieux (2013), Why New International Taxes for Development are Inefficient

166 In South Korea, about 1/3 of the government tax receipts are earmarked, which means those funds cannot be used for other programs that may have more public demand. As a result, earmarked tax revenues pose budget inflexibility and potentially spend taxpayer money inefficiently.

APPENDICES

Tobacco and Taxation

Abbreviations

AWOTE	Average Weekly Ordinary Time Earnings
CIF	Cost, Insurance, Freight
COICOP	Classification of Individual Consumption According to Purpose
CPI	Consumer Price Index
ET	Excise Tax
GST	General Sales Tax
HICP	Harmonized Index of Consumer Prices
IDA	Istituto de Desarolo Agrario (Agrarian Development Institute) – Costa Rica
MET	Minimum Excise Tax
MIP	Minimum Import Price
MPPC	Most Popular Price Category
MRP	Minimum Reference Price
MYO	Make your Own
NEFP	Net Ex-Factory Price
NRP	Net Retail Price
OTP	Other Tobacco Products
PLT	Public Lighting Tax
RSP	Retail Selling Price
RYO	Roll Your Own
SAF	Social Assistance Fund
SCT	Special Consumption Tax
SDRs	Special Drawing Rights
STF	Special Tobacco Fund
VAT	Value Added Tax
WAP	Weighted Average Price

Glossary of terms

Excise tax incidence	Excise tax divided by reference price (RSP, WAP, etc.)
Excise yield	Monetary amount of excise tax
Ex-factory price	Price charged from manufacturer to wholesaler
Net ex-factory price	Price charged from manufacturer to wholesaler excluding taxes (Excise and VAT)
Specific tax ratio	Specific excise divided by the sum of specific, ad valorem and VAT

Appendix I. Elasticity of Demand

COMPLETE DATA AND SOURCES FOR GLOBAL PRICE ELASTICITY OF DEMAND ESTIMATES (TABLE 4, PART I)

Countries	Authors	Data/Year	Price Elasticity Results
High Income Countries	Chaloupka, Warner (1999)	Time series data, multiple periods	-0.14 to -1.23
High Income Countries	Chaloupka, Hu, Warner, Jacobs, and Yurekli (2000)	Time series data, multiple periods	-0.25 to -0.5
High Income Countries	Hu, Wilkins, and Yurekli (2003)	Time series data, multiple periods	-0.3 to -0.5
High Income Countries	Gallet, List (2002)	Aggregated time series data, multiple periods	-0.48
High Income Countries	Remler (2004)	Time series data, multiple periods	-0.3 to -0.5
High Income Countries	Sayginsoy, Yurekli (2010)	Time series data, multiple periods collected from USDA's Foreign Agricultural Services, Commodity Trade Statistics, Economic Intelligence Unit, World Bank tobacco database, and IMF	-0.41
Argentina	Rozada (2006)	Monthly data: Jan 1996 to June 2004	-0.265
Bolivia	Alcaraz (2006)	Yearly data 1988 - 2002	-0.85
Brazil	Costa e Silva (1998)	Annual data 1983-1994	-0.11 to -0.80
Brazil	Iglesias (2006)	Quarterly data 1991-2003	-0.25 to -0.279
Bulgaria	Sayginsoy, Yurekli, de Beyer (2002)	Living Standards Measurement Study household survey of 1995	-0.8
Canada	Gospodinov, Irvine (2005)	Quarterly 1972Q1-2000Q4	-0.11 to -0.31
Canada	Gospodinov, Irvine (2008)	Time series and cross sectional 1997-2005	-0.28 to -0.3
Chile	Debrott (2006)	Quarterly data 1993-2003	-0.21 to -0.45
China (Sichuan province)	Mao ZZ, Jiang, JL (1997)	Aggregate time series 1981-1993	-0.47 to -0.8
China (Sichuan province)	Mao ZZ, Jiang, JL (1997)	Cross section 1995	-0.69
China	Hu TW, Mao Z (2002)	Aggregate time series 1980-1997	-0.54 to -0.64

Countries	Authors	Data/Year	Price Elasticity Results
China	Lance, Akin, Loh and Dow (2004)	Micro-level data, survey, 1993 and 1997 panels	-0.007 to -0.08
China	Mao Z, Hu TW, Yang GH (2005)	Cross section 2002	-0.154
China	Mao Z, Hu TW, Yang GH (2005)	Aggregate time series 1980-2002	-0.18 to -0.61
China	Bai Y, Zhang (2005)	Pooled cross-section/time series 1997-2002	-0.84
China	Mao Z, Yang GH, Ma H (2003)	Cross section 1998	-0.51
China	Bishop, Liu, Meng (2007)	1995 Chinese Household Income Project	-0.47 to -0.51
Egypt	Nassar (2001)	Cross sectional data on family budget 1994/1995 and 1995/1996 surveys	-0.27 to -0.82
Estonia	Taal et al (2004)	Monthly data taken from household income and expenditure study Emro 1992-1999; and Statistical Office of Estonia 1996-1999	-0.32
Europe	Gallus, Schiaffino, et al. (2006)	2000 Tobacco Control Country Profiles (TCCP) Data	-0.4 to -1.00
India	Bhall et al (2005) Unpublished	National Sample Survey Organisation's National Sample Survey 1983-1999; and National Family Health Survey for 1998-1999	Cigarettes: -0.79 to -0.85 Bidis: -0.58 to -0.83
India	John, R.M. (2008)	1999-2000 NSSO Survey	Cigarettes: -0.18 to -0.41 Bidis: -0.86 to -0.92
Indonesia	Adoietomo, Djutaharta, Hendratno (2001)	1999 National Socio-economic Survey data	-0.61
Indonesia	Djutaharta, Surya, Pasay, Hendratno, Adioetomo (2002)	Yearly data 1970-2001 and Monthly data January 1996-June 2001	-0.32 to -0.57
Indonesia	Adoietomo et al. (2005)	1999 National Socio-eEconomic Survey (Susenas), collected by the Central Bureau of Statistics	-0.61
Ireland	O'Riordan (1969)	Time series data 1953-1967	-0.69 to -0.92
Ireland	Walsh (1980)	1953-1960	-0.79
Ireland	Walsh (1980)	1961-1976	-0.38
Ireland*	Madden (1993)	1958-1988	-0.34 to -0.68

Countries	Authors	Data/Year	Price Elasticity Results
Ireland*	Conniffe (1995)	Annual time series, 1960-1990	-0.29 to -0.57
Ireland	Chaloupka, Tauras (2011)	Quarterly data 2002-2010	-1.0 to -2.3
Ireland	Reidy, Walsh (2011)	Time series 2002-2009	-3.6
Malaysia	Ross, H.; Al-Sadat, N.A.M. (2007)	1990-2004	-0.077 to -0.76
Maldives	InfoGlobal Consultants (2002)	Monthly data December 1997-October 2000	-1
Myanmar	Kyaing (2003)	Household level data 2000	-1.619
Morocco	Aloui (2003)	Agg Annual 1965 to 2000	-0.51 to -1.54
Nepal	Karki (2003)	Household level data (2003)	-0.886
Papua New Guinea	Chapman, Richardson (1990)	Annual data 1973-1986	Cigarettes: -0.71 Other tobacco products: -0.50
Philippines	Quimbo et al (2012)	2003 Family Income and Expenditure Survey	-0.87
Russia	Ogloblin et al. (2003)	Household data from national surveys 1996 and 1998	-0.085 to -0.628
Russia	Lance, Akin, Loh and Dow (2002)	Longitudinal household surveys, 1992-2000	-0.02 to -0.176
South Africa	Maranvanyika (1998), van der Merwe (1998)	Annual time series data 1970-1994	-0.59 to -0.68
South Africa	Berg and Kaempfer (2001)	Household survey, 1997	-0.8 to -1.79
South Africa	Van Walbeek (2002)	The Income and Expenditure household surveys of 1990 and 1995	-0.81 to -1.39
Spain	Pinilla (2002)	1985-1994	-0.12 to -0.84
Spain	Fernandez, Gallus, Shiaffino, et al. (2004)	Annual data from Tabacalera, Commission for Trade of Tobacco, and Spanish National Institute of Statistics, 1965-2000	-0.19
Sri Lanka	Arunatilake (2001)	Monthly time series data 1999-2000	-0.227 to -0.908
Sri Lanka	Arunatilake (2002)	Household level data 1999 and 2000	-0.45
Thailand	Supakorn (1993)	NA	-0.67
Thailand	Supakorn (1993)	Linear Expenditure System and household level data of 1988	-0.09

Countries	Authors	Data/Year	Price Elasticity Results
Thailand	Sartinsart et al. (2003)	Household socio-economic survey 2000. Consumer price index from the Department of Business Economics	-0.393
Turkey	Onder (2001)	Household level data survey 1994	-0.41
Turkey	Tansel (1993)	Annual time series data 1960-1988	-0.169 to -0.370
Ukraine	Krasovsky, Andreeva, Krisanov, Mashliakivskyand, Rud (2001)	June 2001 national survey	-0.4
Ukraine	Maksym Mashliakivskyy (2004)	Monthly data 1997-2003	-0.3 to -0.48
United Kingdom*	Chambers (1999)	-	-0.25
United Kingdom*	Duffy (2001) (2002) (2003)	Quarterly aggregate time series data 1964Q2-2002Q3	-0.4 to -0.5
United Kingdom	Czubek and Johal (2010)	Quarterly time series data on duty-paid cigarettes from 1982 to 2009	-0.92 to -1.17
United States	Chaloupka (1991)	National Health and Nutrition Examination Survey 1976-1980	-0.27 to -0.48
United States	Peterson et al. (1992)	Annual data 1955-1988	-0.49
United States	Coats (1995)	Cross sectional, time series data, 1970-1988	-0.17
United States	Stehr (2004)	Behavioral Risk Factor Surveillance System, 1984-2001	-0.092 to -0.382
United States	Chiem et al (2007)	Pooled data Behavioral Risk Factor Surveillance System 1984-2004	-0.22 to -0.45
Uruguay	Ramos (2006)	Quarterly data 1991-2003	-0.34 to -0.55
Zimbabwe	Maranvanyika (1998), van der Merwe (1998)	Annual time series data 1970-1996	-0.85

*Refers to studies that include cigarettes, as well as other tobacco products, in the price elasticity of demand estimate.

Appendix II.
Excise Tax and VAT/GST Tables

As of January 2014

Country	Tax Tier	Specific Rate (in LC)	Specific Rate Base	Ad valorem	Ad valorem Base
Albania	-	4,500	per '000s	-	-
Algeria	-	1,260	per kg	1.4%	of selling price to trade less VAT and excise
		11	per 20 cig.		
Argentina	-	-	-	60%	of (RSP - SAF[2] - VAT- STF[3] total)
Armenia	filter	5,000	per '000s	-	-
	non-Filter	1,400	per '000s	-	-
Australia	<=0.8gram	0.40197	per cig. actual tobacco content	-	-
	Other	502.48	per kg tobacco content	-	-
Austria	-	35	per '000s	42%	of RSP
Bahrain	-	-	-	100%[5]	of CIF

MET (in LC except for %)	MET Base	VAT/GST[1]	Source
-	-	20%	Law on Excise Tax Law on Value Added Taxes
-	-	17%	Article 29 & 36 de la loi de Finances pour 2002
75%	of MPPC Excise	21%[4]	Public Law 24625 SAF: (http://infoleg.mecon.gov.ar/infolegInternet/anexos/30000-34999/31989/texact.htm) Public Law STF 19800. (http://www.fetsalta.gov.ar/?page_id=28) Public Law 24674 Excise tax: (http://infoleg.mecon.gov.ar/infolegInternet/verNorma.do;jsessionid=25B70971FF5F78283D5E-DA355173E7B9?id=38621) Decree 296/2004 MET: (http://infoleg.mecon.gov.ar/infolegInternet/verNorma.do?id=93386) Public Law 23349: (http://infoleg.mecon.gov.ar/infolegInternet/verNorma.do?id=16092)
-	-	20%	Amendments and Additions to the "Excise Tax" Law of Republic of Armenia", N -129- , adopted in 10/07/2010
-	-	20%	Amendments and Modifications to the Law of the Republic of Armenia "On Value Added Tax"" 10/07/2010
-	-	10%	http://www.customs.gov.au/webdata/resources/files/2013-58.pdf
-	-	10%	
117.48	per '000s	20%	http://ec.europa.eu/taxation_customs/resources/documents/taxation/excise_duties/tobacco_products/rates/excise_duties-part_iii_tobacco_en.pdf
10	per '000s	-	GCC Customs Union Agreement 2003, Provision IV

Country	Tax Tier	Specific Rate (in LC)	Specific Rate Base	Ad valorem	Ad valorem Base
Bangladesh[6]	Premium: From BDT 80+	-	-	61%	of RSP
	High: From BDT 42-45	-	-	59%	of RSP
	Medium: From BDT 27.38-28.40	-	-	56%	of RSP
	Low: From BDT 13.69-13.90	-	-	39%	of RSP
Belarus	RSP/000 <400000	125,000	per '000s	-	-
	RSP/000 >400000 BYR & <550000	215,000	per '000s	-	-
	RSP/000 >550000:	250,000	per '000s	-	-
	non filter	93,800	per '000s	-	-
Belgium	-	23.59	per '000s	50.41%	of RSP
Bolivia[7]	Black	-	-	50%	of (RSP – excise tax- distribution margin - VAT)
	Other	-	-	55%	of (RSP – excise tax- distribution margin - VAT)
Bosnia	-	45	per '000s	42%	of RSP

MET (in LC except for %)	MET Base	VAT/GST[1]	Source
		15%	http://www.nbr-bd.org/budget2013-14_vat_gen_ord.html
-	-	20%	Tax Code of the Republic of Belarus
-	-	20%	
-	-	20%	
-	-	20%	
148.11	per '000s	21%	http://ec.europa.eu/taxation_customs/resources/documents/taxation/excise_duties/tobacco_products/rates/excise_duties-part_iii_tobacco_en.pdf
		13%[8]	Law 843 tax reform (http://www.impuestos.gob.bo/index.php?option=com_content&view=article&id=1007:impuestos-presenta-un-compilado-y-actualizados-de-la-ley-843-y-del-c%C3%B3digo-tributario&catid=100)
100%	MPPC	17%	Law on Excise Tax of 2009, Official Gazette no. 49/09; Decision on the Establishment of Specific and Minimum Excise for Cigarettes in 2014, Official Gazette 88/13.

Country	Tax Tier	Specific Rate (in LC)	Specific Rate Base	*Ad valor-em*	*Ad valorem* Base
Brazil	Box	1.3	per 20s	54%	15% of RSP
	Soft	1.2	per 20s	54%	15% of RSP
Brunei	-	250	per '000s	-	-
Bulgaria	-	101	per '000s	23%	of RSP
Cambodia	-	-	-	10%[10]	of (CIF+ Import Duty[11])
Canada[13]	-	1.7	per 20s	-	-
Canary Islands	-	28	per '000s	-	-
Chile	-	105.5	Per 20s .000128803 x Monthly Taxation Unit x 20)	60.5%	of RSP
China	1) Production Stage: 'Gross Ex-factory >= RMB 70/carton	3	per '000	56%	ex-factory price or CIF inclusive of excise but exclusive of VAT
	Production Stage: Gross Ex-factory < RMB 70/carton	3	per '000	36%	ditto
				5%	% of Price to Retailer (excl. VAT)
	2) Wholesale Stage :	-			

MET (in LC except for %)	MET Base	VAT/GST[1]	Source
- -	- -	25%-37%[9]	Decree 7593 Excise tax: (http://www.receita.fazenda.gov.br/ Legislacao/Decretos/2011/dec7593.htm) Medida Provisional 540 Excise tax: (http://www.receita. fazenda.gov.br/Legislacao/MPs/2011/mp540.htm) Law ICMS (VAT). Constitution define that is a State defined tax.
-	-	-	http://tobaccotax.seatca.org/?page_id=72
148	per '000s	20%	http://ec.europa.eu/taxation_customs/resources/documents/ taxation/excise_duties/tobacco_products/rates/excise_du- ties-part_iii_tobacco_en.pdf
		10%[12]	http://www.tax.gov.kh/en/bpl.php http://tobaccotax.seatca.org/?page_id=86
-	-	5%[14]	Federal Excise Tax: (http://www.cra-arc.gc.ca/exciseduty/)
-	-	20%	http://www.gobiernodecanarias.org/tributos/portal/estatico/ info_tributaria/legislacion/pdf/64676_ley_tabaco_actualizada. pdf
-	-	19%	Original Decree Law 828 of Excise Tax: (http://www.sii.cl/ pagina/jurisprudencia/legislacion/basica/dl_828.htm) Excise Tax law reform 2012: (http://www.leychile.cl/ Navegar?idNorma=1043598) Law 825 VAT: (http://www.leychile.cl/Navegar?idNorma=6369)
		17.0%	Finance and Taxation (2009) No. 84

Country	Tax Tier	Specific Rate (in LC)	Specific Rate Base	Ad valorem	Ad valorem Base
Colombia	-	635.75	per 20s	10%	Certified Dec'13 prices x (1 + estimated inflation 2014) - Ad Valorem paid previous year
Costa Rica	-	426	per 20s	95%	of (RSP – Retail Margin - Distribution Margin - VAT - IDA[16] - ET - Discounts)
Croatia	-	197	per '000s	37%	of RSP
Cyprus	-	55	per '000s	34%	of RSP
Czech Rep	-	1,190	per '000s	27%	of RSP
Denmark	-	1,182.5	per '000s	1%	of RSP
Dominican Republic	-	45	per 20s	20%	of (Ex-Factory Price x 1.1)
Ecuador	-	0.0862	per cig.	-	-

MET (in LC except for %)	MET Base	VAT/GST[1]	Source
-	-	16%[15]	Excise tax reform 1393 of 2010: (http://web.presidencia.gov.co/leyes/2010/julio/ley139312072010.pdf) VAT law 633 of 2000: (http://juriscol.banrep.gov.co/contenidos.dll/Normas/Leyes/2000/ley_633_2000)
85%	of MPPC Excise	13%	Agricultural Tax (Earmarked): (http://www.pgr.go.cr/scij/Busqueda/Normativa/Normas/nrm_repartidor.asp?param1=NRTC&nValor1=1&nValor2=72582&n-Valor3=96178&param2=1&strTipM=TC&lResultado=6&strSim=simp) General Tobacco Control law 9028 (includes MET): (http://www.pgr.go.cr/scij/Busqueda/Normativa/Normas/nrm_repartidor.asp?param1=NRTC&nValor1=1&nValor2=72249&n-Valor3=92154&param2=1&strTipM=TC&lResultado=2&strSim=simp) Excise Tax law 7972: (http://www.pgr.go.cr/scij/Busqueda/Normativa/Normas/nrm_repartidor.asp?param1=NRTC&n-Valor1=1&nValor2=41967&nValor3=95518&strTipM=TC) VAT Law number 6826: (http://www.pgr.go.cr/scij/Busqueda/Normativa/Normas/nrm_repartidor.asp?param1=NRTC&n-Valor1=1&nValor2=32526&nValor3=92185&strTipM=TC)
567	per '000s	25%	http://ec.europa.eu/taxation_customs/resources/documents/taxation/excise_duties/tobacco_products/rates/excise_duties-part_iii_tobacco_en.pdf
121.5	per '000s	19%	http://ec.europa.eu/taxation_customs/resources/documents/taxation/excise_duties/tobacco_products/rates/excise_duties-part_iii_tobacco_en.pdf
2,250	per '000s	21%	http://ec.europa.eu/taxation_customs/resources/documents/taxation/excise_duties/tobacco_products/rates/excise_duties-part_iii_tobacco_en.pdf
-	-	25%	http://ec.europa.eu/taxation_customs/resources/documents/taxation/excise_duties/tobacco_products/rates/excise_duties-part_iii_tobacco_en.pdf
-	-	18%	Tax code (law 11-1992) excise tax modified by law 253-2012: (http://www.dgii.gov.do/legislacion/leyesTributarias/Paginas/leyesTributarias.aspx) Ad valorem taxable base General norm 10-2006: (http://www.dgii.gov.do/legislacion/normas/Paginas/normasGenerales.aspx) VAT taxable base modified by law 495-2006: (http://www.dgii.gov.do/legislacion/leyesTributarias/Paginas/leyesTributarias.aspx)
-	-	12%	Ley de regimen tributario interno (update December 2012): VAT Title II, Excise Tax Title III (http://www.sri.gob.ec/de/web/guest/90) Last update of specific rate of excise tax: (http://www.sri.gob.ec/de/web/guest/cupos-de-utilizacion-de-alcohol-excento)

Country	Tax Tier	Specific Rate (in LC)	Specific Rate Base	*Ad valorem*	*Ad valorem* Base
Egypt	-	62.5	per '000s	50%	of RSP
El Salvador	-	0.0225	per cig.	39%	of (RSP -Specific Excise - VAT)
Estonia	-	46.5	per '000s	34%	of RSP
Finland	-	28	per '000s	52%	of RSP
France	-	48.75	per '000s	49.7%	of RSP
Georgia	filter	37.5	per '000s	-	-
	non-Filter	10	per '000s	-	-
Germany	-	96.3	per '000s	21.74%	of RSP
Greece	-	82.5	per '000s	20%	of RSP
Guatemala	-	-	-	75%	of (Ex-Factory Price/CIF
Honduras	-	368.9	per '000s	-	-

MET (in LC except for %)	MET Base	VAT/GST[1]	Source
-	-		General Sales Tax Law
-	-	13%	Decree N°539, «Ley de Impuesto Sobre Productos del Tabaco» (http://www.asamblea.gob.sv/eparlamento/indice-legislativo/buscador-de-documentos-legislativos/ley-de-impuesto-so-bre-productos-del-tabaco) VAT Law 296-1992 (last update Sep-2013) (http://www.asam-blea.gob.sv/eparlamento/indice-legislativo/buscador-de-doc-umentos-legislativos/ley-de-impuesto-a-la-transferencia-de-bienes-muebles-y-la-prestacion-de-servicios-iva)
90	per '000s	20%	http://ec.europa.eu/taxation_customs/resources/documents/taxation/excise_duties/tobacco_products/rates/excise_du-ties-part_iii_tobacco_en.pdf
161.5	per '000s	24%	http://ec.europa.eu/taxation_customs/resources/documents/taxation/excise_duties/tobacco_products/rates/excise_du-ties-part_iii_tobacco_en.pdf
210	per '000s	20%	http://ec.europa.eu/taxation_customs/resources/documents/taxation/excise_duties/tobacco_products/rates/excise_du-ties-part_iii_tobacco_en.pdf
-	-	18%	Tax Code of Georgia
-	-	18%	
192.59	per '000s; MTT (includes VAT)	19%	http://ec.europa.eu/taxation_customs/resources/documents/taxation/excise_duties/tobacco_products/rates/excise_du-ties-part_iii_tobacco_en.pdf
117.5	per '000s	23%	http://ec.europa.eu/taxation_customs/resources/documents/taxation/excise_duties/tobacco_products/rates/excise_du-ties-part_iii_tobacco_en.pdf
		12%	Excise Tax law Decree 61-1977 (Reformed by Decree 04-2012) (http://portal.sat.gob.gt/sitio/index.php/leyes/impuestos.html) VAT law Decree 27-1992 (http://portal.sat.gob.gt/sitio/index.php/leyes/impuestos.html)
-	-	18%[17]	Law Decree 17-2010 (Ley de Fortalecimiento de los Ingresos, Equidad Social y Racionalización del Gasto Público) (http://www.tsc.gob.hn/leyes/Ley%20de%20fortalecimiento%20de%20los%20ingresos,%20equidad%20social%20y%20racio-nalizaci%C3%B3n%20del%20gasto%20p%C3%BAblico.pdf) VAT Law Decree 24 (reformed by Decree 278-2013) (http://www.sefin.gob.hn/?page_id=5395) (http://www.sefin.gob.hn/wp-content/uploads/2013/12/Ley_Ordenamiento_de_las_Fi-nanzas_Publica_Control_de_las_Exoneraciones_y_Medi-das_Antievasion_Decreto_278_2013.pdf)

Country	Tax Tier	Specific Rate (in LC)	Specific Rate Base	Ad valorem	Ad valorem Base
Hong Kong	-	1,706	per '000s	-	-
Hungary	-	12,500	per '000s	31%	of RSP
Iceland		22,650	per '000s	-	-
India[18]	Filter				
	Cigarettes of tobacco substitutes	1,661	per '000		
	>85mm	3,290	per '000		
	>75mm≤85mm	2,725	per '000		
	>70mm≤75mm	2,027	per '000		
	>65mm<70mm	1,409	per '000		
	≤65mm Non Filter	669	per '000		
	>65mm≤70mm	2,027	per '000		
	>60mm≤65mm	764	per '000		
	≤60mm	669	per '000		
	Bidis				
	Hand Made	13	per '000		
	Machine Made	32	per '000		

MET (in LC except for %)	MET Base	VAT/GST[1]	Source
-	-	-	http://www.budget.gov.hk/2014/eng/pdf/e_supplement04.pdf
24,920	per '000s	27%	http://ec.europa.eu/taxation_customs/resources/documents/taxation/excise_duties/tobacco_products/rates/excise_duties-part_iii_tobacco_en.pdf
-	-	25.5%	http://www.althingi.is/dba-bin/unds.pl?txti=/wwwtext/html/lagas/143a/1995096.html&leito=tóbaksgjald\Otóbaksgjald\Otóbaksgjalda\Otóbaksgjaldanna\Otóbaksgjaldi\Otóbaksgjaldinu\Otóbaksgjaldið\Otóbaksgjalds\Otóbaksgjaldsins\Otóbaksgjöld\Otóbaksgjöldin\Otóbaksgjöldum\Otóbaksgjöldunum#word1
		12%-65%[19]	http://www.cbec.gov.in/excise/cxt2013-14/chap24.pdf http://www.cbec.gov.in/excise/cxt2013-14/appxIII.pdf http://www.cbec.gov.in/excise/cxt2013-14/appxV-VII.pdf http://www.cbec.gov.in/excise/cxt2013-14/appexIV-IVA.pdf

Country	Tax Tier	Specific Rate (in LC)	Specific Rate Base	Ad valorem	Ad valorem Base
Indonesia[20]	See table on Indonesia excise taxes that immedi-ately follows this table				
Ireland	-	241.83	per '000s	8.72%	of RSP
Israel	-	398.98	per '000s	270%	of wholesale price net of excise taxes and VAT
Italy	-	10.34	per '000s	53.69%	of RSP
Japan[21]	All cigarettes except "Former 3rd Class products"	12,244	per '000	-	-
	Former 3rd Class products	5,812	per '000	-	-
Jordan	RSP/Pack 1.00 RSP/Pack 1.10 RSP/Pack 1.20 RSP/Pack 1.30 RSP/Pack 1.40 RSP/Pack 1.50 RSP/Pack 1.60 RSP/Pack 1.70 RSP/Pack 1.80 RSP/Pack 1.90	0.32	20 cigs	102%	of Selling price ex distributor + wholesale margin

MET (in LC except for %)	MET Base	VAT/GST[1]	Source
		8.4%	http://www.tarif.depkeu.go.id/Data/Regulation/ PMK1790112012.pdf http://www.sjdih.depkeu.go.id/fullText/2009/28TAHUN-2009UU.htm
275.62	per '000s	23%	http://ec.europa.eu/taxation_customs/resources/documents/ taxation/excise_duties/tobacco_products/rates/excise_du-ties-part_iii_tobacco_en.pdf
764.32	per '000s	18%	Purchase Tax Law (Goods and Services) Value Added Tax Law
115%	of MPPC Excise	22%	http://ec.europa.eu/taxation_customs/resources/documents/ taxation/excise_duties/tobacco_products/rates/excise_du-ties-part_iii_tobacco_en.pdf
- -	- -	5% 5%	https://www.mof.go.jp/tax_policy/summary/consump-tion/127.htm http://www.nta.go.jp/shiraberu/ippanjoho/pamph/sho-hi/201311.pdf
0.327	20 cigs		
0.370	20 cigs		
0.414	20 cigs		
0.457	20 cigs		
0.501	20 cigs	16%	Customs Law 20/1998
0.545	20 cigs		
0.588	20 cigs		
0.632	20 cigs		
0.675	20 cigs		
0.720	20 cigs		

Country	Tax Tier	Specific Rate (in LC)	Specific Rate Base	Ad valorem	Ad valorem Base
Kazakhstan		3,000	per '000s	-	-
Kosovo	-	32	per '000s	-	-
Kuwait	-	-	-	100%[22]	Of CIF
Laos[23]	-	-	-	15%-30%	Net ex-factory price
Latvia	-	39.8406	per '000s	33.5%	of RSP
Lebanon	-	-	-	108%	of CIF+charges[24]
Lithuania	-	148	per '000s	25%	of RSP
Luxembourg	-	17.56	per '000s	48.11%	of RSP
Macau	-	0.5	per stick	-	-
Macedonia	-	1,300	per '000s	9%	of RSP
Malaysia	Imports[25]	250	per '000	20%	(CIF + royalties + import duty)
	Local[26]	250	per '000	20%	(net ex-factory price - security ink exemption)
Maldives[27]	-	-	-	-	-
Malta	-	89.25	per '000s	25%	of RSP
Mauritania	-	-	-	20% 13%[29] 3%[30]	of CIF

MET (in LC except for %)	MET Base	VAT/GST[1]	Source
-	-	12%	Tax Code of Kazakhstan
-	-	16%	Law on Excise Tax in Kosovo Law on Value Added Taxes
8	per '000s	-	GCC Customs Union Agreement 2003, Provision IV
		10%	Department of Tax, Ministry of Finance No. 05045/DoT dated 13 Mar 2013
79.68	per '000s	21%	http://ec.europa.eu/taxation_customs/resources/documents/taxation/excise_duties/tobacco_products/rates/excise_duties-part_iii_tobacco_en.pdf
-	-	10%	http://www.customs.gov.lb/customs/tariffs/national/tariff1.asp
244	per '000s	21%	http://ec.europa.eu/taxation_customs/resources/documents/taxation/excise_duties/tobacco_products/rates/excise_duties-part_iii_tobacco_en.pdf
108.95	per '000s	15%	http://ec.europa.eu/taxation_customs/resources/documents/taxation/excise_duties/tobacco_products/rates/excise_duties-part_iii_tobacco_en.pdf
-	-	-	http://images.io.gov.mo/bo/i/2011/51/lei-11-2011.pdf
1,500	per '000s	18%	Law on Excise Law on Value Added Tax
			http://tariff.customs.gov.my/
-	-	6%	https://www.mira.gov.mv/Gst.aspx
144.25	per '000s	18%	http://ec.europa.eu/taxation_customs/resources/documents/taxation/excise_duties/tobacco_products/rates/excise_duties-part_iii_tobacco_en.pdf
		4%[28]	Law n° 70.019 of January 16, 1970, modified in 1982 and in 2013

Country	Tax Tier	Specific Rate (in LC)	Specific Rate Base	Ad valorem	Ad valorem Base
Mexico		0.35	per cig.	160%	of (RSP - VAT - ET - Retail Margin)
Moldova	Filter	45	per '000s	24%	of MAX RSP
	Non filter	30	per '000s	-	-
Montenegro	-	17.5	per '000s	35%	of RSP
Morocco	Blondes	332	per '000s	40%	of RSP net of VAT
	Brunes	217	per '000s	25%	of RSP net of VAT
Myanmar[32]	-	-	-	100%	of net ex-factory price
Nepal	Filter				
	>85 mm	1,306	per '000		
	>75-85 mm	977	per '000		
	>70-75 mm	763	per '000		
	<=70 mm	597	per '000		
	Non Filter				
	<=70 mm	272	per '000		
Netherlands	-	169.86	per '000s	2.36%	of RSP

MET (in LC except for %)	MET Base	VAT/GST[1]	Source
-	-	16%[31]	Excise Tax law (last update December 2013) (http://www.diputados.gob.mx/LeyesBiblio/ref/lieps.htm) VAT law (last update December 2013) (http://www.diputados.gob.mx/LeyesBiblio/ref/liva.htm)
-	-	20%	Tax Code of Moldova
-	-	20%	
110%	of MPPC excise	19%	Excise Law of Montenegro Value Added Tax Law
53.6%	of RSP	19%	Official Bulletin N. 6113 bis – 17 safar 1434
53.6%	of RSP	19%	
		-	Commercial Tax Law, 1990
		13%	Nepal National Union Budget Announcement - July 2013
176.11	per '000s	21%	http://ec.europa.eu/taxation_customs/resources/documents/taxation/excise_duties/tobacco_products/rates/excise_duties-part_iii_tobacco_en.pdf

Country	Tax Tier	Specific Rate (in LC)	Specific Rate Base	Ad valorem	Ad valorem Base
New Zealand	≤0.8kg/'000 >0.8kg/'000	545.39 777.18	per '000 per kilo of tobacco content (KTC)	- -	-
Nicaragua	-	374.93	per '000s	-	-
Norway	-	2,390	per '000s	-	-
Oman	-	-	-	100%[33]	of CIF
Pakistan	Net RP[34]>=P-KR 2,286/000 Net RP<PKR 2,286/000	2,325 880	per '000 per '000	- -	- -
Panama	-	-	-	100%	of (RSP - VAT - ET)
Paraguay	-	-	-	13%	of (Ex-Factory without ET and VAT)
Peru	-	0.07	per cig.	-	-
Philippines[36]	Net Retail Price[37] (PHP/pack) > PHP 11.50 Net Retail Price (PHP/pack) < or = PHP 11.50	27 17	per pack per pack	- -	- -
Poland	-	206.76	per '000s	31.41%	of RSP

MET (in LC except for %)	MET Base	VAT/GST[1]	Source
- -	- -	15%	http://www.customs.govt.nz/news/updates/Pages/New-excise-duties-rates-for-tobacco-and-tobacco-products-from-1-January-2014-22112013.aspx
-	-	15%	Law 822 (Ley de Concertación Tributaria) (http://www.dgi.gob.ni/documentos/GACETA_241_Ley_822_Ley_de_Concert._Tributaria.pdf)
-	-	25%	http://lovdata.no/dokument/STV/forskrift/2013-12-05-1486#KAPITTEL_2
10	per '000s	-	GCC Customs Union Agreement 2003, Provision IV
- -	- -	17%	http://www.fbr.gov.pk/Downloads.aspx#Acts http://www.fbr.gov.pk/budget/default.html http://www.fbr.gov.pk/budget/FinanceBill/FinanceBill.pdf
1.5	per pack	15%	Law 69-2009 (http://www.asamblea.gob.pa/main/Legispan-Menu/Legispan.aspx) Fiscal Code (reformed by Law 008-2010) (http://www.asamblea.gob.pa/main/LegispanMenu/Legispan.aspx)
		10%	Excise Tax Law (ISC) 125/91 Book three modified by law 4045/10 (http://www.set.gov.py/pset/hgxpp001?6,18,249,O,S,0,S-RC;287;0;66161;N;SRC;MNU;E;108;1;MNU) VAT law 125/91 Book three (http://www.set.gov.py/pset/hgxpp001?6,18,249,O,S,0,S-RC;287;0;66161;N;SRC;MNU;E;108;1;MNU)
-	-	18%[35]	Excise Tax Law (TUO IGV e ISC appendix IV) (http://www.sunat.gob.pe/legislacion/igv/ley/index.html) VAT law (TUO IGV e ISC title I) (http://www.sunat.gob.pe/legislacion/igv/ley/index.html) Additional municipal promotion tax included in VAT law (DL 776-1993) (https://www.mef.gob.pe/contenidos/tributos/tbl_imp_er/DL_00776.pdf)
- -	- -	12%	http://www.gov.ph/2012/12/19/republic-act-no-10351/ http://www.dof.gov.ph/wp-content/uploads/2013/02/RR-17-2012.pdf
392.86	per '000s	23%	http://ec.europa.eu/taxation_customs/resources/documents/taxation/excise_duties/tobacco_products/rates/excise_duties-part_iii_tobacco_en.pdf

Country	Tax Tier	Specific Rate (in LC)	Specific Rate Base	*Ad valorem*	*Ad valorem* Base
Portugal	-	87.33	per '000s	17%	of RSP
Qatar	-	-	-	100%[38]	of CIF
Reunion	-	-	-	64.7% *110%	of the RSP of a given brand in mainland France.
Romania	-	256.46	per '000s	19%	of RSP
Russia	-	800	per '000s	8.5%	of Max RSP
Saudi Arabia	-	-	-	100%[39]	of CIF
Senegal	Premium (NEFP>250)	-	-	45%	of NEFP
	Low (NEFP≤250)	-	-	40%	of NEFP
Serbia	-	2,250	per '000s	33%	of RSP
Sri Lanka[40]	>84 mm	17,100	per '000	-	-
	>72 -84 mm	13,815	per '000	-	-
	>67 - 72 mm	10,953	per '000	-	-
	>60 - 67 mm	8,112	per '000	-	-
	<60 mm	4,037	per '000	-	-
Singapore	-	352	per '000s	-	-
Slovakia	-	59.5	per '000s	23%	of RSP
Slovenia	-	60.79	per '000s	24.55%	of RSP
South Africa	-	546	per '000s	-	-

MET (in LC except for %)	MET Base	VAT/GST[1]	Source
125.3	per '000s	23%	http://ec.europa.eu/taxation_customs/resources/documents/taxation/excise_duties/tobacco_products/rates/excise_duties-part_iii_tobacco_en.pdf
100	per '000s	-	GCC Customs Union Agreement 2003, Provision IV
195	per '000s	8.5%	Article 575 of the General Tax Code
357.26	per '000s	24%	http://ec.europa.eu/taxation_customs/resources/documents/taxation/excise_duties/tobacco_products/rates/excise_duties-part_iii_tobacco_en.pdf
1,040	per '000s	18%	Tax Code of Russian Federation
100	per '000s	-	GCC Customs Union Agreement 2003, Provision IV
8	per cig	-	Loi n° 2009-19 du 9 mars 2009
3	per cig	-	
100%	of WAP excise	20%	Excise Law of Serbia Value Added Tax Law
-	-		
-	-		
-	-	12%	http://www.customs.gov.lk/
-	-		
-	-		
-	-	7%	http://www.customs.gov.sg/leftNav/info/Importer.htm
91	per '000s	20%	http://ec.europa.eu/taxation_customs/resources/documents/taxation/excise_duties/tobacco_products/rates/excise_duties-part_iii_tobacco_en.pdf
97	per '000s	22%	http://ec.europa.eu/taxation_customs/resources/documents/taxation/excise_duties/tobacco_products/rates/excise_duties-part_iii_tobacco_en.pdf
-	-	14%	Customs & Excise Act 91 of 1964

Country	Tax Tier	Specific Rate (in LC)	Specific Rate Base	*Ad valorem*	*Ad valorem* Base
South Korea[41]	-	32,050	per '000s	-	-
Spain	-	24.1	per '000s	51%	of RSP
Sweden	-	1,410	per '000s	1%	of RSP
Switzerland	-	120.95	per '000s	25%	of RSP
Taiwan[42]	-	590	per '000s	-	-
Thailand[43]	-	1	per g.	87%	(Net ex-factory price or (CIF + Import Duty) x [87% / (100% - 87%)]
Tunisia	-	38+65	per '000s	135%	135% of RSP less trade, specific, VAT
Turkey	-	0.13	per pack	65.25%	of RSP
Turkish Cyprus	Imports	150	per '000s	21%	of RSP
	Local Production	100	per '000s	22%	of RSP

MET (in LC except for %)	MET Base	VAT/GST[1]	Source
-	-	10%	Local Excise Tax / Education Tax: http://www.law.go.kr/lsSc.do?menuId=0&subMenu=1&query=%EC%A7%80%EB%B0%A9%EC%84%B8%EB%B2%95#liBgcolor3 Health Fund http://www.law.go.kr/lsSc.do?menuId=0&p1=&subMenu=1&nwYn=1&query=%EA%B5%AD%EB%AF%BC%EA%B1%B4%EA%B0%95%EC%A6%9D%EC%A7%84EB%B2%95&x=0&y=0#liBgcolor2 Green fun : http://www.law.go.kr/lsSc.do?menuId=0&p1=&subMenu=1&nwYn=1&query=%EC%9E%90%EC%9B%90%EC%9D%98+%EC%A0%88%EC%95%BD%EC%99%80+%EC%9E%AC%ED%99%9C%EC%9A%A9+%EC%B4%89%EC%A7%84%EC%97%90+%EA%B4%80%ED%95%9C+%EB%B2%95EB%A5%A0&x=0&y=0#liBgcolor0 VAT: http://www.law.go.kr/lsSc.do?menuId=0&p1=&subMenu=1&nwYn=1&query=%EB%B6%80%EA%B0%80%EA%B0%80%EC%B9%98%EC%84%B8%EB%B2%95&x=0&y=0#liBgcolor0
128.65	per '000s	21%	http://ec.europa.eu/taxation_customs/resources/documents/taxation/excise_duties/tobacco_products/rates/excise_duties-part_iii_tobacco_en.pdf
-	-	25%	http://ec.europa.eu/taxation_customs/resources/documents/taxation/excise_duties/tobacco_products/rates/excise_duties-part_iii_tobacco_en.pdf
214.7	per '000s	8%	http://www.admin.ch/opc/fr/classified-compilation/19690056/index.html.
-	-	5%	http://law.moj.gov.tw/Eng/LawClass/LawAll.aspx?PCode=G0330010 http://law.moj.gov.tw/Eng/LawClass/LawAll.aspx?PCode=G0340080 http://tobacco.hpa.gov.tw/Upload/FTB/UpFiles/tobacco.zip
Ad Valorem/Specific	the greater	7%	http://www.excise.go.th/PEOPLE/KNOWLEDGE/GOODS_KNOW/CIGAR/index.htm click on 3rd item: "อัตราภาษี"
-		18%[44]	Official Gazette of the Tunisian Republic – July 2012
0.1875	per cig	18%	
-	-	20%	Administrative Order #581 published in the Official Gazette #187 in 28.10.2011
-	-	20%	

Country	Tax Tier	Specific Rate (in LC)	Specific Rate Base	*Ad valorem*	*Ad valorem* Base
UAE	-	-	-	100%[45]	of CIF
UK	-	176.22	per '000s	16.5%	of RSP
Ukraine	Filter Non filter	173.2 77.5	per '000s per '000s	12% 12%	of RSP net of VAT of RSP net of VAT
Uruguay	-	38	per 20s	-	-
Venezuela	-	-	-	70%	of (RSP - VAT)
Vietnam[47]	-	-	-	65%	of Net ex-factory price

MET (in LC except for %)	MET Base	VAT/GST[1]	Source
100	per '000s	-	GCC Customs Union Agreement 2003, Provision IV
-	-	20%	http://ec.europa.eu/taxation_customs/resources/documents/taxation/excise_duties/tobacco_products/rates/excise_duties-part_iii_tobacco_en.pdf
231.7 101.6	per '000s per '000s	20% 20%	http://zakon4.rada.gov.ua/laws/show/2755-17
-	-	22%	Excise tax (Law 18083) (http://www.parlamento.gub.uy/leyes/AccesoTextoLey.asp?Ley=18083&Anchor) Ficto Prices Decree 069/2010 (http://www.dgi.gub.uy/wdgi/page?2,principal,_Ampliacion,O,es,0,PAG;CONC;167;1;D;decreto-no-69-010;0;PAG)
-		12%[46]	Excise Tax law (http://declaraciones.seniat.gob.ve/portal/page/portal/MANEJADOR_CONTENIDO_SENIAT/02NORMATIVA_LEGAL/2.4TRIBUTOS_INTERNOS/2.4.08ISCMT/2.4.8.html#) VAT Law (http://declaraciones.seniat.gob.ve/portal/page/portal/MANEJADOR_CONTENIDO_SENIAT/02NORMATIVA_LEGAL/2.4TRIBUTOS_INTERNOS/2.4.03IVA/2.4.3.html)
-		10%[48]	http://vanban.chinhphu.vn/portal/page/portal/chinhphu/hethongvanban?class_id=1&_page=2&mode=detail&document_id=168893 (Decision No 47/2013/QD-TTg on Tobacco harm prevention and control fund – in Vietnamese original text only) http://www.chinhphu.vn/portal/page/portal/chinhphu/hethongvanban?class_id=1&mode=detail&document_id=81144 (Law No 27/2008/QH12 on Special Consumption Tax – in Vietnamese original text only)

Indonesia - 2014 Excise Tax Rates			
Category	Production Volume Tier	Price Tier (1) (IDR/stick)	Specific Rate (IDR/stick)
Hand-rolled kretek			
Tier 1	> 2 bio.	> 749	275
		≥ 550 - 749	205
Tier 2	> 0.3 - 2.0 bio.	> 379	130
		> 349 - 379	120
		≥ 336 - 349	110
Tier 3	≤ 0.3 bio.	≥ 250	80
Machine made kretek			
Tier 1	> 2 bio.	> 669	375
		≥ 631 - 669	355
Tier 2	≤ 2.0 bio.	> 549	285
		≥ 440 - 549	245
White cigarettes			
Tier 1	> 2 bio.	> 679	380
Tier 2	≤ 2.0 bio.	> 444	245
		≥ 345 - 444	195
(1) Note: Price Tier based on Minimum Banderole Price per stick			

Appendix III. Earmarked Taxes

Country	Name	Earmarking Purpose	Tax Base	Rate or Duty	Included in Excise Tax?
Argentina	Social assistance fund	Ministry of Social Development	RSP	21%	NO
Bangladesh	Development surcharge	No further information	landed cost	5.00%	NO
Belarus	Hockey tax	Voluntary payment to support the development of ice hockey in Belarus	ex-importer price	5.00%	NO
Benin	Ecologic Tax on Tobacco products	Environment	NA	NA	NA
Brazil	PIS/COFINS	Program for social contributions	RSP	10.97%	NO
Cambodia	Public Lighting Tax	No further information	Price prior to wholesale	3.00%	NO
Cape-Verde	(1) Ecologic Tax on Tobacco, (2) Custom Tax on Tobacco	(1) Environment, (2) Custom	NA	(1) Specific, (2) Rate of 0.77%	NA

Country	Name	Earmarking Purpose	Tax Base	Rate or Duty	Included in Excise Tax?
Colombia	Coldeportes	Support the development of sportive activities	% of the Specific Excise Tax	16.00%	YES
Costa Rica	IDA	Funding of farming activities	RSP – Specific Excise Tax – VAT	2.50%	NO
Egypt	Health tax	To fund health insurance for students	per 1000 sticks	EGP 5.00	NO
El Salvador	Fosalud	Health fund	per stick	USD 0.0225	YES
Estonia	Cultural Endowment of Estonia	Cultural, physical fitness and sport endowment	Total tobacco excise revenue	3.50%	YES
Greece	(1) Agricultural Insurance Organisation	(1) Financial support of Greek tobacco growers,	(1) per 1000 sticks	(1) EUR 0.06	YES

Country	Name	Earmarking Purpose	Tax Base	Rate or Duty	Included in Excise Tax?
Guatemala	Excise tax	Ministry of health budget	Ex-Factory / CIF	75%	YES
Iceland	No special name	Work aimed to decrease smoking in Iceland	gross tobacco sales	0.90%	YES
India	Education Cess	No further information	base: excise + import duty + import cess (only imports, 2 % of excise)	3.00%	NO
Indonesia	Regional tax	For health service programs and law enforcement on eradication of illegal trade and smoking ban	Excise tax	10%	NO

Country	Name	Earmarking Purpose	Tax Base	Rate or Duty	Included in Excise Tax?
Ireland	No special name	For the services and purposes connected with the performance by the Health Service Executive of its functions	Fixed annu-al sum	Set annual amount not to exceed 167,605	YES
Ivory Coast	(1) Special tax on Tobacco for sport, (2) Special tax on Tobacco for AIDS	(1) Funding of sport federations, (2) National program dedicated to fight AIDS	NA	(1) 2.5% to 10%, (2) 2%	NA
Japan	Special Tobacco Tax	Settlement of debt of the former national railways corporation	per 1000 sticks	YEN820[49]/ YEN389[50]	NO
Jordan	Youth and cancer tax	No further information	pack	JOD 0.03	NO
Lithuania	National (1) Cultural and (2) Sport support Fund	To finance (1) professional and country art, (2) sport	Last year to-tal tobacco and alcohol excise revenue	(1) 3%, (2) 1%	YES
Macedonia	(1) Environ-mental Tax, (2) Health Contribu-tion, (3) Tobacco Growers Tax	(1) No further information, (2) No further information, (3) No further information	(1) per 1000 sticks, (2) per 1000 sticks, (3) per 1000 sticks	(1) MKD 250, (2) MKD 50, (3) KMD 150	NO

Country	Name	Earmarking Purpose	Tax Base	Rate or Duty	Included in Excise Tax?
Moldova	Ecologic tax	No further information	CIF	1.00%	NO
Morocco	Palestine Tax	Collected to provide assistance for Palestians	per 1000 sticks	MAD 2.5/5.0	NO
Panama	Excise tax	Health related initiatives Anti-illicit tobacco trade related activities	RSP – Excise Tax – VAT	100%	YES
Poland	Health Program	Reduction of tobacco consumption	Total tobacco excise revenue	0.50%	YES
Romania	(1) National Health Fund, (2) Sport contribution/Sport Ministry	(1) Public health infrastructure, national health programs, special situations of the MoF, (2) Sport contribution/ National sport programs	(1) per 1000 sticks, (2) (*Ad Valorem* + Specific Excise - Health Tax)	(1) EUR 10, (2) 1%	YES

Country	Name	Earmarking Purpose	Tax Base	Rate or Duty	Included in Excise Tax?
South Korea	(1) Educa- tion Tax, (2) Health Fund, (3) Green Fund	(1) Support of local education, (2) Support of health programs nationwide, (3) Protection of the envi- ronment	(1) per 1000 sticks, (2) per 1000 sticks, (3) per 1000 sticks	(1) KRW 16, 025, (2) KRW 17, 700, (3) KRW 405	NO
Sri Lanka	(1) Port and airport develop- ment levy (2) CESS (3) Nation building tax	No further information	(1) & (2) CIF (3) customs duty + excise tax+PAL + CESS	(1) 5% (2) 10% (3) 2%	NO
Switzerland	(1) Domestic tobacco growing fund, (2) Tobacco Prevention Fund	(1) Contribu- tions to the local tobacco growing, (2) Contribution to a national tobacco pre- vention fund administrated by the Fed- eral Health Office	(1) per 1000 sticks, (2) per 1000 sticks	(1) CHF 1.30, (2) CHF 1.30	(1) NO, (2) NO
Taiwan	Health surtax	To subsidize the National Health Insurance program.	per 1000 sticks	TWD 1,000	NO

Country	Name	Earmarking Purpose	Tax Base	Rate or Duty	Included in Excise Tax?
Thailand	(1) Health Tax	(1) Thai Health Promotion Foundation	(1) Excise tax	(1) 2.00%	NO
	(2) TV Tax	(2) Support Thai Public Broadcasting	(2) Excise tax	(2) 1.5% of excise	NO
	(3) Provincial Tax	(3) Service network general provincial fund	(3) Per pack	(3) THB 1.86 per pack except Bangkok which has nil provincial tax	NO
Turkey	Tobacco fund	To support tobacco growers	per kg on imported tobacco	USD 1.80 (supposed to gradually reduce to 0 by 2018)	NO
United States	Master settlement agreement MSA	Payments to the US states according to the agreement	per pack	approx. USD 0.50	NO
Vietnam	National Fund	Prevention and control of tobacco harms.	Net-ex factory price	1%[51]	NO

Appendix Endnotes

1 Nominal unless otherwise stated

2 Social Assistance Fund: 7% of RSP.

3 Special Tobacco Fund: 8.35% of RSP – SAF – VAT + AR$ 0.3649

4 VAT: 21% of (RSP - SAF - VAT - STF total - ET)

5 Import duty

6 Tax rates based on RP of pack of 10s. Also development surcharge of 5% landed cost.

7 Also: Transaction Tax 3% of RSP – Excise Tax – Distr. Margin

8 of (RSP - ET - Distrib Mg)

9 Varies in different states

10 For locally produced: 65% of ex-factory price

11 Import Duty: 7% of deemed CIF

12 of (Price to wholesaler – excise tax - Public Lighting Tax); Public Lightning Tax = 3% (Price to wholesaler less excise tax)

13 Also: Harmonized Sales Tax: 13% of (RSP - HST), only applicable in Ontario (13%), New Brunswick (13%), Nova Scotia (15%), Prince Edward Island (14%) and Newfoundland (13%); Provincial Tobacco Tax: C$2.47 - 5.80 (Range for all provinces and territories); Provincial Sales Tax: 5-8% of (RSP - GST - PST)

14 GST: 5.0% of (RSP - GST - PST)

15 of (RSP - ET – VAT)

16 Agricultural Tax (IDA): 2.5% of (RSP - VAT – IDA)

17 of (RSP - VAT - Retail Mg)

18 Also: Education cess = 3% [excise + import duty + import cess (only imports: 3% of excise)]

19 Varies across states

20 Also: Regional tax = 10% of excise tax

21 Excise tax includes special tobacco tax: All cigarettes except "Former 3rd Class products": 820 per '000, "Former 3rd Class products": 389 per '000

22 Import duty

23 Import: specific import duty of USD20/'000, Tax Stamp: LC500/pack

24 Bank charges and stamp cost

25 Imports sales tax = 5% of (CIF + excise duty + royalties + import duty)

26 Local produced sales tax = 5% of (net ex-factory price + excise duty - security ink exemption)

27 Maldives has no excise tax on cigarettes but levies an import duty of MVR 900/'000

28 IMF: 4% (VAT-like turnover tax)

29 Droit Fiscal

30 Tax Statistique

31 of (RSP - VAT)

32 Commercial tax equivalent of 5% on invoice price for traders

33 Import duty

34 Net RP= RSP-GST

35 Rate includes municipal promotion tax (2%).

36 For cigarettes packed by machine under Section 5(c) of Republic Act No. 10351 (Revised Excise Tax Law).

37 "Net retail price" shall mean the price at which the cigarette is sold on retail in at least five (5) major supermarkets in Metro Manila (for brands of cigarettes marketed nationally), excluding the amount intended to cover the applicable excise tax and the value-added tax. For cigarettes which are marketed only outside Metro Manila, the "net retail price" shall mean the price at which the cigarette is sold in at least five (5) major supermarkets in the region excluding the amount intended to cover the applicable excise tax and the value-added tax. [Section 5(c) of Republic Act No. 10351]

38 Import duty

39 Import duty

40 Also: Nation building tax = 2%[customs duty + excise + port and airport development levy (5% CIF) + CESS (10% CIF)]

41 Also: Education tax = 50% excise tax; Public health fund = 17,700/'000; Green fund = 405/'000

42 Also Health surtax of TWD 1,000/'000s

43 A de-facto MET. Provincial tax = 1.86/pack (with the exemption of Bangkok which is not subjected to the tax); Health tax = 2% of excise tax; TV tax = 1.5% of excise tax

44 of RSP less trade margins, specific

45 Import duty

46 of (RSP - VAT - ET)

47 Also: National fund = 1% of net ex-factory price

48 on wholesaler price

49 All cigarettes except "Former 3rd Class products"

50 Former 3rd Class products

51 Rate at 1% since 2013. 1.5% from 2016, 2% from 2019

Bibliography

Allen, R. and D. Radev. "Managing and Controlling Extrabudgetary Funds." IMF Working Paper 06/286, 2006.

Andreyeva, T., Long, M., and K. Brownell. "The impact of food prices on consumption: a systematic review of research on the price elasticity of demand for food." *American Journal of Public Health* 100, no. 2 (2010): 216, 2010.

Atun, R., Knaul, F.M., Akachi, Y., and J. Frenk. "Innovative financing for health: what is truly innovative?" *The Lancet* 380.9858 (2012): 2044-2049, 2012.

Australia's Future Tax System Review. "Australia's Future Tax System Report to the Treasurer. Part Two: Detailed Analysis." Australia's Future Tax System, 2010. http://taxreview.treasury.gov. au/content/FinalReport.aspx?doc=html/Publications/Papers/Final_Report_Part_2/Chapter_e6.htm

Australian Government Department of Health and Ageing. "Increasing Tobacco Excise to Reduce Smoking Rates." Australian Government Department of Health and Ageing. http://www. yourhealth.gov.au/internet/yourhealth/publishing.nsf/Content/ factsheet-prevention-01#.U59rVfldWE5

Australian Taxation Office. "Excise and excise-equivalent customs duty - index tobacco excise to average weekly ordinary time earnings." Australian Taxation Office Media Release, 2013. https://www.ato.gov.au/General/New-legislation/In-detail/Indirect-taxes/Excise/Excise-and-excise-equivalent-customs-duty---index-tobacco-excise-to-average-weekly-ordinary-time-earnings/

Barbeau, E., N. Krieger, and M.J. Soobader. "Working class matters: socioeconomic disadvantage, race/ethnicity, gender, and smoking in NHIS 2000." *American Journal of Public Health* 94, no. 2 (2004): 269, 2004.

Barnett, P., T. Keeler, and T. Hu. "Oligopoly structure and the incidence of cigarette excise taxes." *Journal of Public Economics* 57, no. 3 (1995): 457-470, 1995.

Bartlett, B. "Cigarette Smuggling." National Center for Policy Analysis, 2002. http://www.ncpa.org/pub/ba423

Bask, M. and M. Melkersson. "Rationally addicted to drinking and smoking?" *Applied Economics* 36, no. 4 (2004): 373-381, 2004

Baumol, W. and W. Oates. "The use of standards and prices for protection of the environment." *Swedish Journal of Economics* 73, no. 1 (1971): 42-54, 1971.

Becker, G. and K. Murphy. "A theory of rational addiction." *The Journal of Political Economy* (1988): 675-700, 1988.

Bennett, B. "Tobacco Tax has Minnesotans Driving SD to Purchase Cigarettes." KSFY ABC, 2013. http://www.ksfy.com/story/22952695/tobacco-takes-sends-minnesotans-over-the-sd-border-to-buy-cigarrettes

Berka, M. "Nonlinear adjustment in law of one price deviations and physical characteristics of goods." *Review of International Economics* 17, no. 1 (2009): 51-73, 2009.

Bhagwati, J. "The generalized theory of distortions and welfare." Massachusetts Institute of Technology, Department of Economics Working Paper, 1969.

Bird, R. and J. Jun. "Earmarking in theory and Korean practice." ITP Paper 515 (2005), 2005.

Blecher, E. H. and C. P. Van Walbeek. "An international analysis of cigarette affordability." Tobacco Control 13, no. 4 (2004): 339-346, 2004.

Bogdanovica, I., Murray, R., McNeill, A., and J. Britton. "Cigarette Price, Affordability and Smoking Prevalence in the European Union." Addiction 2012 Jan; 107(1):188-96, 2012.

Bowen, C. "Government to Increase Tobacco Excise." Australian Government, The Treasury Joint Media Release with the Hon Tanya Plibersek MP, Minister for Health, Minister for Medical Research, No. 015, August 1st, 2013. http://ministers.treasury.gov.au/DisplayDocs.aspx?doc=pressreleases/2013/015.htm&pageID=003&min=cebb&Year=&DocType=

Breton, A. "Competitive governments: An economic theory of politics and public finance." Cambridge University Press, 1998.

Brøchner, J., Jensen, J., Svensson, P., and P. Sørensen. "The dilemmas of tax coordination in the enlarged European Union." CESifo Economic Studies 53, no. 4 (2007): 561-595, 2007.

Browne, M. "Global Taxation and the United Nations: A Review o f Proposals." RL31405, Congressional Research Service 3 (2002), 2002.

Buchanan, J. "External diseconomies, corrective taxes, and market structure." American Economic Review 59, no. 1 (1969): 174-177, 1969.

Buchanan, J. and R. Wagner. "An efficiency basis for federal fiscal equalization." The analysis of public output, pp. 139-162. UMI, 1970.

Buchanan, J. and W.C. Stubblebine. "Externality." Economica (1962): 371-384. 1962.

Bureau of Labor Statistics. "Covered Employment and Statistics Survey, Total Employment, Not Seasonally Adjusted", 2002.

Burgess, R. and N. Stern. "Taxation and development." Journal of Economic Literature (1993): 762-830, 1993.

Burkhauser, R., Larrimore, J., and K. Simon. "A "second opinion" on the economic health of the American middle class." No. w17164. National Bureau of Economic Research, 2011.

C2ER. "Annual Average Cost of Living." The Council for Community and Economic Research, 2013. http://www.coli.org/

Campaign for Tobacco-Free Kids. "State Cigarette Excise Tax Rates and Rankings." Campaign for Tobacco-Free Kids, 2013. http://www.tobaccofreekids.org/research/factsheets/pdf/0097.pdf

Campaign for Tobacco-Free Kids. "State Excise and Sales Taxes per Pack of Cigarettes." Campaign for Tobacco-Free Kids, 2013. https://www.tobaccofreekids.org/research/factsheets/pdf/0202.pdf

Chaloupka, F. and K. Warner. "The economics of smoking." *Handbook of Health Economics* 1 (2000): 1539-1627, 2000.

Chaloupka, F., Hu, T., Warner, K., Jacobs, R., and A. Yurekli. "The taxation of tobacco products." Tobacco control in developing countries (2000): 237-272, 2000.

Chassin, Y. "Why New International Taxes for Development are Inefficient." Montreal Economic Institute, 2013.

Cheng, K.W, and D.. Kenkel. "US cigarette demand: 1944-2004." The BE journal of economic analysis & policy 10, no. 1 (2010), 2010.

European Commission. "Excise Duty Rate Tables Manufactured Tobacco." European Commission, 1996. https://circabc.europa.eu/sd/a/deb0b777-4f6d-4e72-a1f7-91037db8e002/EDT-%201996-Part%20III-Tobacco.pdf

European Commission. "Excise Duty Rate Tables." European Commission, Directorate General XXI, Customs and Indirect Taxation, 1997. https://circabc.europa.eu/sd/a/d0371627-651c-43d5-ae62-8065080c3e86/EDT%201997%20Tobacco-Energy-Alcohol.pdf

European Commission. "Excise Duty Tables on Tax Receipts for Manufactured Tobacco." European Commission, 2013. (http://

ec.europa.eu/taxation_customs/resources/documents/taxation/ex-cise_duties/tobacco_products/rates/excise_duties_tobacco_en.pdf)

CDC. "State Cigarette Minimum Price Laws --- United States, 2009." CDC, 2009. http://www.cdc.gov/mmwr/preview/mmwrht-ml/mm5913a2.htm

Cnossen, S. "Theory and practice of excise taxation: smoking, drinking, gambling, polluting, and driving." Oxford University Press, 2005.

Cnossen, S. "Tobacco taxation in the European Union." CESifo Working Paper Series No. 1718, 2006.

Cnossen, S. "Excise Systems: a global study of the selective taxation of goods and services." Johns Hopkins University Press, 1977.

Coase, R. "The Problem of Social Cost." Jl & econ. 3 (1960): 1, 1960.

Collis, J., Grayson, A. and S. Johal. "Econometric Analysis of Alcohol Consumption in the UK." HM Revenue and Customs, HMRC Working Paper 10, December 2010. http://www.hmrc.gov.uk/research/alcohol-consumption-uk.pdf

Colman, G. and D. Remler. "Vertical equity consequences of very high cigarette tax increases: If the poor are the ones smoking, how could cigarette tax increases be progressive?" *Journal of Policy Analysis and Management* 27, no. 2 (2008): 376-400, 2008.

Commission of the European Communities. "79/32/EEC: Second Council Directive of 18 December 1978 on Taxes other than Turnover Taxes which Affect the Consumption of Manufactured Tobacco." Council, 1978.

Commission of the European Communities. "Completing the Internal Market." European Commission White Papers, 1985.

Commission of the European Communities. "Commission Report to the Council and European Parliament on the Rates of Duty Laid Down in Council Directive 92/79/EEC of 19 October 1992 on the Approximation of Taxes on Cigarettes, Council Directive

92/80/EEC of 19 October 1992 on the Approximation of the Rates of Excise Duty on Alcohol and Alcoholic Beverages and Council Directive 92/82/EEC of 19 October 1992 on the Approximation of the Rates of Excise Duties on Mineral Oils." European Parliament, 1995.

Commission of the European Communities. "Report from the Commission to the European Parliament and the Council on the structure of rates of excise' duty applied on cigarettes and other manufactured tobacco products." Commission of the European Communities, 2008.

Conconi, P., Carlo, P., and R. Riezman. "Is partial tax harmonization desirable?" *Journal of Public Economics* 92, no. 1 (2008): 254-267, 2008.

Consumers Price Index Revision Advisory Committee. "What should the Consumers Price Index measure?" Ian Ewing, Yuong Ha, Brendan Mai, Statistics New Zealand, 2004.

Cooper, J. "Price Elasticity of Demand for Crude Oil: Estimates for 23 Countries." Organization of the Petroleum Exporting Countries, March 2003. http://15961.pbworks.com/f/Cooper.2003.OPECReview.PriceElasticityofDemandforCrudeOil.pdf

Cour des comptes. "Rapport 58-2 sur la taxe sur les billets d'avion et l'utilisation de ses recettes." November 30, 2010. http://www.assemblee-nationale.fr/13/pdf/rap-info/i3645.pdf.

Cullum, P. and C. Pissarides. "The demand for tobacco products in the UK." HM Customs and Excise, 2004.

Customs, HM and Excise HM Treasury. "Tackling Tobacco Smuggling." HM Treasury (2000): 5, 2000.

Czubek, M. and S. Johal. "Econometric analysis of cigarette consumption in the UK." HM Revenue & Customs, HMRC Working Paper 9, December 2010. http://www.hmrc.gov.uk/research/cig-consumption-uk.pdf

Da Pra, M. and C. Arnade. "Tobacco product demand, cigarette taxes, and market substitution." 2009 Annual Meeting, July 26-28,

2009, Milwaukee, Wisconsin, no. 49210. Agricultural and Applied Economics Association, 2009.

Davis, O. and A. Whinston. "Externalities, welfare, and the theory of games." *The Journal of Political Economy* 70, no. 3 (1962): 241, 1962.

De Gregorio, J. and P. Guidotti. "Financial development and economic growth." *World Development* 23, no. 3 (1995): 433-448, 1995.

De Mooij, R. and M. Keen. "Fiscal Devaluation' and Fiscal Consolidation: The VAT in Troubled Times." No. w17913. National Bureau of Economic Research, 2012.

De Walque, D. "Education, information, and smoking decisions: evidence from smoking histories, 1940-2000." *World Bank Policy Research Working Paper* 3362, 2004.

Deaton, A. and J. Muellbauer. "An almost ideal demand system." The American economic review (1980): 312-326, 1980.

Deran, E. "Earmarking and expenditures: A survey and a new test." *National Tax Journal* (1965): 354-361, 1965.

Duffy, M. "Tobacco consumption and policy in the United Kingdom." *Applied Economics* 38, no. 11 (2006): 1235-1257, 2006.

Dupuit, J. "On the measurement of the utility of public works." *International Economic Papers* 2, no. 1952 (1844): 83-110, 1952.

Economist Intelligence Unit. "World Cost of Living Survey." Available by subscription at http://www.worldwidecostofliving. com/asp/wcol_WCOLHome.asp

European Central Bank. "Harmonised Indices of Consumer Prices, Breakdown by Purpose of Consumption." 1.3.2. Tobacco, European Central Bank. http://www.ecb.europa.eu/stats/prices/hicp/html/ hicp_coicop_inw_022000.4.INW.en.html

European Commission. "Reporting on tobacco product ingredients practical guide." European Commission Health and Consumer Protection Directorate-General, SANCO C6 TPE/ub D(2007)

360206, 2007.

European Commission. "Consultation Paper on the Structure and Rates of Excise Duty Applied on Cigarettes and other Manufactured Tobacco." European Commission Directorate-General Taxation and Customs Union Tax Policy, 2008.

European Commission. "Excise Duty Tables (Tax Receipts – Manufactured Tobacco)." European Commission, Directorate-General, Taxation and Customs Union Indirect Taxation and Tax Administration. REF 1.037, 2013.

European Commission. " VAT Rates Applied in the Member States of the European Union." European Commission, Situation at 13th January 2014, 2014. http://ec.europa.eu/taxation_customs/resources/documents/taxation/vat/how_vat_works/rates/vat_rates_en.pdf

European Commission. "Releases for Consumption of Cigarettes 2002-2013 (in 1000 pieces)." European Commission, 2013. http://ec.europa.eu/taxation_customs/resources/documents/taxation/excise_duties/tobacco_products/rates/tobacco_releases_consumption.pdf

Evans, W., and M. Farrelly. "The compensating behavior of smokers: taxes, tar, and nicotine." *The Rand Journal of Economics* (1998): 578-595, 1998.

Evans, W., Ringel, J. and Diana Stech. "Tobacco taxes and public policy to discourage smoking." *Tax Policy and the Economy*, volume 13, pp. 1-56. MIT Press, 1999.

Farrelly, M., Nimsch, C., Hyland, A. and M. Cummings. "The effects of higher cigarette prices on tar and nicotine consumption in a cohort of adult smokers." *Health Economics* 13, no. 1 (2004): 49-58, 2004.

Farrelly, M., Nonnemaker, J. and K. Watson. "The consequences of high cigarette excise taxes for low-income smokers." PloS one 7, no. 9 (2012): e43838, 2012.

Federal Law Gazette (BGBl). "Tobacco Tax Act of July 15, 2009."

I, p. 1870, 2009.

Federal Law Gazette (BGBl). I, p. 2221, December 21st, 2010.

Francois, J. and L. Baughman. "The Unintended Consequences of US Steel Import Tariffs: a quantification of the impact during 2002." Study prepared for the CITAC Foundation, Trade Partnership Worldwide, Washington, DC, 2003.

Franks, P., Jerant, A., Leigh, J.P., et al. "Cigarette prices, smoking, and the poor: implications of recent trends." *American Journal of Public Health* 97, no. 10 (2007): 1873, 2007.

Foundation for Economic & Industrial Research. "The Greek Economy". Foundation for Economic & Industrial Research, Quarterly Bulletin No. 73, 2013.

Gallet, C. and J. List. "Cigarette demand: a meta analysis of elasticities." *Health Economics* 12, no. 10 (2003): 821-835, 2003.

Gospodinov, N. and I. Irvine. "A 'long march' perspective on tobacco use in Canada." *Canadian Journal of Economics/Revue canadienne d'économique* 38, no. 2 (2005): 366-393, 2005.

Gospodinov, N. and I. Irvine. "Tobacco taxes and regressivity." *Journal of Health Economics* 28, no. 2 (2009): 375-384, 2009.

Grossman, M., Chaloupka, F. J., and I. Sirtalan. "An empirical analysis of alcohol addiction: Results from the Monitoring the Future panels." Economic Inquiry, 36(1), 39-48, 1998.

Gruber, J. "Tobacco at the Crossroads: The Past and Future of Smoking Regulation in the United States." *Journal of Economic Perspectives,* 15(2) (2001): 193-212, 2001.

Gruber, J. and B. Köszegi.. "A modern economic view of tobacco taxation." Paris: International Union Against Tuberculosis and Lung Disease, 2008.

Gruber, J. and B. Köszegi. "Is addiction "rational"? Theory and evidence." *The Quarterly Journal of Economics* 116, no. 4 (2001): 1261-1303, 2001.

Gruber, J. and B. Köszegi. "A theory of government regulation of addictive bads: optimal tax levels and tax incidence for cigarette excise taxation." No. w8777. National Bureau of Economic Research, 2002.

Guindon, G., Tobin, S. and D. Yach. "Trends and affordability of cigarette prices: ample room for tax increases and related health gains." Tobacco control 11, no. 1 (2002): 35-43, 2002.

Harris, J. "Taxing tar and nicotine." *The American Economic Review* (1980): 300-311, 1980.

HM Revenue and Customs. "Anti-forestalling restrictions: cigarettes." HMRC, 2009. http://customs.hmrc.gov.uk/channelsPortalWebApp/channelsPortalWebApp.portal?_nf-pb=true&_pageLabel=pageExcise_ShowContent&propertyType=document&id=HMCE_CL_000185

HM Revenue and Customs. "Measuring Tax Gaps 2010." HMRC, An Official Statistics Release, September 16th, 2010. https://www.gov.uk/government/uploads/system/uploads/attachment_data/file/249154/mtg-2010.pdf

HM Revenue and Customs. "Tackling Tobacco Smuggling – Building on our Success." HM Revenue and Customs, 2011.

Hsu, H.H., Chern, W.S., and F. Gale. " How Will Rising Income Affect the Structure of Food Demand?" China's Food and Agriculture: Issues for the 21st Century, AIB-775, Economic Research Service/USDA (April 2002): 10-13, 2002.

Hu, T. and Z. Mao. "Economic Analysis of Tobacco and Opinions for Tobacco Control: China Case Study." HNP Discussion Paper, Economics of Tobacco Control Paper No.3, 2002.

Hu, T., Xu, X. P. and T. Keeler. "Earmarked tobacco taxes: lessons learned." Applied Fiscal Research Centre, University of Cape Town, Cape Town, 1998.

Huang, B.N., Yang, C. and M.J. Hwang. "New evidence on demand for cigarettes: a panel data approach." *International Journal of Applied Economics* 1, no. 1 (2004): 81-98, 2004.

IMF. "Taxes on Goods and Services (% of Revenue)." Government Financial Statistics Yearbook and Data Files, 2011. http://data.worldbank.org/indicator/GC.TAX.GSRV.RV.ZS?order=wbapi_data_value_2011+wbapi_data_value&sort=asc

Indonesian Excise Law No. 39 of 2007.

Indonesian Minister of Finance Regulation No. 131/PMK.011/2013, dated October 1, 2013. Amending Ministry of Finance Regulation No. 78/PMK.011/2013.

Inman, R. and D. Rubinfeld. "Rethinking federalism." *The Journal of Economic Perspectives* (1997): 43-64, 1997.

International Labour Organization. "Consumer Price Index Manual: Theory and Practice." International Labour Organization, 2004.

International Tax & Investment Center. "The Impact of Imposing a Global Excise Target for Cigarettes: Experience from the EU Accession Countries." International Tax & Investment Center, 2012.

International Tax & Investment Center. "Are Earmarked Taxes on Alcohol and Tobacco a Good Idea? Evidence from Asia." International Tax & Investment Center, 2013.

International Tax & Investment Center and Oxford Economics. "Asia-11 Illicit Tobacco Indicator 2013 Update for the Philippines." International Tax & Investment Center and Oxford Economics, May 2014. http://www.iticnet.org/images/Asia11PHUpdate.pdf

Israel Purchase Tax (Goods and Services) Law, 5712-1952, implemented by the Ministry of Finance.

Jay, J., Hamilton, A. and J. Madison. *The Federalist Papers.* New York: New American Library, 1779.

John, R. "Price Elasticity Estimates for Tobacco and Other Addictive Goods in India." Indira Gandhi Institute of Development Research, Working Paper Series No. WP-2005-003, August 2005.

http://www.eaber.org/sites/default/files/documents/IGIDR_John_2005.pdf

Kan, M. "Investigating cigarette affordability in 60 cities using the cigarette price-daily income ratio." Tobacco control 16, no. 6 (2007): 429, 2007.

Keen, M. "Taxation and Development—Again." IMF Working Paper No. 12/220, 2012.

Keen, M. and J. Strand. "Indirect Taxes on International Aviation*." Fiscal Studies 28, no. 1 (2007): 1-41, 2007.

Ketkar, S. and D. Ratha. "Innovative financing for development." World Bank Publications, 2009.

Kirchgässner, G. and W. Pommerehne. "Tax harmonization and tax competition in the European Union: Lessons from Switzerland." *Journal of Public Economics* 60, no. 3 (1996): 351-371, 1996.

Kovacs, L. "Tax Harmonsation versus Tax Competition in Europe." European Commissioner for Taxation and Customs, Conference Tax Harmonisation and Legal Uncertainty in Central and Eastern Europe, Organised by the Austrian Chamber of Professional Accountants and Tax Advisors, 2005.

KPMG. "Study on the collection and interpretation of data concerning the release for consumption of cigarettes and fine-cut tobacco for the rolling of cigarettes." KPMG, 2005.

KPMG. "Project Star 2010 Results." KPMG, 2011.

KPMG. "Project Star 2012 Results." KPMG, 2013.

Kumar, P., Kumar, A., Parappurathu, S., and S.S. Raju. "Estimation of Demand Elasticity for Food Commodities in India." *Agricultural Economics Research Review,* Vol. 25 January – June 2011: 1-14, 2011. http://ageconsearch.umn.edu/bitstream/109408/2/1-P-Kumar.pdf

LaFaive, M. and T. Nesbit. "Cigarette Smuggling Still Rampant in Michigan, Nation." Mackinac Center for Public Policy, 2014. http://www.mackinac.org/19725?utm_source=Media+List&utm_

campaign=2b03c09fbd-Smuggling_presser_2_17_2014&utm_me-
dium=email&utm_term=0_272f205f74-2b03c09fbd-259481833

Laffer, A. "The Laffer Curve: Past, Present and Future." Laffer
Associates, 2004.

Lal, A., and M. Scollo. "Big Mac index of cigarette affordability."
Tobacco Control 11, no. 3 (2002): 280, 2002.

Lechene, V. "Income and Price Elasticities of Demand for Food",
Section 5 of the "Annual Report on Food Expenditure, Consump-
tion and Nutrient Intakes", Report of the National Food Survey
Committee, London, The Stationery Office, 2001

Lechene, V. "Income and Price Elasticities of Demand for Meat,
Meat Products and Fish", Section 6 of the "Annual Report on
Food Expenditure, Consumption and Nutrient Intakes", Report
of the National Food Survey Committee, London, The Stationery
Office, p87-110, 2000.

Lenihan, B. "Budget Speech by the Minister for Finance." Fianna
Fail (The Republican Party), September 12th, 2009. http://www.
fiannafail.ie/news/entry/budget-speech-by-the-minister-for-fi-
nance/

Lepiarz, J. "With Higher Cigarette Taxes, Concerns About Smuggling". 90.9 WBUR Boston's NPR News Station, 2013. http://
www.wbur.org/2013/07/31/cigarette-taxes-smuggling

Lin, C.-Y., and J. Zeng. "The Elasticity of Demand for Gasoline in
China." Energy Policy, Elsevier, vol. 59(C): 189-197, 2013.

Litvack, J., Ahmad, J. and R. Bird. "Rethinking decentralization in
developing countries." World Bank Publications, 1998.

Manning, W., Keeler, E., Newhouse, J., et al. "The Taxes of Sin:
Do Smokers and Drinkers Pay Their Way?" JAMA 261, no. 11
(1989): 1604-1609, 1989.

Martinez-Vazquez, J. and A. Timofeev. "Choosing between centralized and decentralized models of tax administration." Andrew
Young School of Policy Studies Research Paper Series No. 06-49,

2005.

McCleary, W.. "The earmarking of government revenue: a review of some World Bank experience." The World Bank Research Observer 6, no. 1 (1991): 81-104, 1991.

McLure, C. and J. Weiner. "Deciding whether the European Union should adopt formula apportionment of company income." *Taxing Capital Income in the European Union–Issues and Options for Reform*, Oxford University Press, Oxford, New York (2000): 243-292, 2000.

Mendez, R. "The case for global taxes: an overview." United Nations ad hoc Expert Group Meeting on Innovations in Mobilising Global Resources for Development, pp. 25-26, 2001.

Merriman, D. "Understand, Measure, and Combat Tobacco Smuggling." *World Bank Economics of Tobacco Toolkit*, Tool 7 Smuggling.

Mikesell, J. "International experiences with administration of local taxes: A review of practices and issues." Tax Policy and Administration Thematic Group, The World Bank, 2003.

Mindell, J. and D. Whynes. "Cigarette consumption in The Netherlands 1970–1995 Does tax policy encourage the use of hand-rolling tobacco?" *The European Journal of Public Health* 10, no. 3 (2000): 214-219, 2000.

Ministry of Finance Japan. "Comprehensive Handbook of Japanese Taxes 2010." Ministry of Finance Japan, 2010. http://www.mof. go.jp/english/tax_policy/publication/taxes2010e/

Mintz, J. and J. Weiner. "Exploring formula allocation for the European Union." *International Tax and Public Finance* 10, no. 6 (2003): 695-711, 2003.

Morgan, B. "Burden of Taxation: International Comparisons." House of Commons Library Economic Policy and Statistics Section, Parliament, 2008.

Musgrave, R. "Who should tax, where, and what?" *International Library of Critical Writings in Economics* 88 (1998): 63-80, 1998.

Mundell, R. A. "The Pure Theory of International Trade." *American Economic Review*, March 1960, v. 50, pp. 67-110, 1960.

Nguyen, L., Rosenqvist, G. and M. Pekurinen. "Demand for Tobacco in Europe-An Econometric Analysis of 11 Countries for the PPACTE Project." Raportti: 2012_006, 2012.

O'Shea, T. "Tax Harmonization vs. Tax Coordination in Europe: Different Views." *Tax Notes International*, Volume 46, No. 8 (2007): 811-814, 2007.

Oates, W. "An Essay on Fiscal Federalism." *Journal of Economic Literature*, Vol. XXXVII, pp. 1120-1149, 1999.

OECD. " Economic Survey of Luxembourg 2010." Economic Surveys and Country Surveillance, OECD, 2010. http://www.oecd.org/eco/45025268.pdf

OECD. "OECD International VAT/GST Guidelines: Guidelines on Neutrality. Outcomes of the Public Consultation." OECE Committee on Fiscal Affairs, Working Party No. 9 on Consumption Taxes, Centre for Tax Policy and Administration, 2011.

OECD iLibrary. "OECD.Stat – extract data from across datasets." OECD. http://www.oecd-ilibrary.org/statistics

Ohsfeldt, R., Boyle, R. and E. Capilouto. "Tobacco taxes, smoking restrictions, and tobacco use." No. w6486. National bureau of economic research, 1998.

Peck, R. "Equity Issues, Tobacco, and the Poor." *World Bank Economics of Tobacco Toolkit, Tool 6 Poverty.*

Peretti Watel, P., Constance, J., Seror, V. and F. Beck. "Cigarettes and social differentiation in France: is tobacco use increasingly concentrated among the poor?" Addiction 104, no. 10 (2009): 1718-1728, 2009.

Philip Morris International.

Pigou, A. "The economics of welfare." Transaction Publishers, 1924.

Poterba, J. "Tax policy to combat global warming: on designing a carbon tax." No. w3649. National Bureau of Economic Research, 1991.

Prud'Homme, R. "The dangers of decentralization." The world bank research observer 10, no. 2 (1995): 201-220, 1995.

Puller, S. and L. Greening. "Household adjustment to gasoline price change: an analysis using 9 years of US survey data." *Energy Economics* 21, no. 1 (1999): 37-52, 1999.

Rajan, R. and A. Subramanian. "Aid and growth: What does the cross-country evidence really show?" No. w11513. National Bureau of Economic Research, 2005.

Ramanathan, R. "Short- and long-run elasticities of gasoline demand in India: An empirical analysis using cointegration techniques." *Energy Economics*, Volume 21, Issue 4 (August 1, 1999): 321-330, 1999. http://www.sciencedirect.com/science/article/pii/S0140988399000110

Ramsey, F. "A Contribution to the Theory of Taxation." *The Economic Journal* 37, no. 145 (1927): 47-61, 1927.

Reidy, P. and K. Walsh. "Economics of Tobacco: Modelling the Market for Cigarettes in Ireland." Office of the Revenue Commissioners, Research and Analytics Branch, 2011.

Republic of the Philippines Bureau of Internal Revenue. "Chapter IV – Excise Tax on Tobacco Products." Bureau of Internal Revenue, National Internal Revenue Code.

Sagasti, F., Bezanson, K., Fernando, P., et al. "The Future of Development Financing: Challenges, Scenarios and Strategic Choices." Regeringskansliet, Ministry for Foreign Affairs, Sweden, 2005.

Salmon, P. "Decentralisation as an incentive scheme." Oxford review of economic policy 3, no. 2 (1987): 24-43, 1987.

Sarnsamak, P. "Public Health Ministry Vows Sweeping Reform." The National, 2013.

Selvaraj, S., Karan, A., and S. Srivastava. "Price Elasticity of

Tobacco Products among Quintile Groups in India, 2009-10."
Working Paper, 2013. http://papers.ssrn.com/sol3/papers.cfm?abstract_id=2289221

Singapore Customs. "Revenue Statistics." Singapore Customs, 2013. http://www.customs.gov.sg/topNav/pub/Statistics.htm

Singapore Health Promotion Board. "National Health Survey." Health Promotion Board.

Smith, A. *An Inquiry into the Nature and Causes of the Wealth of Nations*. Nelson, 1845.

Sørensen, P. "International tax coordination: regionalism versus globalism." *Journal of Public Economics* 88, no. 6 (2004): 1187-1214, 2004.

Sørensen, P. "Tax coordination in the European Union: What are the issues?" *Swedish Economic Policy Review* 8, no. 1 (2001): 143-196, 2001.

Spahn, P. "Decentralization in Transition Economies." Paper prepared for the World Bank Seminar on Fiscal Decentralization in Developing Countries, Washington, D.C., May 7, 1997.

Spahn, P. "Decentralized Government and Macroeconomic Control." Paper prepared for the International Institute of public Finance 53rd Congress, Kyoto, Japan, 1997.

Statistics Sweden. "Living Conditions Surveys (ULF/SILC)." Statistics Sweden. http://www.scb.se/LE0101-EN/

Stiglitz, J. and E. Brown. "Economics of the public sector." New York: WW Norton, 1988.

Swedish Customs, Tullverket. "Tullverkets Årsredovisning." Swedish Customs.

 http://www.tullverket.se/2.6e3d73401151cda416380001786.html

Swedish Finance Department Finanstidningen 6/11/1997.

Swedish Government. "Alterations of tobacco taxation due to revised tobacco tax Directives." Swedish Government Budget, 2012. http://www.sweden.gov.se/content/1/c6/14/76/20/5b861e28.pdf

Swedish Government. "Government's Spring Budget 2014." Swedish Government, 2014. http://www.esv.se/PageFiles/14014/ Utfallet%20f%c3%b6r%20statens%20budget_%c3%a4ndrad%20 20140407.pdf

Swedish Government Bill 1997/98:150.

Tait, P., Rutherford, P., and C. Saunders. "Do consumers of man-ufactured cigarettes respond differently to price changes compared with their Roll-Your-Own counterparts? Evidence from New Zea-land." Tobacco control (2013): tobaccocontrol-2013, 2013.

Tanzi, V. "Fiscal Federalism and Decentralization: A Review of Some Efficiency and Macroeconomic Aspects." In M. Bruno and B. Pleskovic, eds., *Annual World Bank Conference on Development Economics*, pp. 295 – 316. Washington, D.C.: World Bank, 1995.

The Council of the European Union. "Council Directive 2002/10/ EC of 12 February 2002 Amending Directives 92/79/EEC, 92/80/ EEC and 95/59/EC as Regards the Structure and Rates of Excise Duty Applied on Manufactured Tobacco." *Official Journal of the European Communities*, 2002.

The Council of the European Union. "Council Directive 2011/64/ EU of 21 June 2011 on the structure and rates of excise duty applied to manufactured tobacco." *Official Journal of the European Union*, 2011.

The Swedish National Institute for Public Health. "Swedish Na-tional Public Health Survey." The Swedish National Institute for Public Health, Folkhalsomyndigheten.

Tian, G. and F. Liu. "Is the Demand for Alcoholic Beverages in Developing Countries Sensitive to Price? Evidence from China." *International Journal of Environmental Research and Public Health* 2011, 8(6): 2124-2131, 2011.

Tiebout, C. "A pure theory of local expenditures." *The Journal of Political Economy* (1956): 416-424, 1956.

TNS. "Pack Collection Study." TNS, 2013.

Trussler, S. and M. Meschi. "A Review of the Economic Literature on Tobacco Taxation." FTI, 2011.

Tsai, Y.W., Yang, C.L., Chen, C.S., Liu, T.C., and P.F. Chen. "The effect of Taiwan's tax induced increases in cigarette prices on brand switching and the consumption of cigarettes." *Health Economics* 14, no. 6 (2005): 627-641, 2005.

UBS. "Prices and Earnings: A Comparison of Purchasing Power Around the Globe." UBS, 2012.

UNITAID. "Innovative Financing." UNITAID. http://www.unitaid.eu/en/how/innovative-financing

UNITAID. "UNITAID Results and Impact." UNITAID. http://www.unitaid.eu/en/impact

United States Census Bureau. "Annual Social and Economic Supplement: Income of Households by State." http://www.census.gov/hhes/www/income/data/statemedian/

Wachtel, H. "Tobin and other global taxes." *Review of International Political Economy* 7, no. 2 (2000): 335-352, 2000.

Wallich, C. "Russia and the challenge of fiscal federalism." World Bank, 1994.

Weingast, B. "The Economic Role of Political Institutions: Market-Preserving Federalism and Economic Development." JL Econ. & Org. 11 (1995): 1, 1995.

WHO. "The Solidarity Tobacco Contribution: A New International Health-Financing Concept Prepared by the World Health Organization." WHO, 2011. http://www.who.int/nmh/events/un_ncd_summit2011/ncds_stc.pdf

WHO. "WHO Technical Manual on Tobacco Tax Administration." WHO, 2011. http://www.who.int/tobacco/publications/tax_administration/en/

Wildasin, D. "Externalities and bailouts: hard and soft budget constraints in intergovernmental fiscal relations." World Bank Publications, 1999.

Wilensky, H. "The welfare state and equality: Structural and ideological roots of public expenditures." Vol. 140. Univ of California Press, 1975.

Wilkins, N., Yurekli, A., Hu, T. "Economic Analysis of Tobacco Demand." World Bank Economics of Tobacco Toolkit, Tool 3 Demand Analysis.

Wilson, J. "Theories of tax competition." *National Tax Journal* (1999): 269-304, 1999.

World Bank. "Final Consumption Expenditure, etc. (% of GDP)." World Bank World Development Indicators, 2013. http://data.worldbank.org/indicator/NE.CON.TETC.ZS

World Bank. "Inflation, Consumer Prices (Annual %)." World Development Indicators, 2013. http://data.worldbank.org/indicator/FP.CPI.TOTL.ZG?display=default

World Bank. "Labor Tax and Contributions (% of Commercial Profits)." *World Development Indicators*, 2013. http://data.worldbank.org/indicator/IC.TAX.LABR.CP.ZS?order=wbapi_data_value_2012+wbapi_data_value+wbapi_data_value-first&sort=asc

World Bank. "Tariff Rate, Applied, Weighted Mean, All Products (%)." World Development Indicators, 2013. http://data.worldbank.org/indicator/TM.TAX.MRCH.WM.AR.ZS?order=wbapi_data_value_2011+wbapi_data_value&sort=asc

World Bank. "Global Economic Prospects." World Bank, 2014.

World Bank Staff. "World development report 1997: the state in a changing world." World Bank and Oxford University Press, 1997.

World Bank Staff. "Curbing the epidemic: governments and the economics of tobacco control." Development in practice. Washington DC; World Bank, 1999.

World Trade Organization. "Thailand – Customs and Fiscal Measures on Cigarettes from the Philippines." World Trade Organization, 2011.

Yurekli, A. "Design and Administer Tobacco Taxes." *World Bank Economics of Tobacco Toolkit, Tool 4 Design and Administration.*

Zee, H. "A note on global taxes and aid for development." *Journal of Economic Studies* 33, no. 1 (2006): 5-11, 2006.

About Dr. Arthur B. Laffer

Arthur B. Laffer is the founder and chairman of Laffer Associates, an institutional economic research and consulting firm, as well as Laffer Investments, an institutional investment management firm utilizing diverse investment strategies. Dr. Laffer's economic acumen and influence in triggering a world-wide tax-cutting movement in the 1980s have earned him the distinction in many publications as "The Father of Supply-Side Economics." His name is attached to the Laffer Curve, a graphical representation that there exists a tax rate between 0% and 100% that will maximize government revenue and above which tax receipts will decline.

Dr. Laffer was a member of President Ronald Reagan's Economic Policy Advisory Board for both of his two terms (1981-1989). He also advised Prime Minister Margaret Thatcher on fiscal policy in the U.K. during the 1980s. During the years 1972 to 1977, Dr. Laffer was a consultant to Secretary of the Treasury William Simon, Secretary of Defense Don Rumsfeld, and Secretary of the Treasury George Shultz. He was the first to hold the title of Chief Economist at the Office of Management and Budget (OMB) under Mr. Shultz from October 1970 to July 1972.

He was formerly the Distinguished University Professor at Pepperdine University and a member of the Pepperdine Board of Directors. He also held the status as the Charles B. Thornton Professor of Business Economics at the University of Southern California from 1976 to 1984. He was an Associate Professor of Business Economics at the University of Chicago from 1970 to 1976 and a member of the Chicago faculty from 1967 through 1976.

Dr. Laffer received a B.A. in economics from Yale University in 1963. He received a MBA and a Ph.D. in economics from Stanford University in 1965 and 1972 respectively.

About the Laffer Center at Pacific Research Institute

Founded in 2012, The Laffer Center at the Pacific Research Institute is dedicated to preserving and promoting the core tenets of supply-side economics. The Laffer Center is named after Arthur B. Laffer, one of the nation's leading economic minds and considered by many to be the "Father of Supply-Side Economics." The Laffer Center houses Dr. Laffer's life's work and seeks to be the leading source for supply-side research and thought, including the research and published works of other economists and thought leaders whose ideas have played an instrumental role in the supply-side movement in the United States and abroad. Most important, The Laffer Center is focused on educating people on economic ideas and ensuring that the lessons of supply-side economics are as relevant and applicable today as they were in the 1980s when the supply-side revolution swept the country.

www.ingramcontent.com/pod-product-compliance
Lightning Source LLC
Chambersburg PA
CBHW050535190326
41458CB00007B/1792